Voices in   Exile

Voices in

The Decembrist Memoirs

G. R. V. BARRATT

McGill-Queen's University Press   Montreal and London   1974

Exile

© McGill-Queen's University Press 1974
International Standard Book Number
0 7735 0183 5
Library of Congress Catalog Number
74-77505
Legal Deposit Fourth Quarter 1974
Bibliothèque nationale du Québec

This book has been published with the
help of a grant from the Humanities
Research Council of Canada using funds
provided by the Canada Council.

Design by Peter Dorn, MGDC
Printed in Canada by Bryant Press Ltd., Toronto

The death of Nicholas multiplied our hopes and energies tenfold. 'Long live reason!' I cried involuntarily ... 'Nicholas has gone; and *Polar Star* shall reappear on the day which is our Good Friday—the day on which *five gibbets became for us five crucifixes.*'
A. I. Herzen, *The Engelsons* (1865)

It was early in the nineteenth century, when there were as yet no railways or macadamized roads, no gaslight, no stearine candles, no low couches with sprung cushions, no unvarnished furniture, no disillusioned youths with eye-glasses, no liberalizing women philosophers ... ; when ball-rooms were illuminated by candelabra with wax or spermaceti candles, when sofas were arranged symmetrically, when our fathers were still young—in those naive days of Masonic Lodges, Martinists and Tugendbunds, the days of Miloradoviches and Pushkins and Davydovs.
L. N. Tolstoy, *Two Hussars* (1856)

We see clearly three generations, three classes acting in the Russian Revolution. First, nobles and landowners, the Decembrists and Herzen. The circle of these revolutionaries was a narrow one. They were fearfully distant from the people. But their cause did not perish.
V. I. Lenin, *Memoirs of Herzen* (1912)

The woman took Nadya by the sleeve of her coat. 'My dear! It was easy to love a man in the nineteenth century. The wives of the Decembrists— do you think they performed some heroic feat? Did personnel sections call *them* in to fill out security questionnaires?'
A. I. Solzhenitsyn, *The First Circle.*

v

Contents

Plates

Endpapers, *On the Senate Square 14
December 1825,* from a watercolour by
K. L. Kol'man

1 *Room of an unknown Decembrist,* water colour by Nikolai Bestuzhev, 1831.
Literary Museum, Moscow

2 The Academy of Arts, 1787

x

3 Prince S. P. Trubetskoy, 1834   4 Baron A. E. Rozen, 1832

5 M. A. Bestuzhev, 1838   6 N. I. Lorer, 1833

7 Main Street, Chita, 1829

8 N. V. Basargin, 1836   9 A. G. Murav'yova, 1825

10 N. Murav′yov, 1836   11 Princess M. N. Volkonskaya, 1828

12 I. D. Yakushkin, 1851   13 Prince E. P. Obolensky, 1857

14 Petrovskiy Zavod, 1833

15 A. I. Yakubovich, 1831

16 N. A. Bestuzhev, 1825

17 M. S. Lunin, 1836

18 I. V. Poggio, 1845

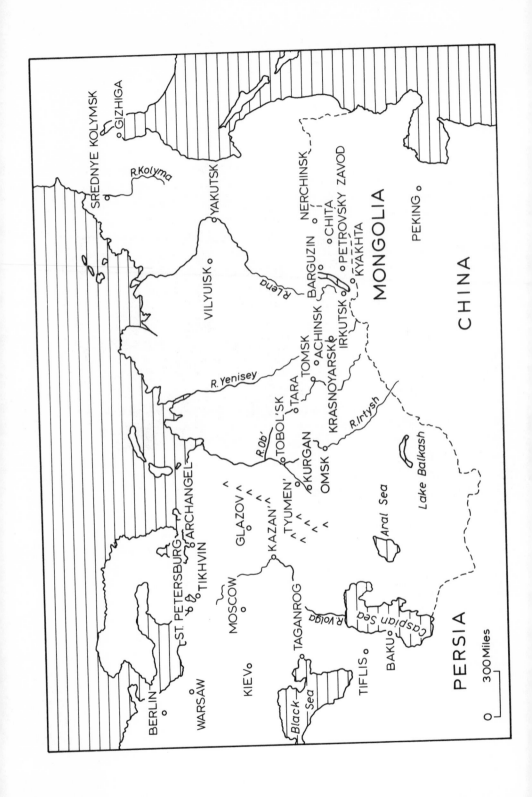

SREDNYE KOLYMSK
GIZHIGA
R.Kolyma
YAKUTSK
VILYUISK
R.Lena
NERCHINSK
BARGUZIN
CHITA
PETROVSKY ZAVOD
ACHINSK
KYAKHTA
TOMSK
IRKUTSK
MONGOLIA
R. Yenisey
TARA
PEKING
TOBOL'SK
KRASNOYARSK
CHINA
R.Ob'
KURGAN
R.Irtysh
TYUMEN'
OMSK
GLAZOV
Lake Balkash
ARCHANGEL
KAZAN
ST. PETERSBURG
Aral Sea
TIKHVIN
MOSCOW
R.Volga
BERLIN
TAGANROG
Caspian Sea
WARSAW
KIEV
TIFLIS
BAKU
Black Sea
PERSIA
0   300 Miles

Preface

1975 marks the sesquicentennial of the Decembrist insurrection in St. Petersburg. In the Soviet Union, the occasion will be widely celebrated, in the West hardly at all, perhaps. Feeling that something should be done to mark that fateful rising, and to honour the Decembrists' memory, I offer the present selection of translations of eye-witness accounts of participants in that revolt against autocracy. It is, I think, appropriate that Canada should make some contribution to the marking of this anniversary abroad: millions of Canadians have Slavic antecedents, and some are the descendants of Decembrists.

This volume is intended for those with no knowledge of Russian, as well as for Russian-readers. It is hoped to interest historians who are not specialists in nineteenth-century Russia, and other than professional historians. To reach that end, it has seemed necessary to include copious footnotes, for which I here apologize to specialists.

My grateful thanks are due to friends and colleagues who have helped me in the preparation of this book, by answering questions, correcting misconceptions, and generally lending me encouragement. Special mention must be made of Dr. Peter Squire, of Cambridge University; of Professor V. I. Grebenschikov, of Carleton University; of the staffs of the Finnish and Royal Swedish Embassies in Ottawa; and of my wife, whose idea the present volume was, and who has always given me support of every kind throughout its writing. Thanks are also due, for assistance of a dozen sorts, to Mr. Jeremy Palin, Keeper of Rare Books at Carleton University; the Librarian of Emmanuel College, Cambridge; Mrs. Helen Mildmay-White, of Holbeton, Plymouth; Dr. Ernst Oppenheimer and Mrs. H. van der Lagemaat, of Ottawa; Dr. Anatole Mazour of Stanford, California; Professor S. B. Okun', of Leningrad State University; Marfa Antonovna Malova, of the *Institut Russkoy Akademii Nauk,* Leningrad; and to the staff of McGill-Queen's University Press.

Ottawa, 1974.

Introduction

December 14, 1825 was the day on which Guards regiments in Petersburg were to swear solemn allegiance to Nicholas I, the new emperor. Less than three weeks before, when news of the death of Alexander I had reached the capital from Taganrog on the Sea of Azov, an oath no less solemn or binding had been taken to Nicholas's elder brother, the Grand Duke Constantine, viceroy of Poland. Constantine, however, had declined to be the emperor, in accordance with two separate acts of renunciation made in 1819 and, secretly, in 1822. The effective interregnum caused uneasiness both in society and in the army. The government feared undefined disorders – with some reason, since police agents reported the existence of various clandestine groups and rumours of a coup to be effected by guardsmen. Nicholas was anxious that the oath be sworn to him promptly and quietly. At first, it seemed that he would have his way; senators, ministers and members of the Council of State took the oath by 9 A.M. In most regiments of the garrison the oath was also taken peaceably. In some, however, troops expressed bewilderment at the swift passage of rulers and the multiplicity of swearings. Seizing upon this mood, some officers, members of a secret society, brought about 3000 men onto the Senate Square, where they formed up ready for action. The officers who led them hoped that such an extraordinary display of discontent and show of military strength would rally all the troops stationed in St. Petersburg, and that their ranks would swell enormously. But this was not to be. Quickly and poorly planned, their scheme was frustrated. Confused, the mutineers waited for orders to act, while their officers merely walked up and down their flanks, telling them to stand firm, have more patience, and to shout for Constantine.

Nicholas, meanwhile, was in the nearby Winter Palace, preparing countermoves. He had no plan. Nor could he help proceeding slowly and with caution, since the troops' mood was unknown to him; he was not sure if even regiments of guards would remain loyal to him. Outside, the mutineers still stood immobile. Nicholas and his generals gathered loyal men, especially artillerymen, and carefully encircled Senate Square. Hours passed, and still the rebels had not moved. Cannon were brought up and trained on them. The military commandant of Petersburg, General M. A. Miloradovich, attempted to persuade the sullen mutineers to disband, but was too forward and too bold. One of the conspirators, P. G. Kakhovsky, shot him dead. What the general had failed to do, a grand duke and an archbishop also failed to do. The mutineers would not disperse; but neither did they make a move. Finally, between 3 and 4 P.M., Nicholas felt confident of the complete superiority of 'his' forces, and ordered the artillery to open fire. Within one minute, no one stood where for six hours insurgent troops, uncomprehending, muskets loaded, had stamped their feet and watched not only Nicholas and his suite, perhaps a hundred yards away from them, but also crowds of curious and sympathetic onlookers. Grapeshot scattered everyone, slaughtering many. Within the next twenty-four hours, virtually all the main conspirators then in the capital had been arrested. The mutinous soldiers had been disarmed, the many dead pushed hurriedly under the ice of the Neva and places where their blood had turned snow red sprinkled with fresh, white snow. The day which had begun in fear, foreboding, nervousness, ended in easy victory for autocracy.

In retrospect it is apparent that the well-born conspirators had little chance or none of a success: their plans to take advantage of the curious interregnum were laid in haste, and their leaders were found wanting. Prince S. G. Trubetskoy, who was to be 'dictator' of post-autocratic Russia, was not to be found where and when he was desperately wanted. Still, the very fact of revolt made a deep impression on the country. Rumours spread rapidly that thousands were rebelling openly against the government and Nicholas. Reaching the Second Army in the Ukraine, these rumours sufficed to precipitate another armed rebellion in January 1826. It, too, was suppressed after a bloody meeting near Belaya Tserkov'. Plans to occupy Kiev came to nothing. By mid-January all was tranquil again in the Empire, the leaders of the risings were imprisoned, mutinous soldiers had been disciplined. But how narrow was the margin of defeat? Several participants believed that it was very narrow, and that a little more balanced determination, a fraction more realism, would have brought over to the insurgents' side the great majority of troops loyal to the government. Perhaps, some argued, a successful insurrection in the capital would have touched off several more in the various army corps. The question is, of course, quite academic. Two solid facts remain: first, the conspirators' defeat resulted in the almost absolute eclipse of liberal hopes for a generation afterwards; second, their fate and example (five leaders were hanged on July 13, 1826, while 121 individuals received sentences of exile with hard labour) created something of a martyrology in Russia, and a summons to more revolutionary action. The end of the Decembrist insurrection, in other words, was only the beginning of that insurrection's rôle in Russian history and thought.

The immediate cause of the revolt of December 14, 1825 was the crisis of succession. Alexander died suddenly, leaving no heirs. Treating the Russian state like a large family estate, members of the imperial family had, in 1822, decided that, because of his morganatic marriage to a Polish noblewoman not of royal blood, Constantine should, so to speak, not have it. The attitudes of the imperial brothers to each other, to the throne and the succession, were complex, and have given rise to endless controversy. Constantine, suffice it to observe here, did not renounce the Russian throne entirely voluntarily; pressure was brought to bear by the dowager empress.

Such matters, however, did not lie at the root of discontent among the educated gentry and nobility. For deeper causes, we must look back to the wars against Napoleon and even to the French Revolution. For it was these events which in the first years of the century, set in motion an accelerated growth of civic, economic and, above all, political consciousness among the Russian landed classes. Most future Decembrists saw some action in Western Europe. Those who did not heard from their fellow-officers how differently matters were arranged in Saxony, Prussia, and France, where even common soldiers and poor peasants displayed a sense of dignity and independence immediately striking to a Russian. Everyone, it appeared, was free from the oppressive restraint to which even Russian officers were perpetually subject; whereas Russian serfs were sullen and distrustful, German peasants were self-assured and, in the main, industrious. Contrasts of every kind were striking. Great was the shock when liberals returned to Russia to discover there oppression, ignorance, petty and corrupt administration, tyranny in many guises. The effect of the discovery was simple: rejection of the autocratic system. What, many reasoned, caused such a deplorable state of affairs if not Russia's plainly evil social structure and oppressive institutions? For the first time, Russian officers saw Russia, and disliked what met their eye.

Partly under the influence of what they had observed abroad, partly in imitation of local precedents, many officers banded together, in the post-Napoleonic years, in small secret or semi-secret societies. Politics, literature, law and a range of other topics were discussed. One of these groups was the Northern Society; another, in the Ukraine, the Southern Society which, in September 1825, merged with the Society of United Slavs. All three were directly involved in the events of December 1825. All three had, for the previous three years, formed centres of attraction for young officers and educated servants of the state who were dissatisfied with actual economic, legal and socio-political conditions in their country, and wished somehow to change them. The Northern and Southern Societies were offshoots of an earlier group, the Union of Welfare, which was itself the offspring of the Union of Salvation (1816–18). As such, they showed the influence of German *Tugendbunden* on which the founders of the Union of Salvation, most of whom experienced at first hand the military campaigns of 1813–14, had modeled their society on their return to Russia. In their constitutions too, as in that of the disbanded Union of Salvation, two principal aims were inherent: the moral self-improvement of the small ruling elite, and the 'enlightenment' of Russia's leadership in order to prepare the ground for (carefully unspecified) political reform. Moral improvement and enlightenment: the very words clearly suggest the intellectual debt of the Decembrists to the eighteenth century. Many indeed were thoroughly familiar not only with the fashions, arts and drama of late eighteenth-century Germany and France, but also with the history, philosophy and intellectual life of those two countries or, rather, of those large patchworks of states. As eighteenth-century men, at least in non-practical training, many Russians born with the new century were well versed in the classics and familiar with the libertarian drama of the Greeks and Romans, as depicted by Plutarch, Titus Livy, Cornelius Nepos. Though linked in intellectual tradition to their fathers' age, however, the Decembrists had seen things and had experiences of which their fathers had not dreamed. Theirs was the age of Bonaparte, of conscious and romantic nationalism, and of idealistic thought. Theirs was a generation that had tasted the heroic, active life. Small wonder that the disillusionment of life in a supposedly victorious St. Peterburg, where in fact the soldier-heroes of one month had returned to the station of serfs within the next, bred endless discontent. Sources of inspiration were not lacking: Karl Sand, Riego and Bolivar provoked no less enthusiasm among liberals than did literary figures of rebellion – Byron's and Schiller's ardent heroes. Not content with merely passively experiencing the influence of the German and English romantics, the Decembrists actively participated in creating a romantic literature in Russia and for Russia. Several of the principal Decembrists, including Ryleyev, Bestuzhev-Marlinsky and V. K. Kyukhel'beker, were writers of great merit. Historical and literary example; ideas gathered in German universities or works in French (by many non-French authors) on political economy, land management, natural law; the spectacle of fellow-countrymen being beaten and methodically oppressed – all added dangerous fuel to the fires of discontent.

It was essentially a sense of disappointment that prompted the returning officers to form secret societies. The fact that government spies attempted vainly to prohibit their formation between 1816 and 1822, when all secret associations were outlawed throughout the empire, merely deepened that bitter sense and gave rise to more societies. The reign of Alexander, as many had occasion to recall by 1820, had opened on a note of optimistic expectation of constitutional and administrative reforms and of the prompt establishment of a firm rule of law in Russia. Such hopes soon proved illusory. But it was not until 1815 that the educated élite's feeling of disappointment grew acute. During the previous three years official statements had been issued that might reasonably have been interpreted as pledges of reform after the war. After Napoleon's demise, constitutional monarchies had been established in France and many German states, and even the truncated Kingdom of Poland, in personal union with Russia, had received a theoretical constitution. Yet for Russia herself nothing was done. And had not Russians *earned* reform, by their glorious part in defeating the Napoleonic armies? Had they not helped other nations to secure the benefits of constitutional government? (Few liberals indeed approved of regicide in Russia; in endless and inconclusive discussions, the members of the Northern Society spoke for political participation by the nobility, a limiting of autocratic power, thorough improvement of all branches of the Russian administration, especially the judiciary, and some improvement of the peasants' lot. Most shied away from plans for murder.)

Far from acting as the discontented officers and bureaucrats hoped he might do, however, Alexander I proceeded to subordinate Russia's own national interests to Metternich's reactionary policy and to use Russian arms to put down liberation movements everywhere. Worse still, he set about restoring the whole army, and especially the Guards, whence came most future Decembrists, to its earlier parade-ground style. It was his 'paradomania,' as Prince Adam Czartoryski put it, that led Ryleyev to attack him in a propaganda poem as 'the Russian German.' Everywhere, educated officers resented the grim process whereby troops who, having fought real battles and lost the habit of precise and clockwork movements, were flogged, knouted and starved until they perfectly remembered all the past. Alexander's was a family obsession with the visible minutiae of army life; in his brother Nicholas, as in Paul I, it assumed a virulent form. The best-known, but by no means atypical, case of savage treatment of troops was perhaps Colonel Shvarts's of the Semyonovsky Guards Regiment, in October 1820. Shvarts's brutality provoked the soldiers of the emperor's favourite regiment to open mutiny, albeit a peaceful one. The emperor reacted violently: far from attempting to appreciate the reasons for such conduct, he punished veteran soldiers with utmost severity, disbanded the regiment and scattered officers and men to Finland and the Caucasus – thus contributing greatly to the spread of smouldering disaffection. Shvarts's was an evil name in Russian liberal circles; but nothing so disgusted and enraged future Decembrists as the conduct of the emperor's factotum and trusted martinet, Count A. A. Arakcheyev, 'the corporal of Gatchina.' Arakcheyev brought to public life the mentality and methods of the murdered Paul I. Under his aegis flourished a large network of so-called military colonies, prevailing conditions in which may be judged by the fact that the death rate in them exceeded the birth rate, despite the fact that women, whose pots and pans were issued by strict military procedure, were officially required to bring forth children annually. No less than pointless militarism, peculation and oppression flourished in such camps.

The social, economic, and political stagnation of the country; the neglect of Russia's true national interests; the military colonies and 'paradomania,' all stemmed, in the opinion of most liberals, from the will and policy of Alexander. Autocracy, in other words, lay at the heart of Russia's problems. Autocracy was arbitrary, capricious, cruel and, even worse, enabled a bureaucracy to operate without adequate controls or supervision. Inherent in autocracy was lack of real respect for human dignity and coupled with it, absence of security. (And here, the liberals had a point; for Alexander and his close advisers had indeed acquired the habit, by 1818, of expressing both distrust and scorn for Russia's landed gentry and nobility.) Autocracy, then, was to be changed. But how could it be changed without precipitating the collapse of the whole state, based as it was on loyalty to the sovereign and on serfdom? For many, the dilemma was insoluble. Simply by being loyal to the monarchy, Decembrists fell into the traps which Nicholas so dexterously set them in their personal interrogations after the revolt. Paradoxically, many nurtured the hope that the new emperor's goodwill might be employed to end abuses; in short, they vainly dreamed that Nicholas might voluntarily impose restrictions on his own imperial power! Had they known his character, they would not have entertained such an illusion. Still more significant than their reliance on the personal nature of kingship, however, proved their unprecedented shift of allegiance from sovereign to state. It was the first time that an influential group in Russian society held a conception of the state as both distinct and separate from the ruler. The Decembrists, to be sure, did not advocate a lessening of the state's authority, as would later revolutionaries and *intelligenty*. For, in their view, the people's welfare was indissolubly tied to the stability and power of the state. The contriteness displayed by so many Decembrists after their failure was perhaps due to a tardy understanding that their enterprise threatened the state no less than the autocracy. Nicholas, for his part, fully appreciated this, if little else, and stressed the fact whenever possible throughout the subsequent investigations. While emphasizing their commitment to the Russian national state, he might also have seen (had he the eyes to see), the Decembrists perfectly exemplified the liberal élite's growing alienation from the government which he himself controlled, led and embodied. It was this positive commitment to the notion of a national state that later generations would discard, ironically, because of the Decembrists' very failure.

It is not easy to speak of the hundred and twenty-one different personalities, sentenced for their involvement in the risings of December 14, 1825 and of January 3, 1826, as a single or homogeneous assembly. The Decembrists, almost axiomatically, had as many individual characteristics as they had common traits. Four of these traits, however, may be seen to have been vital to their enterprise. In the first place, most were of a common class and, in consequence, had shared the same historical experiences in the Napoleonic wars. Many belonged to the same prestigious regiments of Guards, whose officers were stationed in the capital in contact with the court. Most, second, had received the finest education then available, either from private tutors or in schools for the nobility. Many had also taken advantage of their months in Western Europe to improve their education even more, attending lectures, reading widely. Thirdly, most were very young in 1825. Some were adolescents still, or had barely attained their majority. Only two Decembrists were more than forty years of age in 1825, only a dozen more than thirty-five. Most were in their twenties. Lastly, a great many had seriously participated in one or more secret political society. Their arrest affected most of the more prominent aristocratic families, naturally reinforcing Nicholas's suspicion of their class and widening the rift between society and state. Nicholas hardened the bureaucracy's discretionary power.

Many Decembrists broke down during their trial, and repented of their rôle on Senate Square or in the Ukraine. Some had failure of nerve, others felt the effects of small, damp cells and solitude; none were prepared by their own background to resist subtle psychological pressures or police tricks. Yet all such explanations of their conduct are inadequate, when one recalls that those officers tried were courageous, determined men. More undermining than all physical or other deprivations, one perceives, was the fact that many felt, even early in 1826, that their failure to do something good and valuable for Russia stemmed from a wrong approach. Immediately, old notions of their loyalty to the state and emperor revived. Few, significantly, tried to escape from prison or exile, accepting their position as a punishment for failure and a vindication of their inner righteousness.

All educated Russians understood the aspirations of the exiles; many shared their purpose, feeling totally excluded by autocracy from the formulation of state policy – a formulation which their forebears had for many generations known and shared. Such an attitude did much to ease the physical and, even more, emotional position of Decembrists in Siberia. It confirmed their own belief that their five comrades, hanged in ignominy, were indeed martyrs and that they were themselves serving the anti-autocratic cause and the *narod* (the people). Nicholas unwittingly did much to foster that belief and, by extension, to ensure most exiles' mental health. By sentencing them savagely, and accepting as the truth what prisoners said in moments of distress, he somehow justified them in their own sight. Exiled in groups – another major error by the emperor, if he wished to eradicate the Decembrists' memory and ruin them – they kept alive the flame that they had kindled. The native population of Siberia proved far from hostile towards them. When the wives of some of the exiles joined their husbands, Decembrists were enabled to receive news from the West, and to send news. They contributed greatly, in the meanwhile, to the spread of education, medical care, and agricultural expertise in Siberia. By allowing them to live, as one exile put it, 'beyond political death,' and even to prepare eventual memoirs, Nicholas himself changed the Decembrists' joint and common failure into victory. For the happenings of December 14, 1825 were not, as some suggest, the making of the first great revolution within Russia. Rather did they prove, as Herzen, the essential mythmaker, would stress, to be the opening episode of *the* Russian revolution.

Defeat was thus changed into victory; the Decembrist legend grew apace. It is, indeed, precisely because fate gave the material for powerful revolutionary myths to those who followed them that the Decembrists cannot possibly be placed in the same category as Guards groups who effected palace coups throughout the eighteenth century. Unlike those earlier conspirators and king-makers, the Decembrists had discussed, even excessively, ideological questions, and had struggled to establish constitutional plans and reforms. Unlike participants in earlier cabals, they were not moved only by selfish interests; instead, they were sincerely and honestly concerned with the improving of the lot of the majority of Russians. Regrettably, they were unable to agree how best to do so. It was, above all else, their sincerity and their idealistic, if quixotic, passion that made of most Decembrist lives glowing examples to be followed, and inspired their lasting myth and legend for the future. Theories, as Herzen said, inspire convictions, but example can shape conduct. The fate of the Decembrists in challenging autocracy proved, for another ninety years, a summons to more action in the cause of revolution. Yet several Decembrists in the 1860s could already disapprove of the interpretations of which they were themselves the ageing subjects. Perhaps they would have felt more strongly still, had they survived to read simplistic Soviet texts based on their own experience, and their own example.

Memoirs of revolutionaries have often proved mixed blessings for historians. Some, written post facto to justify events or individuals – more commonly than not the authors themselves – turn out to be misleading. So particular are others in their treatment of events, and so generous are their omissions, that they do far less to clarify than to obscure them. But for the memoirs of Decembrists we have reason to be thankful. There are, undeniably, accounts of the unhappy day itself, of the trial and the imprisonment that followed, of the 'Well, I told you so' variety: one thinks of parts of D. I. Zavalishin's and of A. S. Gangeblov's narratives. But these are few and, once identified, may readily be made allowance for. Happily, most participants' accounts of events during and after the ill-fated insurrection of December 1825 are not only tolerably accurate from the strictly factual viewpoint (obviously, all memoirs are 'accurate' insofar as they reflect an individual's true impression of what once happened to him), but are also lucid, sometimes eloquent records. Their authors, after all, were representatives of the best educated, most enlightened sector of Russian society. Like all memoirs, finally, those of the Decembrists fulfil a double function for the reader: they throw light not only on events which their authors once observed (and sometimes instigated), but also, and especially, on the memoirists themselves. That the authors of these memoirs were remarkable and memorable men can hardly be disputed.

Primary sources for all subsequent accounts of 'what actually happened' on Senate Square, in Peter-and-Paul Fortress and in the Winter Palace, in Finnish and Siberian holds, encampments, and settlements, from December 1825 until the death of Nicholas and the accession of his son in 1856, these and all other eye-witness accounts have obvious and undeniable importance to students of the period. They are the bricks that all historians have used to raise their structures, no matter to what plan they have been building. They are the vital records that a dozen generations have interpreted or misinterpreted, scrutinized, re-read and weighed. But even this is not the whole charm and significance of the Decembrists' lucid records for contemporary historians: because there are many of them (see Appendix D), they may reasonably be left to prove their worth and to establish their validity as factually accurate accounts. They cannot be overweening, like some single extant fragment, for each one corroborates or fails to corroborate others. True, the picture of events in, say, Peter-and-Paul Fortress on the last days of December 1825 does grow a little blurred when it is painted variously by different prisoners (though in general it transpires that each saw the reality from different angles, or at different times, or in a different light); but loss of crystalline detail in every phase of the rebellion and its lengthy aftermath, most would agree, is adequately compensated for by the guarantee that broad outlines and major traits, at least, are accurately stated and perceived. It would be foolish to suggest that this abundance of autobiographical writing is automatically of help in clarifying various episodes. It is not. In fact, it sometimes adds confusion. Yet this is rarely so, and by exerting effort and a little common sense we can extract from the enormous mass more insight than confusion, more fresh knowledge than bewilderment.

It is a pity, one may say, that most accounts of what occurred on Senate Square and in the fortress opposite in the first days of Nicholas's reign – *joli commencement de règne*, as he himself apparently remarked – were not written until ten, twenty, even thirty years later; and so, in a sense, it is. Inevitably, the lapse of time obscured some details and made many more look strange. Yet, once again, we see various compensating factors. Would not all perspective have been lost if those so newly separated from their wives and infant children, stripped of all ranks and exiled to Siberia for life, had tried to give a record of events? Necessarily engrossed in their own chances of survival and worried for their own close family, would they not have lost sight of the forest for the trees? Though there are certainly some losses for present-day students in the long delays that preceded the writing of most memoirs (but not all), there are also certain gains. Nor can it be denied, on the same subject, that the exiles were well served by their memories even three decades after the rising. Of this we may convince ourselves by checking one account against another, the authors frequently not having met for years. But of course, it would have been surprising if most of them had *not* kept photographic memories of happenings of long before: they were hardly likely to forget those days and hours in St. Petersburg, even if, as in M. A. Bestuzhev's case, cannon-balls had crashed all round them on a cracking, frozen river, or if, as in Prince E. P. Obolensky's, crowds had stampeded within yards of them. Rather would the tragedy of those and other scenes stamp them deep into the memory.

Only a sense of regularly passing time seems to have suffered noticeably from the many years' delay. In some accounts, such as those of I. D. Yakushkin and Baron A. E. Rozen, which were prepared during the fifties but not published until 1862 and 1869 respectively, hours, days and nights fuse and combine easily, aimlessly, and it is sometimes difficult to know precisely when events being described occurred. But once again, comparison restores proper perspective – here in a temporal, not spatial sense.

Yet for all the occasional misgivings that most memoirs of the period provoke – misgivings which, by forcing us to compare various texts, nudge us closer to the truth, not further from it – there remains the glowing certainty that the personal dimension provides insights unobtainable elsewhere. Such reminiscences, one need not labour, suggest the 'feel' or texture of a period as no later reconstruction can. Not only do the Decembrists' memoirs offer a more sweeping and complete scenario of the times; they show those times from close up, like a magnifying glass trained on one part of a huge canvas.

It would be wrong to think, however, that the reader must be ever on his guard in reading these accounts of chaos, trial, imprisonment, and exile. The chaos, after all, quickly subsided; the exile lasted many years, and no one stood to gain by underplaying or exaggerating its innumerable tribulations. There are, perhaps, no finer or more accurate descriptions of Siberia as it was in the 1830s, of the customs, dress and manners of its polyglot and motley population, than those of Baron Shteyngel' and N. V. Basargin. Always measured in tone, their narratives dealing with Buriat and Tungus tribes, with Old Believers, Poles and other exiles, with the flora, jewellery, commerce, animals, and climate of the districts where they found themselves, form an invaluable record. No less than those of G.–A. Erman, Cottrell, Haxthausen, and other sharp-eyed Western Europeans who visited Siberia in the 1830s and '40s, their balanced, clear, accounts of the vast land that would, they saw, one day become 'the Russian America,' are of interest and value to the anthropologist as well as to the sociologist and the historian. If only for this reason, it is time that the Decembrists' memoirs, or at least a few of them, were brought before a wider Western audience.

Obviously, any selection such as that presented here must be a personal one; inclusions necessarily imply omissions, and not every emphasis can be deliberate. It was decided, then, to limit the scope of this book in three essential ways: there are no narrative accounts of the southern rising or of subsequent events in Pologi and Trilesy in early January 1826; little is said here of the fates of individual exiles after 1837; and only eight of numerous available memoirs are used, in lengthy extracts, to form the body of the book. (Others are used, however, to provide occasional extra dimensions; those of M. A. Fonvizin and A. A. Bestuzhev, for example, in connection with the average Russian officer's frustrated life in the years preceding the rising.) Eight raconteurs, while representing a wide range of attitudes, may be accepted on an individual basis; extra faces in the cast would merely blur into a crowd. By limiting the number of accounts, that is to say, we are more likely to succeed in grasping what they offer as a group *and* individually, and so to gain perspective.

This, then, is the general shape; here are the eight memoirists whose narratives are used: Prince E. P. Obolensky, Baron A. E. Rozen and M. A. Bestuzhev; Prince S. G. Trubetskoy, I. D. Yakushkin and N. I. Lorer; N. V. Basargin and Baron V. I. Shteyngel'. Specific reasons why these narratives and not others have been used are to be found in the short introductions placed before each passage by a hitherto unintroduced contributor, that is, on each memoirist's first appearance. But there are also general reasons why all eight are used extensively, and there are qualities common to all. All eight are, in the main, factually reliable. Certainly there are errors in each one of them, but they are not deliberate; they are errors of fact *tout court,* and not intentional distortions or confusions of the truth. Insofar as there *are* distortions in the texts selected here, they tend to stem not from misstatement but from omission, that commonest of all memoirists' sins. Not one of the Decembrists, being human, failed to present himself, at least occasionally, in a more favourable light than the reality can fairly justify. A good example of such lapses is Sergey Trubetskoy's account of his interrogation by an irate tsar. Trubetskoy, we may recall, was the 'dictator' so conspicuously absent when most needed, and whose swift, abject repentance so delighted Nicholas. Did he indeed, as he pretends, clench his fists and shout at the tsar, 'Shoot me, then! You have the right!'? Possibly; but one somehow doubts if those were quite the words and gestures used. In this case, there is no way of ascertaining; he was alone with the tsar and General Tol', neither of whom cast light on the matter in their own (unreliable) papers. Again, we may consider the case of N. I. Lorer, whom contemporaries describe as a brilliant raconteur. If Trubetskoy suffered from a politic amnesia, Lorer remembered everything when he resolved to. Certainly it is impressive to find whole conversations recalled verbatim after twenty years.

A second quality shared by all eight narratives used here is a sense of fundamental balance. This is not to say there is no passion or *fuoco* in them; there is, most obviously in passages that deal with the protracted interviews that led up to the 'trial' and sentencing. In descriptions of confinement, too, and of the dreaded Alekseyev Ravelin, there are moments of drama and anger. But these moments are controlled, and do not set the tone for a whole memoir, spreading sound and fury everywhere. Purple passages are used deliberately: N. V. Basargin introduces one to excellent effect in a description of the walk from Chita to Petrovskiy Zavod in August 1830 (see pp. 276-78) – and certainly it must have been a curious sight, the exiles wearing fancy-dress, drinking 'brick-tea' by Buriat yurts in the middle of the steppe. But Basargin manages such local colour carefully; it does not manage him. Lorer, too, knows the full value of a splash of exotic detail. Yet it would surely have been difficult not to write interestingly of such events as most Decembrists had personally experienced: of the breaking of their swords at dawn; of hurried journeys to Siberia by sled and post-chaise, over plains, foothills and on the frozen surface of the 'Holy Sea,' Lake Baikal; of semi-professional man-hunters, wife-beaters, projects to escape *en masse* to the Pacific down the Amur. All these elements of drama and adventure notwithstanding, however, a sense of balance is maintained throughout the eight memoirs used here. Exile, it is borne in upon us, was essentially a wearisome, debilitating business. By sending the Decembrists to one place, as Nikolay Bestuzhev notes, the government allowed them 'to survive politically beyond political death'; but it was difficult to keep one's intellectual acuity, still more, emotional resilience, after ten years of exile. True, Siberia did not prove 'the frontier of an uninhabited realm, where ice and cold like Herculan pillars draw the line for Man, saying *non plus ultra*,' of which S. I. Krivtsov wrote with such apprehension, and which many others dreaded. The exiles' sufferings were, in the main, not physical at all, though there were endless petty deprivations, but rather moral and emotional. Still, there were trials enough. It is to the credit of the great majority of the Decembrists in Siberia that their spirits were not broken absolutely. Something of their strength is well reflected in these memoirs.

Plainly, different memoirists give different emphases to the same major events and circumstances. Where there are several clashing versions of a single happening or chain of happenings, as of events on Senate Square between 9 and 11 a.m. on December 14 or in Peter-and-Paul Fortress in the last days of 1825, more than one account is given here. Broadly speaking, Rozen's and M. A. Bestuzhev's accounts of the actual insurrection may be seen as complementary. So, too, are Lorer's and Yakushkin's recollections of their journeys to Siberia. A third double perspective is that of life in Chita and, after 1830, Petrovskiy Zavod as recorded by N. V. Basargin and Baron Shteyngel'. Some Decembrists speak at length of their experiences several years before the rising. Lorer, for instance, gives us insights into P. I. Pestel''s political and social attitudes while both were in the South in 1823–24; Prince Obolensky tells us much about Ryleyev as he was in 1822–23. Again, some speak at length of their confinement in Peter-and-Paul and, in some cases, other fortresses. (Many of those sentenced on July 9, 1826 suffered long months of solitude in damp strongholds in Finland before eventually departing for Siberia; two individuals were ten years in a cell and one, G. S. Baten'kov, twenty.) Others, conversely, scarcely mention their incarceration, dwelling instead on hectic journeys east. Some overlapping is perhaps inevitable: all memoirists have something to relate concerning General S. R. Leparsky, commandant at Chita and Petrovskiy, as of the 'angel-guardians' or wives who joined their husbands in Siberia. (One point that emerges from the extracts given here is that the 'Russian Women' of Nekrasov's poem were entirely mythical; they were heroic, certainly, but only to a point. Nor were they martyrs to autocracy. As Solzhenitsyn has remarked through one of his characters, they were treated everywhere as aristocracy and honoured.) An effort has been made here to avoid unprofitable repetition. In general, the extracts given offer, in the view of one translator, the most balanced and illuminating accounts of any given incident or topic.

As will be seen, the extracts are arranged neither by strict chronology nor simply under authors. An attempt is made, instead, both to suggest a sense of forward movement – obviously, exile follows sentencing, and sentencing rebellion – and to present each memoirist at stages of the whole Decembrist process where his narrative may best contribute, and be seen to best advantage. I. D. Yakushkin, for example, first appears in the 'Aftermath.' Not only is his narrative describing General V. V. Levashev at his card-table in a corner of the Hermitage a particularly brilliant one; his listing of celebrities encountered in the South during the years before the rising (which might have replaced Prince Obolensky's reminiscences in the first chapter), is by and large irrelevant to the purpose of this volume. Yakushkin, Lorer and Basargin are first introduced in 'Aftermath' for another reason, too: all three men were arrested outside St. Petersburg, separated from their comrades and brought to the Winter Palace from considerable distances. The aftermath of the rising affected many officers and others who were far away from St. Petersburg on December 14, 1825.

Memoirs of two non-Decembrist eye-witnesses are cited briefly, but without apologies, in the first pages. These are the reminiscences of Dr. Robert Lee, a shrewd Scottish surgeon who happened to be in Taganrog when Alexander died ('the spleen was enlarged ... '), and of Aleksandr Herzen. The two are complementary, and cast much needed light not on specific incidents, but on the national mood throughout December 1825. Lee, whose journal was eventually published as *The Last Days of Alexander and the First Days of Nicholas* (London, 1854), was a refreshingly objective onlooker. He tells us both how Alexander died and how his death affected the enormous populace; what he had not done for Russia; what might happen to Russia; and the barometric pressure and the temperature in Taganrog from 1817 to September 1825. He was a representative professional, well-educated foreigner. Herzen needs little introduction. Heir to the Decembrist tradition, maker of Decembrist myth, inspirer of the later populists, and teacher of distrust towards all Western bourgeois values, the future émigré champion of socialism was a child in 1825. He was a most observant child, however, and in his later writings tells us eloquently, *inter alia*, how the gentry in both St. Petersburg and Moscow looked on Nicholas in the days immediately after his accession.

Details of texts used here may be found in Appendix D. For the curious, more details are provided in Appendix C on earlier translations of Decembrist memoirs into Western European languages. The texts of Obolensky's, Shteyngel''s, Rozen's and Trubetskoy's memoirs pre-date the October Revolution. Whenever possible, texts have been checked against the manuscripts themselves, which are now kept in the Lenin Library, Moscow, the Central State Archive of Literature and the Arts (TsGALI), also in Moscow, or in Pushkinskiy Dom (Institut Russkoy Literatury Akademii Nauk S.S.S.R.), in Leningrad. Soviet textology is, in the main, first-rate. Details of changes in manuscripts both by the author and in other hands, of punctuation slips, tears, orthographical and other errors are, in an edition such as S. Ya. Shtraykh's *Zapiski, stat'i, pis'ma dekabrista I. D. Yakushkina (The Memoirs, Articles and Letters of I. D. Yakushkin;* Moscow, 1951), of the very highest order. I acknowledge my indebtedness to Shtraykh and other Soviet scholars; their scrupulous attention to minutiae has made my own task the less heavy. It is with an easy heart that I follow their example with regard to minor textual corrections.

Wherever possible, I have made no alterations whatsoever that might possibly affect the tone or meaning of a sentence. Insistent idiosyncracies, conversely, have been kept. This applies, too, in matters of style: thus Obolensky's often rambling sentences, Trubetskoy's high-sounding airs and M. A. Bestuzhev's concrete style are deliberately preserved. Though basic sentence structure and paragraphing is everywhere maintained on principle (and the paragraphing of the manuscripts, not of any one edition, is adhered to), sentences formed of so many clauses that to render them exactly makes the sense elusive in English are, regretfully, split into two. Always the main effort is to present the sense and the flavour of the original, not the precise wording; but of course, 'both are best.' Liberal use of the dash, more characteristic of Russian than of English prose, has also been preserved; there seems to be no reason for 'improving' sentences by replacing dashes with semi-colons, brackets or any other sign.

Trubetskoy occasionally lapses into French, Rozen and Lorer into German. These lapses are not truly lapses, for they are deliberate. As deliberate, words and whole passages given in the original in languages other than English are offered here in footnotes. Short phrases or words given in English in the Russian texts are put into italics. Paintings and books are, for convenience, referred to in their English forms (the Russian name having been given also, in the latter case, if they have obvious historical importance). So, too, are towns and sites with recognized anglicized spellings (thus: Archangel, not Arkhangel'sk; Schlüsselburg, not Shlyusselburg). For names of Russian individuals *and* individuals who viewed themselves as Russian or who made their reputations in that country (such as officers and functionaries of German origin: Generals Tol' and Benkendorf, for instance), the same (British) system of transliteration is used as is employed throughout, with one traditional exception: names of tsars, monarchs and princes are given in their *usual* anglicized forms (thus: Nicholas Pavlovich, not Nikolay). Where German forms occur in Russian documents, however, (in Roman lettering, of course), those German forms are also given *once,* after the Russian form. Women's surnames are kept in their Russian forms (e.g., Mme. Yakushkina), unless memoirists specifically given them a masculine form (Baroness Rozen, in some cases). Shteyngel', Rozen and Lorer so signed themselves; therefore they are not known here as Messrs. Steinheil, Rosen und Lohrer. Count P.Kh. Wittgenstein, on the other hand, and General Roth and Poggio, *customarily* signed themselves in those forms. Their feelings on the matter are respected.

Dating throughout is in accordance with the Julian calendar (employed in Russia until 1918), unless otherwise stated thus: (N. S.). To convert dates to the Western European (Gregorian) calendar, one adds twelve days to nineteenth-century dates, thirteen to twentieth-century dates.

A Setting

The lucid reminiscences of Prince Yevgeniy Petrovich Obolensky are admirably suited to the purpose of setting the broad scene for the Decembrist tragedy. They also show a man of strong conscience and attractive personality. The favourite child of a doting and patriarchal family, 'the wonderful Yevgeniy,' as Ryleyev called him, was a nobleman of natural modesty. Moreover, he was always concerned with the questions of man's natural rights and just relationship with his society; always he held, as he maintained even in 1826 after long weeks of questioning by Nicholas's Commission of Enquiry, that 'there exists in every human soul a kind, mysterious quality, every human being having been born good.'[1] It was his fate, having a far more active conscience than many members of the Union of Salvation or, later, the Northern Society, to spend his life in private moral battles. Than this, nothing emerges with more clarity from all his extant notes, letters and memoirs.[2]

Prince Yevgeniy Petrovich Obolensky   1797–1865

When a young officer, Obolensky volunteered to substitute for a relation, the only son of a poor widow, who was about to fight a duel; he inadvertently killed his opponent.[3] The 'murder' troubled him all his remaining years. It was specifically because of its 'high moral ideals' that he was drawn to the still embryonic Union of Salvation. Indeed, he was more mentally preoccupied by *schöne Seelen* and Schellingian thought than by republican or constitutional designs. Personally close to Ryleyev, the Prince stood in striking contrast to him: Ryleyev spoke magnetically, while Obolensky lisped and sometimes grew inaudible, so softly did he speak; Ryleyev was decisive; he, cautious and deliberate; Ryleyev was a revolutionary; he, a reflective, conscience-hounded moderate. Could Ryleyev have been troubled by 'a notion that ... a state system must contain an expression of higher love, which joins all in a common family'? Or by a doubt as to the rightness of 'imposing *almost by force* a way of viewing the state ... on those who are possibly satisfied with the present'? It is barely conceivable.

And yet, as will be seen, it was this same moderate individual who, with Ryleyev, was most deeply affected by Pestel''s northern mission of 1824, and who as a result most favoured closer union with the South.[4] True, Obolensky's promise to 'work on a plan' by which the two societies would join under Pestel''s effective leadership was all the colonel *did* achieve in St. Petersburg. Nikita Murav'yov's hostility was not to be appeased. But what is of significance is not that Obolensky made small headway with the project, but that he even went thus far; for Pestel' planned a republic, not a constitutional monarchy on a British model. Pestel', it is apparent from so many different memoirs, impressed most members in the North as a man of brilliant intelligence and lofty ideals.

It was, one may infer from Obolensky's own memoirs, essentially out of a sense of obligation to the liberal cause and to his comrades that the prince assumed command of the 'standing rebellion' on Senate Square on December 14, 1825, and so served to increase confusion. Though a staff-officer, his military rank was modest – that of lieutenant in the Finland Foot Regiment. Far worse, he lacked initiative. Accustomed to deliberate discussion and strategy involving army corps, he was both intellectually and temperamentally ill fitted to make swift decisions.[5] The same feeling of duty that prompted him to act on Senate Square would later bring him to a frank and full confession of his guilt before the tsar. Indeed, his repentance would be total and unqualified: there was, as he viewed it shortly after the débâcle in the South, no room for reservations. He was, once more, consistent with himself – for was this not simply another moral challenge to be met with true humility? Such was his attitude.

To overcome *this* challenge was, however, difficult. Nicholas bore him a personal grudge and meant to see that it went hard with him. 'Obolensky,' the new emperor informed his brother Constantine, 'has a black soul. His face has a bestial and mean expression; scorn for him is felt generally and strongly.'[6] Why did the tsar feel such profound antipathy? Because, when Nicholas, as aide-de-camp to General Bistrom, had commanded the First Guards Infantry Division as grand duke, Obolensky had once been in a position to cause his future emperor unpleasantness. The fact that he forebore and did not do so was not greatly in his favour; he had witnessed Nicholas's general unpopularity with his own troops. 'So this,' he exclaimed to General Levashev when Obolensky was brought in before him, 'is the man of whom you spoke to me so highly! God alone knows what I have had to undergo because of *him*!' Like others similar to it, this scene does not appear in Obolensky's memoirs – to have included it would, one supposes, have been a gesture of retaliation. Here, now, is an extract from a letter by the prince to Nicholas, written from a cell in Peter-and-Paul Fortress in early January, 1826:

Having been granted the blessing of Holy Communion, and having thus received the Lord's pardon and been enabled to present myself to Him with a serene conscience, I hold it my primary duty to cast myself at your feet, all-merciful Tsar, and to implore, not your temporal pardon, but your forgiveness as a Christian – your spiritual forgiveness ... now I feel guilty of only one sin: hitherto I have been giving your appointed Committee [of Enquiry] only those names which I could not conceal; the rest remained hidden in my heart. ... But Faith, after reconciling me with my conscience, has also made me conscious of a loftier responsibility, and your generosity, Sire, has won my heart. Seeing in you not a severe judge but a merciful father, and trusting in your mercy, I now place at your feet the destiny of your erring sons.'[7]

No doubt there is a curious kind of logic hidden here; but many men had cause to regret Obolensky's restless conscience and his willingness to furnish Nicholas with a full list of *former* members of the Union of Salvation and Northern and Southern Societies.

Even in exile, conscience did not cease to drive him. Many Decembrists – Mikhail Bestuzhev, for example, and A. Frolov and Falenberg – married Siberian peasant girls; but only Obolensky married one from motives of contrition and deliberate self-abasement. Once, he had dreamed of an ideally pure young woman of extraordinary beauty, a creature of the Schellingian hinterland. Now, in Siberia, he saw the possibility of self-perfection only in terms of marriage with an ugly, virtuous woman. First he proposed to an aged chambermaid of Princess Trubetskaya, who rejected him. Later he was accepted, only half willingly, by a young nurse hired by I. I. Pushchin, his comrade in the hamlet of Yalutorovsk. The girl had been employed to care for Pushchin's illegitimate daughter, and one can hardly doubt that such a stigma, though not hers, made her the more attractive in Obolensky's sight. Even his marriage, which proved happy, gave him another moral challenge: he had to forgive his friends their scarcely veiled hostility towards that marriage. 'My wife,' as he declared defiantly, 'is not from the higher circles, but is a simple, illiterate girl. Honestly and unselfishly did I seek her hand, and she has given herself to me unselfishly and honestly.'[8] His attitude, it soon transpired, was too straightforward for his theoretically egalitarian friends.

Only the memoirs of Yakushkin and the fractious Gorbachevsky reflect integrity like Obolensky's. If only because of their lofty air (and concomitant suggestion of profound impracticality), Prince Yevgeniy's memoirs would be worthy of our notice. But they have other points of interest and value: in them we find detailed accounts, first, of the celebrated duel between Chernov and Novosil'tsev[9] – a duel that led to a funeral which, thanks to Ryleyev's activity, became a political event of some importance – and, second, of Princess Trubetskaya's arrival in Siberia. In them, we see reflected doubts shared by a number of the members of the Northern Society, doubts both as to the rightness of the cause of revolution and, more particularly, as to the likelihood of a rebellion's succeeding. But most of all, the memoirs are of value as reflections of a noble and religious temperament. Obolensky, it emerges from the extract following here, was not merely pious; in piety he was far outshone by such as Baryatinsky and M. S. Lunin. It was, rather, that he viewed all things and happenings from an unhesitatingly religious standpoint; that is to say, he was a man governed by conscience and his duty, as he saw it, to the church invisible. Like N. V. Basargin and Mikhail Bestuzhev, he observed the lack of crime among the criminals toiling and dying at Petrovskiy Zavod. For Basargin, it was a remarkable phenomenon partly explicable by the hypocrisy and immorality of those who had condemned the wretched convicts. For Bestuzhev, it was 'a necessary result of the vicious state of our society.' But to Obolensky no such eminently reasonable, sociological approach suggests itself. To him, it is the natural goodness of the convicts that leaps to the eye; why, he asks, should they 'trouble to assist him in his work,' for which they see no hope of a reward, if not because of 'virtuous instincts'?

Those extracts given here are taken, in the first place, from the first volume of *Obshchestvennyye dvizheniya v Rossii v pervuyu polovinu XIX-ogo stoletiya* (Social Movements in Russia in the First Half of the 19th Century; St. Petersburg, 1905), pp. 233–78, where Obolensky's memoirs are edited by V. Bogucharsky. Though hardly an improvement on the 1861 text,[10] which it follows faithfully, it at least avoids such grave omissions as were earlier committed by Prince P. V. Dolgorukov in his journal *Budushchnost'* (The Future).[11] The printing, too, is admirably clear. It is to be regretted only that V. Bogucharsky's annotation is so marginal.

Prince E. P. Obolensky

With the start of my acquaintance with Kondratiy Fyodorovich Ryleyev also began a feeling of sincere and warm friendship for him. I do not remember for certain, but it seems to me that this was in 1822, that is, after the Guards Corp's return from Besenkovichi and, therefore, after the proposed campaign abroad against the revolutionary movements in Italy.[12] Ryleyev had just published *Voynarovsky* at that time, and was preparing his *Meditations* for the press[13]. His name was well known among men of letters, while the freedom-loving direction of his thought had drawn on him the attention of the members of the Secret Society.[14] Ivan Ivanovich Pushchin seems to have been the first to make his acquaintance and, with the authorization of the Supreme Council,[15] he received him into the Society. Having become the good friend of Kondratiy Fyodorovich in the first days of our acquaintance, I cannot deny having trusted in him with all my heart and found with him that mutual confidence so precious in every stage of life, but which is valued most of all in one's youthful days—days when the inner forces seek expansion and the widest possible sphere of activity. This striving was satisfied in part by becoming a member of the Secret Society. Indeed, the Union of Welfare—for so it was called—satisfied every noble aspiration in those who sought in life not merely amusement, but true moral well-being both for themselves and for all those close to them. It was not easy to resist the charm of a union the aims of which were: the moral perfecting of each of its members; reciprocal aid in reaching that goal; intellectual education as a tool for fostering judicious understanding of everything found in society's civil organization and moral orientation; and, lastly, the directing of contemporary society by means of each member's personal conduct and attitude, in his particular circle, towards solutions of the most important questions—questions immediate and questions of general politics. All this was to be accomplished by that influence that every member *could* have, and by the personal training and moral character that all might be *supposed* to possess. An ultimate and inaccessible object was perceived in the misty future, when all the scattered seeds would have ripened and when general education would be within reach of the masses of the populace; that object was the political transformation of the Fatherland. Given his ardent and poetic soul and his receptive nature, it was not difficult to get Ryleyev to accept these principles. And with his earliest step he made a veritable run into the sphere now opened to him, surrendering himself wholly to that lofty idea that he had made his own.

I will say a few words about his appearance and his early service. Ryleyev was of medium stature. The features of his face formed a fairly regular oval in which no one feature stood out more sharply than another. His hair was black and slightly curled, his eyes dark, with a pensive expression—often brilliant in animated conversation. Together with his measured step, his head, which was inclined a little forward, would show that his thoughts were ever occupied by that inner life which, given form in an inspired song when a moment of inspiration came to him, at other times sought out the realizing of the notion that was the motivating principle behind all his activity.

He had received his education in the First Cadet Corps and begun his service in the artillery. I learnt in conversation with him that his youth had been stormy; but I did not hear details of that period of his life, nor did I even chance to know his service comrades of that time, that is, his comrades in the military field. He married early for love, and not, it seems, with the full approval of his elderly mother, Nastas'ya Fyodorovna, who lived in a hamlet some 60 versts[16] from Petersburg, near the village of Rozhdestveno. His wife, Natal'ya Mikhaylovna, loved him with passion. His little daughter, Nasten'ka, then still only four or five and a slight, swarthy, and lively child, animated his home life by her presence. Of his life in the civil service I can say little. At first, he served as an assessor in the Petersburg Criminal Chambers together with I. I. Pushchin, who had exchanged the greatcoat of the Horseguards Artillery for that modest position, hoping thus to render some substantial service in the field and, by his own example, to prompt others, too, to take upon themselves duties that the nobility avoided, preferring glittering epaulets to any usefulness thay they could bring by introducing to the courts of lower instance that noble cast of thought, those pure motives that embellish men in private life and which, in the public domain, comprise a sure support for all the weak and all the helpless. Always and everywhere such people form the majority, whose needs and sufferings, however, are scarcely audible to the minority of the wealthy and the strong. Subsequently, Ryleyev transferred as a manager to the American Company and occupied a modest apartment in the Company building.[17] As a poet, he enjoyed the friendship or acquaintance of many men of letters of the time. The whole literary family used to gather once a week, in those days, at Nikolay Ivanovich Grech's, and Ryleyev was one of his most constant visitors. He was particularly friendly with Aleksandr Aleksandrovich Bestuzhev whom, it seems, he also received into the Society. Together with the latter, Nikolay Aleksandrovich his brother, and Pyotr their younger brother, whose earthy life was quickly run, also became members of the Society.[18] Aleksandr Bestuzhev was already entering on his literary career then with tales which, in their liveliness of style, promised a brilliant success — a promise which he afterwards so fully justified. Also to be remembered here is Aleksandr Osipovich Kornilovich, an officer of the Guards General Staff who laboured long and lovingly over memorials of the Petrine period, and set forth the fruits of his toil in a simple tale that prompted general sympathy with its subject.[19] At Ryleyev's, too, writers and many of his close friends and acquaintances frequently gathered. Besides those named already, there came Vil'gel'm Karlovich Kyukhel'beker, a Lyceum friend of Pushchin's; Faddey Venediktovich Bulgarin, Fyodor Nikolayevich Glinka and Orest Somov; Nikita Mikhaylovich Murav'yov, Prince Sergey Petrovich Trubetskoy, Prince Aleksandr Ivanovich Odoyevsky and many more whose names I do not recall. Conversation would be animated, and not always on purely literary topics — often it would move on to lively questions of the public life of that time, because such was the common inclination of most of those present at these amicable meetings. As the hostess, Natal'ya Mikhaylovna was considerate towards everyone, and she inspired general respect by her modest manner.

Ryleyev's public activity in the position that he held as manager in the American Company deserves special attention, such was the benefit he brought to the Company by means of it and, doubtless, by yet more substantial services. For not two years had passed since his entering their service before the board of the Company expressed their gratitude to him, presenting him with an expensive raccoon fur coat then valued at 700 rubles.

Of all my impressions of that time I here recall but one: that he was much disturbed by the transferal — of necessity, by virtue of a treaty with the North American Union — of Ross colony, which we had founded in California. This colony, which we handed over to the North Americans, might have been a firm foothold enabling us to participate in the exploiting of the goldfields which afterwards became so celebrated.[20] At that time when this step was taken — an important one for the American Company — Ryleyev, as manager, entered into relations with high government dignitaries, and always afterwards enjoyed their favour. The greatest goodwill was shown to him by Mikhail Mikhaylovich Speransky and Nikolai Semyonovich Mordvinov.

At this time, that is, at the end of 1823 or the beginning of 1824, Pavel Ivanovich Pestel' came to St. Petersburg. He had instructions from the members of the Southern Society to enter into relations with those of the Northern, so as to reach an arrangement on the score of the combined activity of all the Union's members. This arrival had a decisive influence on Ryleyev.[21] Here, attention must be paid to the remarkable personality of P. I. Pestel'. Not having had occasion to grow intimate with him, however, I can only convey the impression produced by him on me.

Pavel Ivanovich was at this time Colonel and Commander of the Vyatka Foot Regiment. Of no great height, pleasantly featured, he was distinguished by his extraordinary mind, his clear appreciation of the most abstract of subjects and his rare gift of eloquence, which acted captivatingly on those with whom he shared his private thoughts. He enjoyed the general confidence of the Southern Society and had been elected to its Supreme Council as soon as the Society had been established. His view of that Society, and of its true objective, corresponded with his intellectual *penchant*, which was to demand clarity in all things, a definite goal, and actions leading to the achievement of that aim. *Russkaya Pravda* (Russian Justice), which he wrote, formed the programme that he was proposing for a political state system.[22] The object of his journey to St. Petersburg was to persuade the Northern Society to coordinate its actions in conformity with those of the Southern Society. The members of the Supreme Council in Petersburg were then Trubetskoy, Nikita Mikhaylovich Murav'yov and myself. In his first meeting with us Pavel Ivanovich explained, with his customary, absorbing gift of speech, that the vagueness of its object and the means for its achievement were giving our Society so *indeterminate* a character that the actions of each individual member were simply being lost in futile efforts, separately; were those actions (he went on) directed to a definite, clearly acknowledged end, they would then serve to reach it in the quickest possible time. This thought was not new to us. Long before, in our own meetings, it had been discussed, and formed a subject of reflection for each one of us. But it had not yet been given definite shape. Pavel Ivanovich's proposal gave it that shape, and was attractive as the fruit of the long, private reflection of a lucid mind — a mind especially adorned by a persuasive gift of speech. It was not easy to resist a personality as charming as Pavel Ivanovich's. And yet, for all the merit of his mind and the cogency of what he said, each of us felt that, once having accepted his proposal, we should all have to renounce personal convictions and, submitting to him, to follow the path indicated. Besides, we could not give a final answer, not having first presented the proposal to those members of the Society who most enjoyed the general confidence. Of these, many were absent, so we postponed making a definite reply until such time as opportunity arose to convey Pestel''s proposal to those members whose trust had placed us in the posts we occupied.

Pavel Ivanovich, who met Kondratiy Fyodorovich through us, soon became friendly with him and, having revealed his secret thoughts to him, won his support for his own view of the Society's objective, and of the means for its attainment. This rapprochement, it appears, exercised a decisive influence on Ryleyev's subsequent political activities. Soon after Pestel''s departure, Prince Trubetskoy was appointed duty staff-officer to the Fifth Infantry Corps which had its headquarters in Kiev. Kondratiy Fyodorovich was elected to the council in his place.

To this same period, that is, to the middle of 1824, we must relate a sad incident in which Ryleyev participated as a witness, and which re-echoed sorrowfully through society at that time. This was the duel between an officer of the Semyonovskiy Lifeguard Regiment, Chernov, and a Lifeguard hussar, Novosil'tsev. Both were youths of little more than twenty — but they stood at practically opposite ends of society. Novosil'tsev, a scion of the house of Orlov, belonged by birth, wealth and connections to the upper aristocracy. Chernov, the son of a poor landed woman, Agrafena Ivanovna Chernova, who lived near the village of Rozhdestveno in her own hamlet, belonged to that category of officer who, having received an education in a cadet corps, enters the army.[22]

For his transfer to the Guards he was indebted to the fresh reconstitution of the Semyonovskiy Regiment, into which merged one battalion each from the regiments of the Emperor of Austria, the King of Prussia and Count Arakcheyev. But Agrafena Ivanovna Chernova had a remarkably beautiful daughter. I do not recall on what occasion, but Novosil'tsev made Agrafena Ivanovna's acquaintance, was struck by her daughter's beauty and, after only a few weeks, decided to ask for her hand. Mother and daughter gave their full assent. Both by his personal distinctions and by his physical appearance Novosil'tsev could and, indeed, was bound to make a strong impression on a maid living far removed from high and glittering circles. Having received her mother's consent, Novosil'tsev treated the girl Chernova as if she were his betrothed fiancée, rode out with her alone in a cabriolet through the surrounding district and, in his conduct with her, behaved with that degree of intimacy permissible only to a bridegroom with his bride. He quite forgot, in the transport of the first days of love and enchantment, that he had a mother, Ekaterina Vladimirovna, née Countess Orlova, without whose consent he could not even think of marrying. He soon collected himself, however, wrote to his mother and, as might have been expected, received a decisive refusal—and strict orders to break off immediately all relations with his bride and her family. Whether from disillusionment in love or fear of his mother's wrath cannot be said, but Novosil'tsev did not ponder long, having received the letter. He bade his betrothed farewell promising to come back quickly, and ended all relations with her, starting then. Kondratiy Fyodorovich was connected with the Chernovs by ties of kinship. Through her brother he heard of all Novosil'tsev's dealings with the girl. After lengthy delays in the hope that the latter would approach his betrothed, but seeing finally that he had completely forgotten her and was apparently ignoring her, Chernov—having first come to an agreement with Ryleyev—addressed Novosil'tsev, first in writing, then in person, with the request that he explain the reasons for his former conduct towards his sister. At first, the reply was evasive; then a few abusive words were perhaps spoken on either side and, finally, a duel was arranged, Chernov's challenge to Novosil'tsev having been delivered by Ryleyev. The adversaries met on the appointed day, paces were measured out, the signal given, both turned to face the other, pulled the trigger, and both fell mortally wounded; both were carried off by their attendants to the latters' quarters—Chernov to the modest officers' quarters of the Semyonovskiy Regiment, Novosil'tsev to the house of his relations. Ryleyev had been Chernov's second, and did not abandon his bed of suffering. Imminent death put an end to the adversaries' enmity. Each frankly concerned himself with the other's condition. Doctors gave no hope for either. Both prepared themselves for the hour of death. Because of my close friendship with Ryleyev, I and many others went to Chernov in order to express my sympathy with the noble act by which, in defending his own sister's honour, he had fallen victim to that sorry prejudice which orders that stained honour must be washed with blood. ... Soon Chernov was no more; he passed away peacefully into Eternity, and Novosil'tsev passed away at the same time. His mother and his relatives comforted his final moments. Struck down by grief, his mother received his last breath and accompanied the bier, with a few near ones, to the ancestral vault—the final dwelling place of her only and beloved son, her only hope of earthly joy. As to the mother of Chernov, she did not know of the sorrowful end of her beloved son. Chernov, it would appear, did not wish her or, especially, his sister to be told of the unhappy event, the outcome of which was so close and so inevitable. Many, many people gathered, on the morning of the day fixed for the burial, by the grave of the now silent man. His comrades bore him out and brought him to the church; and those who had known him and those who had not, who came to pay their final tribute to the dead youth, stretched out in a great column. It is not easy to convey what a multitude accompanied the coffin to the Smolensk Cemetery.[24]

The idea had occurred to Ryleyev, in the second half of 1822, to publish an almanac, the aim being to turn a literary enterprise into a commercial one. His object and that of his associate in the undertaking, Aleksandr Bestuzhev, was to offer more substantial rewards for literary work than were received then by those individuals who devoted themselves to intellectual pursuits. Often the only recompense received by these, indeed, was that of seeing their name in print in a published periodical; though they gained fame and celebrity, still they suffered cold and hunger and existed on a salary for which they toiled, or on their own income from estates or capital. The enterprise succeeded. All the writers of the time agreed to accept payment for articles printed in almanacs; among them was Aleksandr Sergeyevich Pushkin. *Polyarnaya Zvedza* [The Polar Star] had an enormous success, and not only recompensed the editors for their original expenses but provided them with a clear profit of from 1,500 to 2,000 roubles.[25]

So began 1825, which we met with a smile of joy and hope. I greeted it at home, in the circle of my family. Having been granted twenty-eight days' leave, I was using it to renew broken relationships with many of the members of the Society who had moved to Moscow for service reasons. Then, having fulfilled that object of my journey and been solaced by the kindness of my sisters and my father, who was elderly, I returned to Petersburg at the end of January. Ryleyev I found still occupied with the publication of his almanac; as to the Society's affairs, everything seemed in a kind of lull. Many of the original members were far from Petersburg: Nikolay Ivanovich Turgenev was abroad; I. I. Pushchin had moved to Moscow and Prince Sergey Petrovich Trubetskoy was in Kiev; Mikhaylo Mikhaylovich Naryshkin was also in Moscow. So the number of members of the Society on hand in Petersburg was very small. The newly received members, for their part, were still too young and inexperienced to bring the Society's objective and intentions to fruition by their presence—they could only prepare themselves for future activity, constantly drawing closer to each other and exchanging feelings and ideas—all this on days fixed periodically for private gatherings. And so, imperceptibly, 1825 flowed by. I remember at this time the arrival of Kakhovsky, a former officer of the Life-Grenadier Regiment who had come to Petersburg on some family business. Ryleyev was acquainted with him, came to know him rather better and, finding an ardent soul in him, received him into the Society. Personally I knew him very slightly; but I knew from Ryleyev's testimonial that *he* valued his inner qualities highly. Ryleyev saw a second Sand in him.[26] I also know that he greatly assisted Kakhovsky in finding a livelihood, and did not spare his purse for him either.

It was towards this time, that is, the beginning of the autumn in 1825, that there grew in me, either as a result of an unsolved, dark premonition or, possibly, in consequence of thoughts that were continually turned on one and the same subject, a feeling of doubt of some importance for my inward peace. I conveyed it to Ryleyev. It was comprised of this: I asked myself if we had the right, as private individuals who barely formed a noticeable unit of the huge mass of the population of our country, to undertake a revolution and impose our way of viewing state affairs *almost by force* on those who, possibly, were satisfied with the present and were not seeking something better. And if the majority *were* seeking and striving for something better, were they not doing so through an historical development? For a long time this idea gave me no peace in my moments of leisure, when thought itself becomes a process of self-examination. Perhaps it had arisen in me because of the word that we had given to Pestel', because of the decision taken by us to utilize a change of sovereign or some other important political event to execute the Union's final objective, i.e., to bring about a revolution by such means as would be ready at that time.

Having shared my reflections with Ryleyev, I found him hotly opposed to my attitude. His objections were just. Ideas, he said, are not subject to the laws of a minority or a majority; they are born and develop freely in every thinking creature. More than this, they are communicable, and if they tend to the common good, and are not consequences of an egoistic and self-interested feeling, they are only expressions by a few persons of what the majority feels but cannot yet express. For this reason he believed, he had the right to speak and act in the sense of the Union's aim, and to express, by doing so, a general idea not yet expressed by the majority—for he was fully confident that no sooner would these notions be communicated to the great majority than they would both accept them and sanction them with full approval. As proof of the majority's sympathy he adduced countless examples of general and personal dissatisfaction with oppression and injustice, both on the part of private individuals and springing from higher authority. Finally, he cited examples of free-thinking ideas that had grown almost spontaneously in certain individuals of both the merchant and the petty bourgeois classes with whom he was in personal contact. I sensed and recognized the justness of Ryleyev's retorts; yet I also understood that if the *ideas* of freedom, truth, and justice are the necessary property of every thinking creature and thus comprehensible and accessible to all, still the *form* of their expression, their expression as a deed, is liable to certain general laws which must in turn express the general idea alone. A poor man may say to a rich man, from a sentiment of justice: give me part of your wealth. But if, on receiving a refusal, he resolves, moved by the same feeling of truth [sic], to take a part by force, then by his action he destroys the very idea of justice which arose in him when he experienced his poverty. I understood also that a state organization is an expression, or realization, of the ideas of freedom, truth, and justice; but the nature of a state organisation depends not on some theoretical view, but on a people's historical development, which lies deep in the common consciousness. Dimly, too, I comprehended that beside state, criminal, and civil laws as expressions of the ideas of freedom, truth, and justice, a state system must contain within itself expression of the idea of higher love, which joins all in one common family. The Church is the expression of this notion. Long and often did I argue with Ryleyev or, rather, exchange thoughts, feelings, and opinions. Every day for a month, more or less, he called on me or I on him, and we passed hours talking together, parting when we were wearied by our long, late conversations. The themes of these daily discussions were both philosophical and religious. But after many digressions Ryleyev would return to the topic I had raised in the beginning. I could see that he viewed this as a cooling on my part towards the cause of the Society—so his efforts were directed so as not to allow me to cool.

Meanwhile, a sad event was being prepared in the Fates' high secrecy, of which not one of us had dreamt and which struck us like a thunderbolt out of a clear sky. The Emperor Alexander was preparing for a journey to the South. There were many rumours at the time about the reasons for the journey. It was said, among other things, that he had furnished himself with a quiet place away from regal cares in Taganrog, where a palace was being fitted for him and where, with his virtuous spouse, Elizaveta Alekseyevna, he thought of settling in deep seclusion once he had abdicated, and devoting the remainder of his days to peace and calm. For a long time, many signs of weariness with kingly labours and of deep disturbance in the flow of his best innermost strength had been noticeable, not only to those close to his person but also to us, who held lower positions in the hierarchy of government. The disbanding of the old Semyonovskiy Regiment, which was his favourite Regiment, had been the first thing to shake his confidence in the loyalty towards him of those Regiments of Guards in whose affection he had had most faith. Nor can one doubt that he was certain that the cause of the Regiment's open disobedience did not lie merely in the petty oppression of Colonel Shvarts, and in his ignorance of how to treat the men, and his desire to abase the spirit of both troops and officers, but, rather, in the activity of a secret society to which he supposed many officers of the old Semyonovskiy Regiment to have belonged.[27] In this he was mistaken: to my knowledge the only one of the officers then with that regiment who was a member of the Society was Sergey Ivanovich Murav'yov-Apostol, who was also one of its founders. Besides him, I knew not one.[28] Nothing new was revealed in the enquiry later held—only Colonel Shvarts' conduct towards the troops and officers, of which everybody knew, and the latters' opposition to his *noble* treatment of the lower ranks entrusted to him. Yet one could see, starting from then, that mistrust towards his own beloved army had crept into the Emperor's heart.

But to return to his journey to Taganrog and the first news of his ailing condition after his arrival in the Crimea: who could have dreamt, on hearing of his light bouts of Crimean fever, that the illness was dangerous and would lead to a swift end? The telegraph did not exist at that time, so we calmly awaited the latest tidings, which came, however, soon enough and with an ominous air. Then public prayers for the health of the Emperor began in the churches and it was, I believe, during the second service in the Winter Palace that the news came of his death. The service was changed into a solemn requiem.[29] Thereupon Constantine Pavlovich was proclaimed Emperor. Next day all the Guards and all the highest authorities swore an oath of allegiance to him.

All the members of the Society at hand met in Ryleyev's rooms on the eve of this oath-swearing ceremony. It was agreed unanimously that either to oppose the accession or to undertake something decisive in so short a time was impossible. It was proposed, moreover, that the activities of the Society should cease for a while, on this appearance of a new Emperor. Sadly we dispersed to our homes, sensing that for a long time, and conceivably forever, execution of the finest dream of our lives had been postponed. News came the very next day of the possible renunciation of the throne by the new Emperor. Then the late Emperor's testament was made known, and with it the probable accession to the throne of the Grand Duke Nicholas Pavlovich. At this, everything was set in motion; once more, hope of success flashed in all hearts. I shall not speak here of our daily conferences or the activity of Ryleyev who, despite his sickly condition (he had quinsy at the time), put all the strength of his soul into the realizing of a ready-planned objective—the utilizing of a change of reign to stimulate a revolution.

The actions of the Society and of each one of its members have been made public in the Commission of Enquiry's report and the findings of the Supreme Criminal Court. The truth expressed by facts cannot be denied; but I can honestly say, and must say, that a man says things in a delirium that he cannot afterwards recall. So it was then. All that was said in moments when the imagination, carried away by wildly rapturous feeling, spoke in a transport of enthusiasm, cannot and ought not to be taken for the truth. But the Supreme Court could not have witnessed secretly what had occurred during our meetings, and could not go deep into the moral state of every man. It brought a sentence on the facts, and fact was incontestable! Let us cover the past with a veil!

December 14th came. I was at Ryleyev's early in the morning; he had long been keeping vigil. Having agreed on our further actions, I set out for my house, where I had duties to attend to. Coming onto the Square at the same time as the Moscow Regiment, I found Ryleyev there. He had put on a soldier's pouch and a private's shoulder-belt and was preparing to join the ranks of the men. But shortly after this he had set off to the Life-Grenadier Regiment, to hasten its arrival. He went off on this assignment, and executed the commission; but never again did I see him.

Baron Vladimir Ivanovich Shteyngel'   1783–1863

Baron Shteyngel' was a latecomer to the Northern Society.[30] Among the most moderate of the Decembrists, he was also one of the most elderly and, in the view of many fellow exiles in the 'thirties, venerable. Born in Obva, a village in the Western Siberian province of Perm, he received his early education in Kamchatka, where his father had been posted. The family was far from rich; Shteyngel' knew poverty as a cadet in the Imperial Naval Corps in St. Petersburg (1792–99), but overcame it by sheer intellectual distinction. He served, first in the navy, later in the civil administrations of Irkutsk and Moscow, both out of hard necessity and because regular, socially useful service drew him: earlier readings of works by Radishchev, Voltaire and the Encyclopaedists, as well as in Russian history of the post-Petrine period, persuaded him that work was honourable if the majority gained by it. The same mixed reasons of financial need and philanthropic inclination led him, after his marriage, to accept the directorship of a large boys' school in Moscow. Always he was reliable; always appalled by the conditions, political and social, that darkened life in Russia. Like Aleksandr Bestuzhev and Nikolay Turgenev, he viewed serfdom as totally unethical.[31]

From 1802 until 1810 Shteyngel' served in his native Siberia, in Okhotsk and Irkutsk. After the Napoleonic Wars, he was appointed special aide to General Tormasov, military commander-in-chief in Moscow. Already his administrative experience was known and valued. In Moscow, he observed at first hand the malfunctioning of justice and the accompanying legislative chaos. And later, he wrote several balanced, closely argued papers, including a most sensible 'Dissertation on Laws Relating to Blasphemy.'[32] He became known to Turgenev, Nikita Murav'yov, and other liberals. He also found himself the father of a large and growing family which left him little time for active work in any group.

Not until 1824, in fact, did he become closely associated with the St. Petersburg radicals, though he had met and spoken with Ryleyev twelve months previously, in a bookshop. It was, as far as membership of the former Union of Salvation went, a year of triumph for Ryleyev: the three elder Bestuzhevs, Torson and Zavalishin, Batenkov and Kakhovsky, Odoyevsky and Shteyngel', all joined his growing forces. And these were not grandees like Trubetskoy but, in the words of the Russian scholar M. N. Pokrovsky, 'nobly born *intelligenty* who became revolutionaries not by virtue of their noble rank, but because they were *intelligenty* despite their noble origins.'[33]

But was Shteyngel' ever truly a revolutionary? Reading his memoirs, one has doubts. Certainly he was the drafter of the declaration drawn up by the Society 'on behalf of the Senate' which crisply proclaimed the overthrow of the old régime and the establishment of a provisional government – this to be promulgated after the yet unplanned rebellion.[34] But what sweeping changes did this declaration threaten? It breathed no word of presidents, republics or wide suffrage; nor did it intimate that landowners were faced with times of crisis. On the contrary, the populace was asked to keep the peace and to respect all private property! Never, as Nikita Murav'yov saw happily, would Shteyngel' lend support to the republicans. It is, indeed, striking that Ryleyev seemingly failed to foresee the baron's inability to accept his own strident anti-monarchic slogans – failed, that is, until Shteyngel' suggested that Elizaveta Alekseyevna be proclaimed head of state instead of either Nicholas or Constantine. Poor Ryleyev! Shteyngel', at least, was not a wild card like Kakhovsky; but whereas Kakhovsky threatened to career out of control and kill a duke or monarch, Shteyngel' was not inclined to run at all. This became clear on December 14.

Shteyngel' was, in essence, an observer of events on Senate Square. True, he visited Ryleyev early in the day and later lingered in his rooms again; but he played no part in the rebellion itself. Like Baron A. E. Rozen, whose position was in some ways comparable, he was an *onlooker*. So he describes himself three times in his own memoirs. As in the case of Rozen, too, his very temperamental inability to join the desperate carré formed by men of the Moscow Regiment (as he demanded of Nicholas later, how could he have done so, 'with a crowd of children'?), was to become no trifling asset in recording his impressions of the day and of the days that followed. Shteyngel''s memoirs are as admirably balanced as Rozen's, and as factually reliable as any Decembrist's save in the early parts, where dates tend to be shaky. But such, of course, is what one might expect of a well balanced and essentially unviolent former administrator. To deplore Shteyngel''s lack of fuoco is as pointless as to make a condemnation of the simple observation that he was, in general terms, inactive 'on the day.' Better by far to bear in mind that Shteyngel''s stable, calming influence was valuable indeed to Mikhail Bestuzhev, Vasiliy Ivashev and several other younger men less well equipped than he to bear the strain of trial, disgrace, and banishment. Mikhail Bestuzhev, as his memoirs testify, was perpetually grateful:

To this day I cannot fully understand what can have brougrt about my close friendship with Shteyngel'; for it is still beyond my power to explain the friendly feeling entertained by so steady, so intelligent a man as he – the father of a numerous family and one who had passed through the fire and flood of worldly cares and troubles – for a youth practically thirty years his junior, who danced French quadrilles in his irons for the exercise.[35]

Shteyngel''s own memoirs are of special interest in two major respects. First, they reflect the attitudes of a majority in the Northern Society in 1825, that of the constitutional monarchists. The deep hatred of serfdom felt by most for ethical reasons and by some for economic reasons too; the strong impulse towards humanitarian action; the inability to countenance regicide; even the ultimate acceptance of the christian church's dogmas, all, echoed in these memoirs, were shared by the supporters of Nikita Murav'yov. Second, Shteyngel' wrote lucidly and at some length about those aspects of the liberal débâcle that most interested him; and what most interested him was what seemed to him, subsequently, susceptible of analytic scrutiny. There are no grandiose descriptive passages, no flights of eloquence for their own sake in his reminiscences. Even the justly celebrated pages dealing with Siberia, its needs, problems, and likely future, have about them a pragmatic air not present in Volkonsky's or Rozen's or Basargin's various treatments of the theme. Shteyngel', one is reminded frequently, was an administrator, not a poet like Prince A. I. Odoyevsky or a scientist like Pyotr Borisov; his survey of the region of Ishimsk, in the Province of Tobol'sk, where he passed four active years, was fundamentally statistical in direction and, being grounded in research, later appeared under a false name in the publications of the Ministry of the Interior.[36] If only for these merits, his memoirs would be worthy of attention by all students of the period; but there is yet another factor to commend them: they do not dwell on the imprisonment in Peter-and-Paul Fortress, the interrogations by the Special Secret Committee, the journey to Siberia – themes covered by at least a dozen others. Instead, the emphasis is on Shteyngel's own earlier life, his acquaintance with Ryleyev, the illegality of the Supreme Court and, of course, Siberia, which he knew even better than did Zavalishin.

Shteyngel''s chapters on Siberia, it was said, have long been prized; the same, unfortunately, cannot be said of those dealing with the events of 1823–26, and for this reason all three extracts given in this book from Shteyngel''s reminiscences are taken from the 'earlier' sections (although, in fact, the account of December 14 was not written until 1851). The text used is that printed first in *Istoricheskiy Vestnik* (The Historical Herald) for April, May, and June 1900, and reprinted, with a useful introduction and Shteyngel''s own crisp notes, in V. I. Semevsky's, V. Bogucharky's and P. E.

Shchegolev's *Obshchestvennye dvizheniya* ..., pp. 410–46. The text is generally reliable, though minor liberties are taken with the paragraphing.[37]

Here, now, is Shteyngel''s broad account of Nicholas's problems with his brother Constantine, and of events in early December, 1825:

Baron Shteyngel'

When the Tsarevich Constantine, enamoured of the daughter of the Polish chamberlain, Joan Grudzinska, later Princess Lowicz, sought the Emperor's permission to marry her, a law was promulgated by which children issuing from the morganatic marriage of a member of the Imperial family should lose all rights conferred on lawful children. It is hard not to pause over the strangeness of this scorn for unequal matches in a dynasty, the very founder or supposed founder of which[38] was married to a *barin's* young lady, the daughter of a farming landlord, who yet — poor happy girl — brought forth into the world the wise Alexis[39]. Strange, too, when one recalls that in his turn Alexis married a poor orphan, who bore the unexampled Peter, most brilliant of the tsars; and when, finally, the greatness is ascribed to Peter himself of marrying an unknown woman or maid (it is not certain which), and of not only marrying her but leaving her possessor of the Empire! But this is not the only curiosity to have shown that contradiction between concepts, on the one hand, and actions, on the other, is inseparable from the human race.

After the promulgation of this law, the consent of the Emperor and of the chagrined Empress Mother was given to this longed-for marriage, on condition that the right of accession be renounced. The ardent Constantine agreed and in 1823, being in Petersburg, he signed such a renunciation.[40] That he did so not entirely willingly was guessed because, having been present at a ball at the Grand Duke Nicholas Pavlovich's on July 1st, he hid himself of a sudden and left for Warsaw that same night. This was no secret to the highest circle, or even to the English Club in Moscow; it was discussed, in confidence, more than a little ....

In order to cloak the fact of the Tsarevich's renunciation in some proper form, a manifesto was at once drawn up concerning the succession to the throne in the event of the Emperor's death.[41] To this were appended the Tsarevich's original letter, in which he asked permission to renounce his rights in favour of his brother, and a copy of the Emperor's reply expressing sovereign assent. All these documents were placed in a sealed envelope in the State Council, and other copies in the Uspensky Cathedral in Moscow, with the instruction that they were to be unsealed on the Emperor's death. It may be noted here, in passing, that at this point there began various happenings that particularly animated people's minds: the exiling of Labzin, Phoetius's victory over the Bible Society,[42] the duel between Chernov and Novosil'tsev and, in the special magnificence of the former's funeral, the answer of an outraged plebeianism [see pp. 24–26]. Then the appalling flood,[43] recalling that of the year of the Emperor's birth; so deeply did *this* shake the Sovereign's spirit that, of three projects sent in to the Military Governor-General [of St. Petersburg] on the matter of assistance for the victims of the flood, he chose that written by Baten'kov, in a spirit of Christian humility. Lastly, the death of Mar'ya Antonovna's daughter[44] and the Emperor's preparations to leave for the Crimea with the sick Empress; the actual departure, which was accompanied by various omens; and the killing of Nastas'ya Minkina in Gruzino, which so affected the first man of the government, who had been left practically ruler of the state, that he threw up everything and left the capital, filled with a spirit of vengeance.[45] There was something unusual in all this, something ominous! It may be imagined how tense people became when it was broadcast, 'The Sovereign is ill!' Every day state couriers arrived from Dibich, the Head of the General Staff. But still the Petersburg populace did not suspect danger — when suddenly the Grand Duke [Nicholas] moved out of his own Anichkov Palace into the Winter Palace, and occupied the Emperor's rooms with all the appearances of keeping guard. This in itself gave grounds for suspecting something out of the ordinary. Then suddenly, by an early notice on November 27th, the Council, Senate, and all the General Staff officers were invited to a Mass and public prayer for the health of His Imperial Highness in the Aleksandrovskaya monastery.[46] This meant that the courier who had arrived at a gallop at 4 A.M. had brought news that the Emperor's life was despaired of. The Metropolitan was saying Mass and hardly had the Cherubs' Hymn[47] been begun than Neygardt, Chief-of-Staff of the Guards Corps, went up to the Grand Duke and whispered something to him. His Highness at once went quietly out, and everyone set off for the palace after him. There it was learnt that another courier had brought the fateful tidings, 'The Sovereign is dead.'[48] The premeditated public prayers had to be changed into a requiem! As Military Governor-General, Count Miloradovich then had the fateful imprudence to say to the Grand Duke that he, Miloradovich, could not vouch for the city's tranquility, should an oath-taking to His Highness be announced. 'You yourself,' he added, 'will deign to acknowledge that you are not loved.' The Grand Duke at once proposed to swear an oath of allegiance to the Tsarevich. But Prince Lopukhin[49] announced to His Highness that it was necessary first that he fulfil his duty and carry out the will of the late Emperor by unsealing the packet kept in the Council. The Grand Duke agreed, and all the members of the Council set out with him to witness this. The packet was unsealed, the manifesto read, with its appendices, and all turned to the Grand Duke expressing their readiness to acknowledge him as Sovereign and to swear allegiance to him.[50] 'No, no,' replied the Grand Duke, 'I am not ready, I cannot, I do not wish to burden my conscience by depriving my elder brother of his right. I yield to him, and I will swear allegiance first.' ...

A ukase was immediately issued from the Senate ordering, on the basis of a resolution regarding the Imperial family, that allegiance be sworn to the late Emperor's other brother. That very same day and most willingly, the Guards swore their allegiance. Couriers were dispatched to all ends of the Empire, while to Warsaw was dispatched the *Ober-Prokurator* Nikitin, better known to Petersburg in the capacity of gambler.[51] Rumours began, and idle talk also, and the members of the Secret Society roused and bestirred themselves. In normal circumstances, their difference of opinion with the Southern Society would have made them cooler — and they had, in fact, remained inactive up to now: distracted by service and their private affairs, it was as if they had abandoned every thought of the objective for which they had been striving. But from the very first evening the quarters of K. F. Ryleyev,[52] the noble, never-to-be-forgotten author of *Meditations* and *Voyarovsky* (in the building of the Russian American Company, on the central board of which he was a manager) became a centre for news, meetings and debate. Through Colonel F. N. Glinka, who was then with Count Miloradovich and head of the secret department, the members could learn everything that the government, acting on the instructions of the Grand Duke, who was then *de facto* representative of Sovereign authority in the capital, was doing for its part.

In many shops on Nevskiy Prospect portraits of 'Constantine I, Emperor and Autocrat of all the Russias' were displayed for sale the day after the oath-taking. Passers-by clustered in front of them, paying attention mostly to the physiognomy, which recalled that of Paul I. Sarcastic comments were not lacking from the candid.

One of those who did not belong to the Society but had known of it since 1824, though only in vague terms and because of Ryleyev's friendly confidence in him,[53] represented to the latter that a revolution in the republican spirit was not yet possible in Russia, and would bring horrors in its train — in Moscow alone, of the 250,000 inhabitants 90,000 were serfs ready to go for their knives and abandon themselves to every passion. This individual therefore advised that if it were desired to do something to introduce the political freedom for which, it seemed, many thirsted, it would be best to have recourse to a palace revolution and proclaim Elizaveta Empress.[54] She had no heirs.[55] Longinov, who was close to her,[56] had been educated in England, and the very circumstance of a woman reigning was remembered favourably by the public. Ryleyev did not refute this but, sensing freedom, he was longing for the overthrowal of, as he expressed it, a despotism hateful and offensive to mankind.

That time is long past now—more than a quarter of a century has sunk into oblivion, and this is not the place for prejudice or passion. The truth must be stated and the inexorable truth only. Unfortunately, then, Ryleyev had at hand a man greatly embittered by something, a solitary, sombre man, ready to meet his doom—in a word, Kakhovsky.[57] Kakhovsky had elected himself in the event that *sayyids*[58] should be needed. In the heat of passion there is no place for reflection; Ryleyev told the other members of the Society of the proposal, and several were horrified by even the idea! Rostovtsev,[59] the youngest of three brothers serving in the Lifeguard Chasseurs and aide-de-camp to General Bistrom, Commander of the Guards Corps, had been shown much favour by the Grand Duke and, in a noble impulse of the heart, resolved to warn his Highness. To do so was not easy. Entry into the palace was difficult, so he acted as follows: he wrote a letter to the Grand Duke, went to the palace with it and announced at the entrance that he had been sent to the Grand Duke by General Bistrom. Admitted to the Grand Duke's study and handing him the letter, he then asked to be forgiven for presuming to deceive His Highness, and confessed that the letter was from himself and not from the General. In it, he had written that there was a plot against His Highness's life, but that 'he was not a scoundrel' and begged not to be asked to point out individuals. To this, the Grand Duke said that he did not wish to know them, shook Rostovtsev's hand and promised not to forget his noble act. This, at least, was how Rostovtsev himself described everything on a sheet of paper with which he appeared before Ryleyev, early on the morning of December 13th. Acknowledging his fault, he said: 'Do what you want with me.' Ryleyev was greatly indignant and, in the first fit of his anger, was proposing that he should be killed. But Rostovstsev, who protested against *aristocratic notions*, succeeded in calming him and bringing him to reason, so that he said, 'Well, to the Devil with him; let him live!'[60]

It was already known, on Saturday, December 11th, that the Tsarevich had received neither Nikitin nor the Senate's messages. In a letter to the Grand Duke Nicholas Pavlovich, he confirmed his renunciation. They thought in the Council of issuing a manifesto directly in the name of the new Emperor Nicholas I. Speransky was entrusted with its writing. Next day, Sunday the 12th, it being the birthday and also the day of remembrance of the late Alexander, the manifesto was signed—but everyone meant to keep this a secret. ... In discussions of the Secret Society, meanwhile, one of which was held at Prince Obolensky's, a plan of insurrection was formed. The troops that were ready to rise in revolt were to go to the Senate. It was supposed that the Senate would be in session and that, once encircled by bayonets, it would agree to proclaim a provisional government. Prince Trubetskoy, then a staff-officer of the Fourth Corps, was chosen to lead the insurrection. A sort of sombre premonition went about the capital. The very mysteriousness of the apparent bustle on both sides was frightening to one and all and, instead of exchanging greetings, those who met on the sidewalks and boulevards said, 'Well, what'll happen tomorrow?'

Mikhail A. Bestuzhev   1800–1871

No two Decembrists came to a position of political radicalism, or even of liberalism, by the same route. Prince Obolensky, it was seen, passed through a period of enthusiasm for Schellingian philosophy that led him to reflect on 'higher love,' and so on the common good. Shteyngel', while serving with the Commandant of Moscow, witnessed miscarriages of justice that quickly prompted him to take an interest in legal and administrative reforms – an interest taken by Nikolay Turgenev for less demonstrably emotional reasons. (Quite apart from the morality or immorality of serfdom, theory of jurisprudence was Turgenev's speciality; he took a heated intellectual interest in matters of economic chaos and crude legal injustice.) Others who had estates and had observed the long brutality and weariness of peasant life, or who, like N. V. Basargin, saw spectacles of cruelty as children, came to Turgenev's premises by way of their emotions. Readings from Adam Smith, Condorcet, Bignon and Destutt-de-Tracy merely gave intellectual support to what they held already. Again, some grasped the liberal idea after having indulged in Masonry.

Passages might be given here from various memoirs to suggest that a majority of members of the Northern Society were profoundly shaken by the blatant differences between peasant life in Russia and in Western Europe, which they saw as officers stationed abroad during the wars against Napoleon; or that almost all deplored the institution of autocracy, admired Benjamin Franklin, subscribed to French journals, had studied Roman history. The points made would be true, but an essential truth would have been overlooked: each individual, for all his surface similarities with others in the Union of Salvation or, later, the Northern and Southern Societies, passed the years 1820–25 in a unique way, and viewed the prospect of open rebellion against the status quo in a no less independent manner. It would be futile and misleading carefully to nudge all the Decembrists into an all-encompassing design, as it were on an enormous chess board. Instead, three extracts will be given here from the memoirs of Yakushkin and Mikhail Bestuzhev and from the private correspondence of A. A. Bestuzhev (-Marlinsky), to suggest *diversity with underlying unity*. The unity stems from common dissatisfaction with the economic, social and political realities of

Alexandrine Russia; diversity re-emphasizes that while some men were gathering clandestinely in drawing-rooms or clubs, others scarcely troubled to hide their hatred of autocracy, and others again were cruising happily in the warm Mediterranean.

Many Russian officers who had seen service in Germany or France were shocked by the brutality and brutalizing quality of life to which, in 1814–15, they returned. Yakushkin was among them:

From France we returned to Russia by sea. The Guards First Division landed at Oranienbaum and heard a *Te Deum* celebrated by the Archpriest Derzhavin. During the prayers, the police were mercilessly beating people who had tried to draw closer to the lined-up troops. This made the first unfavourable impression on us when we returned to our homeland .... Finally the Emperor appeared, accompanied by the Guard, on a fine sorrel steed, with an unsheathed sword which he was about to lower before the Empress. We looked at him with delight. But at that very moment, a peasant crossed the street, almost under his horse. The Emperor spurred his steed and rushed towards the running peasant with a naked sword. The police attacked him with their clubs. We could not believe our eyes, and turned away ashamed for our beloved Tsar. That was my first disappointment in him; involuntarily I recalled a cat transformed into a Beauty who, however, could not see a mouse without pouncing on it ... Life was tiresome for young men in St. Petersburg. For two years events had passed before our eyes which determined the fates of nations, and we had been participants in them to some degree. Now it was intolerable to see the empty life of Petersburg and listen to the babbling of old men who praised the past while reproaching every progressive move. We were away from them a hundred years.[61]

At home, as Mikhail Fonvizin put it, was found 'slavery of the majority of Russians, cruel treatment of subordinates by superiors, all kinds of government abuses and general tyranny. And all this stirred intelligent Russians, and irked patriotic feelings.'[62] Patriotism, however, was by no means the only sentiment experienced by returning combat officers, as Bestuzhev-Marlinsky makes plain. There were pleasures to distract both mind and body, if one had wealth enough and the determination to be distracted:

I'm back in St. Petersburg! Spent the evening at Sof'ya Ostaf'yevna's [a celebrated madam], and dropped in at Komarovsky's where we played silly games. From there to a magnificent ball at the Vergins. Danced a lot but soon got bored and left ... [Again, ten days later:] Had supper at the Duke's [of Württemberg]. He bade me go and enquire after the Grand Duke Mikhail's health. The latter has injured the unmentionable part of his anatomy with the butt-end of a musket. My English teacher came and tortured me with verbs. Friday must have been a truly marvellous day – I can't remember a thing. Went and ate oysters at the club, drank some of their lethal beverage and messed around there until 4 P.M. ... Was sitting at

Ryleyev's in the evening when a court messenger brought me a gold snuff-box, a gift from the Empress Elizaveta. How sweet of her; she is so kind! Afterwards we all went at once to Bedryaga's and drank a bottle of champagne to her health, [these are all, presumably, *revolutionaries*!] Gave the snuff-box to my mother. Went to pay my respects to the Duchess, who thanked me for *Polar Star* and told me that Karamzin had been singing my praises. Piles of invitations ... Spent the whole day with the ladies and told them countless lies. Saw M. at the ball in the evening; she's adorable![63]

And this was the man whom Nikita Murav'yov appointed to his own place on the Council of the Northern Society when, in April 1825, he left the capital to settle in the country. Vain, physically brave, but with Byronic airs, Bestuzhev proved ill-suited to the cautious and pedestrian work of the professional conspirator; but he was present, when the time for action came.

Here, lastly, are some of the very different experiences, over the same period, of Mikhail, the third of the Bestuzhev brothers. M. A. Bestuzhev (1800–71), who has so utterly and undeservedly been overshadowed by his elder brothers Nikolay and Aleksandr in general histories of the Decembrist movement, was one of the numerous sailors involved in the conspiracy. Having joined the Naval Cadet Corps in 1812 and shone there, he was posted warrant-officer in 1817, at which point the following extract takes up his tale:

M. A. Bestuzhev

On my passing out of the Naval Corps in May 1817, my brother Nikolay and I sailed for France aboard the ship 'Touch Me Not' to pick up Vorontsov's division. It was then that I made the acquaintance of N. I. Grech,[64] who was also aboard and bound for France with the wife and niece of General Jomini. I saw him as a passenger, not as a *littérateur*, while he saw in me a seventeen-year-old cadet without experience of life, a child in the fullest sense. To substantiate this remark, let me mention his gift to me—a box of French plums! (He was throwing all his medicines overboard and found these prunes superfluous too— prunes that had been prescribed by his physicians as the only remedy against death from sea voyage.) It was in the same frame of mind that he treated me not long before December 14th. When, already having joined the Society and been previously warned to be on guard against him as a government spy, I paid him several visits, he tried obliquely and by hints to draw something out of me concerning the existence of something it was *necessary* that he know, but which had escaped his vigilance. Tormented by the demon of curiosity, he invited me into his study one evening after dinner, shortly before the 14th, and spoke to me directly without mincing his words:

'Tell me, Michel, you belong to the Secret Society, after all. ... What're its aims and intentions?' 'You aren't a detective,' I replied, 'and I'm not an informer. But in case I'm mistaken in the former assumption, let me assure you that I'm no Judas, and won't betray the innocent for a few silver roubles.'

Heated with anger, I left him and walked out of his house meaning never to meet him again. He did not forgive me that burning reproach and tried in his own fashion, in his memoirs, to wound me with a venomous remark about my character.

The equipage, or battalion, in which I found myself serving was sent to Archangel to meet the Emperor, as the best ship's company to have seen service at the front. My brother Nikolay remained in Kronstadt while I, as if leaving for exile, was obliged to set out for the North and spend two years there. On my return from Archangel, I lived with K. P. Torson, and grew as close as a brother to him. He and I were one. It was by him that I was received into the Society.

Torson submitted a project at this time for reorganizing the fleet, and I laboured on that project with him. One whole winter, frozen and dying of ennui, we spent drawing up an establishment according to the new plan. Finally a ship, the 'Emgeyten,'[65] was assigned to us to realize Torson's ideas, and it was decreed by special order that, on the completion of her armament, she should be taken out for sea trials and commanded by the author of the project, that is, by Torson himself. So once again we plunged into murderously exhausting work, this time concerning the ship's armament; and one has to have beheld the pettiness and miserliness of our Admiralty to conceive the difficulties that we encountered at every step, in making innovations. With every move we came across obstacles and stones thrown in our path by the Admiralty foremen—those rats who smelt an end now to their unaccountable gnawing away at the interests of the state.

But finally we overcame all difficulties. 'Emgeyten' was fitted out like a bridegroom for the wedding. And splendid it was to see that beauty of the Russian fleet, now equipped without regard for 'classical' regulations, but simply, cleanly, in a way that fully corresponded to her warlike purpose. But then what? A few days before she was due to put out to sea the Guards Equipage arrives on steamboats from St. Petersburg, is given quarters on 'Emgeyten' and—the ship goes out to the roads! Kachalov, Commander of the Guards Equipage, assumes command of her and prepares her for a meeting with the Grand Duke Nicholas! And so the project that would have brought the government economies of a million roubles or more on one ship alone was put aside, and Torson, like some person who had never been, was banished. Of me and the Commission that had laboured a whole year no mention was so much as made! 'But what kind of a rum affair is this?' you may ask. A very simple one, it may be answered, and one in no way different from those which ever and anon occurred under the *beneficent* rule of the Blessed Alexander. On this occasion his little brother, Nicholas Pavlovich, had decided that he wished to see his father-in-law, the King of Prussia; but he had no stomach for the journey by land, on miserable roads! Well (said he), I'll go by sea! In consequence of which, an order: to prepare a ship to convey the Grand Duke and his family to Prussia. Easier said than done, this. All the ships then in Kronstadt harbour were rotting away, painted and prettified on one side only—along which the reviewing monarch would invariably be led. It did not take much working out: 'Emgeyten,' that beauty, was ready. The Grand Duke would set out in her! And so he did.[66] The Blessed One saw his little brother off, was in raptures over the arrangement of the ship, thanked Kachalov for the pleasure of having seen over the ship so splendidly prepared by him, rewarded him and his crew—and us? *We* were all sent away from Kronstadt under different pretexts and received nothing! Torson, do not forget, was senior adjutant to the Acting Naval Minister. And these and similar low intrigues were being brought about without his knowledge. You may imagine the vexation in so pure a soul as Torson's, and the storm that he raised when he discovered what a pitiable rôle he had played in this comedy. Straightaway he told the Minister he would approach the Tsar and 'inform him of everything concerning the fleet, and especially of how his special ukases were trifled with, even when the exchequer's interests would suffer ... ' Like any German who imbibes the ways of Holy Russia, the German Moller[67] understood that such pills as Torson had swallowed might well cause indigestion of the stomach. He therefore hastened to calm him by all possible means. He referred to the state of our fleet, to the necessity of 'Emgeyten's' mission, soothed and assuaged his annoyance and finally, to calm him down completely, proposed a scientific expedition to the North Pole! The command would be Torson's. The frigate and the brig allotted for this purpose would also be under his command. (Captain-Lieutenant Vasil'yev's unsuccessful voyage to the Pole was given as a pretext for a fresh attempt.)[68] Thorough German that he was, Moller quite sank to baseness to control the storminess of Torson's anger, giving solemn promises to load him and all who should participate in the voyage with rewards, at the conclusion of the expedition; he even proposed to Torson that he himself draw up the orders for his coming voyage.

Well do I remember those blessed moments when, on an autumnal night, by the dim light of a tallow candle, Torson and I would lay courses all over the terrestrial globe, discovering unknown islands and lands which we christened with Russian names. I remember, too, how we puzzled to find a pretext for visiting the Mediterranean as well, to which my ardent fancy drew me—and finally even those regions were included in an order, and the order was confirmed by the sovereign authority. The frigate and the brig were built in Petersburg. I and the officers selected for the voyage were to supervise the building of the ships. But in my heart dissatisfaction seethed, and aversion for a service in which, for all one's keen performance of one's duty, nothing secured rewards. Sympathizing with my situation and foreseeing that the fateful hour was near—and, probably, wishing to see me an active collaborator in the imminent events—my brother Aleksandr suggested that I exchange the sea for the dry land and enter the Guards, specifically, the Moscow Regiment, in which my naval rank would give the rank of first lieutenant and in which, vacancies opening up continually, I should quickly and indubitably find promotion. Swayed by my feeling of disgust still, I agreed. I was transferred to the Moscow Regiment as first lieutenant. Il'ya Gavrilovich Bibikov, then senior aide to the Grand Duke Mikhail Pavlovich, did much to facilitate this transfer, and to ensure that the Grand Duke would be well disposed towards me. And the Grand Duke did take a liking to me. On being promoted staff-captain, I was entrusted with Captain Mart'yanov's company, a company trained by the threat of canes, birch rods, and gun-sticks. Many were the wearisome days that it took me to retrain that company on more humane principles; but finally I had the happiness of having the Grand Duke Mikhail Pavlovich himself wish to take it from me because, according to the bulletin of penalties, not a single man in it had suffered punishment. It was with this company that I appeared on the Square on December 14th. ...

As you will see from this short sketch of my life from the time of my promotion to lieutenant to the fateful 14th of December, that life was passed outside Petersburg. Although I shared rooms for a little while, after my transfer to the Guards, with Ryleyev and my brother Aleksandr, and met many remarkable individuals, nevertheless my days were swallowed whole by the tasks of active service and, especially, by the taking on of a company; only the evening hours were left for short rests. When I happened to be present at literary dinners or soirées at Grech's, Prince Shakhovskoy's, Bulgarin's, Prokof'yev's, Somov's and elsewhere, but most particularly at Ryleyev's evenings and late breakfasts, I certainly met masses of interesting men; but I had neither time nor motive then to study their biographies. And in prison we lived the lives of shades in the Elysian Fields. True, we often, very often, heard of highly entertaining episodes in the lives of all the prisoners; but these only occupied us while the tale was being told. Afterwards, they fused into the chaos of a thousand similar stories, leaving no impression on the memory.

Robert Lee 1793–1871

Here, to conclude this section, are two eye-witness accounts of the first days of Nicholas's reign by individuals who were not and could not have been revolutionaries: Dr. Robert Lee, private physician to Count M. S. Vorontsov (1782–1856), the dictatorial and anglophile governor-general of New Russia (and Pushkin's chief in Odessa), and Aleksandr Herzen, then a boy of just fourteen. A few words are apposite to place the Scottish doctor.

Dr. Lee, a distinguished obstetrician who served briefly with the East India Company, was appointed personal physician to Count Mikhail Vorontsov in 1824.[69] He arrived in Odessa, seat of the governor-general, on January 8, 1825; was present when the numerous Imperial suite arrived in late October; travelled with the tsar to Taganrog; ate with the tsar two days before his death; was with him at the end, and attended the autopsy in company with Dr. James Wylie, special physician to the dead monarch and his fellow-countryman. Returning to London in 1826, Lee wrote a paper which was published in 'The Athenaeum' only in 1845. That paper was designed 'to counteract impressions that the Emperor did not die naturally.' But Lee decided not to publish it while controversy was still rife – a curious decision, some may feel. Using the same private journal that he kept throughout his stay in Russia's southern territories, the doctor then expanded his original paper. *The Last Days of Alexander and the First Days of Nicholas* appeared in London (Richard Bentley and Co.) in 1854. It is an exceptionally shrewd and sane account of life in Russia in a time of national crisis, and deserves far wider recognition.

The entries in Lee's journal are direct, terse and reflect no small intelligence.

Robert Lee

Thursday December 10th, 1825. Taganrog.
At 11 o'clock this forenoon I went to a wooden church where all the public authorities were assembled to swear allegiance to the Emperor Constantine. This was done by an ukase from St. Petersburgh. The body of the church was

filled with people of the lowest order and mouziks, who shewed no enthusiasm for the occasion.

Friday, December 11th.
This morning at nine o'clock the body of the Emperor Alexander was conveyed from the house in which he resided to the church called St. Alexander Newsky, which had been fitted up for its reception. The streets were lined with troops. A small party of gendarmes commanded by the Master of Police led the procession. Then followed the valets, cooks, and others employed about His Majesty. Next, the persons employed about the quarantine and others of the town. Then came a number of priests with flags, torches and crosses, usually carried in funeral processions. Then came a band of singers. After these, a number of generals bearing the orders, crosses, etc. of His Majesty. ... The day was bitterly cold, and the effect was not great. ... And this was all that remained of the mighty sovereign who had reigned over 40 millions of slaves, and whose empire had extended from China to the Baltic Sea, and from the confines of Persia and Turkey to the Arctic Ocean.

24th, Thursday.
... It appears that a regiment of guards at Petersburgh refused to take the oath and broke out into an open revolt. The Emperor Nicholas went to them, and reasoned with them calmly in the midst of the tumult; but all his arguments proving ineffectual, force was obliged to be had recourse to, to bring them into subordination. Nicholas remained among them several hours, in the utmost danger of being murdered; and the Count Miloradowitch was shot dead by a person not in military uniform. ... The number of lives lost I have not heard, but it must have been considerable as the sedition was not quelled until several pieces of artillery were brought to play upon them. They were chiefly young men who were engaged in this affair; but that an extensive conspiracy was formed to prevent the accession of the present Emperor there cannot, I think, be a doubt. This is an ominous commencement of the reign of Nicholas, and will not be forgotten, though it should be equally prosperous as that of his predecessor and of still longer duration.

26th, Saturday.
... Affability and benevolence Alexander certainly possessed in an eminent degree, and had he not been a great monarch he would have been beloved and respected by all who knew him. But I have met with none here who have endeavoured to form an estimate of his public and political life. Of his conduct in regard to Greece, Italy and Spain, there can be but one opinion; and in respect to Russia few will hesitate to express their conviction that his blind attachment

to the army, and his dread and hatred of all free institutions in the country, have been two of the greatest errors which a sovereign could have committed. The former passion led to the ruin of the commerce of the country and the finances of the empire; and the latter to the proscription of every species of public instruction. The state of the universities is truly wretched; every man of talent being either driven out or forced to quit them owing to the restrictions to which they have been subjected. ... If, instead of wasting the last ten years in exercising his unwieldy host, in planting military colonies and in crushing the rising liberties of Germany and the south of Europe, he had directed his mind to the improvement of the laws and civil institutions of the country, and to the amelioration of the 40 millions of slaves in his empire, what a magnificent and imperishable monument would he not have raised to his fame. ... The Emperor Alexander undoubtedly gained the affection of those immediately around his person, because he was most attentive to their feelings and wants, and by them he is no doubt sincerely regretted; but of his tender mercies to the people at large I can see no evidence. ...

Many of the officers detest the present form of government, and desire a representative and constitutional government, and long to see the slaves educated and gradually emancipated. The soldiers cannot feel any attachment to the government which has dragged them from their homes and doomed them to a life of the severest hardship. Slight circumstances might effect the most important changes in the whole structure of society in Russia, and it is hardly possible that good should not spring from any change. All power being vested in the army, the changes will begin first in that quarter.

Aleksandr I. Herzen[70]

Nicholas was completely unknown until he came to the throne; in the reign of Alexander he was of no consequence, and no one was interested in him. Now, everyone rushed to enquire about him. No one could answer questions but the officers of the Guards, and they hated him for his cold cruelty, his petty fussiness, and his vindictiveness. One of the first anecdotes to circulate in the city confirmed the officers' opinion of him. The story was that at some drill or other the Grand Duke had so far forgotten himself as to try to take an officer by the collar. The officer responded with the words, 'Your Highness, my sword is in my hand.' Nicholas drew back, said nothing, but never forgot the answer. After the 14th of December he made inquiries on two occasions as to whether this officer was implicated. Happily he was not.[71]

The tone of society changed before one's eyes; and this rapid moral deterioration was a melancholy proof of how little the sense of personal dignity was developed among Russian aristocrats. Except women, nobody dared to show sympathy or to utter a warm word about friends or relations whose hands they had shaken only the day before police had carried them off by night. On the contrary, there were savage fanatics for slavery, some from motives of abjectness, others, still worse, for disinterested reasons. ...

The accounts of the rebellion and of the trial of its leaders, and the horror in Moscow, made a deep impression on me; a new world was revealed—and that world became increasingly the centre of my moral life. I do not know how it came about, but though I had no understanding of what it all meant, or only a very dim one, still I felt that I was not on the same side as the grapeshot and victory, prisons and chains. And the execution of Pestel' and his associates finally scattered the childish dream of my soul.

Everyone expected some mitigation of the sentence on the condemned men —the coronation was about to take place. Even my father, despite his caution and his scepticism, said the death penalty would not be carried out and that all this was being done merely to impress people. But he, like everyone else, knew little of the youthful monarch. Nicholas left Petersburg and, not visiting Moscow, stopped at the Petrovsky Palace. ... The citizens of Moscow could scarcely believe their eyes when they read in *Moskovskiye Vedomosti* [Moscow News] of the terrible event of July 14th.

The Russian populace had grown unaccustomed to the death penalty. Since the days of Mirovich,[72] who was executed instead of Catherine II, and of Pugachov[73] and his companions, there had been no executions; men had died under the knout, soldiers had run the gauntlet (contrary to the law) until they fell dead, but the death penalty *de jure* did not exist. The story is told that in the reign of Paul there was a rising of some of the cossacks of the Don in which two officers were implicated. Paul ordered them to be tried by court martial, and gave the Hetman or general full authority. The court condemned them to death—but no one dared confirm the sentence. The Hetman submitted the matter to the Tsar. 'They're a pack of women,' said Paul; 'they want to throw the execution onto me—much obliged to them!' and he commuted the sentence to one of penal servitude. Nicholas re-introduced the death penalty into our criminal proceedings, illegally at first, though afterwards he included it in the Code.

The day after the terrible news was received, there was a religious service in the Kremlin.[74] After celebrating the executions, Nicholas made a triumphal entry into Moscow. I saw him for the first time then; he was on horseback, riding beside a carriage in which sat the two Empresses, his wife and Alexander's widow. He was handsome, but there was a coldness about his looks; no face could have more mercilessly betrayed the character of the man than his. The sharply retreating forehead and lower jaw developed at the expense of the skull were expressive of iron will and weak intelligence, and rather of cruelty than sensuality; but the chief point in his face was the eyes, which were wholly without warmth, without a trace of mercy; wintry eyes.[75] I do not believe that he ever passionately loved any woman as Paul had loved Anna Lopukhina[76] and Alexander every woman but his wife. He was 'favourably disposed towards them,' nothing more.

The Rising

Of all the many aspects of the movement known (post facto) as **Decembrism**, none is more generally familiar than the actual insurrection of December 14, 1825. All histories of the development of liberalism in Russia, indeed, all histories of Russia, spare it a paragraph or two; all studies of the reign of Nicholas, whether for scholarly or popular consumption, published in the USSR or in the West, allude to it if they do not give a chapter to it. And such a situation is most proper: on Senate Square, liberal tendencies in Alexandrine Russia came to an unexpected crisis. It was, in political terms, the high point of the radical-liberal movement in St. Petersburg, the martyrs' day, the *joli commencement de règne.*

Yet on what sources have all studies of the movement, from general works such as A. G. Mazour's, A. N. Pypin's and M. N. Pokrovsky's, to specialized volumes such as A. E. Presnyakov's *14 Dekabrya 1825 goda,*[1] relied essentially? To glance through any one of these scholars' contributions to the field is to appreciate the answer: it is on two sets of memoirs, those of A. E. Rozen and of the Bestuzhev brothers, that all modern appreciations of the rising have been grounded.

Because of this, and also because the happenings on Senate Square are tolerably well known to many readers, only three short accounts of the revolt itself will be presented here: those of Baron Rozen (the value of whose narrative cannot well be denied), Mikhail Bestuzhev (whose account is no less accurate or lucid than his brother Nikolay's), and, to give added depth of perspective, Baron Shteyngel'. There are a number of good reasons why the narratives of Rozen and M. A. Bestuzhev should be included here. Both men saw more than most, because of their positions on St. Isaac's Bridge and on the Square, and recorded what they saw and heard with greater accuracy than most. Reasons for introducing Baron Shteyngel''s less familiar account are less self-evident but may be briefly stated. Shteyngel' was present on the Square for a few minutes in the morning and again towards 2 p.m. He was personally acquainted with Ryleyev yet did not care to view himself as one of the insurgents. While theoretically approving of any means by which autocracy might be abolished and a constitution introduced to Russia, he yet described his comrades as mere *insurgenty.* But on the other hand he censured Yakubovich[2] for referring to those comrades as *buntovschiki,* or rebels. Again, he could admire the new tsar's calm and poise – but wished to see him driven from his throne in great disgrace. The baron was, in fact, confused. Though his impression of events was a fragmentary one, however, he was a most intelligent, exceedingly perceptive individual, and his account of the rebellion has two over-riding virtues from the modern student's viewpoint: it is extremely clear; and it is typical of many narratives deliberately and carefully assembled from assorted scraps of evidence by men who, like himself, saw something but not everything. Like his attitudes, his errors and his prejudices were widespread among contemporaries, and this, too, is of interest and value.

First, however, here is Mikhail Bestuzhev's account of *der Tag:*

M. A. Bestuzhev

It was a noisy, turbulent meeting in Ryleyev's rooms on the eve of the 14th.[3] Those present, and there were many, were in a feverish, somehow exalted state and there were heard desperate statements, impracticable instructions and suggestions, words without deeds for which many, although guilty of nothing and before no man, would pay dearly.[4] The boastful exclamations of Yakubovich and Shchepin-Rostovsky were frequently audible. Though a brave officer, Yakubovich was a braggart and would trumpet abroad his feats in the Caucasus; [5] but discretion, it is justly said, is the better part of wisdom — and this he proved on Senate Square on December 14th. The bravery of the soldier and of the conspirator are not one and the same. In the first case, honour and rewards may be expected even in the event of failure, whereas in the second even success brings an uncertain future, and should the cause be lost one may expect disgrace and an infamous death. But I had brought Shchepin-Rostovsky to the meeting on purpose, though he was not a member of our Society, to see if he would draw back from us. [6] Galvanized by me perhaps even excessively, and feeling the irresistible force that now drew him into a vortex, he slapped his arms and legs as though attempting, by spraying and splashing some invisible water, to stifle or cloud over his reason.

But how fine Ryleyev was that evening! He was not a handsome man, nd, although he spoke simply, he did not speak fluently. But when he touched on his favourite theme, love of the motherland, his face would grow animated, his jet-black eyes light up with an unearthly glow, his speech flow as smoothly as molten lava; and *then* one could never tire of gazing at him.

So on this fateful evening too, during which that cloudy question, *To be or not to be*, was resolved, Ryleyev's countenance, pale as the moon but lit up by some supernatural light, would vanish, reappear and vanish once again in the stormy waves of that ocean seething with various passions and convictions. Sitting to one side with Sutgof,[7] with whom my brother and I were talking and confiding our innermost thoughts, I admired him. Ryleyev approached us then and said, taking us both by the arm, 'Peace be with you, men of action and not words! *You* don't rave like Shchepin or Yakubovich, yet I'm certain that you'll do what has to be done. And we. ...'

'I find all this showing off,' I interrupted him, 'and these parades of vanity extremely suspect—especially on Yakubovich's part. It's very well to tell him to raise the artillery and the Izmaylovskiy Regiment, come with them to me, and then lead them all onto the Square and up to the Senate but believe me, he won't carry all *that* out. And if he does, any delay once the troops' enthusiasm has been roused may well damage our chances of success or completely ruin them.'

'But how can you imagine that a courageous Caucasian...?'

'The soldier's bravery is not the same as the conspirator's. But he's intelligent enough to appreciate that difference. To be brief, *I'll* lead the regiment, try to get it to swear the oath[8] and let the other regiments join up with me on the Square.'

'I know the men of your company will follow you through fire and water,' said Ryleyev, after a moment's reflection. 'But what about the other companies?'

'My men have been working hard for the past two days among the other companies, and the company commanders have given me their word of honour not to hinder their men if they come out with mine. I've persuaded the commanders themselves not to go onto the Square, increasing the number of victims to no purpose.'

'And what will *you* say to them?' asked Ryleyev, turning to Sutgof.

'I'll repeat what Bestuzhev has said to you,' said Sutgof, 'and lead my company onto the Square as soon as even a part of the troops are assembled.'

'And the other companies?'

'Perhaps they'll follow me too; but I can't answer for them.'

These were the last words I exchanged with Ryleyev on this earth. It was almost midnight when we left him and I hurried home in order to be ready for the fateful day then dawning, and to husband my strength, which was debilitated by intense activity, if only by a few hours' sleep. Things worked out otherwise, however. Ever pointlessly on the simmer by his nature, Shchepin had suddenly been plunged into a sphere unknown to him. Not understanding that the question was by no means whether we should have Constantine or Nicholas for Tsar, he had been shouting the most desperate phrases in favour of Constantine—and so was placed by the Commission of Enquiry among the most desperate members of our Society, when he did not even know of its existence! Seeing his overwrought state, I regretted having introduced too much steam into that engine and, afraid lest the boiler should actually burst, decided to spend the night with him and see that safety valves were opened periodically. I shall not describe that night, his ragings or my own attempts to quieten them.

Dawn came on finally, and we were asked to attend on General Fridrikhs, [Friedricks] the Regimental Commander. With him we found Captain Kornilov (the elder brother of the hero of Sevastopol'). I watched Kornilov as Fridrikhs read out to us Constantine's renunciation and Nicholas's manifesto, and noticed the pallor that came over his crimson face. So utterly astounded was he by Constantine's renunciation that he left the General on unsteady legs. I stopped him going down the staircase that led to Fridrikhs's first floor, and asked him: 'Well? What do you mean to do now?'

'I can't act with you; I withdraw my word.'

'But you have forgotten one condition,' I exclaimed, showing him the butt of a pistol which I had hidden in the sleeve of my greatcoat.

'Well, kill me then! I'd sooner agree to die than to take part in an illegal undertaking!'

'No, why die? Live! But don't prevent the men in your company from coming out with mine if they go onto the Square.'

'I promise,' he said, at last—and he kept his word.[9]

But let me say a few words here to cast some light on what may be obscure in the foregoing conversation. Kornilov was in all respects an excellent fellow: educated, kindly, and a splendid colleague; but he was utterly possessed by politics, and held his own deep reasoning to be indisputable. And Constantine's renunciation was inconceivable according to that reasoning—all Russia had sworn an oath to him! But Kornilov had readily agreed to collaborate with me earlier, and when I had asked, 'Suppose Constantine refuses?' he had replied, 'Then I shall let you shoot me. I'll swear to no one else.' Thus the sagacious politician found himself in a tight corner.

I found my brother Aleksandr waiting for me impatiently, on returning to my rooms. 'Where's Yakubovich?' I asked.

'Still in his rooms, working out how to betray us most courageously,' replied my brother. 'When I urged him to go to the artillery and the Izmaylovskiy, he just repeated stubbornly, 'You've taken on something impracticable. You don't know the Russian soldier as I do.'

'So we've lost our hopes of artillery and of other regiments, too.' Tears almost came to my eyes. 'Well, plainly God wills it so. There's no point in delaying—let's join the regiment. I'll lead it onto the Square.'

'No, wait a little,' said my brother. 'Ryleyev had serious doubts when he heard Yakubovich's boasting yesterday, and he promised me to go to the artillery, the Izmaylovskiy, the Semyonovskiy and the chasseurs himself, and lead them here.'[10]

'No, delay will ruin everything. Let's go, and take the regiment out for the oath-taking.'

My brother gave way, and we left. He told the men he was an adjutant of the Emperor Constantine, that the Emperor had been held up on the road to Petersburg, and that they wished to force the Guards to swear allegiance to Nicholas. The men replied with one voice: 'We don't want Nicholas! Hurrah for Constantine!'

After this, Aleksandr went off to the other companies, but I, having issued live cartridges, drew my company up in the courtyard. Then, sending trusted agents off to those other companies with instructions that they, too, bring live ammunition, march out and join us, I gave the order to move out. We went out into the main courtyard,[11] drums beating. There, a lectern had already been brought up for the oath-taking ceremony. The colours, too, were there already, and rows of colour-bearers waited for us to emerge onto the main courtyard so as to join the companies proceeding to the Square. Shchepin drew up his company behind mine; behind us all, soldiers just then running out from their contingents formed an unruly crowd. There was no opportunity even to form them up in a massed column; we were afraid of losing time. I moved ahead with my company. As we approached the archway of the gates to which the colours had been brought (that is, where the exit from the lecture hall is situated), the bearers all at once came into sight. The colour of my own battalion was placed at the head of my company, as was appropriate; but the other one was carried further on to join the companies of the other battalion. And this became the cause of a confused scramble that halted the whole movement of the regiment and very nearly ruined everything which had begun so well! (For, a chaotic mob of soldiers from other companies, supposing that the colour was being carried to the lectern around which already stood those men of the Moscow Regiment who were not willing to join us, threw themselves onto the colour-bearers intending to seize the colour from them. A fight began, each side believing that the other was an enemy, when in fact all were our men.) I was already crossing the Fontanka bridge when an under-officer of Shchepin's company ran up to me.

'Your Excellency,' he gasped, 'for God's sake go back and stop ... stop the mêlée.'

'But where's your company?' I asked, halting my men. 'And where's the Prince?'

'Where, Your Excellency? On the courtyard, as you know.'

'And what are they doing there?'

'Fighting for a banner, the fools!'

'And that Prince of yours, why doesn't he stop them?'

'Oh, the Prince. ... He's chopping left and right at his own men — and everybody else. He's already wounded, in the arm, Lance-corporal Fyodorov of his own company.'

'Right foot forward, march!' I ordered. 'Come on, lads, we'll calm them down.' We entered the courtyard by another gate a little behind the bustling crowds, which now spread practically over the whole area. And there was the colour, now vanishing, now appearing once again over the shaken plumes and bayonets of soldiers! Once having plunged into *that* raging sea, it seemed, there was no possibility of getting to the colour which had caused the whole affair. But in one way or another action had to be taken.

'Close ranks, lads,' I shouted to my men. 'Stand tight against each other!' As if fused into a single mass, my men cut a path to the centre of the crowd and, moving forward irresistibly, flung off to either side seething masses of soldiery. 'Gently!' I commanded, having reached the colour. So the enraged soldiers calmed down, and ordered arms. And I went up to Shchepin, when I had taken the colour from its bearer's hands. 'Here's your colour, Prince. Now lead your men onto the Square.'

'Behind me, lads!' yelled Shchepin furiously. And all that turbulent mass of troops, ready to cut each other's throats a minute earlier, moved as one man through the barrack gates and flooded Gorokhovaya Street,[12] to its full width.

As we were leaving, we caught sight of my brother Aleksandr. He was standing beside General Fridrikhs and attempting to persuade him to be gone; but seeing that his protestations were futile, he threw open his greatcoat and showed the General a pistol. Fridrikhs galloped off to the left, but stumbled upon Shchepin who cut at him so deftly with his sharp sword that he fell to the ground. Thereupon, approaching the exit of the archway now, Shchepin ran up to Brigadier Shenshin, who was haranguing a quite separate group of disaffected men, and dealt with him in the same fashion. Under the archway itself stood Colonel Khvoshchinsky, arms raised high and shouting at the troops not to advance. Shchepin shook his sword at him. Hurrying off in great alarm, Khvoshchinsky brought himself down to the ground, so that Shchepin only succeeded in giving him a long blow on the back with the flat of his sword. 'I die! I die!' cried the Colonel in a pitiful voice, still running off. The men burst their sides with laughter.

Minutes later, passing down Gorokhovaya Street and past the quarters occupied by Yakubovich, we caught sight of that individual as he was hurriedly running down a staircase and onto the street to join us.

'What might this mean?' said my brother Aleksandr. 'Still, we must try him out.'

Yakubovich, his sword drawn and his white-plumed hat waving magnificently on its tip, approached us with triumphant cries: 'Hurrah!' he yelled, 'Constantine!'

'By your right as a brave Caucasian, take command of the troops.'

'Why all the ceremony?'[7] said he, vexed. Then, having reflected an instant: 'Very well, I accept.'

Coming onto Senate Square, we found it completely empty.[13]

'Well, am I *now* in my rights to repeat that you've undertaken something quite impossible?' he then said. 'You see? Not one man, as I thought.'

'You couldn't have said that,' burst out my brother, 'if you'd kept your word and led either the artillery or the Izmaylovskiy here before us.'

Shchepin and I hastened to count up the men and then form them into a carré. My company, including privates from other companies, made up two sides of it, one facing the Senate, the other facing the monument of Peter I. Shchepin's, which also contained men from other companies, formed the two sides facing St. Isaac's and the Admiralty. It was already about nine o'clock.

For more than two hours we stood, and no force appeared against us. The first troops that we saw nearby were horseguards, who approached us quietly in groups of three from the right while keeping close to Admiralty Boulevard. Having wheeled, they drew themselves up with their backs to the Admiralty and their right flank towards the Neva. Then men of the Preobrazhenskiy Regiment appeared, advancing from the Palace Square, artillery ahead (for which they had forgotten or not managed to get ammunition, and which was sent after them. Still towards evening they were bringing ammunition!) The first battalion of the Preobrazhenskiy closed off the exit from St. Isaac's Bridge, passing behind the horseguards. Taking the same route, mounted pioneers sealed off the exit to English Embankment, while the Pavlovskiy Regiment formed up with its rear to Lobanov-Rostovsky's mansion,[14] the Semyonovskiy along Horseguards' Manège, and the Izmaylovskiy along the street formed when they built Lobanov's house. Other regiments were placed along the main streets leading to St. Isaac's, Palace, and Petrovskiy Square. But the arrival and the disposition of these troops, far from being simultaneous, was accompanied by lengthy pauses and much bustling. And men of the Izmaylovskiy Regiment who had stoutly refused to swear an oath to Nicholas—and who had beaten Rostovtsev without mercy when he thought to persuade them to do so[15]—

were led against the troops whom they were every moment waiting some good opportunity to join! As Commander of this regiment, the new Emperor had not even received a formal response to his thrice-repeated greeting: 'Well done, children!' and had retired in confusion. And this same regiment they left to stand against us until evening! The Preobrazhenskiy men too, also drawn up against us by St. Isaac's Bridge, were left until the evening, despite the fact that, won over by Chevkin, they had firmly refused to swear the oath to Nicholas. As for the horseguards three times sent off to attack us, but who succeeded only on the third occasion in galloping through to the Senate, where they formed up backs towards it, they too were simply left to stand there; and this was a regiment so well prepared by members of our Society that, had we moved, it would most probably have joined us! Like those of the Preobrazhenskiy, the men of the Izmaylovskiy Regiment had let us know their intentions by means of the crowd surrounding us.

Once having completed that difficult manoeuvre, the forming of a carré out of units from various companies (around which many of our members had already gathered), but still not seeing Yakubovich, I asked why he was missing.

'He told me,' said my brother, 'that he was leaving the Square because of a fearful headache. But just look at him!' he added, pointing towards the Tsar's suite. 'The atmosphere round the new Tsar has probably had an improving effect on his sensitive nerves.'

My brother was not wrong in that supposition. Quite overcome by feelings of the deepest loyalty, Yakubovich had approached the Sovereign and sought permission to conduct us back to the path of lawfulness. The Sovereign had agreed. Tying a white kerchief to his sword, Yakubovich then came promptly up to our carré, whispered to Mikhail Kyukhel'beker, 'Hold on! They're terrified of you!' and went off. Shortly after this incident, a squadron of horseguards broke formation and rushed down on us. They were met by the crowd with a hail of stones from the carriageway and a hail of sorted firewood from behind the fence by St. Isaac's Cathedral.[16] The cavalrymen, who had attacked unwillingly and without spirit, returned to their front in disorder.[17] A second and third attack were withstood by the Moscow men without the crowd's assistance, and with cool fortitude. After the third had been repulsed, the horseguards galloped over to the Senate; and my men, supposing that they meant to attack us from that side, where they were now starting to form a front, immediately took aim, wanting to fire a volley which would very probably have felled them to the last man. Ignoring the danger, I ran out in front of the side of the carré, shouting: 'Let them alone!' Rifles were lowered, but several bullets whistled by my ears and a few horseguards fell from their mounts. A little later, God knows by whose order, the mounted pioneers rushed past my side and past the horseguards. My men fired volleys at them, and forced them to retire. Being on the other side of the carré, I could neither foresee nor stop this. Regrettable though these two incidents certainly were, however, they had happy results for us: the shots were heard in the Guards' barracks, whereupon the Guards hastened to our assistance.

Almost at the same moment that this occurred in the Life-Grenadiers' barracks, similar events were taking place in the Guards' Staff quarters. Here is Pushchin's account of them:[18] 'General Shchipov, Regimental Commander of the Semyonovskiy Regiment and Head of the Brigade of which the Guards' Staff formed a part, was in the Staff's quarters. Shchipov, who had been an ardent member of the secret society not long before and had been wholly devoted to Pestel', chose this moment to play the rôle of mediator between those officers of the Guards' Staff who did and those who did not wish to swear the oath to Nicholas. As their Commander he gave no orders, but begged them not to ruin themselves and a good cause. He then assured them that they would postpone indefinitely, by their reckless undertaking, what might in any case be hoped for from the new Emperor. But all entreaties were in vain— resolutely the officers told him that they would never swear the oath, and went out to the troops who were waiting for them. Nikolay Bestuzhev, meanwhile, was persuading these not to swear allegiance to Nicholas. Suddenly shots were heard. 'They're killing our men, lads,' shouted Kyukhel'beker; and the whole group, as of one mind, moved off after our good Nikolay, who led them onto the Square.

On the Square itself, the Staff drew itself up to the right of the Moscow Regiment and sent out its marksmen under the command of Lieutenant Mikhail Kyukhel'beker.[19] With the Guards' Staff, besides the company commanders Kyukhel'beker, Arbuzov and Pushkin,[20] came the two brothers Belyayev, Bodisko, Divov and Captain-Lieutenant Nikolay Bestuzhev, brother of Aleksandr and Mikhail. He, however, was not a member of the Guards' Staff ...' Here, now, in Pushchin's just account of it, is the rebellion of the Life-Grenadiers:

'Konovnitsyn of the Mounted Artillery, meanwhile, having escaped arrest somehow, galloped towards the Senate building and encountered Odoyevsky,[21] who had just then been relieved from the inner watch and was on his way to the Life-Grenadiers with the news that the Moscow Regiment had already been some time on the Square. Konovnitsyn rode with him. Arriving at the barracks only to find that the Life-Grenadiers had sworn allegiance to Nicholas Pavlovich and that the men had been dismissed to eat, the pair went off to Sutgof to reproach him for not having led his company to the assembly place, where the Moscow Regiment had been standing a long time already. But Sutgof had known nothing about this till then. Without further words, he went off to his company and gave orders that the men take up their shoulder-belts and arms. The men obeyed, [live] cartridges were issued there and then, and the whole company, leaving the barracks without hindrance, set out towards the Senate. Battalion Adjutant Panov, who happened to be present, then rushed off to the other seven companies in an attempt to persuade the men not to be separated from those of Sutgof's company. As if by magic, all the seven companies seized arms and cartridges and poured out of the barracks. Panov, who was a small man, they carried out aloft. As to the threats and, later, admonitions of Styurler [Stürler], Commander of the Regiment, they produced no effect on the men whatsoever. Panov led them through the Fortress, which they could have seized with ease and, bringing them out onto Palace Embankment, would have turned into the Palace itself; but someone told him that his comrades were not there but by the Senate, and that in the Palace there was a battalion of sappers. So Panov went further along the Embankment, turned to his left and, coming out on Palace Square, went past the cannon standing there which, as it was remarked later, he could have taken. And all this time Styurler was marching with his regiment and trying to persuade the men to return to barracks! When the Life-Grenadiers drew level with the Moscow Regiment, Kakhovsky took a shot at him, wounding him fatally.[22] This Styurler was a Swiss by birth. La Harpe sent him to Russia in 1811 with a request of his royal pupil, the Emperor Alexander, that he protect his fellow-countryman. So Styurler was appointed a lieutenant in the Semyonovskiy Regiment. He was an intelligent and outstandingly brave man, but a thorough condottiori. He spoke poor Russian, and he was an insufferable pedant in service matters; neither officers nor men liked him. Moreover, he dearly loved money.

The Life-Grenadiers formed up on Senate Square to the left and a little in front of the Moscow Regiment. Odoyevsky joined his comrades just before these new troops came.

But now completely unexpected help was approaching us. As I walked along the side of my carré facing the Neva, I saw cadets of the Naval and First Cadet Corps coming towards us.

'We are sent as deputies from our corps to request permission to come onto the Square and fight in your ranks,' said one of them breathlessly. I smiled involuntarily. And for a moment it crossed my mind to grant them their request. The presence of those fledglings on the Square, standing side by side with mustachioed grenadiers, would certainly have embellished our rising in an original way. But the participation of children in the revolt is the only imaginary fact in the annals of its history. I withstood the temptation, on reflecting that I should subject the lives and futures of these children to danger.

'Thank your comrades for their noble intention,' I answered seriously, 'and save yourselves for future feats.'[23] They went off.

While omitting all other details of the events of December 14th, I will mention the slap in the face with which Odoyevsky rewarded Rostovtsev as the former was returning to the Square from the mounted artillerymen. Rostovtsev was coming from the Izmaylovskiy Regiment, where the troops had pretty well trampled him, when he thought he would hold forth on Nicholas's behalf.

The day was overcast and a chilly wind was blowing. The men, in full dress uniform since five o'clock in the morning, had already been standing more than seven hours on the Square. We were surrounded on all sides, without a high command (because dictator Trubetskoy had not appeared),[24] without artillery, without cavalry—in short, deprived of all moral and physical support for the courage of the soldier. Yet all this notwithstanding, our men stood firm and showed great fortitude. Shivering with cold, they stood in their ranks as if on parade. To test their spirits, I approached Lyubimov, a lance-corporal and a fine and handsome fellow married just three days before—I myself had pronounced the blessing as he stepped under the crown.[25] 'Well, Lyubimov,' I said, 'you've grown very thoughtful. Or are you dreaming of your young wife?' I patted him on the shoulder.

'Ah, Your Excellency, is this the time for women? I'm racking my brains to see why we're standing on one spot. Look—the sun's setting, my legs are stiff from standing, my hands are numb from the cold, and still we stand.'

'Just wait a bit, Lyubimov, we'll be moving. Then you can unfreeze both your hands and your feet.'

I moved away from him with a heavy heart indeed. Meanwhile, Kyukhel'beker and Pushchin had been trying to persuade the crowds to clear the Square; they were preparing to shoot into us. I joined them, but there was only one response to all our exhortations: we'll die alongside you. Sukhozanet galloped up to us to deliver the Tsar's latest demand—that we lay down our arms, otherwise they would shoot us.

'Get back to where you came from,' we yelled. 'And send someone who's less of a dirty dog than you!' added Pushchin.[26]

Sukhozanet took the plume from his hat while still galloping back, which was the pre-arranged signal to fire, and a round crashed out. The canister was aimed over our heads. The crowd stood stock-still. Another shot, this time into the very centre of that mass, brought down many innocents. More rounds of canister were sprayed in all directions. I ran to my line facing the Neva. A third volley followed, and many men in my company fell to the ground groaning and writhing in their final agony. Others ran off towards the river. Lyubimov appeared by my side. 'I shan't leave you whatever happens, Your

Excellency,' he said with brotherly warmth in his voice, then collapsed at my feet, struck in the chest by canister-shot. Blood welled up from his deep wound. I gave him my kerchief, which he pressed to his breast. But now, suddenly, a crowd of running soldiers caught my eye. I rushed forward.

'Behind me, lads!' I cried to the Moscow men, and went down onto the frozen river. Reaching the middle of the river, I halted them and then, assisted by my splendid under-officers, began to form a massed column, with the intention of crossing the ice all the way to Peter-and-Paul Fortress, and taking it. Could we only manage that, we should have an excellent *point d'appui* where we might gather all our forces, and from where we could begin negotiations with Nicholas with cannon aimed at the Palace. Already I had succeeded in forming up three platoons; but suddenly a cannon-ball whistled, striking the ice and bouncing, ricocheting, down the river.[27] I turned to see where they were firing from and, following the gunsmoke with my eye, caught sight of a battery positioned near the centre of St. Isaac's Bridge. I went on forming the column, although cannon-balls would tear a row from it now on the left side, now on the right. Nor did the troops themselves despair, the old men even ribbing younger ones and asking them, when they stooped on hearing the whine of a cannon-ball, 'What are you bowing for? Or are you acquainted with it?'

But even as the rear of the column was being formed, a shout went up suddenly: 'We're sinking!' I saw a huge patch of unfrozen water in which men were floundering, drowning. The ice could not hold under the weight of all the men assembled on it, and now, broken up by cannon-balls, it was giving way. Soldiers threw themselves towards the bank, reaching it by the Academy of Arts building.

'Now where do we go?' asked a colour-bearer, seeing me. I glanced through the open gateway of the Academy, and saw the circular courtyard that I remembered so well.[28] I also remembered the halls of antique statues and paintings that surrounded that courtyard. If we seized *those*, the thought flashed on me, we could defend ourselves for a considerable time. 'This way, lads!' I shouted—and the leading group of soldiers ran over to the gates and past a doorman who stood thunderstruck—but who, nevertheless, recovering from his alarm, released the weights of those same gates so that, alas, they slammed shut right before our noses. Next I gave orders to seize up a log from the bottom of a wooden barge lying broken in the river so that, by using it, we might knock the gates from their hinges. And the good fellows set to it together. The gates were already splintering under their blows when we caught sight of a squadron of Guards bearing down on us at full gallop. My men's hands were quite empty. Could we have thought of resistance amidst such confusion, when all were lumped together in a disorderly crowd?

'Save yourselves as best you can, lads!' I shouted. The men scattered in various directions. I walked up to the colour-bearer and embraced him. 'Tell your comrades in the Moscow Regiment that I take my leave of them forever in your person. Now take the colour and hand it to that officer over there who is riding ahead. That way you'll avoid being punished.'

For a few moments more I stood there, and saw the colour-bearer go up to the officer in the middle of Rumyantsev Square, give up the banner, and collapse from a blow from that officer, who struck at him with all his might. The bearer fell, and I fought back the tears that I felt welling up. I have forgotten the name of that despised hero, but I seem to recollect that it began with a Von-, and that once he had received the Order of St. Vladimir with a ribbon for bravery, having cast down at the Emperor's feet a banner which he had recaptured in the heat of battle ....

As I slowly made my way along the sidestreets to my sisters' peaceful abode,[29] the feverish excitement left me gradually. I felt it flow away. And somehow an indefinable weight, which had been oppressing my spirits, left me. I knew that I had done my duty blamelessly, and even found a pleasure in imagining the most humiliating, awful sentences. Then a healthy metabolism came into its own; having passed three days with neither food nor sleep,[30] I felt hungry and ready to fall asleep immediately. My sisters met me with tears and interrogations.

'Now's not the time for weeping, chattering and sighing, *mes soeurs*—time is precious. Give me a bite to eat and let me rest a while and then I'll try to satisfy your curiosity. I shall be leaving you forever.'

I ate hurriedly and was soon asleep, having asked my sisters to warn our mother of my presence when she should awake. Whether or not I was asleep long I can't say, but when I woke it was completely dark. It was essential to think of the future while no one was preventing me. Should I run, or give myself up to arrest, causing no trouble? Let's try the first approach first, I decided, and the second only in the case of failure. I dressed myself up in my brother Nikolay's[31] old naval half-coat, put his raccoon fur-coat on top of it and, in this fancy-dress, presented myself to my mother. I knelt down and asked for her blessing. 'May God bless you,' said my mother, 'and arm you with patience to bear all the sufferings awaiting you.' I embraced my sisters, ran out through the gates and jumped at the first cab, telling the driver to go to Isaac's Square. I meant, if possible, to make my way to Torson.

'But will they let us onto Isaac's, master? That's the question!' said the driver. 'They're washing and scrubbing away, and there are guns and soldiers all over.'

'What washing are you talking about?' I asked.

'Why, everybody knows—they're washing out the blood. Sprinkling fresh snow, they are, and smoothing it out!'

'Was there a lot of blood, then?'

'Oh, enough. I mean, plenty—of dead, that is. Look there,' he added, pointing at a cart covered with bast matting. 'That's all dead men. God grant 'em peace. They were just men, after all, and they stood up for a just cause. Now they're shoving 'em under the ice without a proper Christian burial.'[32]

'But just what *did* happen here? Will you tell me?'

'Huh, will you tell me! In one word, it was horrible!'

A gendarme stopped us. I paid the driver and began to make my way from the other end of the Square, zigzagging and taking roundabout routes, down towards Galernaya Street, where Torson lived.[33] It was a strangely animated scene on the Square itself, which was illuminated here and there by blazing bonfires round which infantry and artillerymen were warming themselves. Gleaming muzzles of guns placed at all the main streets that led to the Square could be seen occasionally through the smoke and flickering flames. Slow matches smouldered by each gun like so many glimmering stars. And in the middle of this circle, where a few hours earlier the fate of the Tsar and of Russia had been settled, working folk were diligently washing away every remaining trace of the unlawful attempt made by misguided men—men who had dreamed of lightening, if only by a little, the burden of the bitter lot of those same working folk! Some scraped the red snow, others sprinkled white snow on the scraped and cleansed patches. The rest were gathering up bodies of the dead, and carrying them off towards the river.

Not without great difficulty, practically stealing along, I reached Galernaya Street; and I had gone halfway along it almost running when a picket of the Pavlovskiy Regiment halted me. 'Wait here 'til an officer comes to question you,' they told me.

'Now I've had it,' I thought. I had said I was skipper of the Eighth Equipage[34]—but what if this officer should recognize me? Instinctively, I leaned towards the lamp-post nearest me so that the light should not fall on my face. On the other side of this same lamp-post stood a little group of Life-Grenadiers, Moscow Regiment men and sailors of the Guards' Equipage. They had been searched out in the houses bordering Galernaya Street and taken to the picket so as later to be sent to some assembly point. The Izmaylovskiy men, at this juncture, brought in further detainees.

'So, you've caught the mice again!' said one of the Pavlovskiy men, a wag and joker who amused the whole company with his highly diverting sallies. 'Did you find it easy, stooping into every hole and burrow? Just look at him— he's as tall as that lamp-post!'

'You'd have done the same as us if they'd sent you!' retorted the Ismaylov-skiy private.

'On the contrary, my friend—you're talking through your hat. In the first place they wouldn't have sent *us*. *We* didn't swear to your chieftain, and we don't mean to betray our oath. We sent to the Moscow men that we were ready to march with 'em—and now *you're* catching 'em so as to string 'em up. No, my friend,' he said, stepping forward with his arms akimbo, 'I may have a brass forehead, but I'm not a blockhead. And if I'd said, 'I'll go, I'd have gone...'

'And we'd have gone too,' interrupted the Izmaylovskiy private.

'So why didn't you come and join us?' asked one of the Moscow Regiment men.

'And why did you just stand there on the spot, as if you'd frozen to the road?'

Baron Andrey Yevgen'yevich Rozen   1800–1884

Alone of the memoirists whose narratives are offered in this book, Baron Andrey Yevgen'yevich Rozen (1800–84) published his entirely in a Western language, German. *Aus den Memoiren eines russischen Dekabristen,* which appeared in Leipzig in 1869,[35] was the first monograph dealing with the imprisonment and exile of Decembrists, by a Decembrist, to be published in the West. Well informed European readers were, of course, aware that there had been an insurrection in the Russian capital in 1825. Not only had it been described in generally accurate detail by Baron M. A. Korf and J. H. Schnitzler, and in a more fragmentary and superficial manner by Dupré de St. Maure, Lesure, Ancelot and others;[36] Decembrists themselves had made their contribution, in the West, to a knowledge of the rising. But, though Nikolay Turgenev's two-volume *La Russie et les Russes* (Paris, 1847–48) cast new light on the whole liberal movement in Russia, and on Nicholas's reign in particular, Turgenev himself – happily for him – was an absentee Decembrist. Again, M. S. Lunin caused a stir with his essay, 'On the Russian Secret Society from 1816 to 1826,' which found its way to London and to Herzen's *Kolokol,* and which Lunin himself later translated into Russian.[37] But Lunin had nothing to say in that work of his own massive misfortunes, or of life in Siberian exile. It was, in short, with some justification that Rozen prefaced his book with the remark: 'The subject of this work will be new to many of its readers; the rising of the soldiers in St. Petersburg in 1825 is but little known or remembered.' His book did much to change that.

Rozen had not always intended, however, that his memoirs form a book. Having settled under strict police surveillance in the Province of Kharkov, in 1855, he had reworked a long series of notes and reminiscences made several years before, first in Siberia, then (1837–39) in Georgia. After the (almost) general amnesty granted to the now elderly Decembrists in August 1856 by Alexander II, he began to concentrate on them. But still these polished memoirs were intended for his relatives and children. Matters changed greatly between 1856 and 1866. In fact, as he declared with typical modesty in his preface of 1869, 'Times and circumstances are so wholly changed that one may think that an account may be of interest to the general public. ... The recalling of such happenings cannot be viewed as revolutionary or dangerous to the State in any way.' With the new reign, there had also emerged a new official attitude towards such men as Rozen. The son of Nicholas, one may recall, had himself met Decembrists while travelling in Siberia in 1837, and subsequently took a certain interest in their fates.

There was, moreover, a second and a far more pressing reason why Rozen felt disposed to give a public reckoning of his life, by publishing. As he put it:

I feel that many of my old companions, had they wished to do so, would have been far better qualified than I to describe our lives. But it is most unlikely that those still alive will trouble themselves to give any account of their experiences; and so it has fallen on me, one of the few survivors, to spend a part of my remaining time on earth in giving a plain but truthful account of what I have myself been through and what I have seen and heard. I have confined myself almost entirely to my own experiences, only adding here and there what I have heard from authentic sources and reliable authority.

In the event, Rozen proved over-pessimistic: there was a spate of reminiscing by Decembrists and others connected with their exile in the late 1860s and another in the early eighties. Many of the accounts appeared in two new periodicals, *Russkiy arkhiv* and *Russkaya starina.* Nor by any means, were all the Decembrists dead by 1870 – triumphant at the last, D. I. Zavalishin was alive in 1892.[38] Rozen's anxieties, however, spurred him to take immediate action and to publish his corrected notes; for that we may be grateful.

Rozen's memoirs are, in the main, highly reliable. Rozen himself was of a steady, careful temperament; his reminiscences mirror a calm, prudent, and unempassioned nature.[39] This was no flaming revolutionary, no Estonian Ryleyev or Riego, but a rational and somewhat cautious junior officer. His German prose style is even, occasionally verging on the dispassionate, as in his balanced summary of reasons why the revolution failed. No less dispassionate is his approach, as seen throughout his memoirs, towards the political radicalism so widespread among liberal Russian circles in his own late adolescence and early manhood. Consider, for example, the following two statements. It is virtually inconceivable that the Bestuzhevs, or Lorer, or Yakushkin should have made them: 'I know well enough that men's characters and actions are very much determined by the spirit of the times and by the circumstances in which they happen to be – a fact that may make us bitter towards those men who have acted harshly towards ourselves ...'; 'So it may be seen that the conspirators and rebels of 1825 were young enthusiasts who should be judged by other standards than strictly political ones. The cruel fate they were obliged to suffer atoned for their crime, and now it is possible, for those who read their history, to take a kindly and compassionate interest in the first attempt to draw Russia along the path of Western European liberalism.' What a yawning gulf at first seems to divide Rozen's own later life from his earlier service years, separating the returned exile of the 1850s and sixties from the youthful officer! Yet even as one looks, the gulf becomes illusory. Rozen did not change essentially during those thirty years that fell between the rising and the amnesty. Admittedly, one has the feeling that the author of the memoirs, by some curious act of will or by the action of his temperament, manages almost to dissociate himself from the hard realities of his own early manhood – standing aside and watching as his youthful wraith performs. Yet the same Lieutenant Rozen drove and shadowed Baron Rozen all his life, bringing him first to Chita and Petrovskiy Zavod, then to the hot, malaria-ridden township of Belyy Klyuch in the Caucasus. Rozen's temperament and character were stable, and changed little, as he aged. Deliberate and cautious in 1869, he was cautious and deliberate in 1825; balanced in outlook and approach in 1869, he was hardly less so as a subaltern. He took no foolish risks in later life; nor did he do so on 'the day' in 1825 – and here is another reason why his scrupulous account of the rebellion itself is of unusual value. Unable to decide to leave the scene and drive away, but equally unable to advance onto the Senate Square, hemmed in by government and by his own men, Rozen saw everything as from a grandstand.

For three hours he stood immobile on St. Isaac's Bridge with three full companies of the Finland Foot Guards at his back – his own men; for three hours, from that vantage-point, he watched the tide of fortune ebb and flow two hundred yards away, until eventually his comrades lost the day and were scattered by canister-shot. To his left was the Admiralty, by the far corner of which appeared the tsar and all his suite; to his right was the Senate and Galernaya street, by which onlookers had gathered by the dozen and on which cannon opened up as dusk approached. In front of him was the rebellion itself. Six hours before, he had himself made an impromptu hasty effort to incite his own men to revolt, but had lacked the vital boldness. His hesitation was infectious. He objected to the swearing of an oath to Nicholas, then he took the oath himself. He then drove up to the insurgents in a sled but, gnawed by doubt, quickly drove off again. Having brought several hundred men to a full stop on Isaac's Bridge by an earth-shaking 'Halt!' he stood glued to the same spot, neutral to all intents and purposes. That same lack of the erratic element that makes his reminiscences so pleasantly consistent and reliable also resulted in his loss to the Decembrists in their desperate hour.

Rozen, in short, was admirably positioned to observe events on Senate Square. The Bestuzhevs and Prince Obolensky undeniably *did* more; but they also rushed around far more. There is, perhaps in consequence, a jerking quality and hurriedness and tension in the three Bestuzhevs' recollections of the day totally missing from the Baron's measured prose. At times, indeed, the very sense of *Ordnung* in his memoirs in those places where they deal (supposedly) with rage and passion can oppress. He may 'hurriedly return' to his regiment, and whole units may 'traverse the ice at a charge,' but still, as though controlled by the baton of a conductor, events unfold with easy dignity. One has to read Mikhail Bestuzhev's account of the same hectic afternoon fully to grasp the fact that many things were happening simultaneously, unplanned, and that confusion reigned supreme by one o'clock.

These very shortcomings, however, if they are indeed shortcomings, are changed into positive virtues in the later parts of Rozen's narrative. Not all was drama for the rebels, after all. The few hours of intense and rushed activity were followed by long months of wearisome incarceration, which in turn gave way to longer years of exile. Not always happy when describing sudden turns of circumstance, quick movements and volte-faces, Rozen comes splendidly into his own as a narrator when sustained and pure narration is required. Thus his descriptions of Siberian life, its climate and geography, peoples, commerce and industry, are unequalled by his fellow memoirists.[40]

All this, however, comes later. Here, now, is part of Rozen's clear account of the rebellion of December 14, 1825.

Baron A. E. Rozen

All the officers of the Regiment assembled at the Colonel's house at dawn; he welcomed us with the announcement of a new Tsar, and thereupon read out Alexander's will, Constantine's resignation of the throne and Nicholas's latest manifesto. I stepped forward in the presence of all the officers and said to the General:[41] 'If all the documents just read by Your Excellency are authentic, which I have no right to doubt, how can it be explained that we did not swear an oath of allegiance to Nicholas on November 27th?' Visibly embarrassed, the General replied: 'You are making an unnecessary difficulty. This has been considered by older and more experienced men than yourself. Gentlemen, return to your battalions and administer the oath.'

Our Second Battalion, under Colonel Moller,[42] was on guard duty in the

Winter Palace and at posts in the city's first district. The First Battalion took the oath in barracks, with the exception of my section of sharpshooters, who had the day before assumed sentry duty at Galley Port and had not yet been relieved. From the barracks I proceeded to the Palace for the parade, which took place without ceremony. Everything was still quiet; there was no disturbance to be seen. Then, on returning to my house, I found a note from Ryleyev saying that I was expected in the quarters of the Moscow Regiment. It was between ten and eleven o'clock.

As I approached St. Isaac's Bridge in my sled I saw a dense mass of people at the other end of it, and on the Square a division of the Moscow Regiment drawn up in a carré. I pushed through the crowd on foot, went straight to the carré, which had been formed on the other side of the monument to Peter the First, and was met by loud cheers. There stood Prince Shchepin-Rostovsky, leaning on his sword and quite exhausted from a conflict in the barracks where, after meeting with the greatest difficulties, he had refused to swear the oath, severely wounded the brigadier commanding the regiment and battalion, and finally led out his company under its colours. Mikhail Bestuzhev's company and a few groups from the other companies had followed him. The two captains stood side by side, waiting for aid. Pushchin stood dauntless and immovable in the carré; he had left the army two years earlier, but the men obeyed him willingly although he wore civilian dress. I asked him where I could find Trubetskoy, the dictator. 'He's vanished,' he replied; 'if you can, bring us more men. If you can't, there are enough victims already without adding you.' I hastily returned to the barracks of my regiment (the Finland Chasseurs), where only the First Battalion and my section of sharpshooters remained. The latter, in the meantime, had been released from guard duties. I went through all four companies, ordered the men to dress at once, screw in their flints, take cartridges with them and start immediately in rank and file, with the understanding that we must make haste to help our comrades. In half an hour the battalion was ready; only a few officers, however, fell in. No one knew by whose command the men had been turned out. Adjutants on horseback incessantly galloped about: one was sent to our brigadier with instructions to lead our battalion onto St. Isaac's Square. We marched in columns of companies. At the Naval Cadet Corps we found the General-Adjutant, Count Komarovsky, who had been sent to meet us on horseback. We were halted in the middle of St. Isaac's Bridge, and ordered to load sharp; almost all the troops crossed themselves. Confident of the spirit of my men, my first effort was to attempt to cut a path with them through the Regiment of Carbineers before us, and through a company of the Preobrazhenskiy Regiment which had possession of the bridge where it joined Senate Square. Convinced now that the rising had no leader and was wholly without unity, and determined not to sacrifice my own men needlessly (while it was out of the question, of course, that I should join the ranks of the rebels' opponents), I decided to halt my men where they stood at the instant that Count Komarovsky and the Brigadier gave out the order to advance. By this, I meant not only to prevent my men from being turned against my friends, but also to deprive those regiments pursuing us of the possibility of crossing the bridge now occupied by my section and acting against the insurgents. The result was quite successful. My men shouted 'Halt!' with one voice, so that the Regiment of Carbineers in front of us could not form up. Only by dint of personal exertion and unsparing use of his fists, indeed, did Captain A. S. Vyatkin manage to lead his section further. Twice the Brigadier came back to make my own section advance, but his threats and his persuasions were alike without results. The Commandant had vanished; I commanded the position on the bridge[43]. Three whole companies standing behind my section were brought to a halt. Not only did the men in those companies not obey their captains—they expressed their feeling openly that the officer at the front knew what he was doing!

The clock struck two. Police drove the onlookers from the Square; the people then crowded against the rails of the bridge near Vasil'yevskiy Island. Many passers-by begged me to hold out for an hour and all would go well.[44] Because of this backward movement of the crowd, the captain of our third company, D. N. Beleyev, succeeded in retiring with his company, crossing the Neva from the Academy to English Embankment and then effecting a junction with the first section of our battalion in front of the bridge. For this he was awarded the Vladimir Cross.[45] The other columns remained behind my section until the final moment. This painful state of uncertainty lasted more than two hours. Every moment I was expecting that my friends would cut their way through to the bridge, so that I might come to their aid with my 800 men, who were prepared to follow me anywhere.

Meanwhile, 1,000 men of the revolted Moscow Regiment had formed a carré on Senate Square. M. A. Bestuzhev's company stood opposite the Admiralty Boulevard, and there, under his orders, formed three sides of the carré. The fourth, opposite St. Isaac's Cathedral, remained under the command of the weary and exhausted Prince Shchepin-Rostovsky. This circumstance allowed M. A. Bestuzhev to save two troops of Guards cavalry from the fire of his own men—cavalry who had advanced from the Square behind and placed themselves at short range from it. The carré front facing the Senate building was about to fire a salvo, but was hindered by Bestuzhev who placed himself before the line and gave the order, 'Reverse arms!' A few bullets whistled past his ears, and a few cavalrymen fell from their horses. The horsemen turned away then, not having brought their charge to a conclusion. A good hour after this, a whole battalion of marines hastened down Galernaya Street to the aid of the insurgent Moscow men.

When this battalion had been assembled in the courtyard of their barracks, there to take the oath [to Nicholas], and when the several officers opposed to this had been arrested by their brigadier, General Shchipov, M. A. Bestuzhev had appeared by the entrance of the courtyard at the very moment when the few shots fired during the cavalry attack were audible. 'We're attacked, my lads!' he cried; 'follow me!' And they all streamed after him to Isaac's Bridge. In his haste he had neglected to bring some cannon from the arsenal, expecting to be reinforced by the Guards artillery who were to bring their guns with them. Arriving at the Palace, the battalion at once formed up in column of attack, and placed itself near the carré of the Moscow Regiment; the column was turned towards St. Isaac's Cathedral.

A little later more assistance came: three companies of the Guards' Grenadier Regiment, led from their barracks by Lieutenant A. M. Sutgof, Battalion Adjutant N. A. Panov and Sub-Lieutenant Koshchevinkov, came onto Isaac's Square and joined the insurgent regiments. These troops had come at a charge over the ice of the Neva and then entered the inner courtyard of the Winter Palace, where they hoped to find some allies. Instead they found Colonel Gerun, who had placed his battalion of Guards sappers in position; in vain he tried to bring the grenadiers to obedience to the new Emperor. They, perceiving their mistake, cried out, 'This isn't our party,' and, turning out at once, hastened up to Senate Square to aid their fellow-insurgents. On the way, by Admiralty Boulevard, they met the Emperor, who asked them, 'Where are you bound? Are you on my side? If so, turn right; if no, turn left.' 'To the left!' a voice answered, and they all hurried on to Isaac's Square without keeping in their rank and file. Here, the grenadiers were placed inside the hollow carré of the Moscow Regiment, so as to enable them to be formed up into companies under the cover of that carré. Hardly was this arrangement completed than the final catastrophe took place.

There were already more than 2,000 men in the ranks of the insurgents.[46] With so large a force, and surrounded as they were by thousands of the populace ready and willing to cooperate, it would have been a simple thing to bring the rebellion to a more favourable issue had there been one efficient leader, the more so as the opposite party was wavering and certain regiments assembled round the Emperor seemed inclined to join the rebels. But able generalship was not to be found among the insurgents: for hours the men were kept standing motionless in nothing but their simple uniforms, and this in ten degrees of frost, with a sharp east wind blowing. The elected dictator, Prince Trubetskoy, was nowhere to be seen; nor were his appointed aides at the posts assigned to them, though they were present on the Square. These offered the command to Colonel Bulatov who, however, turned it down.[47] They then offered it to N. Bestuzhev who refused, as he was but a navy captain, and did not understand infantry service. Finally they forced the high command on Prince E. P. Obolensky, who was certainly no tactician but was well known and liked by the troops. Complete anarchy reigned; no dictator being at the head, everyone shouted commands which nobody obeyed, and the confusion was total. Still expecting aid which did not come, they were obliged simply to defend themselves, not daring to make an attack which, at so early a stage, might have produced the most significant results. To surrender they obstinately refused, proudly rejecting terms of mercy. Gradually, forces of the opposite party gathered. The Guards cavalry was first on the Square. Battalions of the Izmaylovskiy and Jäger Regiments came down Voznesenskaya Street to the Blue Bridge, the Semyonovskiy Regiment along Gorokhovaya Street.[48]

On Admiralty Boulevard stood the carré of the Preobrazhenskiy Regiment. The Emperor was there, prominent on horseback, with a numerous suite.[49] The Tsarevich, a seven-year-old boy, was in the middle of this carré with his tutor. In front of it were placed cannon of Colonel Nesterovsky's Brigade, covered by a section of the Chevalier Garde commanded by Lieutenant Ya. A. Annenkov. Behind the Imperial carré stood a battalion of the Pavlovskiy Guards; as mentioned earlier, sappers were ranged in the courtyard of the Winter Palace.

But the loyalty of these troops was not to be relied upon. At the critical moment, they wavered. When the Second Battalion of Jäger Guards received the order to advance over the Blue Bridge and moved off, Yakubovich gave the order, 'Left about face,' and the entire battalion turned about, though the commander of the battalion was known to be thoroughly trustworthy and loyal. Because of this, Colonel Buss [Busse] was not appointed fligel'-adjutant[50] to the Emperor, a distinction given to all officers commanding regiments of Guards which held out for the Emperor that day — with the exception, of course, of Tulub'yev, who commanded my battalion and was compromised by the conduct of my section. The Izmaylovskiy Regiment, too, was wavering in its allegiance now. But the Guards cavalry, on the other hand, led by A. Ya. Orlov, charged the carré of the Moscow Regiment five times, and was five times repulsed by bayonet and shot.

Once the troops so arrayed had encompassed the insurgents on all sides with close columns, the crowd on the Square around them became thinner. The police grew bolder in dispersing people, who at first had filled three faces of the Square: those on the sides of Isaac's Square, Senate Square and the

Admiralty. As for the Emperor himself, he continually rode up and down these two last-named squares at a quick trot, now sharply ordering, now good-humouredly begging the people to disperse and hinder the troops' movement no longer. In the meantime, various higher officers were doing all they could to win over the hesitating troops to the Imperial cause. The Emperor himself was averse to any bloodshed, and ardently hoped to see the insurgents brought to obedience again, before it came to the worst. General Bistrom stopped the companies of the Moscow Regiment, which had remained in barracks, from uniting with their insurrectionary comrades, and even managed to persuade them to assume sentry duties that night. General Sukhozanet rode into the midst of the carré and entreated the men to disperse before cannon opened up. They replied that 'he might run away himself, and fire at them if he chose.'

Next, the Grand Duke Mikhail Pavlovich, who had only a few hours before returned from Neumal[51] (where he waited for the Grand Duke Constantine while the latter tarried quietly in Warsaw), galloped up to the carré of insurgents and did his best to induce the men to submit.[52] He was in danger of becoming a sacrifice to his own bravery, however, for V. K. Kyukhel'beker, fearing that he might succeed in persuading the men, fired at him with his pistol, which happily misfired. Count M. A. Miloradovich, the best-loved leader of the men, also attempted to induce the insurgents to follow him off the Square. Prince E. P. Obolensky then seized the bridle of the Count's horse to lead him out of the carré and stuck a bayonet from one of the soldiers' muskets into the horse's flank, hoping to save the rider in this way. Regrettably, three bullets fired that moment by Kakhovsky and two other soldiers struck the brave Miloradovich, who had fought with great renown in many battles without being injured once, so that he fell mortally wounded. Colonel Styurler, Commandant of the Grenadier Guards Regiment, also fell from a bullet of Kakhovsky's as he struggled to recall to their obedience the Grenadier company which had mutinied. At last, the Metropolitan Serafim appeared in full vestments, accompanied by Yevgeniy, the Metropolitan of Kiev, and several other priests. Lifting the consecrated cross, he asked the soldiers to return to barracks, for the love of Christ, and, as the Grand Duke and Count Miloradovich had done before, promised in Nicholas's name an unconditional pardon to all conspirators, save only the inspirers of the rising. But the Metropolitan's prayers were of no avail. The men only replied, 'Go home, Father, and pray for us there; pray for all. You're out of place here.'

A December day does not last long in the far north. Towards three o'clock, it began to get dark; without doubt those who had been forcibly dispersed would, with the twilight, rejoin the insurgents. But no time was given them to do so. It is supposed to have been Count Tol' who, as the dusk was gathering, approached the Emperor and said to him, 'Sire, give orders that this Square be swept by cannon, or resign the throne!'[53] The first cannon shot, loaded with blank cartridge, thundered out; a second and a third cannon fired balls, which hit the walls of the Senate or flew off over the Neva in the direction of the Academy of Arts. The shots were answered by ringing hurrahs from the insurgents! The guns were then loaded with grapeshot. Colonel Nesterovsky aimed them straight into the carré, the gunner crossed himself, the Emperor gave the command and Captain M. Bakunin took the slow-match from the soldier's hand. A moment later grapeshot fell like hail across the densely crowded Square; the insurgents fled down Galernaya Street and over the Neva to the Academy. At once the guns were dragged into Galernaya Street and to the bank of the Neva, whence they fired canister which trebled the number of the dead, mowing down innocent and guilty, soldiers and mere casual onlookers alike.

Three sides of the Moscow Regiment carré under M. Bestuzhev threw themselves onto the banks of the Neva, pursued by flying shot. Bestuzhev hoped to collect the fugitive soldiers on the ice, but cannon-balls came roaring down on them from Isaac's Bridge, smashing the river ice and making watery graves for numbers of the men. But for this, Bestuzhev would have been in a position to seize Peter-and-Paul Fortress. As for the marines of the Guard, grenadiers of the Bodyguard and the other section of the Moscow Regiment, they all made for Galernaya Street, where they were followed by cannon which cut down many men in that defile.

It is a marvellous fact that not one of my companions in misfortune, the compromised officers, was killed or wounded, although many had their furs and cloaks shot through by bullets. Whole rows of soldiers fell in the marines, but the officers were unhurt. All took to flight in the two directions named, one alone remaining on the Square where he approached General Martynov and begged him to deliver up his sword to the Grand Duke Mikhail. This was M. K. Kyukhel'beker. At the same instant Colonel Sass, of the Pioneer Guards unit, sprang at him with drawn sabre. General Martynov restrained the Colonel, saying, 'My brave friend, you see he has already given me his sword!'

Later, I saw my men forming a circle, and a priest beginning to address them. I at once broke into the circle and publicly declared that my soldiers were in no way to blame for anything; they had only done their duty in obeying their superior officer. I then withdrew while they took the required oath of allegiance to Nicholas. Stars were shining brightly in the sky, bivouac fires burned in every square, and foot- and mounted-patrols roamed through the streets. ...

As I review the events of that memorable day, I am even now of the opinion that with very little trouble the insurrection might have been successful. More than 2000 soldiers and an even larger number of civilians were ready to obey a leader's call. A leader had, indeed, been nominated; but it was not a happy choice. I lived for six years with Prince Trubetskoy; and many of my comrades have known him for far longer; and we are all agreed that he was both an able and an energetic man on whom one could rely in an emergency. Why he was missing from his post at the appointed time, no one has yet discovered. I believe he himself does not know — that he lost his head. Yet this single unforeseen factor settled the issue. Prince Obolensky, who was chosen in Trubetskoy's stead, felt himself unfit for the position. While others tried to overcome his scruples for him, the most precious time was wasted and all cohesion of action was lost. The officers and men then flocking to the standard of the rebels did not know to whom to turn, or under whose command to place themselves; the troops on the Square stood passive and inert. But these were the same men who had so bravely driven off five onslaughts by the Guards cavalry! As if bound by some spell, men who had earlier shown themselves so ardent now stood idle when, with relatively little difficulty, they could have seized the very cannon being used against themselves.

V. I. Shteyngel'

At last the fateful 14th of December came — a noteworthy date: it was cut into the medals with which deputies to the popular assembly for the drawing up of laws in 1776, in the reign of Catherine II, were dismissed. It was a gloomy December morning in Petersburg, with eight degrees of frost. The whole active Senate was already at the Palace by nine o'clock. There, and among the regiments of Guards, an oath of allegiance [to Nicholas] was given. Messengers continually galloped to the Palace reporting how and where all was proceeding. All seemed quiet. Only a few mysterious individuals were appearing on Senate Square in a state of quite apparent agitation. One of these, who knew of the Society's instructions and was then walking across the Square facing the Senate, met with Mr. Grech the publisher of *Syn otechestva* [Son of the Fatherland] and *Severnaya pchela* [The Northern Bee]. To the question, 'Well, will anything be happening?' he uttered a phrase of out-and-out *carbonarism*. Not an important incident, but one that characterizes armchair demagogues: this person, like Bulgarin, reviled assiduously all who perished — because he himself had not been compromised. Shortly after this encounter, at about ten o'clock, the beat of a drum and 'hurrahs!' repeated many times, suddenly rang out on Gorokhovaya Street. A column of the Moscow Regiment with its colours and led by Staff-Captain Prince Shchepin-Rostovsky and the two Bestuzhevs came out onto Admiralty Square and swung towards the Senate, where it formed up in a carré. Soon afterwards, the Guards equipage came[54] briskly up to join it, enthused by Arbuzov; and then came a battalion of Life-Grenadiers, brought out by Adjutant Panov[55] and Lieutenant Sutgof. Many of the common people gathered round, and at once pulled down a pile of firewood that was standing by the barricade surrounding the building site of St. Isaac's Cathedral.[56] Admiralty Boulevard filled up with onlookers. Then, all at once, it became known that the entrance to the Square had already been stained by blood. Prince Shchepin-Rostovsky, beloved of the Moscow Regiment and, although not openly a member of the Society, dissatisfied and conscious that a rising was prepared against the Grand Duke Nicholas, had succeeded in convincing his men that they were being tricked — and that they were bound to defend their allegiance sworn to Constantine, and so should march to the Senate. Generals Shenshin and Fridrikhs and Colonel Khvoshchinsky had tried to change their minds for them and stop them. Shchepin had sabred the first two and wounded the third, as well as one under-officer and a certain grenadier who wished not to give up the colour, hoping to draw the troops away. Happily, these men lived.

Count Miloradovich, who had remained unharmed in so many battles, fell, the first victim, shortly after this. Hardly had the insurgents managed to form up in a carré than he appeared, galloping from the Palace in a pair-horse sled; he was standing, wearing nothing over his full-dress coat and blue ribbon. From the boulevard he could be heard ordering the driver, by whose shoulder he held himself with his left hand as he pointed with his right, 'Go round the church and then right, to the barracks.' Not three minutes had passed before he returned in front of the carré on horseback[57] and began persuading the men to obey and swear allegiance to the new Emperor. Suddenly a shot rang out, the Count folded up, his hat flew off, he collapsed onto the pommel and, in that position, his horse carried him to the quarters of the officer who was his master. Rebuking the troops with the presumption of an old *paternal commander*, Miloradovich said he himself would gladly have seen Constantine Emperor;[58] but there was nothing to be done, he said, since Constantine refused. He himself, he then assured them, had seen the renunciation, and he did his best to make the men believe him. Seeing that such a speech might well have its effect, Prince Obolensky, one of the members of the Secret Society, left the carré and attempted to persuade the Count to move away—otherwise danger would threaten him. Seeing, however, that the Count was paying no attention to him, he inflicted a slight wound in his side with a bayonet. At this instant the Count made an about turn and Kakhovsky fired the fateful bullet at him—the bullet cast the night before.[59] When he was taken from his horse by the barracks and carried into the quarters of the officer just mentioned, Miloradovich had the last consolation of reading through a note from his new Emperor, written in the Emperor's own hand and expressing his regret. By 4 P.M. he was no more.

At this, the true significance of the rising became fully clear—a significance by which the rebels' feet were, so to speak, chained to the spot that they were occupying. Lacking the force to advance, they saw that there was no salvation at their rear either; the die was cast. The dictator did not show himself. In the carré there was dissention. Only one thing was left: to stand, defend themselves and wait for the dénouement destined for them. This they did.

Meanwhile, on the new Emperor's orders, columns of troops loyal to the Palace were assembling every moment. Heeding neither the Empress's persuasions nor the representations of those seriously warning him, the Sovereign himself went out [to Admiralty Boulevard], carrying the seven-year-old heir to the throne in his arms. Him he entrusted to the keeping of the men of the Preobrazhenskiy Regiment. This scene produced its full effect: transports among the troops, a pleasant, hopeful consternation in the capital. Then the Sovereign mounted a white steed, rode out before the first platoon[60] and marched the columns from the drill-hall on the boulevard. His stately although somewhat sombre air of calm immediately drew everyone's attention. The insurgents, at this juncture, had their hopes raised momentarily by the approach of the Finland Regiment, in whose sympathy they had great confidence. This regiment was moving over Isaac's Bridge,[61] to join others that had already sworn an oath [to Nicholas]; but the commander of the leading section, Baron Rozen, reaching the centre of the bridge, shouted the order, 'Halt!' The entire regiment stopped, and nothing, right to the conclusion of the drama, succeeded in making it move. Only the section that had not come onto the bridge crossed over on the ice to English Embankment and there, from the Kryukov Canal side, joined up with troops that had skirted the insurgents.

Shortly after he had ridden out onto Admiralty Square, the Sovereign was approached with a military salute by a stately officer of dragoons whose brow, beneath his hat, was bound with a black kerchief, and who, a few words having been exchanged, went up to the carré.[62] But he soon came back with nothing. He had volunteered to persuade the *rebels* to submit, but received only abuses and reproach. Thereupon he was arrested, on the Sovereign's instructions, and suffered the common fate of the condemned men. After him, the insurgents were approached by General Voinov, at whom Vil'gel'm Kyukhel'beker the poet and publisher of the journal *Mnemozina* [Mnemosyne], who was then in the carré, shot with a pistol, so obliging him to retire. Colonel Styurler [next] appeared before the Life-Grenadiers, and the same Kakhovsky wounded him with his pistol.[63] Finally, the Grand Duke Mikhail himself rode up, also without success: to him the insurgents replied that they wanted a reign of law at last. With this, he was obliged to withdraw because of a pistol raised at him by the hand of that same Kyukhel'beker. The pistol was ready loaded, too.

After this failure, Serafim came out from the St. Isaac's church, constructed temporarily in the buildings of the Admiralty complex — a Metropolitan in full vestments, with cross preceded by gonfalons. Serafim approached the carré, and began an admonishment. But out to meet him came the other Kyukhel'beker, the brother of the one who had obliged the Grand Duke Mikhail Pavlovich to retire. A sailor and a lutheran, he did not know the *high entitlements* of our Orthodox *humility*, so said simply but with conviction: 'Go away, Father, it is not your business to interfere in this matter.' The Metropolitan turned his procession towards the Admiralty. Speransky, who had watched all this from the Palace, said to *Ober-Prokurator* Krasnokutsky, who was standing with him:

'So that trick didn't work either!' Krasnokutsky was himself a member of the Secret Society, and later died in exile. No matter how insignificant, this incident nevertheless reveals Speransky's mood at that time. Nor could it have been otherwise: on the one hand were his recollections, as one who had already suffered innocently, on the other — mistrust of the future.

When the whole process of curbing the rebellion by peaceful means had thus come to an end, recourse was had to strength of arms. With utter intrepidity, General Orlov twice went into the attack with his horseguards. Though he did not prevail against the carré, still he earned by this performance an entirely spurious ennoblement as count. Slowly shifting his columns, the Sovereign was closer to the centre of the Admiralty building now. And at the north-east corner of Admiralty Boulevard the *ultima ratio* had appeared — the guns of the Guards' artillery. General Sukhozanet, who was then commanding them, rode up to the carré and shouted to the men to lay down their arms; otherwise he would fire canister-shot. Even at him muskets were being aimed, but a scornfully authoritative voice was heard in the carré:[64] 'Don't touch that one — he isn't worth a bullet.' Naturally this outraged him to the utmost and, having galloped off towards the batteries, he ordered that a volley of blank rounds be fired; but this was not done! Canister-shot began to whistle; everything and everyone, save those who had fallen, trembled and scattered in different directions. Even at *this* they could have drawn the line; but Sukhozanet fired several more shots down the narrow Galernaya Street and across the Neva towards the Academy of Arts, for which more among the crowd of onlookers were running!

So this accession, too, was stained with blood. ... The troops were dismissed. Look-outs encircled Isaac's and Petrovsky Squares, and many fires were made by the light of which the dead and wounded were removed throughout the night, and spilt blood washed from the Square. But stains of that variety are inerasable from the pages of inexorable history. Everything was done in secret, and the true number of those who lost their lives or who were wounded is unknown. Rumour, as usual, assumed the right to exaggerate. Corpses were thrown into ice-holes: it was affirmed that many had been drowned while half-alive.[65]

3

Aftermath

As those on Senate Square had reached that socially, politically, and physically dangerous position by many varied routes, so, after the débâcle, they
went their different ways to death or exile. Some voluntarily confessed their
sins to Nicholas, and in some cases, blacker sins than they had committed;[1]
others simply went off to bed, like Trubetskoy; others again made ill-con-
sidered or (in four cases) serious attempts to leave the city. Best-known of
the would-be fugitives are certainly Mikhail Bestuzhev and the poet Kyukhel'beker who, in an extraordinarily haphazard way, all but vanished into
Poland.[2] But all the men immediately responsible for the rebellion were soon
delivered up to Nicholas. Most were arrested within forty hours of Sukhozanet's cannonade, some in the street, others at home or in the rooms of
friends, many far from the scene of conflict. Perhaps the most remarkable
aspect of the rebellion itself was that not a single ringleader was so much
as scratched, though many bullets flew and, as was seen, whole rows of
soldiers fell. All the instigators were reserved for other fates.

Here now, to give some notion of the spectrum of reactions to disaster
among Nicholas's *amis du quatorze*, are extracts from the memoirs of
Mikhail Bestuzhev and Baron Rozen, who were arrested in the capital, and
of Baron Shteyngel', Yakushkin, Lorer, and Basargin, who were arrested far
away from it. Once fetched back to the Winter Palace and interrogation,
their paths converged once more, many sombre experiences being shared
by all the detainees.

Mikhail Bestuzhev we left on Galernaya Street surrounded by a picket of
Pavlovskiy Regiment men. Here is the continuation of his story:

M. A. Bestuzhev

'So why didn't you come out and join us?' asked one of the Moscow Regiment men.

'And why did you just stand there on one spot as if you'd frozen to the road?'

'We were ...' The appearance of an officer interrupted this interesting scene.
He came up to me.

'Who are you? And where are you going?'

'I am the skipper of the Eighth Equipage. I was in Galley Port on official business and now I'm returning to my family.'

'Very well, we'll check that up. Now proceed to your family. Move!'

'Your Excellency, they've brought in some more detainees.' This was the senior under-officer of the picket reporting, standing at attention.

'And when'll they stop bringing them?' burst out the officer. 'Well, send them to the assembly point, and designate someone to accompany this gentleman to his home.'

'Sorry, Your Excellency, but who can I designate? The men with the last batch haven't got back yet—and there won't be many spare pickets for *this* crowd.'

'Well, Devil take him. Let him go where he wants. You send off the detainees.'

They let me go and I, though in communion with the Devil, was quite unspeakably happy to have escaped the claws of that blessed man. Practically at a run I reached the barracks of the Eighth Fleet Equipage where Torson lived[3] and entered, panting, without being announced. In the hall, dimly lit by one candle, sat a venerable old woman, his mother. She sat at a round oak table and wore a white bonnet that I still remember well. In her hands were a stocking and a book which she was reading, paying no attention to the knitting. Facing her sat Torson's sister, a beauty and a woman of some sense; she was laying out *grande patience*. Leaning on her elbow, she was so plunged in thought that she did not even hear my rather noisy entry. Seeing me in such fancy dress she gasped, leapt from her chair and ran over to me.

'So! It's all over,' she said, sobbing. 'And where is my brother?'

'You've started on the Christmas festivities early,' said the simple-hearted old woman, laughing merrily. 'Tell us why you've got yourself up like that."

'Be calmer, Katerina Petrovna, for heaven's sake,' I said. 'Your brother was not on the Square. Calm down and be seated; your mother is watching us.'

'She's deaf and can't hear anything of what we say.'

'But she's intelligent and experienced, she will read on your face the unhappiness that you're concealing from her.'

'Well, aren't you going to tell us why you're so dressed up?' said the old woman again, glancing in turn at me and at her daughter.

'For the simplest reason. I was travelling to see my sisters and a clumsy driver tipped me up on the Neva into a pool. So I'm wearing this costume until my uniform has dried out, and I've come to see your son about a matter that can't be delayed.'

This prepared lie I shouted into her ear, then settled down between her and her daughter, feeling unusually weak from my excitement and from the experiences that I had undergone. Had I the pen of a Schiller or a Goethe, or the brush of a Bryulov, what a scene of high drama, how spectacular a picture would I draw, depicting our conversation by the flickering light of that one snuffed candle — a conversation among three individuals so dramatically and so fortuitously brought together! All the feelings of the old woman, who was completely deaf, were concentrated in her glance. Over her imperturbable, angelic face sensations ran like clouds, unfamiliar sensations of inward distress, as her gentle gaze moved from my face to that of her daughter who, swallowing tears, was struggling to stifle her moans, or at least to conceal them with forced laughter. My position was no better. Knowing that they both idolized Konstantin Petrovich and knowing, too, that by his loss they were deprived both of emotional, inner contentment, and of material support, I found myself obliged to calm his sister even while his ruin was inevitable. So as to hide somehow what was going on within me I took a little penknife that was lying on the table and began to draw and carve on the oak. Not knowing how or why, I carved an anchor, a spindle, and a stock, which I then transformed into a cross and which came out as the Christian symbol of faith and hope.

'Here,' I said, hearing Torson's footsteps approaching, 'is what must be your guiding star in your future life.'

So ended the 14th of December, so memorable a day for us. But when the next day dawned Torson and I had still not stopped talking. Knowing what lay in store for us in the future, we felt the need experienced by dying men to express our most secret thoughts — our final testaments.

'So you mean to flee across the border?' he said. 'But how? Which way? You know how hard it is to do that in Russia, and especially in winter.'

'You're right — it's hard, but not entirely impossible. I've already thought all the essentials over. The details I can consider later. Listen: I'll change into a Russian peasant's costume and play the part of a bailiff who's entrusted with bringing a train of wagons once a year from Archangel to Petersburg. I know this particular bailiff, and he'll do anything to save me. I know that from my time in Archangel. He'll take me on as his assistant. I just have to get hold of a passport, and I can leave all that to Boretsky.[4] I'm off to see him now — he has the clerk of the district in his pocket!'

'But who is this Boretsky? And how can you so boldly put yourself into the hands of the first person you meet?'

'Well. Boretsky, as you must know, has a passion for acting. His real name is Pustoshkin and he's a Novgorod landowner and a distant relative of ours. A simple fellow, but irreproachably honest. He loves our family even more than the theatre, for which he exchanged his future as a first-rate army officer. And he'll obtain a beard, a wig and other costume props for me.'

'Very well, and what then?'

'I've only to get myself outside the city gates and I'll get to Archangel safely. I shall hide there until the ice breaks up on the islands. I'll hide among the pilots, some of whom are my good friends and will help me get aboard an English or French ship.'

'God grant that your plans succeed! But I somehow have grave doubts.'

'Well, *something* must be done, however that may be,' I said in conclusion. 'If I succeed, good; if I don't, they'll put me in the same place. Let's go! Petersburg's awake already. You'll come with me, won't you?'

'All right. Since on the way I'm dropping in on a tailor who's an Old. Believer. If he agrees, you'll find the safest of shelters with him.'

We went out. Mounted patrols were riding in various directions along streets. Though several questioned us, we passed them without trouble. Torson called on a tailor in Koz'oye Boloto. [5] I waited for him, pacing up and down like a crane in a bog. At last he rejoined me, and told me he had failed in his attempt. The tailor had said, 'If you'd come yesterday the matter could have been arranged. But last night the police made a list of all available workers already with masters, and strictly forebade us to hire any more without their permission.'

There was nothing to be done. We set off towards Boretsky's. Torson accompanied me as far as the gate, and said farewell until our next meeting — in Siberia.

Bestuzhev met with many difficulties, in the next twenty-four hours, in his efforts to escape unseen from St. Petersburg. Boretsky's plan involved collaboration with one Zlobin; but this, too, posed grave problems.

'So you play your part to perfection but still can't go with this Zlobin?' demanded Boretsky.

'No; and I don't want to go anywhere. I'm tired of hiding! Tomorrow I shall give myself up voluntarily to the government.'

'But why? We'll think it over, rack our brains. If you can't do it one way, maybe you can in another.'

Boretsky thereupon told me in detail of all the trouble he had gone to in order to arrange things. 'First I came to terms with the bailiff Zlobin, whom you knew well in Archangel, and got him to give me the passport of a companion of his who'd just died in hospital. Then, once I'd arranged how and when you'd join him, I went up onto the gateway to see if there'd be any difficulty in leaving the city. And it's just as well that I did! You'd have been caught as sure as eggs are eggs. The officer of the watch told me they'd received an order to let no one through, on foot or otherwise, without a special note from Commandant Bashutsky; and before *he* issues a pass, he questions and inspects everyone personally. So you see, it would have been a shambles. Not knowing how long this order was going to last I went to see your mother to calm her on your account and to assure her that you're safe in my hideout. But I didn't see her. As I was going up to the house I saw it was surrounded by secret police spies and detectives. It was dangerous to risk it. So I went back home, and saw a sled carefully following me. I let the driver go, went into a house with a through passage, came out into another street and so, tip-toeing along, met you. And now, my good friend, let's go home! We're completely worn out. Let's give our bodies and spirits a rest. And the main thing is to get some supper! I'm as hungry as a wolf.'

Just then, very distinctly, I heard the dull crash of a shot.

'Did you hear the boom of that cannon?' I asked, stopping him.

'What boom? I didn't hear any boom.'

'Listen carefully.' We stopped and listened. 'There it is again! Don't say you can't hear it now. Who's shooting and where?'

'Ha! ha! ha!' my host burst out merrily. 'Who's shooting and where! Just take a look,' he went on, rubbing his eyes from mirth and pointing at the gate of the building. 'Our yardman—look: he's going through the wicket-gate now. Careful you don't get caught by the shot coming any moment now!'

And sure enough, hardly had the yardman banged the gate than the dull sound of a shot rang out. Only then did I understand what was up. The courtyard gate was fitted in a vaulted corridor that ran right through the building. The wicket-gate itself, which was stout and made of oak, shut with a bang, the echo of which resounded a number of times when someone came in or went out. I could not help laughing merrily in my turn at so prosaic a conclusion to all my exalted hopes and agitations.

While the table was being laid for supper, I told Boretsky of my firm intention to deliver myself into the government's hands. I told him, too, how awkward it would be for me to get hold of my service harness from my mother's place, where I had left it hanging while I changed into my naval skipper's costume; and I could not possibly present myself at the Palace in *that*.

'So, farewell! I'm on the march again ...' he said, putting on his cap and making for the door.

'Ah, you're crazy! Have some supper first. You've probably eaten nothing since morning.'

'We'll have a drink sometime,' he shouted, already at the bottom of the staircase.

Peace be with you, best of mortals! There were no bounds to your attachment to our whole family or your kindness to me in particular. Every time I recall that attachment, the memory draws from my heart an involuntary sigh and a sincere prayer that the Lord, albeit in another world, may grant you there the solace of which you were deprived here on this earth. Family troubles drove Boretsky to insanity, and brought him to an early grave.

It was already late at night when he returned, exhausted, hungry and shivering with cold, and told me what danger and difficulty he had encountered before entering my mother's house, thereby defeating the vigilance of all the spies. Once inside, he had done his best to calm down my relations, dispel their ignorance as to my fate and tell them of my intention to present myself in the Palace. He had also conveyed my request that they send my military harness with him. He told me, too, what fear and horror seized him when the chief of city police called, and how, hiding behind the door of an adjoining room, he heard my relations asked, in the name of the government, if they knew the place of concealment of Bestuzhev, Mikhail, of the Moscow Lifeguard Regiment. Then, he said, having received a negative reply the officer walked by that very room in which that same deserter's provisions were even then being prepared, and in which, had he troubled to glance through a door that was practically wide open, he would have found the end of the thread which he was trying, strenuously, but so vainly, to unravel! It was with satisfaction that Boretsky told me of his daring escapade with the detectives who were indefatigably following all who left and went into our house, and how, having gathered up all my supplies into a bundle, he ordered that the gates be flung wide open and flew through them with a dare-devil driver. Though pursued, they successfully shook off the spies by driving half-way round the city.

To me, the few remaining hours of night seemed an eternity. I could not fall asleep, but merely sank into an unhealthy state of oblivion and then, in feverish, burning agitation, dreamed with the clarity of one awake that I beheld a scaffold and a gibbet and, set by the edge of a grave into which my mortal remains were being cast, a column or an executioner. I opened my eyes and plainly saw twelve rifle-barrels covering my chest. In an attempt to tear a bandage from my eyes I scratched my face. ... But *these* horrors were swallowed up by scenes that made me shudder with disgust: I dreamed that I was seized and arrested on my way to the Imperial Praetorium and that, surrounded by an idle curious mob, in the middle of the street, I was bound with ropes in full-dress uniform of the Guards and led off to the Palace under escort, like a night-time thief.

'No!' I thought, leaping off the bed where I had found nothing but torment instead of some soothing effect and fresh strength to face the coming storm. 'No, I'll do my best to avoid *that* humiliation. Very well! To the Palace! Come what may!'

Hardly had the uncertain light of dawn begun to filter through the ash-grey atmosphere of the Palmira of the North than I was dressed in full uniform. At a tea-table set with various viands my good hostess was waiting for me — and she was by no means willing that I go without having tried the patties specially prepared for me. Soon afterwards, my good-hearted host also appeared, yawning and still half-asleep. And because it was so very early I had to sit at the tea-table for several hours that seemed to have no end, submitting to my hostess's almost tearful entreaties, and eat and drink willy-nilly — this when every sip of her fragrant tea and every mouthful of her patties stuck in my dry throat and choked me. Yes, that little tea-table divided two worlds: on one side was a world of comfortable tranquillity, of family life, and of the certainty of tasting present joys unhindered; on the other, one of awful turmoil and a dreadful future. To complete the picture you must add the figure of my host who, worn out by the worries of the preceding day and not yet having slept enough, appeared in dressing-gown and slippers. He was a man who had tasted a sufficiency of earthly blessings — in the form of glasses of tea by the half-dozen, and patties by the dozen; sitting there, he slept the sleep of the just.

The clock struck nine. The time to go approached. Haunted by the thought of being recognized and arrested on the street, I put on the raccoon fur-coat instead of my uniform greatcoat; beneath it, I concealed my shako, putting on my head a simple forage cap. My sword I did not take, foreseeing my inevitable arrest. Quickly taking leave of my good hostess, who made the sign of the cross over me and blessed me with tears in her eyes, and carefully kissing my host so as not to break his sweet slumber, I ran out onto the street and leapt onto the first droshky I saw. The day was overcast and my heart heavy, for there was not one single ray of hope to lighten a gloom rent only by occasional flashes of lightning when I recollected the specific facts of my guilt in the government's sight. Those facts, combined, made up the single, solid mass of my crime, my unpardonable crime: to have been the author of all the riots of December 14th. (For certainly the day would have passed quietly out of mind, perhaps with a few disturbances, as in other regiments, had I not been with my regiment that day; and the troops would have sworn allegiance to the new Emperor. As to the populace, there would have been no need to worry, and still less need as to the conspirators. Stealthily, without publicity and one by one, the secret police could have seized us and we should have rotted, unknown, in the damp basement of some prison. But now it was another matter. The pointed spanner which, in the form of a bayonet, I had thrown into the government's wheel, was not to be ignored; and even if they were indulgent, the authorities could only, in their kindness, exchange shooting for disgrace or pains of torture.) Not losing heart, but with a clear appreciation of my fate, I approached the Golgotha that was the Winter Palace's grey mass. I walked briskly. Inwardly kissing the cross on which I would be spread, I swore by that cross in my heart—by the symbol of love for one's neighbour—that, if I died, still I should not have caused the ruin of a single one of those who knew our plans. By that oath I was condemned to the unenviable rôle of one who would disavow and deny even what passed before his eyes—a base rôle, and one that has frequently made me blush for shame, but one that seems noble when, looking back with a feeling of pride and joy in my heart, I can count not just a dozen comrades but many many more, saved by me from the strap, jail or Siberia.

Stepping from the sled by the Commandant's porch, I automatically, from habit, asked Van'ka how much he wanted. 'Well, master,' said he, 'ten kopeks would cover it.' I dug my hand into my pocket to discover I had left my small change on the bed-table. My hand closed round a five rouble bill. I thrust it into Van'ka's cap. His mouth dropped open from astonishment — and across his face, which had been beaming contentedly, there flashed a fleeting suspicion that the bill might be a counterfeit. 'Master! Hey, master!' he shouted after me, stretching the bill and smoothing it out on his knee; and even as I was going up the steps his cries still reached me: 'Come back, master! Well, I'll be. ... What's all this?' These exclamations, and the misplaced generosity that stupefied the poor peasant who had received fifty instead of ten kopeks, were entirely natural. I paid no attention to them—and acted wrongly in doing so. For sighing and groaning, the disconsolate Van'ka came with his bill and, stretching it out with both hands, thrust it under the nose of everyone leaving and entering the Palace. Finally he ran against a platz- or fligel'-adjutant[6] who, having soothed him on the matter of the bill's validity, wished to know whom he had driven to the Palace, and from where. Van'ka could answer only the second question, but this was enough for the house to be searched, for it to be discovered from the yardman with whom I had been hiding for two days and, in the end, for Boretsky to be brought to admit to what was practically a criminal offence. Happily for him, his report was taken down by General-Adjutant Levashev, the most scrupulous of all the interrogators. So unconcerned and tranquil was Boretsky even though arrested, so great the air of quite unworried innocence conveyed in all his answers, that he was sent off home in peace with this godly admonition: that he conceal his natural feelings when feelings of loyalty alone should guide him!

I saw Boretsky being brought in for interrogation several hours later. This I saw through the rusted and dusty panes of the door dividing me from the Palace guardroom. But by what means, I asked myself in vain, had they been able to find out so quickly he had hidden me a full twenty-four hours? I had not indicated that I had been with him during my own interrogation; how, then, could they have discovered it? Running over even the minutest circumstances of the previous twenty-four hours, I stopped involuntarily on Van'ka as the sole being who could possibly have pointed out the house from which he had taken me to the Palace. I was confirmed in this by tales that I heard later about Boretsky. Thus an insignificant incident, an innocent act of Christian charity, all but ruined the most innocent of men and deprived me, at the very outset of the questioning, of all intent I might have had of answering truthfully. Indeed, could any man give credit to my statements when at the very start of my interrogation, once having reverently made the stereotyped remark that 'the sole path to the sovereign's mercy was through frankness in everything,' he had begun with the question, 'With whom did you hide yesterday?' I replied, with calm naiveté, 'In Galley Port'; but the yardman had told the police even the early hour of morning at which I crossed the threshold of his house. After this, I saw the need to sink, snail-like, to the very bottom of a bed of unconditional denials and, in drowning, to be the cause of no one else's doing so by a superfluous word of mine.

But to resume: casting off the fur-coat and forage cap, I went into the inner apartments of the Palace, my shako in my hands. Crossing the hall adjacent to the room which is generally assigned to the officer of the Horseguards, Cuirassiers or Chevalier Garde (who have always been entrusted with the inner watch), I saw the Preobrazhenskiy watch drawn up in three files. They had been relieved from duty. 'Well done, lads!' I said, going by. 'We wish you health, Your Excellency!'[7] they replied, recognizing me. I went through to the Chevalier Garde officer's room.

Sprawled in an armchair, that officer was engrossed in a French novel. Now, hearing the Preobrazhenskiy's loud salute and expecting to see a general, he raised himself to see his chief — but instead saw me in front of him, asking that the sovereign be told I wished to see him.

'What are we to say?' he asked.

'Say that Staff-Captain Bestuzhev of the Moscow Lifeguard Regiment wishes to speak with him,' I replied.

'Bestuzhev!' he pronounced inaudibly, falling back into his armchair.

'Yes, Bestuzhev,' I said. 'What's remarkable about that name?'

Meanwhile a bustle and a scurrying was developing throughout the Palace. Fligel'-adjutants, lackeys and court officials rushed about and, spoken in a whisper, the name Bestuzhev could be heard on every side. Several minutes passed while I insistently demanded to see the sovereign and while the duty officer replied disjointedly. Finally, I heard behind me the voice of the Preobrazhenskiy Colonel, (Mikulin, as I recall.)

'Staff-Captain Bestuzhev! I arrest you, sir! Your sword, please.'

'Forgive me, Colonel,' I replied, 'for depriving you of that pleasure. But I am already under arrest.'

'Who arrested you?'

'I arrested myself. You see that I have no sword.'

'That's all very well,' (he continued, walking beside me to the main guard-room, together with two escorts); 'what is not good is that you didn't present yourself in the main guardroom, but went through into the sovereign's inner chambers.'

'And what do you find 'not good' about that?' I asked.

'Merely that your laudable intention of voluntarily giving yourself up to the government may be interpreted to your disadvantage, and that you may suffer for it.'

'But you, Colonel, can quite remove such an *offensive* suspicion by your testimony. You see that I wear no sword, and can now see that I carry neither dagger nor pistol.'

'All quite true—but you'd have done better to report in the main guardroom as your brother Aleksandr did.'

They led me into the Palace guardroom and, leaving me in my uniform, tied my hands behind my back with a thick rope.

I felt unbearably sad, and my heart ached painfully, from the moment I was visited by a humble spiritual pastor, that grey-haired priest, pitiable arm of despotism. ... Nor could I be in doubt as to the fate predestined for me, so I waited calmly, even impatiently, for death—and indeed, could I expect mercy? Could mercy be expected by a man who had caused a rebellion in the regiment the head of which was the future Tsar's own brother? In which there was not a single member of our Society? Where the very preparation for the rising was accompanied by incredible difficulty because a suspicious government had covered all the regiments of Guards with myriads of spies? And when even Shchepin-Rostovsky, who acted so decisively on December 14th, was not only not a member of our Society but had not even the least grasp of its intention, aim, or workings? So it was that, on the third day, I who had *voluntarily* made my appearance in the Palace to be tried by my enemies, was arrested in full Guards uniform, tied up with ropes like the lowest street rowdy and obliged to pass forty-eight hours in that condition in the Palace guardroom, without sleep and almost without food. In that guardroom I had every other hour to swallow, like some potion, doses of insult and humiliation. When, finally (during my third night's questioning), I persisted in replying, 'I know nothing and will say nothing,' in order not to implicate others—with the result that the enraged despot, running out of his study with a bunch of papers in his hand, scribbled, 'To the Fortress with him, in irons!'; and when, carrying out the sovereign will, Commandant Sukin fettered me and buried me in one of the graves of the Alekseyev Ravelin—after all this, I say, could I have awaited anything but death?

Baron A. E. Rozen

On the morning of the 15th of December, as I said earlier, I was arrested. The Regimental adjutant was sent for me; after a short farewell to my wife (I had only been married eight months), I went with him to the Colonel of the Regiment,[8] where I found all the officers assembled. 'Which of you gentlemen,' asked the General, 'would care to accompany Baron R., who is under arrest, to the Commandant?' No one offered. The General thereupon turned to the orderly officer, Captain D. A. Talubeyev, and told him to accompany me in a carriage to the Commandant's house. In an outer room my sword was taken from me, and I was led to the main guardroom in the Winter Palace, where a battalion of our regiment was on duty. I begged Colonel Moller's permission to write a few lines to my wife. The Colonel seemed embarrassed, and said it was impossible, but that if I had any verbal message to send he would communicate it to her, which accordingly he did. I was taken to the duty officer's room.

The field officer of the day, Colonel Mikulin, then came up to search me with Captain Repin,[9] who had been brought in shortly before, to see if we had any hidden weapons. He then informed us that he had instructions to take us to the Emperor.[10] We were escorted by troops. Ascending a flight of stairs, I felt someone tugging at the flaps or hind pocket of my uniform: it was Colonel Mikulin, who had extracted a letter from it. When we had reached the Emperor's anteroom, through which fligel'-adjutants and general-adjutants were continuously passing to and fro, the Colonel asked me who had written the letter that he found upon me. I asked to see it, and replied that it was from my wife. After the cannonade of the day before, I had begged Repin to set my wife's mind at ease; two hours later I had sent a soldier to her, who brought me back a note with the words: 'Sois tranquille, mon ami, Dieu me soutient, ménage toi.' Mikulin replied that it was impossible, or else that my wife did not know French. It was apparent that it could not have been written by a lady to a man, but must be from a man to a lady. 'How else can anyone writing in the masculine spell *tranquille* with two l's and an e?' persisted the Colonel, not seeing in the least that for me, on the point of being brought before the Emperor for examination, it must be unbearable to be troubled by grammatical minutiae. To my delight, the Emperor's adjutant, P. A. Brovsky, came up and put an end to this disagreeable conflict concerning words, remarking to the learned Colonel,

'Cessez donc, mon cher, vous dites des bêtises.' Prince Ya. V. Vasil'shchikov then left the Emperor's room in tears. A. Ya. Neygardt, the Chief of Staff, followed him, tears in his eyes also. They both returned my salute courteously. A fligel'-adjutant then appeared to say that the Emperor could receive no one more, and had given orders that I be conducted by a detachment of feldjägers[11] to the guardhouse of the Chevalier Garde Regiment, and my comrade Repin to the guardhouse of the Preobrazhenskiy.

I spent the next eight days in that guardhouse without being ordered up for questioning. My wife's uncle lived in the neighbourhood: he sent me a bed and a screen to make my condition more endurable. On the third day of my detention, Ya. A. Annenkov went on guard duty — the same who, on December 14th, had covered the guns used against the insurgents, and was later sentenced to forced labour for life as a member of the Secret Society. Most of the members of these societies had served in the Chevalier Garde, the regiment attached to the household of the Imperial family.

On the afternoon of the 21st, a feldjäger at last arrived to fetch me for examination. The duty officer accompanied me to a sled, and wished me a speedy release.

On arriving at the Winter Palace I was once again taken behind the partition with glass doors, which had been my resting place before, there to await my turn for examination. At ten o'clock in the evening an escort of ten soldiers conducted me into the Palace's inner apartments. Half an hour later I was brought before the General-Adjutant on duty that day, V. V. Levashev.[12] He sat at a writing-table and began to examine me by putting previously prepared questions to me, writing down all my replies. But just as this interrogation had begun, a sidedoor of the room opened and the Emperor came in. I went a few steps forward to salute him; he said, in a loud voice, 'Halt!' came up to me, laid his hand on my epaulet and repeated the words, 'Stand back; back, back!' following me until I reached the spot where I was standing earlier, in the full glare of the candles that were burning on the table. Then he looked me searchingly in the face for a minute, expressed his satisfaction with my former services, and said he had observed me many times. Heavy charges were laid against me, he added, and he expected me to make a full confession. He ended by promising to do everything possible to save me, and withdrew. The questioning was resumed as soon as the Emperor had left the room. I found myself in a most painful position. There was no ground or possibility of my denying the facts on my own account; but neither could I tell the whole truth, for fear of implicating any of those who had taken part in or originated the rebellion. Half an hour later the Emperor came in again, took the paper with my answers on it from General Levashev's hand, and read it. No names were given in my deposition. He looked at me kindly, and encouraged me to be candid. He was wearing, as he had done earlier when Grand Duke, an old uniform of the Izmaylovskiy Regiment with epaulets. His pallor and bloodshot eyes showed clearly that he worked a great deal; he heard, read and investigated everything for himself. Returning to his study he again opened the door, and the last words I heard him say were, 'I would willingly save you' — 'Dich rette ich gern.' Having ended his report, Levashev handed me the paper to read through, so that I might attest to the truth of my evidence with my signature. I asked him to spare me such a signature.

Day after day passed in this situation, and each seemed interminable. On the afternoon of the third day of the Christmas holiday,[13] the Grand Duke Mikhail suddenly came in to me, stood in the doorway and exclaimed, 'What! Is he still here?' I had made up my mind not to complain of either cold or hunger, though my daily food was restricted to a bowl of soup and a scrap of white bread. This was a consequence of my exceptional situation: while most of those under suspicion were brought to the Winter Palace as soon as they arrived in Petersburg, and waited there a few hours only before being questioned, or one day at the most, this same corner of the Palace guardroom was assigned to me as a temporary residence, which lasted fourteen days, however. For those who were to stay only a few hours in the Palace, to be sure, the bowl of soup from the court kitchen sufficed; but I and those who, like me, were detained for many days, but were allowed no other food, were scarcely kept from starvation. One of my companions, M. N. Nasimov,[14] was bold enough to tell the Emperor during an interrogation that he was being left to starve there in his Palace. 'That does not matter,' replied Nicholas; 'all are treated in the same way here — it is only for a short time.' For me, the most trying part was that I could not sleep: the chair, the only piece of furniture in the room except a table, was so uncomfortable, and the floor, despite my warm cloak, so dreadfully cold. I had no choice but to spend fourteen days sitting on the chair. Often it happened that the soldiers doing guard duty were sorry for me in my hunger; they would wake me up at night and secretly give me some of their bread. My sole diversion was to listen to the conversation of these men, who always treated me with the greatest respect and civility. And frequently these conversations were rather interesting: 'It's a pity about these poor young fellows. Now they'll be shut up in the Fortress.' 'We're no better off,' replied another; 'our barracks are worse than the Fortress, and even when we leave them it's only to be tormented with guards and drill. At least these good young fellows'll be left in peace in their dungeons.'

I remained in my miserable corner until January 3rd, 1826. On the afternoon of that day the Grand Duke Mikhail arrived. Again he came into the guardroom and again expressed his astonishment at finding me still in confinement. On his orders, I was taken to another room, where a bed and some clean linen were given me; two soldiers with drawn swords were posted by my door. Greatly did I relish the pleasure of stretching my legs on a bed once more! I remained in this room for two days, sharing it with another compromised man, Colonel Rayevsky.[15] As the sentries stopped any talking, we conversed by singing in French: we both hummed to ourselves as though paying no attention to the other. On the afternoon of January 5th, I was at last taken by a feldjäger to the Fortress.

With beating heart I passed through the door of Peter-and-Paul Fortress. The carillon of the Fortress clock saluted me—a piece of skilful mechanism which slowly, tediously rang out the tune 'God Save the Tsar.' In the Commandant's house I found Andreyev, Myuller, and Malintin, three officers of the Izmaylovskiy Regiment who had been arrested and who were, like me, to receive sentences of imprisonment.[16] After half an hour the Commandant, Sukin,[17] came in, opened a packet that the feldjäger had handed him, and told us that, by high decree, we were to be placed in the casemates. In the same room with us stood a man wearing civilian dress with the Order of St. Anna in diamonds round his neck. The Commandant turned to him and said, in a sad and irritated voice, 'So you're also mixed up in this affair, and leagued with these gentlemen?'

'No, Your Excellency,' said the other; 'I find myself here under court-martial for peculation of timber in ships' materials.'

'Oh, I'm relieved if *that's* all it is, my dear nephew,' said the Commandant, and cordially pressed the hand of the more fortunate man. The Town-Major,[18] Lieutenant-Colonel E. M. Podushkin, now led us one by one to the casemates. He asked me if I had a pocket handkerchief with me as, according to instructions, he must blindfold me. This was done immediately and, grasping me by the arm, he led me down some stairs and there placed me in a sled. After a short journey, we reached our destination. The Town-Major helped me out of the sled, saying, 'Here is the threshold, and there are six steps after that.' Then he called out, 'Open no. 13, gunner.' Keys jingled, locks rattled, we went in, doors slammed behind us. The Town-Major took the bandage from my eyes now, and wished me a swift release. I asked him to order me something to eat; I had not tasted food all day and had been starving in the Palace for a whole fortnight. He made some difficulty, the dinner hour being already over, and gave as his excuse the poor arrangements in the Fortress kitchen; but finally he promised to send me some dinner, though I had only asked for a bit of bread.

My cell was almost pitch-black. The window was covered by a thick iron grating through which I could see only a narrow strip of horizon and a part of the glacis. Against the further wall of the three-cornered cell stood a bed with a blue-grey coverlet; against the other, a table and a bench. My triangle was six feet in the hypotenuse. There was a little window in the door, with a linen curtain on the outside which the sentries could lift up at any time to observe the prisoners. Shortly after I had entered this cage and sat down, I heard a sentry's footsteps drawing near; the keys and locks rattled again; the prison warder entered, bringing me a lamp (a wick burning in an ordinary glass filled with oil and water), a basin of soup, and a good large piece of bread. I asked the man a question, but received no answer. Then, with the greatest haste, I devoured two pounds of bread and the potato soup flavoured with bay-leaves. The warder looked at me in amazement. I explained to him why I was so hungry. He left the room like a dumb man, taking the emptied basin, and closed the door.

Ivan Dmitriyevich Yakushkin   1793–1857

Very different from Baron Rozen's experiences after the rising were those of I. D. Yakushkin, N. I. Lorer, and N. V. Basargin. All three remained at liberty some days before being arrested, and were seized outside the capital – Yakushkin while 'at home, tranquilly drinking tea' in Moscow; Lorer and Basargin in the South.

The memoirs of Ivan Dmitriyevich Yakushkin (1793–1857) are perhaps the best known in the West of all Decembrist memoirs, and need little introduction. First published in extract form by Herzen in the periodical *Polyarnaya zvezda* (Polar Star 1862), and in full first by E. I. Yakushkin (Moscow, 1905), and again by S. Ya. Shtraykh (Moscow, 1951), they are among the most reliable as well as the most readable of all contemporary accounts of the rebellion and its aftermath. Written in a lively style, they cover all phases of the Decembrist movement as well as Yakushkin's own early experiences and later life in Siberia. The *Zapiski* themselves are complemented by short essays on December 14, 1825, on A. Murav'yov's journal, and on Aleksandra Murav'yova and K. P. Ivasheva, as well as by almost two hundred letters, all of which are to be found in Shtraykh's splendid edition.

Despite the relative celebrity of his own memoirs, however, considerably less is generally known of Yakushkin himself, and for that reason a few words may usefully be intercalated here.

The Yakushkin family, of distant Polish origin, had lived at Zhukovo, seven miles south of Pskov, since 1422. It was a family of middling means. Yakushkin himself, having been taught briefly by A. F. Merzlyakov, Zhukovsky's friend and colleague, entered Moscow University in 1809. He joined the Semyonovskiy Regiment two years later and fought in several major battles between 1812 and 1814. He was twice decorated for valour, at Borodino and at Kul'mo. In February 1816, together with the Murav'yovs, Murav'yov-Apostols and Sergey Trubetskoy, he founded the Union of Salvation. Already he was contemplating the assassination of the tsar and, disappointed that his colleagues in the Union disapproved of the intention, withdrew from it and them in 1817. Not until 1821 was he persuaded to rejoin. Meanwhile he had attempted to emancipate his serfs, causing only general confusion. He had also learnt Brutus's letters to Cicero by heart. Once arrested, he remained loyal to his views. Only Lunin, indeed, equalled his calm performance under close interrogation by the emperor. Although 'put in chains so that he could not move' and 'treated severely and not otherwise than as a scoundrel' (on Nicholas's personal instructions),[19] he revealed little to the authorities that they did not know already. His, like Lunin's, was a character quite strong enough to bear the strain of solitary confinement in a fortress. Far from succumbing to despair, when in Siberia, he founded a school in Yalutorovsk that graduated 1,600 pupils, and then, for good measure and despite the opposition of the local police, established one of the first girls' schools in Siberia.[20] Pardoned under the amnesty of 1856, he went to Moscow and began to make the acquaintance of his own two sons. But he had little time to spare in which to do so; he was dead within eight months.

Yakushkin's reminiscences of his interrogations by Levashev and the tsar and of his first days of confinement are followed by the comparable passages in the memoirs of Baron Shteyngel', Lorer and N.V. Basargin.

I. D. Yakushkin

Many of the members of the Secret Society were arrested in Petersburg after December 14th; I remained at liberty until January 10th.[21] On the evening of that day I was at home, tranquilly drinking tea, when the superintendent of city police, Obrezkov, called for me and announced brusquely that it was necessary that he speak with me alone. I showed him into my room. He demanded my papers of me. I informed him that I had no papers whatsoever, and that even if I had had some that might have interested him, I had had ample time to burn them. I expected to be arrested, and deliberately placed on a table my leaflet with my reckonings for the redeeming of serfs in Russia; I hoped the leaflet would be taken with me, and that Obrezkov would draw it to the government's attention. I then proposed to Obrezkov that he take these calculations, but he replied that the figures were entirely unnecessary to him; after which he advised me to dress more warmly and invited me to go with him. Everything in the house had been prepared earlier for my departure.

Accompanied by the police chief, I called to say farewell to my wife, mother-in-law and son. Obrezkov led me away to the Chief of Police, Dmitriy Ivanovich Shul'gin, who met me with the words: 'You have done yourself much harm by burning your papers.'[22] I replied that I had kept no papers, but that had I had any that were dangerous to myself I had had time enough to destroy them, knowing that various people were being seized each day. 'It's impossible that you never had no papers' [sic], said the official, 'because you were taught how to read and write. Most likely you both get and reply to *some* letters.'

'There are two letters on my table,' I replied, 'one from my sister, the other from a village elder in the country.'

Joyfully, Shul'gin said that nothing more was necessary. Obrezkov was immediately dispatched to fetch these two letters. Left alone with Shul'gin, I had a conversation with him and he admitted to me that he needed at least one letter because it was stated in the document on the basis of which they would send me away, and which was signed by Prince Golitsyn,[23] that they were also to send off 'papers found with me.' Obrezkov quickly returned with the letters and the works of Teyer[24] which, being drunk, he had also seized from my desk.

I was sent to Petersburg with a special police officer, who led me straight to the General Staff Building. There, some adjutant or other took me in to Potapov,[25] who was very courteous and sent me off to Bashutsky, Commandant of St. Petersburg, in the Winter Palace. One soldier, with an unsheathed sword, was posted at each door and window [of my room]; and there I passed the night and the following day. Next evening I was taken upstairs and found myself, to my extreme amazement, in the Hermitage! Almost in the corner of the huge hall, by the spot where the portrait of Clement IX used to hang, stood an open card-table; and behind it sat General Levashev,[26] in full uniform.

Levashev invited me to sit down facing him, and began with the question, 'Did you belong to the Secret Society?'

I replied in the affirmative. He then continued: 'Which activities of the Secret Society to which you belonged were known to you?'

I replied that I knew personally of none of the activities of that Society.

'My dear sir,' said Levashev, 'don't imagine that we know *nothing*. The events of December 14th were simply a premature explosion. And you were to have delivered a blow against the Emperor Alexander as early as 1817.'

This made me hesitate; I had not supposed that the Moscow meeting of 1817 could be known of.

'I will even,' continued Levashev, 'give you details of your proposed regicide. Out of a number of your comrades who were present at that meeting the lot fell upon you.'

'Your Excellency, that is not entirely true. I volunteered to deliver the blow against the Emperor, and did not wish to cede that honour to any of my comrades.' Levashev began noting down my words.

'Now, good sir,' he continued, 'would you care to name those of your comrades who were present at the meeting?'

'That I am unable to do, since I promised to name nobody when I entered the Secret Society.'

'Then you will be forced to name them. I assume the duty of a judge in saying to you: there is torture in Russia.'

'I am most grateful to Your Excellency for such confidence. But I must tell you that now even more than before I feel it my duty to name no one.'

'This time I speak to you not as your judge but as a gentleman, your equal; and I cannot conceive why you wish to be a martyr for people who have betrayed you and named you!'

'I am not here to judge my comrades' conduct, nor can I think of anything but fulfilling the engagements that I made on entering the Society.'[27]

'All your comrades testify that the aim of the Society was to replace autocracy by representative government.'

'That may be,' I answered.

'What do you know of the constitution that it was proposed to introduce into Russia?'

'About that I know absolutely nothing.' (And indeed, I did know nothing of Nikita Murav'yov's constitution at that time. Though Pestel' *had* read me excerpts from *Russkaya Pravda* while I was in Tul'chin,[28] these, as far as I can remember, had been about the organizing of regional and rural societies.)

'What, then, were your own activities with the Society?' continued Levashev.

'I was mainly concerned with searching for a way of ending the condition of serfdom in Russia.'

'And what can you say about that?'

'That serfdom is a knot that the government itself must untie. Otherwise, undone by force, it may have the most pernicious consequences.'

'But what can the government do about it?'

'It can redeem the serfs from landowners.'

'That's impossible! You yourself know how little money the Russian government has.'[29]

After this came another suggestion that I name members of the Secret Society. When I refused, Levashev gave me to sign a sheet of note paper that he had dirtied; I signed, not reading it. Levashev then asked me to go out. I went out into the hall where Salvator Rosa's 'Prodigal Son' used to hang. During Levashev's questioning I had felt fairly at ease. Throughout the whole interrogation, indeed, I had been admiring Dominikin's 'The Holy Family';[30] but now, as I went out into another room where a courier awaited me, and found myself alone with him, the threat of torture troubled me. Some ten minutes having elapsed, the door opened and Levashev made a sign to me to walk into the hall in which I had been questioned. The new Emperor stood by the card-table. He told me to approach him, and began to speak as follows:

'You broke your oath?'

'I am guilty, Sovereign.'

'What awaits you in the other world? Damnation! The opinion of men you may scorn, but what awaits you in that other world must terrify you! However, I do not wish to destroy you once and for all: I shall send a priest to you. Why do you make no reply?'

'What do you want of me, Sovereign?'

'I seem to be making myself quite clear. If you do not wish to ruin your family and be treated like a swine, you must make a full confession.'

'I gave my word of honour to name no one. Whatever I knew on my own account I have said to His Excellency,' I replied, pointing to Levashev, who stood a little way off in a dignified position.

'What have 'His Excellency' and your contemptible 'word of honour' to do with it?'

'Sovereign, I can name no one.'

The new Emperor leapt back three paces, stretched out his hand towards me and said: 'Put him in chains so that he cannot move!'

I was calm throughout this second interrogation. I had feared at the beginning that the Tsar would ruin me by speaking in a measured and sympathetic manner—that he would attack the weak and childish aspects of the Society, and conquer through his magnanimity. But I was calm, because I was stronger than he throughout the questioning.[31] Still, when I went out to the courier at a sign from Levashev, and when the courier delivered me into the Fortress, the thought of torture struck me still more forcibly than earlier. I was convinced that the new Emperor had not pronounced the word 'torture' without positive intent.

The courier brought me to Sukin, the Commandant; the courier and I were then led into a little room fitted up as a church. This impressed itself deeply on my imagination. Servants dressed in black for mourning,[32] too, augured nothing good. I sat there for an hour and a half with the courier. He yawned from time to time, covering his mouth with his hand, but I only prayed to God to grant me the strength to bear torture. At last, the sound of iron and of many people approaching could be heard in nearby rooms. Before everyone appeared the Commandant, with his wooden leg. He went up to a small candle. held a sheet of note-paper by it, and said in measured tones: 'The Sovereign has ordered that you be put in irons.'

Several men threw themselves on me, sat me down on a chair and began to place hand-fetters and irons on me. My joy was indescribable. I was convinced that a miracle had been accomplished for me; for irons are not quite torture. Then I was handed over to the Town-Adjutant, Trusov, who tied two ends of his handkerchief together, placed it over my head and conducted me to the Alekseyev Ravelin. Crossing over the drawbridge,[33] I remembered the famous line of verse: 'Abandon hope, all ye who enter here'; for it was said of the Ravelin that only 'the forgotten' were put there, and that no one ever left it. I was pulled out of the sled by soldiers of the Alekseyev Ravelin unit, and they took me into cell no. 1. Here I saw an old man of seventy, the chief officer of the Ravelin and one immediately responsible to the Emperor.[34]

They removed the irons from me, stripped me, dressed me in a thick ragged shirt and trousers of the same material. Then the Commandant knelt down, placed the irons on me again, wrapped up the manacles in a piece of torn cloth and, putting them on me, asked me if I could still write. I replied that I could. Thereupon the Commandant wished me a good night, adding, 'God's mercy saves us all.' Everyone went out, the door was shut, and the lock clicked twice.

This room in which I had been put was six paces long and four paces wide. The walls were covered with stains from the flood of 1824,[35] the windows painted over with white paint; a firm iron grille was set into the wall in front of them. By the window, in a corner, stood a bed, and on this was a mattress and a cotton hospital blanket. A little table stood by the bed, with a mug of water on it. On the mug were engraved the letters 'A. R.' There was a stove in another corner opposite the bed, and in a third corner, a latrine. There were two chairs besides all this, one with a night-lamp on it. Left alone, I was perfectly happy: torture had been passed over this time, and I had opportunity to pluck up courage and even ask myself what they hoped to achieve by the irons placed on me which, as I knew, weighed twenty-two pounds. At nine o'clock in the evening I was brought something to eat; moreover, the soldier who fulfilled the functions of a butler bowed to me most respectfully each time. Not having eaten for more than forty-eight hours, I ate the cabbage-soup with considerable enjoyment. I could not walk about the cell because in irons it was impossible; also, I was afraid that the sound of my fetters might give my neighbours an unpleasant feeling. So I lay down to sleep and would have slept extremely soundly were it not that my manacles woke me up from time to time.

The next day, according to the rule established in the Ravelin, its chief official visited me in the morning accompanied by an under-officer and lance-corporal. He asked after my health, then proceeded further along the cells. I did not leave the bed all morning. Once, at about twelve, I heard footsteps approaching the door and the question, practically whispered: 'Who's in there?' The answer was, 'Dmitriyev.' My door opened and in came Stakhiy, Archpriest of St. Peter and St. Paul Cathedral,[36] an old, stalwart man and as white as the moon. I was sitting with my feet on the bed. He took a chair and, after a few words about my pitiable condition, said that the Tsar had sent him. Thereafter began a formal interrogation and admonition.

'Do you attend confession and Holy Communion every year?'

'I have not been to confession or received the Eucharist for fifteen years.'

'But that, of course, was because you were occupied by service duties and had not time to fulfil that Christian duty?'

'I have already been in retirement eight years; I have not confessed or received the Eucharist because, knowing there is more tolerance of religious convictions in Russia than anywhere else, I did not wish to fulfil that duty as a kind of ritual. In a word, I'm not a Christian.'

Stakhiy exhorted me to the faith as best he could, reminding me at last of what awaited me in the other world.

'If you believe in divine mercy,' said I, 'then you must be convinced that we shall *all* be forgiven: you, and I, and my judges.'

The old man was a good fellow; he began to weep, and said he much regretted that he could not be of use to me. And with that, our meeting ended. Stakhiy went out. My imagination started to run higher and still higher, from time to time positively reaching a state of exaltation; when Stakhiy had arrived he had reminded me of the inquisitor in *Don Carlos*,[37] but after our conversation I recognized a simple Russian priest in him. When he had gone, the lance-corporal brought me, instead of supper, a piece of black bread. He brought it with his usual courteousness, and I thanked him no less civilly. The day passed without further incidents.

On the morning of the third day (January 16th), Town-adjutant Trusov came in to see me, with his usual suite. Except for the priest, everyone was obliged to enter a cell accompanied by a lance-corporal and an under-officer. Trusov brought me a pipe and some tobacco. When I told him that they were not mine, he took them away again. At the time I did not have the least suspicion that all this was by way of temptation. That same day, in the evening, the doors were unexpectedly flung open and in came P. N. Myslovsky, Arch-priest of Kazan' Cathedral[38] and a man even more stalwart than Stakhiy. But *his* methods were quite different: he threw himself on my neck, embraced me tenderly and asked me to endure my situation with patience, remembering how the Apostles and the first Church Fathers suffered.

'Father,' I said, 'have you come to visit me on the instructions of the government'? This took him aback somewhat.

'Of course,' he replied, 'I could not have visited you without the government's permission. But in your position, surely, you would be glad if even a dog somehow managed to run in, so I supposed that my visit would not be superfluous.'

'In my position, certainly, a visit by a man who came to talk would be most pleasant; but you are a priest. So I feel obliged to speak with you plainly at the start of our acquaintance. As a priest you can bring me no solace, whereas for a number of my comrades your visits may be very comforting and you may well allieviate their situations.'

'It is of no matter to me what your faith is,' replied Myslovsky. 'I only know that you are suffering, and would be very glad if my visits, not in the capacity of priest, but as a man, could prove even a little pleasant for you.'[39]

After such a mutual explanation, I gave him my hand and thanked him. He came to see me every day, and in our conversations there was no mention of religion. He behaved simply and straightforwardly with me. Coming over to the Fortress from Kazan' Cathedral on foot, and going through numerous cells, he would eat a hunk of bread with hearty appetite, washing it down with the excellent water from the Neva, which we afterwards called our champagne.

It was, I think, on the seventh day of my sojourn in the Ravelin that I very clearly heard the steps of two men approaching my door. There was a tiny glass window in the door, protected by a grille on the inside, and covered over on the outside by green flannel sacking. The sentries usually came up to this window wearing felt shoes and moved the sacking only slightly in order to look into the cell, so it was practically impossible to observe their approach or inspection. This time, however, all the sacking was raised and I could plainly see a moustache and part of Levashev's face. He said to someone, 'This one has fetters on his arms and feet.'[40]

I was later assured that this other person was the Tsar, which is not wholly probable; it may very well, however, have been the Grand Duke Mikhail Pavlovich. That same evening the usual silence of the Ravelin was broken by a fairly lengthy commotion three cells away from mine. I discovered from Myslovsky that the unfortunate Bulatov was taken from the Ravelin that night only half-sane and half-alive. For eight days neither threats nor entreaties had succeeded in making him eat a thing. He was carried out to the Land Hospital where he died the following day or the day after that. Before his death, he was allowed to see his two little daughters, whom he passionately loved. The girls did not recognize him and ran away from him in fright.[41]

Next evening, after all the doors had already been locked, the lance-corporal came quietly in to me and gave me a roll made of coarse flour. He asked me, in the name of his officer, to eat it all up, because if so much as a crumb of that roll were seen the next day, that officer might suffer for it. For my part, I asked the lance-corporal to take the roll away; but he left it on my table and went out. There was nothing left for me to do but eat it, though I did not in the least want to; and the consequence of this kindness by the officer was that I suffered the most violent stomach spasms. All night I groaned and only in the morning did I find relief in violent vomiting. The Fortress doctor came and asked after my health at the time of the usual morning visit. I said I had had spasms, but was better now. He advised me to abstain from dry food, to which I replied that I always washed down my bread with water.

Two hours later, Commandant Sukin came in to my cell. Having, as a preliminary, expressed regrets as to my present situation, he begged me, with tears in his eyes, to have mercy on myself and name all my comrades. I told him that I could not name them for him, or for anyone else in the world. Still, I was touched by the old man's tears and regretted that I could not oblige him. He expatiated at great length on the goodness of the Tsar, even calling him an angel. 'God grant that that's the truth,' I replied.

'You embarked on a futile[42] business,' he said. 'Russia is a vast country and can only be governed by an autocratic Tsar. Even if the 14th had succeeded, so many disturbances would have followed that order would scarcely have returned ten years from now.'

'We never proposed,' said I, 'to build everything at a stroke.'

All this time I was sitting with my feet on the bed, while the old man stood facing me on his wooden leg. When he had finished his discourse, he said, 'Well, despite your stubbornness, I order you to take dinner. And since you haven't eaten for some time, I order you to drink tea first of all.'

I assured him this was quite unnecessary, but he repeated what he had said and would not listen to me. That same day I was given some very watery tea and cabbage-soup with beef, which I hardly touched. Next day, Trusov came in to me and informed me in the name of the Commandant that I was so obstinate that His Excellency would never visit me again.

Often, at this time, thoughts of my wife and son would enter my mind; but since such thoughts could give no consolation to a man in my position, I dismissed them.

Early in February, Trusov brought me a letter from my wife in which she told me that she had successfully given birth to a son,[43] and that she and the children were well. Reading that letter I almost went out of my mind—I was so happy that I threw myself at the door, pounded it with my fist and demanded to see an officer. My thought was to demand a pen and paper and express sincere gratitude to the Tsar for such happiness; but there was no officer in the Ravelin at the time, so my letter remained unwritten. Now I was absolutely calm, no longer needing to drive off the thought of my family, and I held myself the most fortunate fellow in all of Petersburg.

Baron V. I. Shteyngel'

So carried away was Ryleyev that he was no longer able to draw back. Rostovtsev had brought him an account of his action,[44] on the morning of the 14th, and said, 'Do what you want with me — I couldn't have acted otherwise.' Ryleyev was exceedingly embittered against him. Meeting me immediately after his visit, he showed me Rostovtsev's note and said with feeling, 'He should be killed as an example.' I tried to calm him, however, and prevailed on him to make no move against Rostovtsev. 'Well, let him live, then,' said Ryleyev in a tone more scornful than malicious. Ryleyev told me, besides this, that Kakhovsky had volunteered to be a regicide in some kind of despair — and that if an oath had not been sworn immediately to Nicholas Pavlovich it was because of Miloradovich, who had informed the Grand Duke beforehand that such was the hatred that the Guards nourished for him, Nicholas Pavlovich, that he would not answer for the tranquillity of the city. But nothing of what spies reported to the secret police reached Miloradovich. Ryleyev, on the contrary, was told of everything in advance. I had been witness, furthermore, to Captain Repin's vouching that the greater part of the Finland Regiment would rebel, though Moller asked that his battalion not be counted on. Until the very night of the 13th and even on the morning of the 14th of December, it had been impossible to expect anything. But in the shout of the Moscow Regiment a storm was borne down Gorokhovaya Street, and the Square was stained with blood. Like many others, I was an onlooker. Later, I learnt that Rostovtsev had been clubbed with rifle-butts and carried off to his home; I immediately went off to him, and witnessed the visit of the fligel' — adjutant and doctor sent from the Sovereign.

Ryleyev was arrested that same evening. I thought myself completely safe. I had sworn allegiance to the Sovereign in the Church of the Ascension; I had left Petersburg on December 20th and was in Moscow on the 23rd. I was arrested early in the morning on January 3rd, 1826, and brought into Petersburg at five o'clock on the morning of the 6th, and straight into the Palace.

Here matters began with the general-adjutant on duty, Chernyshev, insulting me with his menaces and coarse tone. From an adjoining room where, it was evident, he had been sleeping and had only just got dressed, he shouted in a Skalozubian bass:[45] 'What have you been plotting in there? We know everything! Take him off to the couriers' room.' It is not easy to describe with what indignation this insolence filled me. I was taken across into a large room where the duty courier was rattling his spurs. And there I was obliged to sit until close on six p.m., eating only one slice of white bread with caviar. At six o'clock I was brought before General-Adjutant Levashev for questioning; then I had the honour of seeing the Sovereign himself.

'Shteyngel', you're here too?' he said.

'I was merely acquainted with Ryleyev,' I replied.

'How are you related to Count Shteyngel'?'[46]

'I am his cousin; but neither in thought nor in feeling have I been party to revolutionary designs. Indeed how could I have been, with a crowd of children?'

'Children signify nothing,' interrupted the Sovereign. 'Your children shall be my children. So you knew of their designs?'

'I knew from Ryleyev, Sire.'

'You knew but said nothing. Are you not ashamed?'

'Sire, I could not give anyone the right to call me scoundrel.'

'But what will they call you now?' asked the Sovereign with sarcasm and in an irate tone. Irresolutely, I looked him in the eyes, and dropped my glance. 'Well, please do not be angry — you see that my position is not enviable either,' said he, with perceptible threat in his voice. He gave orders for me to be taken off to the Fortress.

Merely the recollection of that minute brings a trembling on me even now, after so many years. 'Your children shall be my children' and that 'please do not be angry' seemed a death sentence to me. Starting from that moment, I was no longer in a normal condition. And here, by the by, I may give an account of a remarkable psychological phenomenon.

Pacing from one corner of my cell to another in a tense mood, on the evening of my second or third day of confinement, I was testing myself to see if I should be able to die on the scaffold with complete presence of mind. I traced the whole process backwards. Having put myself to death in this way, I lay down and fell asleep. I dreamt that I and some others were being brought back from beyond Baikal in troikas, and that, coming onto the knoll of Nikol'skaya[47] landing-stage, I saw Zagoskin[48] running towards me out of the first house there, his arms outstretched. Throwing himself on me, he exclaimed, 'My dear friend, you've returned.' Quite naturally, I took this dream to be a consequence of an unsettled imagination and, preparing to die, resolved not to give up my life cheaply. This thought revived my daring.

I asked for some paper, to which we had been given the right, and wrote to the Sovereign in person a quite voluminous letter,[49] which contained a brief but strongly-worded outline of the previous reign, divided into three epochs: that of philanthropy, that of the military, and that of mysticism. In it I managed, among other things, to predict what later happened in a military colony.[50]

In my replies themselves I no longer showed any caution whatsoever. Thus, for example, in a supplementary answer giving every proof that I could, in all justice, be indicted only for having unexpectedly and quite against my will become the guardian of another's secret and not turned informer—a type always despised even by those to whose profit they inform—I concluded: 'You, good sirs, who must bring judgement against me according to your consciences, will certainly recall to your conscience the events of 1801, from March 11th to 12th.[51] There have been and will always be some circumstances beyond all human laws, duties and resolutions.'

In other replies written to question points I said such things as were regarded as too daring (giving reasons, for example, why I was not an adherent of the Grand Duke's); I was summoned before the Committee, where the member sitting furthest to the left, General–Adjutant P. V. Kutuzov, yelled: 'How do you *dare* to write such loathsome things about the Sovereign, my good sir?' 'So good, so merciful,' added the President, the War Minister Tatishchev, in a drawling, plaintive voice, as if wishing to imply incomprehension as to why I should so incite people against myself. Tatishchev knew I was aware of circumstances the discovery of which might have been most unpleasant. On another occasion, when I was led to a large room for a confrontation [52] with Semyonov, Tatishchev came out after me and assured me kindly that I need not be afraid; He attempted to persuade me that he was trying to save me in every way. I glanced at him with bitter mistrust and placed no confidence whatever in his words, having already had several collisions with him. As far as Kutuzov was concerned, his exclamation could not fail to strike me as a piece of shamelessness: for this present judge of rebels, I knew, had formerly been in a crowd of drunken regicides, so I answered calmly; 'I had not the least intention of insulting the Sovereign; but you yourselves demanded full and frank confessions in all cases, so I wrote what it was that obliged me to wish by preference that Elizaveta Alekseyevna should reign.'

'But you may change that,' Benkendorf gently caught me up; 'we must append this to your case, after all.'

'Very gladly,' I replied.

'Well then, we shall send you the questions in another copy, and you will make the same replies, omitting everything offensive.'

'Would you have me not mention Elizaveta Alekseyevna either?'

'No, you may leave that in.' And so it was done.

On my oath I asseverate that until the actual announcement of our sentences I neither knew nor imagined that we were being tried. When the Supreme Court had detailed its members to enquire of those held in the Fortress if 1) the replies had indeed been signed in each individual's own hand and 2) if there were any claims, the Town–Adjutant's summons had been phrased as it always was: 'Today you will kindly go before the Committee ...' In just the same way I was struck with amazement when, instead of being taken to Siberia, I was taken off to Finland and placed in Svartgol'm Fortress,[53] which was later blown up by the English during the Crimean War. Here I was conducted into cell no. 1 of the special block. It was a low casemate, eight paces long and six wide, with two iron doors and a small window with an iron grille. 'This is *your* place,' callously said the officer who was acting as warder, and noisily locked the doors with keys and bolts. That was the most terrible moment in my life. I imagined I was to die there... But all this was later.

Nikolay Ivanovich Lorer   1795–1873

Like Shteyngel', Nikolay Ivanovich Lorer (1795–1873) knew hardship as a child. After his father's early death, he was brought up by family friends. He was of an energetic, even liquid, temperament: to the rectitude of his paternal forebears who, as protestants, were persecuted in France before settling in Germany two centuries before, was added the élan and cheerfully imaginative nature of his mother, by birth a Georgian princess of the Tsitsianov line. He was, moreover, a southerner, raised and educated far from St. Petersburg. On joining the Guards, his attachment was to Constantine Petrovich, commander of the Lithuanian Corps and viceroy of Poland, not to his brother in the Russian capital. Later, he served in the Second Army, in the South, and there became a member of the Southern Society and an intimate of P. I. Pestel', not of Ryleyev and the Northern leaders.

One of the greatest values of Lorer's memoirs, indeed, is precisely that they faithfully reflect his intimacy with Pestel', and the situation in Tul'chin, *in 1825* – not several years before. Others served in the South at the same time and left memoirs, to be sure: Basargin and Sergey Volkonsky spring to mind. But neither man was as close as Lorer to 'all the most important actions of the Southern Society,' or as personally close to its effective leader. Lorer, as his memoirs emphasize, was with Pestel' at the end, in the fateful early days of 1826, and paid the penalty.

For other reasons, too, Lorer's memoirs are most worthy of attention: they contain valuable information concerning the revolt of the Semyonovskiy Regiment on October 17, 1820; on the brutal realities of life as an army private in the reign of Alexander I; and on the general situation in Lintsy, Zhitomir and elsewhere in the South in the years 1822–25. Lorer was a distinguished *raconteur*, and if the fluent manner of the *skazochnik* occasionally leads one to question the entire factual authenticity of certain incidents (he simply omits mention of his own collapse under interrogation in 1826, it may be noted), there is no doubting the authenticity of mood: Lorer 'the burning Romantic' and 'cheerful sufferer'[54] spoke for a generation of high-minded liberals in exaggerating the infernal baseness of Count Arakcheyev, the wretchedness of General Chernyshev, the grandeur of Pestel'.

Nor do his memoirs deal with the period 1820–35 only; no less than one

third of their bulk, indeed, is given over to narration of his life in the Caucasus and fortunes in the 1840s and later years. Sent to Tbilisi (Tiflis) as a
private soldier in 1837, (like Rozen) Lorer saw active service and extended
his acquaintance to a dozen writers, including Nikolay Rayevsky, Lev Pushkin, and Lermontov, whose funeral he attended. The value of his reminiscences to literary historians need not be laboured.

The following and all subsequent extracts from those reminiscences are
taken, in the first instance, from *Zapiski dekabrista N. I. Lorera*, edited by
M. N. Pokrovsky and published in Moscow in 1931. The notes in that edition,
by M. V. Nechkina, are strictly textual with few exceptions and represent a
critical-historical tradition now dead in the Soviet Union. Since S. Ya.
Shtraykh's superb edition of the memoirs of Yakushkin (Moscow, 1951), all
Soviet annotators have inclined towards more detailed biographical and
'background' information – a trend to be welcomed, no doubt, by students
in the West.

N. I. Lorer

There were many remarkable men serving at Second Army Headquarters in
Tul'chin in my day—officers of the General Staff particularly; and it may be
said with justice that that Second Army had been brought to such a level of
perfection that it quite excelled all other Russian corps in organization and
structure. The Sovereign himself did it due justice in conceding this fact at the
Imperial review of 1823.

Because of his advanced years, the Commander-in-Chief,[55] whom the Army
idolized, left the direction of all military affairs to his worthy aides and mainly,
of course, to Kiselyov, his Chief-of-Staff. It is with respect that I pronounce
the name Kiselyov—a name that inspires such warm feelings not in myself
alone, I think. P. D. Kiselyov was then[56] thirty-seven years of age, and all
the time that he discharged so important a function he was good, kindly,
accessible, indulgent, and handsome to boot. At this time he had just married
the Polish beauty Sof'ya Potocka.

Another remarkable man was Pavel Pestel'. When I had familiarized myself
with the regiment and made myself at home in it, I became, for two years,
almost inseparable from Pestel' right up to the moment, indeed, when Fate so
cruelly separated us forever; I came to know him intimately, and can say that
he was one of the most extraordinary persons of his age. Pestel' lived openly.
I, and the Staff regiments, were always dining with him. He lived in a very
simple apartment on the square opposite the drill-hall, and all along the walls

of his few rooms stretched shelves of books, political, economic and generally academic in content for the most part, as well as texts of every conceivable constitution. Quite apart from this, I simply don't know what the man had not read in his time, and in many foreign languages. He was twelve years writing his *Russkaya Pravda*.[57] Pestel' also had a vast memory, I should add. This *Russkaya Pravda* was often lodged with me when he had to leave his rooms for a time, and in this manner he protected his offspring for a while. I read through his constitution for Russia several times, and remember that its introduction was captivatingly, masterfully written. What, indeed, had he not pondered on while adapting it to our Russian ways?

More than once, chatting face to face with him during long winter evenings, I would ask him: 'Pavel Ivanovich, how is it that you're a brilliant fellow, yet seriously think it possible to introduce a republic into Russia?'

'And in what way are the United States better than us?' he would reply.

'But there are different elements at work there,' I would retort. 'The United States were a colony of England for a long time, for heaven's sake, and paid tribute to her; only when they felt themselves strong, and when Washington arrived among them, did they resolve to break away. Let's suppose that Washingtons and Franklins are found amongst us; even so, our society isn't ready for that revolution. And I at least, I'll admit to you, see no good outcome. Don't be alarmed: I shan't betray your aims, having joined the Society, but I sense that we're playing a dangerous game. I see no preparation of any kind. And as if *that* weren't enough, one member or another is received here or there every day.'

'You're right,' said Pestel', 'but things are going better in Vasil'kov. The regiment loves Sergey Murav'yov-Apostol and I'm certain it will follow him.'

'Well, let me tell you now that *your* way of commanding a regiment will never lead to the same results. The men don't know you and perhaps don't like you either, while the officers are nervous of you. Be more popular yourself!'

In this way we whiled away our time. Pestel' was undoubtedly a man of great capabilities; but even then we thought him too self-sufficient, while he had insufficient qualities[58] in him to bring about the republic of which he dreamed. True, he was a defender of freedom, but at the same time he was too much drawn on by ambition. He told me once how, when an adjutant to Count Wittgenstein and serving with his corps at Mitau[59], he had made the acquaintance of the eighty-year-old Pahlen who, as is well known, played a part in the murder of Paul I.[60] The old man took a liking to Pestel' and was frank with him. Once, observing the germ of revolutionary ideas already then developing in him, he said: 'Listen, young man! If you wish to do something through a secret society, it's folly. For if there are twelve of you, the twelfth is invariably a traitor! I have experience, and I know the world and men.'[61] How true it proved! The ominous prophecy was fulfilled.

It was pleasant to listen to Pavel Ivanovich, for he spoke masterfully and could always persuade you of something; yet often an excess of vanity and of ambition could be detected in his words. He himself admitted once that many had remarked on this to him, whereupon he answered, as a rule: 'A little *more* ambition is required in our affair, for only ambition can impel even you to a quicker start. As for myself, I give you my word: when the Russian people are happy and have received *Russkaya Pravda* I shall remove myself to some monastery in Kiev and live out my days as a monk.'

'Yes,' I replied smiling, 'so that you can be carried out in triumph, shoulder-high!'

Pestel' sent for me early one morning to tell me an important piece of news about which he could not take it upon himself alone to decide. This important news was that Count Vitt [Witte] had sent to Pestel' to inform him that he knew of the existence of the Secret Society and wished to offer his services and himself be received as a member of it.[62] Vitt hinted at his own usefulness to us, since 40,000 men were under his command. In addition to this, he warned Pestel' to be careful and to beware of an individual close to him who was already a traitor. What a state we were in at that moment you may easily imagine! Who could this Judas be? For a long time we talked together, thinking it over. Pestel' decided to send me to Tul'chin, where Headquarters were, with a letter for A. P. Yushnevsky,[63] the Society's principal member, asking him for his advice.

Carrying out this instruction, I went to Headquarters as though on my own affairs and stayed with the C.-in-C.'s adjutant, Prince Baryatinsky[64]—to whom, as to the other members, Pestel' asked me to say not a word as to my mission. Yushnevsky was General-Commissary of the Second Army then, and had an outstanding reputation as a serious, unmercenary, practical individual, of considerable knowledge. He was, it may be said, on amicable terms with Count Wittgenstein and liked by Kiselyov, the Chief-of-Staff (and now our ambassador in Paris).[65] On my appearing with Pestel''s letter, he locked the door behind me and plunged into reading it. I tried to read his reply on his face, but it expressed nothing, and he simply shrugged and said, turning to me: 'Can Vitt be trusted? Who doesn't know that famous charlatan? I happen to know that at this very moment Vitt is unable to answer for several million roubles that he's wasted. He hopes to ingratiate himself with the government by delivering us up tied hand and foot like so many partridges. I shan't write to Pavel Ivanovich; be so good as to tell him verbally what you've heard about Count Vitt from me, and advise him not to be intimate with him.'

I returned at once to Lintsy, and told Pestel' of my conversation with Yushnevsky. Pestel' reflected a moment, but it was clear that the idea of reaching a rapprochement with Vitt preoccupied him greatly, for he said to me even then: 'Yes, but what if we're making a mistake? How much we shall be losing!' With that, the enigmatic incident ended.

Later I grew to be on intimate terms with Yushnevsky, and always I respected him. In my view, he was the most pure-minded of republicans, and one who never betrayed his opinions, convictions, or calling. His advice was of great help to Pestel' in composing *Russkaya Pravda*.

So passed the two years of my service in the Army and as a member of the Southern Society. I was often amazed by Pestel''s memory and his ability to be continually occupied both by the matter of which he was prime mover and by the regiment, which he commanded excellently and very easily—so easily, indeed, that it seemed almost negligently, so that the Corps Commander, Rudzevich [Rudziewicz], once said of him: 'I'm surprised that Pestel' should so concern himself with parading when with his brains he should only have been a minister or an ambassador!'

Once, calling on Pestel' in the evening as usual, I found him lying down. He sat up when I came in and, after a brief silence, his brow preoccupied and gloomy, said in a somehow mysterious way: 'Nikolay Ivanovich, everything I'm going to say to you is to remain a secret between ourselves. I haven't slept for several nights now, thinking over an important step on which I've decided. I receive bad news from our boards more and more frequently, and I'm convinced that the members of our Society are steadily cooling towards *notre bonne cause*; moreover I see that no one does anything to further that cause, and that the Sovereign even knows of the existence of our Society and is waiting for some plausible pretext for seizing us all. So I've decided to wait until 1826 (we were in November 1825 then), and to go to Taganrog and give myself up to the Sovereign to make him heed the absolute necessity of destroying the Society. I went to Berdichev and Zhitomir not long ago, to discuss matters with the Polish members, but I found nothing to rejoice over there.[66] They won't even hear of helping us and want to elect a king for themselves in the event of our rebelling. The Emperor Alexander himself has obviously changed in his liberal sympathies since 1817, and has completely fallen under the influence of Metternich who croons in his ear that kindness and indulgence can only shake thrones and destroy them ... . And the King of Prussia, who promised so much and did nothing when things went badly for him, was at the head of his *Tugendbund* himself in 1813 and 1814, but now even he has grown cold. What do you say to my plan?'

'Pavel Ivanovich, I must tell you that you're entering on a risky business. It's all very well if the Emperor receives your warning indulgently and allows himself to be swayed by your arguments; but what if he doesn't? After all, it concerns the tranquillity and happiness of the entire country. And since the interests of states linked by Machiavelli's principle will win him over, what will come of it? In my opinion you shouldn't decide to take such an important step alone; most certainly you should tell at least a few of the members of your plan—Yushnevsky and Murav'yov,[67] for instance—so that no one can suspect you of seeking to save yourself by informing on a society of which you despair.'

Pestel' squeezed my hand and fell silent.

Shortly after this evening one more circumstance hastened the fateful moment of our secret's discovery. Pestel' said to me one morning: 'I've issued an order today by which you will receive the First Battalion, in proper form. Your predecessor is asking to be sent on leave and he won't return to the regiment, it seems. The battalion is billeted in Dankov,[68] fifteen versts from Lintsy, so you can take up your duties forthwith. But we'll see each other again this evening and can talk about one thing and another.' And so it was; that evening he continued: 'You'll have a splendid battalion—the second company of Grenadiers in particular; a real Guard, and with those people much can be done *pour notre cause*. The other companies will follow their lead with no trouble, and I'm hoping that you, with your ability to attach people to you, will easily achieve our aim if ever there should be the need of that. I shall transfer Captain Mayboroda to your battalion in order to lighten your military duties a little, and for the better synchronizing of our actions I shall take him into the Society.'

I had not quite expected this last phrase, and it made an unpleasant impression on me. Always I had felt a certain antipathy towards this individual and always I was on the alert with him, so even then I replied to Pestel': 'Don't be in a hurry, Pavel Ivanovich. Let me get to know him better. Up to now he's struck me as a mean, insignificant fellow, and I've already heard plenty of bad things about him. You probably don't know that the Moscow Regiment, in which he served earlier, forced him to leave the regiment because of a trick he played on one of his comrades. This comrade gave him 1000 roubles to buy horses. Returning from leave, Mayboroda assured him that a horse had been bought but had fallen, and he didn't return the money either, though all the cash had been made up. On top of that, he's no comrade of mine even in the service; he doesn't go easy on his men. However, as Battalion Commander I shan't let him be so harsh without my consent.'

Pestel' did not care for my objections. But I objected more and more strongly, insisting that at least Mayboroda not be told of all our secrets, and even remarking: 'And couldn't he perhaps be the traitor against whom Count Vitt has warned you?' Pestel', however, simply brushed aside that notion and, in his stubbornness, finished by confiding our entire situation to Mayboroda, who so succeeded in gaining his confidence that he surrendered himself to him entirely.[69] A little time elapsed and the traitor, noting down at home all he had heard at Pavel Ivanovich's of an evening, even introduced another member to the Society, Starosel'sky, the better to convince us of the sincerity of his sympathy with our common cause; so Starosel'sky was a traitor too, though only half a one.

One evening two officers of the General Staff, Kryukov and Cherkassky,[70] came from Tul'chin with the news that Chernyshev had arrived there. The day before the Jews[71] in Dankov had been claiming that the Sovereign had died in Taganrog. No one believed this, and yet everyone felt something unusual must have happened, for not a day passed without three or four couriers galloping to Warsaw and back. Pestel', however, managed to find out through a certain officer, who heard it from the fifth or sixth courier, that the Sovereign had indeed died. Still, Chernyshev's unexpected arrival, Kiselyov's sad and preoccupied face and the whole secret by which we were enveloped caused us no little anxiety.

After a long meeting held one evening to decide what steps to take, what course to settle on, in the event of the Society's being discovered, it was resolved that *Russkaya Pravda* would be hidden some way off, buried in the ground. For that purpose it was placed in a strong box, sealed, nailed up and entrusted to Kryukov and Cherkassky in order that they might conduct the funeral rites over it in Tul'chin cemetery at the first suitable opportunity. All night long we burnt Pestel''s letters and papers. Returning to my own rooms, I kept myself busy in the same way there and, for the sake of sureness, burnt everything written in my possession. The custodians of *Russkaya Pravda* rode away, and we awaited a dénouement. But even at the very turning point of our destinies, at that very moment when the Society was ready to commit itself to its fate, no one could push danger aside: Captain Mayboroda had already made his denunciation.

An order came to the Second Army to swear allegiance to the Tsarevich, Constantine Pavlovich, and this was done by companies. As if now, I can see Pestel', sombre and serious, the fingers of his raised hand placed together. Could I then have dreamt that I was seeing him for the last time at the front, and that soon I should be parted from him forever? That day, after the oath-taking ceremony, everyone dined at Pestel''s, and the dinner went off silently and sadly, not without reason. A terrible uncertainty weighed on us. In the evening, as was our custom, we were alone, sitting in a study. There was no fire in the hall. Suddenly, and wholly unexpectedly, the figure of a staff-officer materialized on the threshold of the dark room and handed a small, pencil-written note to Pestel': 'The Society has been found out: if a single member is taken, I shall begin the affair.[72] S. Murav'yov-Apostol.' Our affair, it meant, was already being played out! It may easily be imagined how we spent that night.

Next day we learnt that the Society had been discovered through a denunciation by Mayboroda. My premonitions had been realized. The first part of the report that he had handed to the Emperor Alexander, it was said, had been cast unread into the fire by the latter, who said: 'Villain! He wants to curry favour.' But when Count Vitt appeared before the Sovereign shortly afterwards he was met severely with the words: 'What is going on where you are? And around you? There are plots and secret societies everywhere, but you and Kiselyov know nothing of it! And if all this is true, you shall both answer to me for it dearly!' Vitt then replied that he did know of a secret society, and had come before his Sovereign with the very purpose of presenting a list of the conspirators in the Southern Society, at the head of whom stood Pestel'. The Tsar, then, apparently sent off Chernyshev, to find out about the matter in more detail, but himself died in the meantime of a Crimean fever, having caught a chill on the southern shore. It was also said that Doctor Wylie[73] did not treat him as he should have, not having understood at first the illness which, assuming an inflammatory aspect, brought the Sovereign to his grave on November 19th, 1825.

Chernyshev, meanwhile, carrying out his weighty mission and arriving at Tul'chin, appeared before the Commander-in-Chief and announced, with his natural insolence, that he was going through the Army's regiments to arrest the members of a secret society according to a list. The C.-in-C., a venerable old man, told him he could not permit this not having seen signed orders to that effect, and that he was afraid that the troops, paralyzed by such an indiscriminate arrest of the commanders who were closest to them and whom they loved and respected, might defy orders and arrest Chernyshev himself. 'At least take my Chief-of-Staff with you,' he said; 'him they know.' On this they settled, but then changed their minds and ordered the regimental commanders to assemble in Tul'chin. An order to this effect reached our regiment too. Suspecting no societies, our Brigade Commander himself announced the C.-in-C.'s desire, and arranged to travel with Pestel', to which the latter agreed.

Sensing a coming storm but not being quite certain of our ruin, we spent much time that evening trying to detect some ulterior motive, some poorly concealed hint in the order that related to the Corps; but we saw nothing in particular, unless it was that Pestel''s name was repeated in it three times. In our perplexity we did not know what steps to take, and Pestel' decided to abandon himself to his destiny.

I would have gone to my rooms, but Pestel' detained me and sent me to request the Brigade Commander to see him. This good old man was on cordial terms with him. When he arrived, Pestel' said to him: 'I shall not be going; I am unwell. Tell Kiselyov that I am very ill and cannot present myself.' With that we parted, long after midnight. But I had not even arrived back in my quarters and lain down on my bed before Pestel''s servant ran up to me once more with the request that I call on the Colonel, and with the news that the Colonel was leaving for Tul'chin immediately. Not understanding such sudden changes of plan, I dressed in haste and ran down to the Colonel. He was already in his travelling clothes, his carriage waiting by the steps.

'I shall go. What will be, will be.' Those were the words with which he met me. 'Nikolay Ivanovich, I wanted to see you again to tell you that I may be obliged to give you instructions in the form of a little note, even written in pencil. Please carry out instructions that you read in it without delay, if only out of affection for me.' At these words, we embraced. I walked with him to his carriage and returned to my rooms, alarmed. The candles were still burning. All around there was a deathly quiet; only the rumble of the wheels of the departing carriage shook in the air. It was with a leaden weight on my heart that I sat at the place where Pestel' had sat and, with presentiments of trouble now, involuntarily gave a little thought to my own position. What would happen to me the next day? One cannot escape one's fate, however, so I set off home, weary both physically and spiritually. This was the 14th of December, the very day on which there was a rising in St. Petersburg.

Early next morning my servant reported to me that Pestel''s valet had been brought in in chains and was under strict guard. Excited by the thought that I might somehow manage to see him, I dressed briskly and set off for the unfortunate fellow's temporary jail. My full-dress coat gave me free access to the arrested man, who was in heavy irons. Having seen him, I could not help asking myself what they had done with Pavel Ivanovich. 'They've put him under strict guard in a monastery, Your Excellency,' was the answer. 'But the trouble came about like this: I was driving into Tul'chin with the master when I saw — from a hill a fair way off — a platoon with drawn swords, standing by the gates. When I told the master this, he stopped the carriage, wrote some little note or other and then, letting me down, told me to give it to you without fail; he himself went into the town. I carried out the master's orders and started to run straight off, but I hadn't run a verst before I was overtaken by a troika in which some official or other was galloping. And this official told me to stop and sit with him, and took me off to Tul'chin. I didn't see the master there, but

General Chernyshev took the note off me that was sent to you and asked me what my master did with himself at home; if he did a lot of writing; who visited us most often and who stayed with us. How should I know all that, Your Excellency, says I. It was *my* business to follow master and clean his boots, but as to all this. ... And who stayed with us? Oh, we had quite a few gentlemen — you couldn't remember 'em all!'

I never saw this faithful and sharp servant again after my conversation with him, and do not know what became of him.

That day I set out to dine with my Brigade Commander's wife, and had to endure a yet more awful torment. The General had still not come back, but rumours of the arrest of Pestel' and his valet and others were already running through the little place. Small wonder that the poor woman was anxious for her husband! Hardly had I entered than she gave herself up to weeping and despair and threw herself on me with the question: 'Tell me, for God's sake, what have they done with my husband? You must know! They say Pavel Ivanovich has been imprisoned as a state criminal.'

'I myself know nothing for certain,' I replied, 'but it seems that we've reached a time when many will be taken from among us. As far as your husband is concerned, I give you my word that he is out of reach of any accident. Don't despair—believe me when I say that he'll be dining with you tomorrow.' I tried my utmost to console the wretched woman. Dinner time came round and we went in, but no one had an appetite. The time was passed in reminiscing about Pavel Ivanovich, who was on friendly terms with this household. Both the General's wife and her sister wept throughout dinner. After the meal, to distract the ladies a little, I asked the General's sister-in-law, an excellent musician, to play me Oginsky's 'Pol'skiy'[74] on the pianoforte. She complied with my request, but again burst into tears and went off to her room.

The next day was a Sunday and, as usual, I went to the Roman Catholic church, where our music was generally performed.[75] But here the Regimental adjutant told me, in great confusion, that he had just seen a carriage, with Chernyshev and Kiselyov in it, drawing up at Pestel''s house. Home I went to put on the full uniform of a regimental commander, seize two orderlies and then hasten to the authorities with a report. I found both generals in full-dress uniform, with sabres, pacing about the hall. They had come, it seemed to me, for some joyous feast or other, so festive were their expressions.

All the military formalities having been executed, Kiselyov ordered me to assemble all the officers at Headquarters at once, and to present them to Chernyshev. All this had been done within an hour, and we dispersed to our quarters. Expecting some instruction every minute, I was unable to absent myself from my rooms, but I discovered in the evening that the generals had not been wasting their time: they had rummaged through all the chests of drawers, drawers, and boxes in Pestel"s house, lifted floors, been in the bath-house, even dug up the kitchen-garden with the aid of servants who, no doubt, were wondering what kind of buried treasure these gentlemen were searching for. But this treasure was *Russkaya Pravda*. It was in reliable hands, and Chernyshev did not succeed in laying our accusatory document at the foot of his new sovereign's throne!

For three days the general-adjutants lived in Pestel"s house and, not taking off their coats, worked diligently. ... On the last night I discovered that Mayboroda had been brought in and, as he feared for his own life, locked in his rooms. No matter how our Regimental adjutant tried to get in to him, he did not succeed. Pestel"s other domestics said that the generals were treating Mayboroda very roughly and even yelling at him, and that he was dining apart from them. God preserve me from such a humiliation, I thought then. Better to drain the cup with my noble comrades, no matter how bitter, than to be in his position.

Someone woke me up softly during the night. I opened my eyes and saw an officer holding a candle, and wearing a grey full-dress coat with silver tabs and a captain's epaulets.

'Major, the generals are asking for you.'

'Right away. Allow me to dress; and for that I would ask you to wake my servant and to send him to me.'

We went off. It was a light and tranquil night; the little place was sleeping and only the generals and we two kept vigil. In Pestel"s quarters, by the fire-place in the hall, stood a lamp which dimly lit the spacious room. Kiselyov came out to me, and said severely:

'Major! According to all the information that we have in our possession, you are a member of a secret society. Don't refuse to speak. ...' Chernyshev came in at this point, with the words:

'We know that you were Pestel"s confidential agent and his friend. And I know that you are an excellent staff-officer, as even Pavel Dmitriyevich bears witness; so admit that you belong to the Society and have been received into the Northern Society as well. You are so young that you may have been car-ried away, and the sooner and more promptly you acknowledge your mistake, the more you will be mitigating your own fate.'

I kept silent, guessing that they knew everything from Mayboroda. Seeing my stubbornness, Kiselyov asked Chernyshev:

'Do you give orders to arrest him?'

'Not just yet. But you, Major, will not now wash your dirty linen in public.'

So ended our midnight meeting; and I imagined I had shaken off a fearsome interrogation!

The next day there took place an inspection parade of the First Battalion. Chernyshev was questioning people in the hope of worming something out of them about Pestel'. But the private soldiers, the good fellows, gave no evidence that might harm their good colonel. At last, the generals rode off to Tul'chin, having sent quantities of messengers down every highroad. The storm, it seemed, had passed—for me at least.

But not two days elapsed before I was summoned to Tul'chin. I left in my own carriage, in the evening. The night was frosty but calm, and there was no snow. This was December 22nd. The little village of Lintsy is surrounded by oak woods where more than once, a book in my hand, I have found delicious calm in solitude. Farewell, dear spots, I shall not see you again! Farewell, white hut belonging to the eighty-year-old from the Black Sea with whom I often shared a modest supper. As if expressly for me, the first ray of the rising sun lit up the wood and the cabin alike for the last time—the cabin with its trace of blue smoke. It was in a sad mood that I reached the last station but one, where I learnt from a state courier of the accession to the throne of Nicholas; of the events of December 14th I knew nothing.

In Tul'chin, having put up at a Jewish tavern (there being no other lodgings in the town), I discovered that many regimental commanders who were to have helped Murav'yov-Apostol had been arrested, and that Sergey Murav'yov himself, Povalo-Shveykovsky and Tizengauzen were already under guard.[76] In the morning, I presented myself at the house of the C.-in-C., where Chief-of-Staff Kiselyov also lived and where Chernyshev was staying. Out of weariness and agitation, I sat down on a sofa until they should announce me, and dozed off.

I awoke to find General Kiselyov standing in front of me. When I had reported in due form, I was ordered to appear before Chernyshev. At this meeting of ours I found the General sitting at a writing-desk with a sheaf of papers, which he was reading carefully. He immediately addressed me:

'Major, I am growing more and more convinced that you are a member of the Secret Society. The longer you deny it, the worse it will be for you, and I shall be forced to confront you with Captain Mayboroda.'

This last argument greatly troubled me, and I at once asked General Chernyshev for a few minutes in which to reflect. I then went to our noble Chief-of-Staff, having decided to reveal everything that concerned me to him simply to avoid meeting the scoundrel Mayboroda, whom they wished to place on the same level as an honourable man. When Kiselyov had heard me out attentively, he shrugged his shoulders and said he could do nothing for me now, since Chernyshev alone was arranging everything.

'If the [former] Sovereign were alive,' he said, 'I would have gone to Taganrog myself, surrendered my sword to him and laid myself open to his just anger, but perhaps saved many of you. ... Pestel' acted ungratefully towards me: I gave him everything that one can get by way of ranks and titles, and myself? What have I received for bringing the Army to the splendid state it is now in? General-adjutant's epaulets—and even they, at this moment, are slipping off my shoulders.'

Kiselyov, I saw, was in a most disquieting situation; to his anxieties about disturbances in units under his control had been added news of a rebellion in St. Petersburg on December 14th. I resolved to repeat to Chernyshev exactly what I said to Kiselyov; and from him I heard something that slightly reassured me. He handed me some questions and ordered me to answer them frankly in an adjoining room. So I was left to my fate, and was myself laying hands upon myself! Some kind of functionary was in the room with me, having plainly followed me there, but with whom I exchanged not a word. When I had finished my task, I asked this individual to hand the sheet covered with writing to General Chernyshev, who promptly sent in Kiselyov to me to say:

'You confess to nothing! Everywhere you've written, 'I don't know', 'I cannot say'; is *that* being frank?'

'Your Excellency, I have admitted to being a member of the Secret Society, and so indicted myself. Even for that I can be shot within twenty-four hours, according to the military articles. But I will tell you nothing more, and all your questions will be futile.' Tears flowed down my cheeks involuntarily. Kiselyov shrugged his shoulders and went off. It was about eleven at night. Weary, exhausted, I asked permission to return to my quarters—this through the functionary who was my Argus—and permission was accorded. I noticed sentries posted outside many houses down the road, probably outside the temporary quarters of my unhappy comrades. At my own quarters, the functionary demanded the key to a box of mine, inspected it, took my sword, and bore it off together with my freedom.

The next morning a young courier ran in to me with the same official who had arrested me the previous evening, and ordered me to prepare for departure to St. Petersburg.

'In my carriage, I hope?' I asked.

'No, by relay.'

'For heaven's sake, you won't get me there alive that way.'

'I'm ordered to follow General Chernyshev with you, and we can't do that in a heavy carriage.'

But I insisted and, seeing my guards' intractability, wrote a letter to Kiselyov in which I set forth the complete impossibility of my making that journey by post-chaise because of my poor health. Shortly after, I was told that permission had been granted for me to travel in my own carriage provided that I did not lag behind Chernyshev. My preparations were brief. I said farewell to my good servant, having first given him a letter to my brother[77] in which I asked him to give the man his freedom. I also gave him all my belongings.

In the early stages we sped along after Chernyshev's carriage, but then I found we were forbidden to arrive at posting-stations simultaneously with him! Quite often, indeed, we found ourselves obliged to stop in a field within sight of the General's carriage, when he took it into his head to have a little dinner, and once we were caught by a terrible snowstorm; but there was no change made in this incomprehensible cautiousness.

At Makhnovka we found a winter road,[78] and I left my carriage with a tavern keeper. At Zhitomir I dined in peace for the first time, in a posting-station, for Chernyshev had called on General Rot [Roth]. But soon we were again speeding after Chernyshev, who had likewise left his carriage with Rot and taken a kibitka[79] from him. At one station this kibitka broke, and we involuntarily caught up with him. My travelling companion received an order to send two post-chaises for the General from the station, which was quickly done. I myself lay down to rest behind a partition in the station. When Chernyshev arrived, he immediately asked the courier: 'Where's the Major?' 'Resting behind this partition.' Then I heard him lock his door, securing it with a hook, having made quite sure I was there. Vain precautions! Did he really suppose that I could or wished to flee?

Along the road, I learnt from my escort of the happenings of December 14th, of the death of Miloradovich, and the seizure of many people on the Square. Chernyshev, I was told, had been in a state of anxiety throughout the journey, questioning every passer-by about these happenings, and that he was concerned especially to discover who enjoyed the Tsar's confidence and who was closest to him. And he hastened to replace the favourite, Levashev. Oh, the empty vainglory of a pitiable intriguer!

We drew near Petersburg on the fifth day, and at one station, on New Year's Day or January 1, 1826, Chernyshev summoned me to him. I wished him a happy new year, at which he stiffly bowed to me. Not yet having been tidied up, the silver articles of his toilet were still in the room—quantities of combs, pomatum and scent filled it with their aromas. The General was in full-dress uniform and wearing a painstakingly curled wig. By a stove stood his secretary, with a St. Anna round his neck.

'I wish to try once more,' said Chernyshev, 'to lighten your fate. I will represent you to the Sovereign as one who has truly repented if you will tell me where *Russkaya Pravda* is.'

'General, you yourself know very well that even if I knew where *Russkaya Pravda* is kept I could not tell you. Every decent man's honour forbids him to do so, and I have already testified in my answers that I know nothing about it. One cannot evade one's fate, however, and it is in vain that you try to give me hope of pardon or of commutation.'

'Well, your philosophy will bring you to no good,' concluded Chernyshev.

One hour after midnight we drove up to the gates of Petersburg, and after Chernyshev had whispered some words with the officer of the watch — an officer of the Lifeguard Chasseurs Regiment, as far as I recall — we went into the capital. The city was not yet asleep; we came across carriages, and lights were still burning in houses.[80] Never did I think to enter Petersburg in such sad spirits. And all became particularly, unendurably, burdensome when we drove past the house of my uncle, D. E. Tsitsianov, where I had passed my time so gaily and where, on Thursdays, I had stuffed myself on his Homeric dinners.

Chernyshev, I seem to recall, lived on Pod'yacheskaya[81] [Scrivener] Street, and I was led up a dark and narrow staircase to a room where I was quickly given supper and, at last, allowed to fall asleep on a sofa, guarded by an officer who had emerged from somewhere or other. Next morning I was not permitted to walk up to the little window — why I cannot say. The courier suggested that I shave and, when I told him that I did not have my razors, recommended a barber to me who actually performed the operation on me. I understood then that I was no longer to hold a razor in my hands.

The courier told me that Chernyshev was very sad and that his eyes were red from weeping when he came back from the Palace, moved, probably, by the Imperial mourning. I spent a whole day and a night most tediously, and slept a lot.

Next day, while it was still dark in the street, I was ordered to follow the courier. The escort was in full-dress uniform with white gloves, the detainee in a frock-coat and service cap! Chernyshev's town carriage was standing by the porch of the house; when we reached the carriage door, I civilly asked the courier to enter before me, but he let me pass in front of him, and I remembered Marshal Ney. When *he* was being taken to the place of execution, he said to the priest who was accompanying him, pointing to the cart: 'Be seated! After all, I shall be going there before you!' — and he raised his eyes heavenwards.[82]

I asked the courier on the way: 'Are you taking me to the Fortress?'

'No, to the Palace, where the Emperor wants to see you.'

'But for heaven's sake, everyone's still asleep.'

The courier then told me he was setting out for Moscow the next day to fetch another arrested man. I asked him to be no less kind and civil to him than he had been to me. 'You're young,' I added, 'and God will not abandon you; but if we're destined never again to meet, I would ask you to take a silver tumbler from among my possessions, as a memento of me.'

I was taken into the main guardroom of the Winter Palace. A candle had burnt down on a table, and on a sofa slept an arrested officer, not one of ours. He sighed and moaned a great deal.

How many times, when serving in the Guards, had I not stood here on watch with my company! The same greenish walls, the same armchair—and the officer of the watch, with a scarf and buckled-up cap, dozing as always. Soon this officer, who had gone out when I appeared, returned with eight privates in grey uniforms and bared swords; and all this group clustered around me. I was watching these manoeuvres in amazement when the officer of the watch, of the Preobrazhenskiy Regiment, came up to me. I surrendered to him my snuff-box, a small medallion of my beloved sister and, I think, twenty-five roubles in change—everything, that is, that I had on me. At this moment, in ran a courier, short in stature and ginger-haired, to say breathlessly: 'The prisoner's to see the Emperor, sir.' I would have followed him but, seeing that these eight guards were intending to escort me, halted and said to the officer of the watch that 'for the time being I was still a major in the Russian service, wearing a uniform worn by the entire army with honour, and not a criminal sentenced by law, and so I would not voluntarily take one step with this escort.' The Captain excused himself, saying that this was the procedure there.

'Of your own choosing, you make a market place of the Palace,' I said in vexation. 'Who is the General-Adjutant on duty?'

'Levashev.'

'Be so good as to send someone, this courier if you like, to ask the General to allow me to appear before the Emperor without an escort.'

The man sent soon returned with my permission, and I went into the Hermitage with him. The Hermitage was lit up as though for a ball. Levashev was sitting at a table. When I entered he stood up and we exchanged bows. He asked me why I was not willing to submit to the common procedures of the guardhouse. I repeated my reasoning to him, and added that I would not leave, either, unless alone, until I had been sentenced by law. Levashev smiled and twirled his moustache. I had known him when he was commanding a regiment of Life-Hussars—he was always one of the most brilliant officers, and considered one of the best horsemen in the Guards. The General recognized me, too, and said at the end of our conversation:

'I knew you as an excellent officer and you might have been useful to your Fatherland; but now I only regret that I discover you in this unpleasant situation. Chernyshev is displeased with you, and has complained to the Sovereign of your insincere confession. Be so good as to wait here, behind this screen [until His Highness enters.]'

With these words he indicated a screen placed in a corner. Here I found an armchair, sat down in it and began mentally to prepare myself to be able to answer the Sovereign becomingly, but with a sense of my own worth. I did not wish to try to justify myself, nor was there any point. ... My preparation did not last long; a noise was heard and Levashev, glancing behind the screen at me, asked me to present myself. From the opposite end of a long hall walked the Sovereign, in a frock-coat of the Izmaylovskiy Regiment, done up by all its hooks and buttons. His face was pale, his hair dishevelled. Never before had I succeeded in finding him so ugly.

I would have gone to meet him with firm steps, but he stopped me with a movement of his hand when I was still some way from him, while he himself approached me quietly, looking me up and down. I bowed deferentially.

'Do you know our laws?' he began.

'I know them, Your Highness.'

'Do you know what fate awaits you? Death!' And he drew his hand across his neck, as though my head were to be separated from my torso there and then. To this eloquent gesture there was nothing that I could reply, and I remained silent. 'Chernyshev spent some time trying to convince you that you must admit to everything, but you kept shuffling about. You have no honour, my good sir!' At this, I flinched involuntarily, my breath was taken away and I said quickly:

'This is the first time I have been told so, Sire.'

Nicholas collected himself then, and continued far more gently: 'You yourself are to blame, you yourself. Your former regimental commander is ruined, there is no saving him. And you must tell me everything, do you hear? Otherwise you will perish like him.'

'Your Highness,' I began, 'I can add nothing to the depositions given in my written replies. I was never a plotter or a Jacobin. I was always an opponent of the republic, loved the late Emperor and only wished for just and fundamental laws for the good of my Fatherland. Perhaps I was in error, but I thought and acted in accordance with my convictions.'

The Sovereign listened to me attentively and suddenly, coming up to me, grasped me abruptly by the shoulders, drew me towards the light of a lamp and looked me boldly in the eyes. At the time, this movement and action certainly surprised me; but afterwards I guessed that, in his superstition, the Sovereign was looking for black eyes in me, supposing that all true carbonari and liberals had them; but in me he found grey eyes, and not at all terrible ones.

Nicholas later exiled Lermontov for this reason—he could not bear his look.[83] The Sovereign next said something in Levashev's ear, and then went off. So ended my audience. But how cruelly I had been deceived in him! Being so young—and kindness and humanity are proper to youth—I had supposed he would speak very differently with me, in the language of humanity and not that of a brigade commander.

What reason had he to shout, to frighten those already in his hands? As if we did not know that with one autocratic stroke of the pen, he could commit us all to death! I subsequently learnt from many of my comrades, however, that with me the Sovereign had deigned to speak most graciously—many of us he simply abused. It is said that after December 14th he had wanted to shoot, within twenty-four hours, everyone seized on the Square, but that Speransky had prevented him from executing that intention by hastening to the Palace and saying: 'For pity's sake, Highness; you are making heroes and martyrs of every one of those unfortunates. They will know how to die—and this is a public matter. All Russia and all Europe are watching your actions.'[84]

Nikolay Vasil'yevich Basargin   1799–1861

Nikolay Vasil'yevich Basargin (1799–1861) passed a strange childhood and a still stranger adolescence. His father, an old-fashioned landowner of the Province of Vladimir, regarded education as a luxury that all his sons could do without; his mother, on the other hand, who was far younger than her husband, regarded it quite differently and hired several tutors for her children who were then unceremoniously driven off. The tension that resulted from this clash of attitudes was not resolved until, in 1813, E. K. Basargina died. The boys were left to their own devices. For three whole years Basargin 'frittered time away on the estate,' as he himself put it, while his father grew his barley. Finally, he found the situation wearisome, and resolved to take himself off to a city. His father gave him money and he made his way to Moscow, where at first he planned to audit lectures at the university. The university, however, disappointed him: the students were as rowdy as his brothers, and but little brighter. For a time he did nothing at all. Next, having met A. A. Tuchkov, and through him N. N. Murav'yov, he joined the school for future officers of which the latter was director – the so-called *kolonno-vozhataya shkola.*

N. N. Murav'yov, father of the Decembrists Aleksandr and Mikhail, was a well-liked and skilful teacher. Under his care, young men received a liberal education with a heavy emphasis on natural and military science. Still greater emphasis was placed on high standards of moral conduct, and a sense of loyalty towards others and the state was carefully instilled into Basargin. He did well in the examinations of March 1819, and was invited to stay on a year and teach geometry, for which he had a gift. He agreed to stay. At last, early in 1820, he joined the Second Army in Tul'chin, there meeting southern liberals for the first time. Promotion was not long delayed: by 1821 he was a full lieutenant and an aide-de-camp to P. D. Kiselyov, the chief-of-staff. Within three years he was both senior lieutenant in the Life-guard Chasseurs – a far more socially prominent regiment than the Thirty-first Chasseurs from which he had been speedily transferred – and senior aide-de-camp in Southern Army Headquarters.

Professional success turned into ashes, however, when personal disaster came to him. In September 1824 he had married, for love, an impoverished

Princess Meshcherskaya. The girl was very beautiful. In August 1825 she died of puerperal fever, leaving an infant on Basargin's hands. The blow was terrible. Basargin played no further part in the social life of his regiment, and only a mechanical and passive one in liberal circles.

Not only this personal tragedy, however, led him to keep his distance from the radical society in which he had been welcome and at home until 1821. Even before his marriage he had cooled towards the fervid anti-monarchism of his own earlier years. No longer was he willing to condemn autocracy and all its workings outright, as he had in Moscow. His changing attitude towards secret political societies in general, moreover, and towards hopes of revolution in Russia, typified that of many dozen middle-ranking, middle-income officers once active, like himself, in the Union of Salvation or still earlier societies and groups. If only for this reason, Basargin's clear account of his decreasing radicalism in the years 1822 to 1825 is of value and significance to students of the period.

'Infected by the spirit of free-thinking then reigning in Russia,' he informed Chernyshev eight years later, 'and brought up in an establishment where such sentiments took root in me, I pondered the question of the introduction of free government to Russia.'[85] No doubt the milieu of the Murav'yovs did foster such reflections in idealistic youths. It was reality, however, and not theory, that drove Basargin to become a member of the Union of Salvation. 'While drawing up a survey in the Province of Moscow in 1819,' he further told Chernyshev, 'I chanced to find myself on the estate of a certain land-owner whose treatment of his serfs first gave me the idea or, rather, the *desire* to set them free.' No doubt there had been earlier occasions when Basargin witnessed physical cruelty to serfs – a long knouting, perhaps, to go with a particularly loathsome drowning that he once observed. Received into the Union in Tul'chin, he was at first extremely active on committees: 'I felt a strong desire to be of use; I was attracted by the opportunity to draw closer to right-thinking individuals, as by the Union's (as it then seemed to me) just object.' Part of that object was, of course, the abolition of serfdom throughout Russia and the empire.

Such a pitch of energy was not long to be sustained. Within a year, Basargin's zeal for meetings had decreased; he began to take less interest in the Tul'chin radicals' attempts to link up with the members of the Polish Patriotic Society than in his own future career. Of course, he joined the newly-formed Southern Society; not to have done so would have been a little difficult. But he found less time for it than many. His very attitude towards autocracy was undergoing change in 1822.

'While not ceasing to view all that was *bad* in the same light,' (he would explain when all was over for Pestel' and his companions), 'I often asked myself if everything would actually *be* better if the Society achieved its end – if Russia would comprehend the advantages of representative government. I conceded inwardly that it would be far better if the government itself would seize the initiative and move forward, not hampering but encouraging intelligence and the achievements of education.' Once started on this course, Basargin's mind moved on predictably. By the late autumn of 1823 it had grown apparent to him that 'there is no government whatever without *some* faults. ...' More, 'those faults should be corrected by a government itself, and not by private individuals.' Not 'may be' but *'should* be corrected.' It was, from any liberal standpoint, a reactionary view.

But Basargin was not a reactionary, nor did he ever break his earlier liberal connections. By 1824 it was in any case too late to break them and avoid the consequences of a friendship with Pestel'; the point, however, is that he did not attempt to sever them or to conceal in any way his earlier links and attitudes. In this respect also he typifies the middle-ranking members of both Northern and Southern Societies, many of whom, it is not always justly stressed, had lost much of their earlier fire and enthusiasm by 1824. Arrested on January 8, 1826, he was imprisoned, 'tried' and sentenced to hard labour in Siberia for fifteen years.

Like Rozen, Basargin seems to have made notes or jottings while still living in a settlement (Kurgan, in the Province of Tobol'sk), of which he later made good use. Not until the late 'fifties, however, did he set his memories in order. The manuscript in which he did so has survived. It is a bound notebook containing eighty numbered and fourteen un-numbered sheets.[86] Written in an even, sloping hand, it is remarkably free from corrections and blots, a fact that would suggest that Basargin was correcting and improving on an earlier manuscript, now lost. He was a highly self-critical writer; his essay, 'Recollections of the Educational Institution for Officers and of Its Founder, N. N. Murav'yov,' for example, is known to have gone through three drafts. When Basargin was satisfied with his notebook, he gave it to his (third) wife, Ol'ga, who in turn entrusted it to the historian and Pushkinist P. I. Bartenev. Bartenev edited it and published most of it in a collection entitled *Devyatnadtsatyy Vek* (The Nineteenth Century: Moscow, 1872). The Moscow Censorship Committee demanded various alterations and omissions. In particular, a chapter on Siberia and its future was removed, possibly on Bartenev's own initiative.

Ol'ga Basargina was born a Mendeleyeva, and was the sister of the celebrated chemist. Another member of her family, I. P. Mendeleyev, decided to commit Basargin's notebook to the literary historian and critic P. E. Shchegolev, in order that it might be published in toto. Edited by the irascible, sickly Shchegolev, *Zapiski N. V. Basargina* appeared in Petrograd in 1917.[87] Though even now not quite intact, Basargin's notebook had acquired some 'apparatus': Shchegolev wrote an introductory article and added an index of proper names. He did not, however, annotate it, a fact the more regrettable because no subsequent edition of the memoirs has been published either in the Soviet Union or in the West.

The chief value and interest of those memoirs lies not in any autobiographical content, though there is much of this, but rather in a set of attitudes reflected faithfully in every chapter. Basargin wrote well, but not about himself; dealing with other prisoners and other lives, the feel of Peter-and-Paul Fortress, even the (excessively abused) climate of Western Siberia, he is always lucid, frequently compelling. But the light that worked so well when all its beams were shining outwards made him falter, when turned in upon himself. There are, to be sure, arresting passages dealing with his personal experiences, in the Ukraine in 1820–24, for example. Yet when one most longs for sincerity and self-revealing frankness – for instance, in the section covering his several interrogations in the Fortress – few details are forthcoming. Rather than deal with his own personal conduct when faced by Chernyshev and Levashev (and, as Shchegolev notes, 'he showed but little staunchness under questioning'), he chooses to treat the sham legal proceedings, and the very trial itself, in general terms. For us, the fact is vexing. Basargin was an optimist, except when all was hopelessly depressing and all light appeared extinguished, but he was also of an introspective temperament. He knew himself better, indeed, than Trubetskoy knew Trubetskoy, or Lorer the gay Lorer. It seems that he was not content with what he found inside himself. Did he, perhaps, regret having been acquiescent when faced by the Commission of Enquiry, feeling that he might have been more stubborn? The supposition partially explains the general superficiality of his narrative where it touches on his own interrogations.

There is one passage in his memoirs, however, in which such superficiality is wholly missing; it is, indeed, the only place in which Basargin quite *deliberately* reveals his inner self, under the impact of a memory of horror. We see his secret fears and dreads as he paces a black cell in the grim Kronverk Curtain of the fortress. Basargin suffered more, in his first hellish days and nights of close confinement, than almost any other of the prisoners who lived. The thick stone walls that muffled sound and hope remained with him throughout his life; ever afterwards he suffered from suggestive claustrophobia. Here, now, is his account of his arrival in the capital, his first appalling night of silence, panic, and despair, and his struggle to maintain his sanity.

N. V. Basargin

I went to Headquarters as usual on the morning of January 8th, 1826, and sat down to my work.[88] The duty general called me in to him and, having shown me some instructions from the War Minister,[89] told me that there were orders that, with many others, I should be arrested and then brought to Petersburg. He told me almost in tears, and asked if we should meet again. 'God knows,' I answered. He thought a little, then said:

'At least you don't have anything on paper, do you? In that case, deny it, deny it and keep on denying, and we'll meet again. Tomorrow I shall come and seal up your documents, so be ready. You may set off when you wish. But you've probably not rested from your journey yet — you can wait a day or two.'

'The sooner I leave the better, Your Excellency,' I replied; 'the unknown is worst of all. If you will permit me, I'll go after breakfast and, if possible, with Vol'f.[90] He readily agreed to this.

Things were sad for me all during this time, but especially so when I recalled my earlier happy life. I found comfort in the sympathy and endearments of my wife's relations, with whom I was then living, and in the kind consideration shown me by my fellow-officers who did not belong to the Society and so were not afraid of being arrested. But at last the day of departure dawned.

I spent the last evening at my mother-in-law's house. There, some of our closest friends had gathered and even the duty general came to bid us farewell. We had supper, sadly made our adieus, and embraced for a final time. Then I sat in a wagon together with Vol'f, two gendarmes sat in another, and we set off. As if it were just now, I recall how I was moved by my late wife's very much younger sister, an intelligent, sharp-witted girl of eleven. She wept inconsolably, then, seeing I was packing two English books in my suitcase, asked why. 'I shall study English in the Fortress to keep off boredom, my friend,' I said. 'I'm afraid you'll forget even Russian in there,' she broke out; and with these words, tears flowed from her eyes.

Not infrequently along the way we came upon arrested men and their couriers and gendarmes. But we could not speak to even one of them. Besides, Vol'f and I had agreed at the time of our questioning to keep silent and say nothing that might implicate our comrades. This proved ill-calculated and of no use.

At last we arrived in Petersburg. We were taken to the building of the General Staff and there received by the senior adjutant—Yakovlev, as far as I recall. Yakovlev jotted something down and gave instructions for us to be taken to the Palace guardroom. Here, the gendarme from the General Staff who was sent with us handed a note to the duty officer, who sent for the Town-Major.[91] The Town-Major, in his turn, saw to it that our servants and possessions were sent off to some place unspecified. Then he searched us, took our money, and sat us separately in some little dark room or other with glass doors. And here occurred a minor incident which embarrassed the Commandant and Town-Major and which showed the loyalty of my servant, an eighteen-year-old lad. When he had searched me and placed me in the dark room, the Town Major ordered this lad to go off in the wagon to whatever place the gendarme might direct. My Vasiliy replied that he had come to be of service to his master, and that unless I ordered it, he would not leave me. The Town-Major would have shouted at him but he, not losing his control, calmly repeated what he had already said, adding that he did not mean to insult His Excellency by simply doing his duty. Bashutsky, the Commandant, came in just at this moment. The situation was explained to him and he, going up to my servant, commanded him to carry out the Town-Major's instruction. Vasiliy's reply was the same.

'How dare you speak to me in that manner?' yelled Bashutsky; 'don't you see who I am?'

'I've said nothing offensive, Your Excellency,' retorted my servant. 'I can see you're a general, but what I say to you I'm ready to say to anybody.'

'Like master, like servant,' remarked Bashutsky.

I was a witness to this scene from behind the glass doors. Bashutsky and the Town-Major, it was clear, were perplexed as to what to do. Finally, having exchanged a word or two, they decided to address me, opened the doors, and told me to instruct my servant to obey their orders. 'Do what the general orders, my good Vasiliy,' I said; 'you can't remain with me.' Tears welled up in his eyes, and he could barely utter, 'Yes s—.' I then turned to Bashutsky and asked his permission to give my lad some money from the wallet that had been taken from me. (I guessed from their conversation that the boy would have to stay in Petersburg until the trial was over.)[92] To this the Commandant readily agreed, gave me my wallet and I, taking out one hundred roubles, handed them to my Vasiliy, embraced him, and went back into the dark room.

During the day, several more arrested men were brought in. Two of them I had met earlier, in Moscow: Colonel Grabbe[93] and Murav'yov (Aleks. Nik.); they, too, were put in separate rooms. That evening I was ordered to the Palace and the Sovereign's chambers for interrogation. People were ceaselessly running about with trays and cups in the room where I was placed (behind a screen). After five minutes, an officer of the Corps of Couriers came, took me by the arm, and led me into a large hall hung with paintings. I recognized the Gallery of the Hermitage. There was a little table set up by one wall, and at it sat General Levashev; before him was an inkwell and a few sheets of clean paper. Levashev was about to ask me to be seated facing him when suddenly the same courier reappeared, announcing that Prince Volkonsky (the General-Major and a member of the Society) had arrived. Levashev thereupon excused himself most civilly for having to postpone my questioning until the morrow. They took me back to my old place in the guardroom.

Next morning I was taken back once more for questioning. Levashev was sitting at the same spot, and I had barely sat down facing him when the Tsar entered, wearing a frock-coat and no epaulets. I stood and bowed to him.

'Speak the whole truth,' he said severely. 'If you conceal anything, you'll reproach yourself for it.'

With these words he went out by an opposite door. Levashev indicated that I should be seated again, and began the questioning:

'When did you join the Society, and who received you into it?' he asked, preparing to note down my answers.

'Your Excellency,' I said, 'not considering myself a member of a secret society, I am at a loss what to say to you.'

'Then you wish to say nothing, I take it?' returned Levashev. 'Think a little; this can only do you harm. Even without you the government knows everything.' I remained silent. 'You gentlemen are unwilling to entrust yourselves to the Sovereign's mercy. So you force him to act towards you with all the severity of the law. You have only yourself to blame, as he told you.'

At this, he wrote a note of some kind, went out of the room for a moment and then, handing the note to a courier, ordered me to follow him. Most probably the note was to the Commandant of the Fortress, and signed by the Tsar.

Many, perhaps, will accuse us of stubbornness and feel that by acting in this way we deprived ourselves of hope of the Sovereign's mercy. But I am convinced, on the basis of the late Tsar's character, that not only would a frank admission of the truth not have softened his heart or attitude, but that even the most complete repentance would have failed to do so. His intentions with regard to us had been thought out and determined earlier. In view of his policies and autocratic power, the rising of December 14th had blocked the path to sympathy and mercy in his heart. Its sequel proved this; and certain of our comrades who had recourse to frankness and repentance shared the same fate as the rest of us. As to those few whom the Tsar did pardon, such as the young Wittgenstein, Suvorov, Lopukhin, Shipov and Orlov, this was the working of his policy, and proves still more decisively in what cold blood he could both act and calculate at our trial and in 'administering justice' to members of the Secret Society. But the best proof of his inflexibility is to be seen in his own words to his heir at his death.[94]

But to return to my account: passing through the guardroom and seizing up some of the things, I set off for the Fortress with a courier. There, I was brought before the Commandant, who was handed Levashev's note. We proceeded with him and the Town-Adjutant into the Kronverk Curtain and, following various dark corridors, came to the casemate assigned to me — a room four paces long and wide in which a little window was covered with chalk and in which there stood a folding bed, a little table and a small iron stove. The Town-Major stripped me completely in this casemate, inspected everything on me — removing even my wedding ring — and took all this away with him, leaving me with two shirts, a coat, trousers, and a hospital smock. The door was locked after him, on the outside. Up and down the corridor walked a sentry who would frequently look in at me through a tiny window in the door, a window curtained on his side with rough cloth.

Whoever has not experienced confinement in a Russian fortress cannot imagine that dark and hopeless feeling, that failing of the spirit, I will say more, even the desperation, which not gradually but suddenly seizes the man who has once crossed the threshold of a casemate. All his links with the world are broken, all ties snapped. He remains alone against autocracy, against an unlimited power which is ill pleased with him and which can do with him as it pleases — first subject him to every deprivation, then even forget him; and from nowhere would there come assistance, from nowhere so much as a sound in his favour. Before him stretches gradual moral and physical exhaustion; no longer has he any hopes for the future; every moment it appears to him that he has been *buried alive*, with all the attendant horrors of that situation. Even now, after thirty years of exile, years filled with numerous tribulations, I cannot recall the first day that I passed in Peter-and-Paul Fortress without shuddering. And I marvel that in our time, when notions of philanthropy are not thought dreams or Utopias, when earthly princes and rulers themselves try, more or less, to act in accordance with precisely those ideas — and when torture has been everywhere abolished, being held by everyone to be a useless cruelty — still solitary confinement in fortresses remains. For it is moral torture, more cruel and more destructive of a man than any physical torture.

What I experienced, what I lived through on my first day of confinement it is not possible to describe. On the one hand: memories of a past still so fresh; on the other: all the horrors of the present and a hopeless future. Several times I leapt up from the hard couch in the night not knowing where I was. Nor was there any slumber, only a wearisome drowsiness that agitated one's disturbed thoughts even more. With what impatience did I wait for the light of dawn, already imagining that I was mad! The morning found me totally exhausted. At nine o'clock, they unlocked the cell doors and brought me rolls, two lumps of sugar, a cup, and a teapot full of very watery tea. I remember how this overjoyed me. My first thought was: well, they haven't forgotten about me, they remember I'm alive, they care about my existence! I began to drink the tea while the guard re-arranged something in the cell; he made no reply to some question of mine. I asked the sentry, through the door, what time it was—the same silence. A clock answered me itself: at that moment it struck nine in Peter-and-Paul Cathedral belfry.

I admit frankly, so morally weak, so dispirited did I become during the first two weeks of my confinement that to this day I thank God that I was not summoned before the Committee. In that condition, I would probably have given testimony that would now be troubling my conscience. Throughout those two weeks I continued to imagine I was mad or, at the least, must grow insane. I would consider every act and every movement I performed, and find it incompatible with common sense. If I asked the guard a question or requested him to do something, it struck me straightaway that this was quite unnatural—that a rational person in my position would not occupy himself with such trifles. If, forgetting myself, I started to sing a familiar tune, this immediately struck me as a sign of my insanity. Finally, even the thought of madness, which I was totally unable to shake off, began to trouble me; and it appeared to me that I might easily go mad through thinking that thought and that, having no strength to drive it off, I was already then losing my mind. I thank Thee, my Creator, that Thou didst grant me strength to overcome that disastrous mental state.

But although I passed two weeks in this way, still I thought determinedly how to escape my situation. The only way of *not* dwelling on madness, I saw clearly, was to find some other occupation for myself; but what other occupation could I find in that close, dark, stuffy cell? No books were given to me, nor was I allowed paper or pen or ink. At first, I was allowed to speak to nobody. The sentinel did not answer my questions but walked the corridor like an automaton, lifting the scrap of cloth once every fifteen minutes to see what I was doing. The guard, little by little, grew accustomed to me; it was evident, however, that he feared to enter into any conversation with me and was nervous of remaining in my company without a reason. So I racked my brains, and came up with the following plan.

Everything I had studied was still fresh in my mind. My memory was good then, so I decided to set myself questions in all those branches of knowledge of which I knew something—to consider and resolve those questions as if they were propositions that I had to bring into effect. Often these questions would be purely moral or religious; sometimes they would be mathematical problems, at other times plans for military action, administrative measures, political instructions or plans for industrial enterprise. First, I decided on the data that would serve as the basis of my deliberations. Then I reflected and decided how to organize myself and act, according to the data, so as to bring about a given outcome. I found a splinter of glass, which I used to make marks on the window, wall or table to remind myself of what should be remembered. In this fashion, I could pass several hours and continue with what I was doing even in darkness. Having got up in the morning and prayed mentally to God (because I disliked being watched by the sentinel), I would tidy my bed and cell, summon the sentinel, drink the tea which he generally brought me at the same time every day, and settle down to my occupations until lunch. After lunch I would sleep a little, then, getting up, go about my business again, starting with that very point, deduction or conclusion on which I had stopped earlier. In that cell I understood easily how the blind and deaf-and-dumb learn to communicate, to speak and hear; but this will not be comprehensible to those who never experienced that sharpening of the physical senses and the mental capabilities produced by the removal of all situations in which both might function easily. Later, many of us who were in solitary confinement invented a method of communicating with each other by means of signals knocked on the stone walls, which were of massive thickness. This we did with the aid of an alphabet not easily devised, nor even readily explained in words.

Starting about this time, my thoughts began to regain their normal sequence, even becoming clearer in a certain sense. Terror of going mad, which was little by little weakening, completely disappeared. In spirit I became still calmer; the conviction that this transitory life has no significance whatever compared with that awaiting us after our death—and that this present life is not even worth thinking of—bolstered my moral forces once and for all.

The Trial

Most of those arrested in connection with the rising of December 14, 1825 or with the later insurrection in the South, were brought in person before the emperor who, after a few questions, issued an order indicating to the commandant of Peter-and-Paul Fortress how each prisoner was to be treated: whether he should be kept in chains, placed under close surveillance, or allowed more liberty. These orders, one hundred and fifty of them, have survived and constitute an extraordinary record.[1] They show the avid interest that Nicholas took in the entire affair, and his determination to squeeze from every prisoner the last possible drop of evidence. 'Ryleyev,' read the note accompanying him, 'to be placed in the Fortress but his hands not tied. Give him writing paper and deliver personally to me whatever he writes each day.' 'On receiving Bestuzhev [A.A.], as well as Obolensky and Shchepin,' read another, 'order them to be manacled.' 'Yakushkin to be treated severely, and not otherwise than as a scoundrel.'

The hatred that Nicholas felt for these men was personal and intense. The mere thought of them annoyed him. Prince Obolensky had 'a black soul' and 'a bestial and mean expression.' Artamon Murav'yov was 'nothing but a murderer, an outcast without merits.' As for Prince Sergey Volkonsky, who alone among the Decembrists had a certain and secure niche in the highest court society, his mother being the empress's confidante, he was 'a stuffed fool, a liar and villain in the full sense of the word ... and a *repellent* example of an ungrateful scoundrel.'[2] The emperor's artistry in posing for each prisoner in ways best calculated to extract the desired confession was such as to deceive even La Ferronays, the French ambassador; small wonder, then, that he succeeded even better with the prisoners who, with occasional exceptions such as Lunin and Yakushkin, took his pretended sympathy at face value.

Such an interrogation process was inadequate, however, to meet Nicholas's demands. Almost immediately after the rising was suppressed, he instituted a Commission of Enquiry with himself as its director. (A. I. Tatishchev was nominal chairman, but he followed orders.) In itself, incarceration in the damp and wretched casements of the Alekseyev Ravelin or Kronverk Curtain was occasionally enough to break a spirit, or a life: what with the meagre diet, ponderous chains, and all-pervading silence, many found themselves hard-pressed to bear their situation and, breaking down, involved others. Even today, these cries of 'guilty!' represent oppressive documents, written by men obviously on the verge of physical or mental collapse.[3] But physical discomfort was a trifle when compared with the more subtle pains induced by 'loyal' priests, coming with 'spiritual consolation'; long periods of total isolation from the outside world; and, worst of all, sudden interrogation sessions in the night. Always there was suspense, always some fear, and always ignorance of what others had already said to implicate their comrades. Many collapsed under the strain. Here is Mikhail Fonvizin's recollection of that time:

Methods were used against the prisoners which struck their imagination and destroyed their spirit, irritating them either by false hopes or by fears of torture, and all with one purpose only – the extortion of confessions. The door of a cell would suddenly be opened at night; over the prisoner's head a blanket would be thrown abruptly; then he would be led through the corridors and passages of the Fortress into a brightly lit courtroom. And here, after the blanket was removed, members of the Commission would suddenly ask questions of the prisoner and, giving him no time to think, roughly demand immediate and affirmative replies. In the Tsar's name, they would promise a defendant pardon if he would confess 'straightforwardly.' They accepted no self-justifications, invented fictional testimonies by other prisoners and frequently refused to call those other prisoners in to testify to their statements. Whoever did not give the requisite replies, whether because of ignorance of events about which he was questioned or because he hesitated to ruin some innocent man through a careless word of his, was then transferred to a dark, damp cell, put on a bread and water diet and burdened with weighty arm and leg fetters. The Fortress physician would be ordered to ascertain whether or not the prisoner would bear the most acute physical pain.'[4]

Small wonder that some prisoners, their nerves tangled and frayed by such ordeals, collapsed and then revealed all that they knew, sometimes adding incredible exaggerations and implicating men only remotely linked with the apparently collapsed Decembrist movement. Such was the case with P. I. Falenberg, who, in his dark and isolated torment, gave distorted evidence and went most innocently to Siberia, and with Aleksandr Bulatov, who took his own life in his cell. The commission, one need hardly emphasize, made no attempt to analyze the underlying social forces of the radical movement in Russia or its no less complex psychological aspects. As Prince Obolensky put it: 'They took for truth what had been said or done in moments when imagination had been guided by some feverish outburst – and used this as hard evidence of terroristic plans and evil thoughts.' Why did they make no effort to appreciate the underlying forces that had led the prisoners to conspire against autocracy? Because no such attempt was called for by the tsar; it was not their brief. Even Benkendorf disliked the arbitrariness of the proceedings, a fact suggestive of the suffering that Speransky must have undergone.

For five months the commission was engaged in its supposed investigations, unwilling to report to Nicholas in case some detail had been overlooked. (Also, time had to pass before it could grow clear whether or not such suspect foreigners as the Austro-Hungarian Ambassador, Count Loebzeltern, or such celebrated military figures as Generals Yermolov and Kiselyov' or such writers as Pushkin and Griboyedov were involved in any way.) Finally, a report was made and presented on May 30. Two days later, Nicholas appointed a special supreme court, which held sessions for nine days beginning on June 3. Prince P. P. Lopukhin, whom Nicholas named chief justice of the Russian empire, was conveniently deaf, but there was never doubt, in any case, that the supreme court would do anything but docilely confirm the findings recently submitted by the commission of enquiry. Prisoners were not called before the court, and therefore did not know that their own trials were under way, but were visited in their cells by members of a special sub-committee who merely asked each man whether or not the statements read before the commission of enquiry had been correct, and if the signature beneath them was authentic. If a defendant did not recognize, or refused to acknowledge his signature, he was unceremoniously informed it would make very little difference anyway.[5] Throughout their times in Peter-and-Paul Fortress, prisoners were kept in ignorance of the significance of what they did, wrote or affirmed. Thus most believed that what they said before the commission of enquiry would determine their whole future; in fact, their (often hastily) written replies to a set of multiple questions *(voprosnyye punkty)* played a more vital part in their cases. Some of those replies will follow here.

At last, on July 9, 1826, the court passed sentence on the prisoners. Altogether, 579 persons were brought to trial, of whom 290 were acquitted. Of the remaining 298, 121 were selected as the most responsible conspirators, sixty-one being ex-members of the Northern Society, thirty-seven of the Southern and twenty-three of the Union of United Slavs. The sentence in respect to these main criminals recommended that five, namely Pestel', Sergey Murav'yov-Apostol, Ryleyev, Kakhovsky and Bestuzhev-Ryumin, be quartered alive. The rest were to be treated according to eleven different categories of guilt, thirty-one persons of the first category to lose their heads. For all its savagery, this sentence was too mild for some state dignitaries, such as the infamous Senator Lavrov, who demanded that no less than sixty-three men be split and quartered, 'three parts to perish shamefully and one honourably.'[6] Alone of all the judges, the elderly Admiral N. S. Mordvinov, whose own record was stained by liberal sympathies, refused to ratify capital punishment.[7]

Predictably, the sentence recommended by the court was modified by Nicholas. He had, after all, to demonstrate his clemency. The five leaders would be spared the block and axes, and would hang; the thirty-one would die off in Siberia, where they would serve hard labour terms for life. The fate of the Decembrists was determined long before the court began its sessions, but the 'act of clemency' was very much in keeping with the imperial mind: the world had to be shown all the formalities of due legal procedure. It was, in several senses, the first modern grand 'political trial' in Russia.

The Commission of Enquiry, it was seen, demanded written answers to a standard set of questions from each prisoner. Three questions in this ponderous document – most 'points' were sub-divided into three or even more parts – throw interesting light on the Decembrists' changing intellectual outlook and evolving liberalism:

Excerpts from Individual Testimonies

The following statements, by thirteen different Decembrists held in Peter-and-Paul Fortress in 1826, are replies to Questions 4, 6 and 7 of the commission of enquiry's questionnaire. The questions were:

4. Where were you brought up? If in a public institution, which one specifically? If at home with parents or relatives, who were your teachers and tutors?

6. Did you audit special lectures in addition to your regular schooling? If so, in which subjects, when, with whom and where? Indicate the textbooks used in studying those subjects.

7. When and from where did you acquire liberal ideas? From contact with others or from their suggestions, or from the reading of books or works in manuscript form? Which ones specifically? Who helped to reinforce these notions in you?

Prince S. P. Trubetskoy[8]

4. I was brought up in my father's house. My governor, from infancy to the age of sixteen, was an Englishman named Easenwood [?]; my teachers were Pastor Lundberg for German, and Stadler, an émigré captain in the royal French service, for French. The latter lived in my father's house four or five years. My teachers in Russian and mathematics came from the gymnasium of Nizhniy-Novgorod. When I was seventeen, my father took me to Moscow where I attended some lectures at the University. At the same time an instructor in mathematics and in fortifications came to our house.

6. I did audit a special course of lectures, on the statistics of Russia and political economy, given by Professor German[9] in the winter of, I believe, 1816–17. Perhaps I am mistaken about the year. ... In Paris I several times heard all the famous professors out of curiosity—all, that is, except the professors of natural science, whose courses of lectures I heard in full. I was guided in my studies ... by the best recognized textbooks in those fields.

7. I gained my liberal ideas at the conclusion of the war against the French and as a consequence of the events that had occurred since the establishment of peace in Europe, such as: the transformation of the French Empire into a constitutional monarchy; the promises of other monarchs in Europe to grant constitutions to their peoples, and the actual introduction of a constitution in a number of countries; the annexation of the Kingdom of Poland, and the establishing there of constitutional government; and the first speech of the late Emperor at the Polish *Diet* in Warsaw, from which one might infer that His Imperial Majesty proposed to bring Russia also, in due time, to a similar condition. We were confirmed in this last view by (1) the freeing of the peasants in the German provinces,[10] which led us to think that this measure would be extended to the Russian and the Polish provinces, and (2) the returning of its rights to the former province of Finland. Discussions of these matters that I heard in society, conversations with the members of former secret societies, and the reading of books and journals dealing with the histories and legislation of various states, contributed to this liberal way of thinking. I was strengthened in it by my own conviction that such was Russia's actual condition that an upheaval would unavoidably occur in due time. I based this view on (1) the frequent peasant revolts against their landlords, and the increasing length and number of these risings; (2) universal complaints of extortions by officials in the provinces; and (3) a certain feeling that the setting up of military colonies would also, in due time, become a reason for upheaval.

K. F. Ryleyev[11]

7. I was first infected by liberal ideas during the French campaign, in 1814–15. Later, my liberalism gradually grew from readings of a number of contemporary writers, such as Bignon, Benjamin Constant and others.[12] My criminal cast of mind was set from the day I became a member of the [Northern] Society and for a period of three years had almost daily conversations with people of the same frame of mind, at the same time continuing with the authors I have named. No particular individual reinforced these notions in me. I must blame myself alone for everything.

E. P. Obololensky[13]

4,6. I was educated in my parents' home. My tutors were ... French governors who changed from year to year and even twice a year, and left no trace of their teachings, so that I now barely recall the names of two or three of them: Chevalier d'Ayanger and Comte Tilly; the others I cannot remember — there were sixteen or eighteen of them.

On entering the state service, and in particular after my promotion to officer, I grew conscious of my own deficient grounding in political science, which became a theme of general discussion after the Guards' return in 1814. I therefore started to study ancient and modern history, political economy, and law. In 1819 I attended Professor Kunitsyn's lectures[14] on political economy; where this occurred I truly cannot say. As far as I remember, Professor Kunitsyn relied on the textbooks of Shtorkh and Say.[15]

7. I acquired a liberal outlook from the time that I entered the service, through intercourse with men who had participated in the campaign of 1812; through the reading of various political works; and through reflection and my membership of a society that had political objectives. This way of thinking was confirmed in me by the spirit of the times and by my observation of events which, during recent years, had punctuated the development of almost every country in the world (except in Africa) with all kinds of revolutions. I cannot, I regret, say which specific books had influence on my way of thinking, for my reading was rather wide. In general, however, it was furthered by the reading of such publicists as Benjamin Constant and Bignon.

N. M. Murav'yov[16]

7. The proclamations of the Allied powers, in 1813, offering the peoples of Germany a representative government as a reward for their earlier efforts and efforts yet to come, first focused my attention on the question. In this I was later encouraged by the late Emperor's speech before the *Diet* of the Kingdom of Poland, in which he stated his intention of introducing representative government to Russia. I read no manuscripts. Neither books nor individuals influenced me.

P. G. Kakhovsky[17]

7. Ideas develop with age. I cannot say specifically when my ideas were forming. Having studied Greek and Roman history from childhood, I was fired by ancient heroes.[18] The recent revolutions in the whole political structure of Europe also affected me profoundly. Finally, the reading of everything known in the field of politics gave clear direction to my thoughts. I was abroad in 1823 and 1824, and had many opportunities to read and study — solitude, observation, and books were my teachers.

A. A. Bestuzhev[19]

7. I acquired my liberal ideas mainly from books. Advancing gradually from one opinion to another, I became so engrossed in the writings of English and French publicists that speeches in the House of Commons and the Chamber of Deputies gripped me as much as they would have gripped an Englishman or a Frenchman. Among modern historians, the greatest influence on me was exercised by Heeren,[20] and among the publicists, Bentham. As far as Russian works in manuscript are concerned, they were too slight and insignificant to make an impact on me; I read none of them except 'On the Necessity of Laws' by the late Fonvizin, two letters of Mikhail Orlov to Buturlin[21] and a few poetic sparkles by Pushkin. I do not wish to accuse anyone of inseminating this manner of thinking; I was searching for such leads myself. I will say, moreover, though not in my own defence, that scarcely less than a third of all the nobility thought as we did, although they were more circumspect.

M. A. Bestuzhev[22]

7. I graduated from the Naval Cadet Corps in 1817 and was sent in the same year to France, with the fleet commanded by Vice-Admiral Crown. There I made the acquaintance of many French officers and English travelers, and gathered the principles of liberal ideas. Returning to Archangel in 1824, we stopped in Copenhagen where I had the opportunity to meet Danish and English naval officers. Ideas that I had acquired in France were strengthened in their company. Since our own fleet had been in England since 1812, moreover, and since our naval officers paid visits to England each year, as well as to France and other foreign countries, those officers had gained a notion of the forms of government there. Their descriptions, which I, involuntarily, had opportunities to hear, fostered the ideas that I had acquired already, while the revolutions that occurred practically everywhere in Europe—and of which one could obtain adequate information in the Russian newspapers—were cause enough for the ideas and concepts I had earlier received to grow stronger.

A. N. Murav'yov[23]

7. I acquired my insane liberal notions during my stay in foreign countries and from the spirit of the time, that is, during and after the War of 1813–14. This led me to read various works on politics—Machiavelli, Montesquieu, the *Contrat Social* of J. J. Rousseau and so forth. I read no manuscripts. All these and many other works written not under the guidance of God's true Light (which illuminates only the souls of His true worshippers), but rather under the influence of man's defective reason, devoid of the light of faith, sowed in my heart and mind the pernicious seeds of their errors and fancies which, until 1819, kept me under their nefarious influence. But the Commission knows already how, in May 1819, through the grace of God and His great mercy, I was converted, confessed, and solemnly and openly renounced the criminal Society, and how the Lord saved me from the deep, dangerous chasm over which I was then standing. ... Not only have I not participated in the Society's activities during the past seven years; I have tried to persuade others to leave it.

I. D. Yakushkin[24]

7. I cannot recall that any particular person or the reading of particular books in themselves aroused liberal ideas in me. It was perhaps my stay abroad during

the military campaigns that first drew my attention to the social structure of Russia, and compelled me to see its defects. After my return from abroad, serfdom struck me as the only obstacle to the rapprochement of all classes and ... to Russia's civil reorganization. Living for a period in the provinces, and frequently observing the relations that existed between serfs and landowners, I was more and more confirmed in my opinion.

I indicated in my first testimony how I became one of the first to agree to the organizing of a secret society. I cannot say that anyone's acquaintance or persuasion obliged me to forget all my commitments and surrender to a foolish and a criminal vexation with the government; it was rather the doings of my youth, my unbridled temperament, my passions, and a feeling of superfluous energy.

M. S. Lunin[25]

7. A liberal cast of mind took shape in me from the moment that I started to think; natural reason reinforced it.

P. I. Pestel'[26]

4. I was brought up in my parents' house until I was twelve. In 1805 I went with my brother, who is now a colonel in the Chevalier Garde, to Hamburg, and from there to Dresden, whence I returned in 1809 to my parents' house. During our absence from the Fatherland our education was directed by a man called Seidel who, having entering the Russian service, was in 1820 on the staff of General Miloradovich. I was admitted to the *Corps de Pages* in 1810, graduating the next year as a lieutenant in the Litovsky [Lithuanian] Lifeguard Regiment. ... I had not the least conception of political science until I began my preparation for entry into the *Corps de Pages*, where that subject is required for admission to the upper grade. I then studied it under Professor German, of the Academy, who was teaching the subject in the Corps at the same time.

7. I cannot name anyone to whom I would credit imparting my first free-thinking and liberal ideas to me, nor can I state that precise time when they started to take shape in me. For this happened not suddenly, but imperceptibly. ... When I had acquired a pretty good grounding in political science, I grew passionately interested in the subject. I was aglow with enthusiasm, and desired what is good with all my heart. I saw that both the happiness and the misery of

states and nations depends in large measure upon their government; and this conviction inclined me even more towards those sciences which deal with just such questions, and which point to the means of solving them. But at first I studied those sciences and read works on politics in all humility, without free thought and wishing only to become, in due time and a suitable capacity, a useful servant of the Monarch and the State. ... I also bore in mind and gave consideration to the condition of the Russian people. Here, I was always deeply affected by the slavery of the peasants, as by the privileges of the nobility; the latter I saw as a wall standing between the Monarch and his people, which hid the true condition of the people from the Monarch for the sake of selfish advantages. ... The return of the Bourbons to the throne of France and my reflection on its consequences marked an epoch in my political development, my attitudes and forms of thought. Most of the fundamental institutions brought in by the Revolution (I began to reason) had been kept after the Restoration of the monarchy, and were acknowledged to be good; yet everyone, myself included, had opposed that revolution. This judgment gave rise to the idea that, seemingly, a revolution is not so bad a thing as it is said to be, and may even be quite useful. The judgment was confirmed when I observed that states that have not known a revolution continue to exist deprived of such advantages and institutions as France had. ... In this way, constitutional as well as revolutionary notions began to form in me at the same time. ... I was led from a monarchic-constitutional outlook to a republican one chiefly by these facts and considerations: the works, in French, of Destutt de Tracy[27] made a great impression on me. All newspapers and books were so full of praise of the increased happiness of the United States of America, ascribing this to their political system, that I took it as clear proof of the superiority of the republican system of government. Novikov[28] told me of his own republican constitution for Russia; at the time I was still arguing in favour of a monarchy, but later I recalled his arguments and found myself in full agreement with them. I recalled the happy period of Greece when it consisted of republics, and its wretched subsequent condition. I compared the glorious destiny of Rome in the time of the republic with its lamentable fate under the Emperors. Great Novgorod's past also confirmed me in republican ideas.[29] I believed that in France and England the constitutions served only as covers, and did not stop the English Cabinet or the French King from doing as they chose. And in this respect I preferred autocracy to such a constitution; for in an autocratic government, I reasoned, limitless power is openly observable by all. In constitutional monarchies, on the other hand, limitless power also exists, but acts more slowly — and therefore cannot speedily correct evils. ... The main tendency of the century, it seemed to me, consisted in a growing struggle between popular masses and aristocracies of every kind, whether of wealth or of birth. I calculated that these aristocracies would eventually grow stronger than the monarchs, as in England, and that they formed the major obstacle to a country's happiness and could be done away with only through a republican form of government. Events in Naples, Spain and Portugal had a great impact on me at the time.[30] I saw in them irrefutable proof of the lack of stability of constitutional monarchies, and quite sufficient reason for distrusting the sincerity of monarchs who accept a constitution. These last reflections strengthened me considerably in my republican and revolutionary outlook.

P. I. Borisov[31]

7. No one imparted free thinking or liberal ideas to me. Having read Greek and Roman history and the lives of great men by Plutarch and Cornelius Nepos since my childhood, love of freedom and of popular sovereignty had been implanted in me. In later years, the cruelty shown by commanding officers towards subordinates nourished that love in me, and fanned it by the hour. In 1819, not long before the Georgian campaign, the commander of my company sentenced men to flogging for embezzlement and drunkenness. ... I was so moved that I left the ranks and swore to myself to abolish that variety of punishment, should it cost me my life. The oppression, violence, and injustice, shown by landlords towards their peasants always prompted similar feelings in me, and strengthened my liberal ideas. To this were added personal grievances and discontent. ... The desire to be of use to humanity always possessed me. I made it a rule always to seek the truth. ... *The general good is the highest law* — on this maxim rested my religion and my ethics.

M. M. Spiridov[32]

7. I served mainly in the Army, and was billeted in peasants' houses. And I confess: examining their condition in detail, and seeing how their masters treated them, I was often horrified. I felt guilty, and I saw the cause of it all in their *belonging* to the landowners. In the same village in the Ukraine, I saw crown peasants who had everything in plenty and lords' peasants who were suffering from poverty. When I was transferred to the Province of Zhitomir, I grew even more distressed by the peasants' general poverty. It was there that I saw how a fertile province pays its tribute to the landowners alone; I watched the ceaseless labour of the peasants, whose fruits served to enrich those land-

lords. I saw the latter's untold wealth in grain, while at the year's end peasants lacked grain, not only for sale but even for their sustenance. ... My heart, I will confess, was seized with pity for them. ... I was outraged, too, by the procrastination and the maladministering of justice, and by cruelty towards soldiers.

Accounts of Imprisonment

Here, now, are five accounts of life in Peter-and-Paul Fortress during the months December 1825 to July 1826: those of Basargin, Yakushkin, Lorer, Rozen and Trubetskoy.

N. V. Basargin

I was summoned before the Committee for questioning at the end of January. It was at night, around eleven o'clock. I was already sleeping when the Town-Major came in and ordered me to dress. My eyes were bandaged, a cowl placed over my head so that I should see nothing, my arms tied, and in this way I was led out of the Curtain. We went in a sled to the Commandant's house; the Town-Major took me along a corridor into a little room and sat me behind a screen. I heard people moving around me and speaking in whispers. Finally, someone came up to me and took me by the arm once more, telling me to follow him. 'Take off the bandage,' he said, stopping. I took the kerchief from my eyes, and saw a priest before me. Suddenly the idea struck me that we were all to be shot and that the priest was to prepare me for death, but in a moment I perceived the groundlessness of such a thought. The man, Archpriest Myslovsky (of Kazan' Cathedral), with whom many of our comrades subsequently became friendly and whom they still consider to this day a man who took a real, sincere interest in our fates (which *I* did not observe in regard to myself, however, and which, to be quite frank, I doubt), invited me to sit on a divan and started a conversation. It was *by no means* his intention in seeing me, he said, to try to arouse repentance in me or to persuade me to confess; nor, although this was precisely his instruction from the Committee and therefore formed his duty, could he fail to understand that such instructions must quite necessarily inspire mistrust in us towards him. Still (he continued), it would be a great comfort to him to be able to destroy that same mistrust — something which, by the way, he hoped to accomplish as a consequence of his *sincere* disposition towards us; *then* we would be perfectly convinced that he was nothing but a zealous servant of the altar sent by God to give us solace in our sad confinement. To this, he added that he might also be of some use to us, conveying our requests to the Committee and doing his best in our favour when he was in the company of those on whom their satisfaction must depend. This, said he, was the sole object that had forced him to take upon himself the execution of the Committee's and the Sovereign's instructions. Perhaps I am mistaken, but I did not believe those words then and I do not believe them now. I could even give reasons for my mistrust of Myslovsky; but having subsequently heard much in his favour from a number of my comrades, I fear I may have been unjust, and so I leave open the question as to whether he was acting with sincere, pure motives, or was acting indecisively and hypocritically. He is no longer alive. I, in any event, answered him somewhat coldly, perhaps even with evident mistrust. Our conversation was brief, and he was afterwards in my cell only once, for confession at Lent. I saw him on no other occasions. Now I was led away from him by the same route and made to sit behind the screen again. But soon I was conducted somewhere else and ordered to remove my bandage. All at once I found myself in a brightly lit room, standing before a table covered with red cloth around which sat all the Committee members in full-dress uniform with orders. The chairman's seat was occupied by General Tatishchev. On his left were Prince A. N. Golitsyn and Generals Dibich, Chernyshev and Benkendorf; on his right the Grand Duke Mikhail Pavlovich, Kutuzov (Military Governor-General of Petersburg) and Generals Levashev, Potapov and Fligel'–Adjutant Adlerberg. To one side sat Bludov (now Count, formerly clerk to the Committee of Enquiry).[33] This whole setting was inevitably bound to produce a great, sudden effect on an arrested man led in blindfold. And certainly it did on me. I became a little confused on finding myself before a tribunal composed of individuals of such exalted station, and stood silent, waiting for a question. Glancing at me severely, General Chernyshev took up a sheet of paper and said, addressing me: 'So-and-so and so-and-so testify (he was lying) that you belong to the Southern Secret Society, the aim of which was to change the present form of government in Russia. Tell us all you know and speak the truth.' Not yet having fully recovered from my first impression, I answered thus:

'It is true that I was a member of the Union of Salvation in 1820, but after 1821 I played no part in its activities; therefore I know very little – and part even of that has slipped my memory. Since Your Excellency is pleased to ask me what I know, I shall reply in all frankness with regard to my own activities and remain silent only on what concerns others. To do otherwise would be dishonourable.'

'You, sir, have no conception of honour,' retorted Chernyshev, twirling his moustache. Then, with the same cold look: 'The man who breaks his oath and who rebels against lawful authority cannot speak of honour.' There was no replying to this. I remained silent. 'Do you know anything about *Russkaya Pravda*, that work of a misguided mind?' he continued.

'Nothing,' I replied firmly.

'You'll be put in shackles and *made* to talk if you don't confess voluntarily,' he shouted heatedly. All this time, the Grand Duke and the other members of the Committee were still silent. Some sat with heads lowered, others whispered among themselves. Adlerberg noted down something with a pencil. Kutuzov had been dozing but, on hearing the word 'shackles,' rubbed his eyes and repeated, 'Yes, yes, in shackles!' This made me so indignant that, forgetting the extent of my dependence on them, I turned to Kutuzov and said:

'Your Excellency was so weary that you probably didn't quite hear what General Chernyshev was asking me; yet you share his anger with me! Now I ask you, is that just?'

The Grand Duke smiled ironically, several Committee members began whispering more vigorously and General Dibich, turning to Chernyshev, said with warmth.

'One cannot lock *everyone* away in fetters, Aleksandr Ivanovich; perhaps Mr. Basargin speaks the truth.'

Although this whole episode of my first interrogation lasted no more than ninety minutes, still it exhausted me. I was even glad to return to my melancholy quarters.

Next day, the Town-Adjutant brought me a printed form, inkwell, and pen. It was a set of questions from the Committee. No one had signed it, and I was told to write out my replies on the clean half-page of the same sheet of paper. All the time that I was writing, the Town-Adjutant stayed with me and hurried me on every moment. When I had finished, he seized the questions and answers from me. Answering without preparation, I had thought only of causing no one harm by a single superfluous word. After this, I was left in peace for a time.

Built not long before I was imprisoned in it, my cell was extremely damp. The walls ran and the darkness hindered me from taking exercise. Being of poor health and having suffered many serious illnesses already, as well as a profound emotional shock, I proved incapable of bearing it. I fell ill with chest pains, and I started to spit blood. The Fortress doctor gave me some kind of powder and prescribed a half bottle of beer, to be taken towards dinner time. Finally he told the Town-Major that I would never recover while I stayed in this cell, and should be moved to a less damp place where I could take exercise. In consequence, I was removed to the other end of the Curtain and there placed in a cell certainly larger, but also so dark that for a long time after entering, I could not make out the objects in it. Here, my neighbours were the celebrated Bestuzhev-Ryumin, later sentenced to death, and Andreyev, of the Guards. We soon made each other's acquaintance and, as soon as our cells were locked and the officers' evening rounds were over, would start to chat and often talk until after midnight. The guards and sentinels did not prevent our talking and they, too, came, more or less, to know us.

Towards the beginning of our confinement we were visited, by order of the Tsar, by Generals-Adjutant Martynov, Sazonov, and Strekalov. They came into each cell for a moment and asked if anyone had some request to make, and if we were content with our treatment. There were no requests, of course, except for permission to smoke or to receive letters from relatives; nor could there be complaints. Officials in the Fortress treated us fairly civilly and as to food, probably no one had thought about it. In fact, they fed us badly. Watery veal soup and a morsel of roast meat, also veal, comprised our dinner; and it was unvarying. Moreover, the bread was generally stale. So much did this food disgust me that I ate practically nothing except tea and rolls, which were excellent, with dried black bread and water, which was also tasty. The government cannot be held responsible for this, however, for it allowed quite enough money for the upkeep of detainees; for a general, five roubles a day were granted; for a staff-officer, three; for a senior officer, one and a half. But more likely than not a good half of the allotted sum found its way (as is always the case with us in Russia), as a result of peculation on the part of those entrusted with our maintenance, into their own pockets. Accustomed to smoking tobacco, I began to feel the need of it, so spoke to General Martynov about it. I was allowed a pipe and given a quarter pound of passable smoking tobacco a week.

The holy feast of Christ's Resurrection was approaching. It was sad to meet it in confinement. What a difference between this feast and that of the preceding year! Although I had already begun to grow used to my situation and was stronger in spirit, I could not compare the present with the past with equanimity. On the Thursday of Holy Week I was ordered before the Committee for a confrontation with Pestel'. They read his statement to me. It consisted of an admission that, during a meeting in 1821,[34] he had apparently spoken of introducing a republican form of government to Russia, and that the members of the Union of Salvation then present, not accepting the decisions of the Moscow group, had agreed with his opinions. I replied that we had had no formal meeting, but that we had indeed been brought together by Burtsev, who told us of the Moscow members' decision; and that, as far as I recalled, I was walking in the courtyard with young Wittgenstein when this took place; and that when Burtsev left we had decided to stay in the Society, and had then spoken of various things.[35] What Pestel' had said then I could not recall distinctly. Consequently I could neither substantiate nor refute his statements. 'So you accept it?' said Chernyshev; 'in that case no confrontation will be necessary. Just sign this paper.' I signed it. As I did so, Benkendorf looked at me sadly, and I understood the reason later. It was the Committee's pleasure to transform our meeting at Pestel''s in 1821 into a formal assembly, and a simple conversation — the very occurrence of which, I must say honestly, now leaves me in some doubt — into a positive proposal by Pestel', and an acceptance on our part. There was the awful crime, the 'intention hostile to the Tsar and the Imperial family,' for which I and others like me were to be sentenced to twenty years of hard labour, and then to permanent exile in Siberia. I will speak frankly on this matter, as if before God's judgement seat. We talked a lot of nonsense among ourselves (in 1821), and not infrequently, in friendly conversation over a champagne glass, and especially when we had just heard rumours of some cruel, arbitrary action by the higher authorities, expressed ourselves immoderately concerning the Tsar. But certainly neither I nor any one of those with whom I was most friendly ever entertained a thought of any personal attack on him. I will say more: each of us held it his duty to defend the Tsar, not thinking of his own life.

On entering a room, I found some twenty of my comrades there in various attire. Some were in uniform, and full-dress too; others were in frock-coats, and others again in their smocks. Among them were my friends and acquaintances Vol'f, Ivashev, and the two Kryukovs. Some I knew by report or had met in society, others I did not know at all. In a word, these were the prisoners sentenced in the second category. We were all very gay, greeted each other, talked, embraced, and quite forgot the fate awaiting us. After six months of solitary confinement, we were delighted even with a momentary meeting.[36]

Soon, the Town-Major approached us with a sheet of paper and, considering what he read on it, began to place us in order. Having done so, he instructed us to walk, in that order and one after another, into the adjoining room. The doors of a third room were opened; suddenly we found ourselves in a large hall and before all the members of the Supreme Criminal Court, who sat on benches in two rows around a large table covered with red cloth. In all, there were some hundred persons present.[37] In the middle stood a mirror, and opposite the mirror sat the clergy, metropolitans and bishops (members of the Synod), then members of the State Council and senators. Before the table and on our side of the mirror stood something like a lectern, behind which the executor or secretary to the Senate read sentences on each of us in a great voice. We heard absolutely nothing and only looked at each other, so happy were we with our meeting. Church dignitaries, I noticed, raised themselves to take a look at us, since the mirror stopped their doing so with ease. On the side where I chanced to be standing M. M. Speransky was sitting at a table. He knew my father and all my family, and I myself had called on him on one or two occasions when in Petersburg. It seemed to me that he glanced at me sadly, lowering his head, and that a tear fell from his eye. When his sentence was read out, Nikolay Bestuzhev tried to say something, but he was hushed by many of the onlookers and we were hurriedly led out through an opposite door.

But now I did not find myself back in my old cell. At our request, the Town-Major had placed me with Ivashev[38] in a laboratory; our third comrade was Lieutenant Zavalishin, a distant relation of Ivashev's whom I had not known before. All that day I spent with Ivashev in a kind of daze, not sparing a thought for the sentence. We could not talk for long enough, telling each other everything that had happened to us since we parted—and we had been parted almost twelve months earlier. Ivashev had left me in Tul'chin when my wife was still alive. Zavalishin, too, told us the whole story of his participation in the activities of the Society, and in this way we talked not just all day but almost all night too.

So young were we then that our sentencing to twenty years' hard labour in Siberian mines did not make a profound impression on us. Truth to tell, it was so incompatible with our degree of guilt, and represented such unjust harshness towards us, that it somehow raised us even in our own sight. On the other hand, so totally did it separate us from the past and from our earlier existences, indeed, from all that we held dear in life, that it necessarily made each man summon up his inward strength and stoutness of heart in order to endure that change with honour. Even now I am convinced that had the government awarded milder punishments instead of judging us so cruelly, it would have served its own ends better—we should have felt our punishment the more, perhaps even regretting our lost importance in society and the distinction of our former positions, now gone. By depriving us of everything and placing us abruptly on the lowest and least enviable rung of the social ladder, it gave us the right to regard ourselves as sacrificial victims to the future transformation of Russia; in a word, the government made political martyrs of the simplest and most ordinary of people, and by doing so excited general sympathy for us while taking on itself the rôle of a remorseless, bitter persecutor.

For a long time after dinner I could not fall asleep, but had just begun to drowse when the door was opened with a bang and Trusov[39] and his usual suite came in. They had brought me my own clothes and fur-coat, removed my shackles, then, when I had dressed, put them on again. Trusov took the four keys to my locks from an officer while, on his advice, I made a handkerchief into a suspender by means of which my leg-irons could be held. Trusov then put his handkerchief over my head and conducted me to the Commandant's house. There, someone took me out of his hands and sat me behind a screen, in spite of which and the handkerchief I managed to see a servant carrying dishes into a side room.

At about midnight I was grasped by the arms and taken to the rooms where someone had been dining earlier. In the first of these rooms I could see nothing through the handkerchief but a great number of candles and tables, behind which people were sitting and writing. From this room I was led into a fairly sizable hall, also lit brightly. My arm was released, I stood still and the handkerchief was taken off.

I was standing in the middle of the room. Some ten paces from me stood a table covered with red cloth. At its very end sat Tatishchev, Chairman of the Commission of Enquiry, and beside him sat the Grand Duke Mikhail Pavlovich. To one side from Tatishchev sat Prince Golitsyn [Aleksandr Nikoloyevich] and Dibich. The third chair there [Levashev's] was vacant; Chernyshev occupied a fourth. On the other side of the table, by the Grand Duke, sat Golenishchev-Kutuzov, Benkendorf, Potapov, and Colonel Adlerberg who, not being a member of the Commission, was noting down anything remotely important in order to be able to inform the Emperor immediately of the course of events. When my handkerchief had been removed, silence reigned throughout the whole room for about a minute. Finally Chernyshev waved a finger at me and said, in the most solemn voice: 'Come closer.' Approaching the table, I broke the silence in the room with the clank of my chains. Once more a formal interrogation began.

Chernyshev asked me if I confessed and took Communion every year. I answered him as I had answered Stakhiy.

'Did you swear an oath to the Emperor Nicholas Pavlovich?'

'I did not.'

'Why not?'

'Because an oath is made with such a ritual and such a vow that I did not think it proper for me to do so, the more so as I do not in the least accept the sanctity of such oaths.'

Only now, appearing before the Committee, did I fully understand that they had hoped to ensnare me by giving me a letter from my wife; I looked at all the members of the Commission with loathing.

Chernyshev asked me to name all the members of the Secret Society. I answered him as I had Levashev.

'What can be making you behave so stubbornly over this?' asked Chernyshev.

'I have already said that I gave my word to name no one.'

'You wish to save your comrades, but you'll not succeed.'

'If I were thinking of saving anyone, surely it would be myself; in which case I would not have said what I said to General Levashev.'

'My dear sir, you cannot save yourself. The Committee must tell you that if it asks for the names of your comrades, it is only because it wishes to give you opportunity to lighten your own fate. But since you are obstinate, we will name for you all the members of the Secret Society who attended the 1817 meeting at which it was decided to kill the late Emperor: Aleksandr, Nikita, Sergey and Matvey Murav'yov, Lunin, Fonvizin, and Shakhovskoy were there. Some of your comrades testify that when it was considered who should kill the Emperor the lot fell upon you, others that you volunteered to do so.'

'The latter are correct. I did indeed volunteer.'[40]

'What an awful condition to be in,' said Prince Golitsyn, 'to have a soul so burdened with sin! Has a priest been with you?'

'Yes, a priest has been visiting me.'

At this moment Kutuzov, who had been dozing, woke up and, not quite grasping what was going on, exclaimed:

'What, he wouldn't even let a priest see him?'

Golitsyn calmed him down, telling him I had seen one. Then, when I announced in reply to another question that I was not an Orthodox Christian, Dibich (a Lutheran) cried out:

'Just so—we're more intelligent than were our forebears; how are we to act and believe as our fathers did?'

'At the beginning,' continued Chernyshev, resuming the questioning, 'you were one of the most ardent members of the Society. What made you drift away from it?'

'When we had received a letter from Trubetskoy which troubled us a great deal, and when it was generally agreed that Russia could not be more wretched than she was under the government of the Emperor Alexander, I said that, in that case, each man should act quite independently in accordance with his conscience, and not as a member of the Secret Society. I also said I had resolved to kill the Emperor.[41] On the evening of the meeting no one opposed my intention. The next evening, however, the same members met and begged me not to carry out my plan. But I answered that they had no right to hinder me, that I should be acting quite independently of the Secret Society—and that I could in no event decline to do what they themselves had thought necessary just a day before. After persistent and repeated requests had been made to me to postpone my plan which, in their view, might ruin all of them, I agreed to do so. I added that I would no longer be a member of the Society because they either incited me (as the day before) to the most awful crime or (as today) removed the possibility of executing the most splendid possible deed for a man who truly loved Russia.'

'And was there no one,' asked Chernyshev, 'who tried from the beginning to dissuade you from your plan?'

'There was indeed: Mikhaylo Fonvizin, with whom I was then living, spent all night trying to dissuade me.' I named Fonvizin thinking that my testimony might be useful to him.

When the questioning was at an end, the thought of torture came to me again, and I was almost certain that this time I should not escape it. But to my huge surprise Chernyshev, who had watched me threateningly throughout the whole interrogation, now glanced smiling at the Grand Duke Mikhail Pavlovich and told me rather gently that I should be given written questions to which I should have to give written replies. So the handkerchief was placed over my eyes again, and I was led away back to the Ravelin.

Next morning Trusov brought me these written questions from the Committee. The questions were the same as had been put to me orally the night before. Here was another respite; for I knew quite well I should be left in peace for as long as I was writing answers. They gave me pen and inkwell, and I started to compose replies—slowly, and for something like ten days! Several times Trusov came in to ask if I had finished yet.

I replied to all the questions as I had done [earlier] to the Commission; but when I came to answer the question as to which members of the Society were known to me, I hesitated. Besides those named to me by the Committee I would have to name just a few. However, even in naming these I should be exposing them to practically no danger, because some of them were then abroad, others had played too small a part in the affairs of the Society. Sometimes it seemed to me that I was playing the rôle of Don Quixote, advancing with an unsheathed sword against a lion which, on seeing me, yawned, turned aside and tranquilly lay down. At other times I pictured my family, reunion with whom I was myself making impossible, perhaps through empty vanity.

Myslovsky was now visiting me daily, as he had before, and we came to know each other well. He brought me letters from my people. Sent by the government, he came over to our side completely. At first, I had no wish at all to read the letters that he brought, being afraid that he might suffer for it; but at this he took extreme offence, saying that he would never regard it a crime to help a neighbour in such straits as me. And so deftly and decisively did he act on all these occasions that I finally stopped worrying on his account, and corresponded with my family through him. Being in some perplexity whether or not to name members of the Secret Society whom I knew, I asked Myslovsky his advice. One might have thought that he was only waiting for the question: not without gravity, he replied that I was 'not conducting myself in the most noble fashion'—since everyone had confessed, I was merely slowing down the work of the Committee by my stubborness. To which I could only say: 'So even you are against me, father.' At these words, he seized me in an embrace and replied: 'Dear friend, act in accordance with your conscience and as God may direct you.'

Finally I sent off my answers, naming no one. But I myself felt that my earlier intention to name nobody was weakening with every hour. Prison, irons, and torture of a different kind had all had their effect—they had corrupted me. Now there began a whole series of bargains with my conscience, of sophisms of my own devising. And I endeavoured to convince myself that, naming members of the Society known to me, I could harm no one but might be of use to many through my testimonies.

Having sent off these answers in which I named no one, the next day I requested pen and paper and wrote to the Committee that at last I had convinced myself that, by naming no one, I was depriving myself of the chance of being useful to those individuals who might wish to call upon me as a witness in their own defence! This was the first stage of prison corruption. Of course, I straightaway received those very questions to which I had so long refused an answer. I named those men whom the Committee had itself named to me, and two more: General Passek, whom I had received into the Society, and P. Chaadayev.[42] The first had died in 1825, while the second was abroad. Neither had cause to fear a court. After this, I was forgotten for a long time.

Lent approached; I was asked whether or not I would eat meat. I replied I was indifferent, and throughout Lent they fed me on cabbage soup with sour cream. As earlier, Myslovsky visited me but never started a religious conversation. Once I remarked to him, for some reason, that our government demands of no one that he make a confession of Orthodox faith. Myslovsky replied that, indeed, the government demanded nothing, but that many people earlier baptised into the Orthodox faith but who had later proved 'not to be Orthodox believers,' had been sent off to Solovki or to other monasteries for detention. These words opened up another path to temptation: for if (I began to argue

soundly), the government *demands* of the Orthodox that they *always* remain
Orthodox, obviously it only demands that a rite should be observed. So, on the
sixth day of Lent I told Myslovsky that I wished to take Communion and confession. 'My dear friend,' he replied, 'I've been wanting to suggest it for a long
time but, knowing you, I haven't dared.' It was agreed that he would come in to
me with Bread and Wine on Palm Sunday, and so it was; on that day he came
to me with the stole. He would have started with some formality, but straightaway I said he knew my mind on that account! So he only asked me if I believed
in God. I replied that I did. He muttered some prayer or other to himself, and
gave me the Eucharist. Afterwards, I learnt that this had been a day of great
triumph for the Archpriest of Kazan' Cathedral. In my cell, he acted like a
quite simple, goodnatured and by no means foolish man; but *outside* the Fortress walls he reported his doings in a light not at all unfavourable to himself.
He could not resist the temptation to tell everyone that he had just converted
the most stubborn atheist to Christianity.[43]

When the Commission of Enquiry had submitted its report to the Emperor,
the whole matter was placed before a Special Supreme Court.

During the trial I was granted meetings with N. N. Sheremeteva,[44] then with
my wife and sons. Since summer had begun, all those held in the Ravelin had
been allowed to stroll, one by one, in the small triangular garden which is
situated in the middle of this Ravelin. Here, according to Fortress legend, was
buried Princess Tarakanova (the daughter of the Empress Elizaveta Petrovna
and of Razumovsky), she having been most treacherously kidnapped by Count
Aleksey Orlov from Italy. When she arrived in Russia, the princess had been
put in the Ravelin; she drowned in her cell during a flood in the 1770s.[45]

Early in July I was taken to the Commandant's house. I already knew from
Myslovsky that we would be called before the Special Supreme Court to bear
witness to our testimonies. They led me into a little room in which, in the
chairman's seat behind a table, sat Prince A. B. Kurakin, former Minister for
Internal Affairs. To his left and to his right sat six or seven people, members of
the Court. Benkendorf was present as a representative of the Commission of
Enquiry.

Senator Baranov very civilly requested me to look over some papers which
lay in front of him, and asked if these were my testimonies. It would have been
impossible to read so many sheets in a short time, besides which I could see
that I had not been summoned there to read them through, since 121 defendants were to verify their testimonies and papers within a day or, at the most,
two days. Glancing over a few pages, which Baranov did not even release from
his grasp, I saw my own handwriting on some, but an entirely unfamiliar hand
on others. Baranov asked me to sign something, and I signed it without reading

it. On this occasion, plainly, the Special Supreme Court wished to preserve, if not the forms required in judicial circles, at least the shadow of those forms.

At one o'clock on July 12th, I was again taken to the Commandant's house. This time I was greatly surprised when Trusov, having led me into a room giving access to another, vanished, and I found myself face to face with Nikita and Matvey Murav'yov and Volkonsky. There were two others present also, whom I did not know. One was wearing an adjutant's uniform—this was Aleksandr Bestuzhev (—Marlinsky); the other, wearing the most comical outfit that one could imagine, was Vil'gel'm Kyukhel'beker, the editor of *Mnemosyne*. Kyukhel'beker wore the very clothes in which he had been seized on entering Warsaw, complete with torn sheepskin coat and thick boots.[46]

This meeting with the Murav'yovs, Nikita in particular, was a great pleasure for me. Matvey was sombre; he had a presentiment of what was awaiting his brother. But no one else was gloomy. Whether I myself had grown thinner during my six-month confinement I could not judge, but I was deeply struck by the leanness of not only these comrades, but of all the defendants who passed through our room. Soon after this Myslovsky appeared, drew me aside and said: 'You'll hear a death sentence, but don't believe that the sentence will be carried out.'

For some time the six of us remained in our room; then Trusov led us through a row of empty rooms and we came before the Special Supreme Court. Metropolitans, bishops, members of the State Council and generals were seated at a red table; behind him stood the Senate. All were facing us. The six of us were ranged in single file. Prince Lobanov, Minister of Justice, was taking great pains that everything should be done in the proper manner.

In front of the table stood a reading-stand, on a single pedestal. There were some papers lying on it. A chief secretary of the most ludicrous appearance then started to call the roll; but Kyukhel'beker was slow in replying to his name, whereupon Lobanov shouted in an imperious voice: 'Well answer! Well, answer!' Then began the reading of the sentences. When my own name was read out among those sentenced to death, it struck me as a ridiculous farce—and, indeed, the death sentence was commuted for all six of us to twenty years' exile with hard labour.[47] After this, I was again led off to cell no. 1 in the Ravelin. The priest had promised to call, but did not come. Scarcely had I been undressed before the Fortress doctor appeared to ask after my health. I said I had a slight toothache; he expressed surprise and left. (He had been sent to all who had been at the sentencing, in order to assist those who were taken ill on hearing it.)

We were given supper a little earlier than usual, and I immediately fell sound asleep. At midnight we were woken up and I was dressed in my own clothes and led onto the bridge linking the Ravelin and Fortress. Here I again met Nikita Murav'yov, and a few other acquaintances. We were all taken into the Fortress; from every cell and all directions, sentenced men were being brought. Then, when everyone was assembled, we were taken through the Fortress to the Petrovskiy Gates under an escort of the Petropavlovskiy Regiment. Leaving the Fortress, we caught sight of something strange on our left, but it occurred to no one then that it was a gibbet. It was a platform, above which soared two pillars. On the pillars lay a crossbeam, and to this they were attaching ropes. I remember that someone seized one of these ropes and swung on it as we went by; but Myslovsky's words had convinced me there would be no executions. Most of us were of the same conviction.

Several dozen people were standing on the Kronverk, most of them attached to foreign embassies. It was later said that they were much amazed that men who would in ninety minutes be stripped of everything commonly prized in life should be walking not at all reflectively, but exultantly, and cheerfully talking among themselves. In front of the Gates we were all — except those men in Guards and naval uniforms — drawn up, backs to the Fortress by our escorts; a general sentence was read out. Army men were ordered to remove their greatcoats; we were made to kneel. I was standing on the right flank, and the execution started with me. The sword which they were to break over me, however, had not been properly filed through; quite rashly, an under-officer gave me a blow across the head with it and I collapsed. 'Give me another blow like that,' I said to him, 'and you'll kill me outright.' At this instant I glanced at Kutuzov, who was mounted on a horse a few steps from me, and I saw that he was laughing. All our military uniforms and orders were carried a hundred paces forward and cast into the bonfires made expressly for the purpose. But the execution had ended so early that nobody had seen it. There was practically no crowd in front of the Fortress. I was led back to my cell inside the Ravelin.

N. I. Lorer

I had passed a week in confinement when I was woken up one night by a sort of running about and a noise in our corridor. I listened carefully: footsteps were approaching my cell; the bolt moved aside, the lock rattled and Podushkin, accompanied by an under-officer and two guards, appeared before me carrying my uniform and ordered me to dress and follow him! For me, the most murderous thing about my confinement was always the mystery by which we were continually surrounded. On this occasion, too, I wanted to ask: where am I being taken, and why? But I did not ask, knowing they would not say. Such was the institution.

Soon we entered the Commandant's house, I with my eyes bound by a handkerchief, and I was led into a brightly-lit room. Behind a long table, there appeared in front of me the figures of twenty generals in stars and ribbons, sombre and stern like fifteenth-century knights at a secret court such as the 'Council of Ten' in Venice or at an inquisitorial session. Only the Bridge of Sighs was missing, followed by death in the water![48]

Chernyshev promptly began to ask me the usual questions: who had founded our Society, in what year had it been formed, and so forth. This lasted about a quarter of an hour. Chernyshev rang, the ubiquitous Podushkin appeared, and I was led back. Not a single carriage belonging to messrs. the judges was visible by the porch of the Commandant's house, and I afterwards learnt that they were generally hidden in an inner courtyard, so that coachmen should not see who was being brought in for interrogation.

In the short time that I took to walk across to my casement, a fresh breeze blew in my face and greedily I filled my lungs with it; but the inexorable prison soon reclaimed me. I could not fall asleep for a long time. To crown everything, huge water-rats, reddish and plump, had grown so bold that they walked right over me and the remainder of the night was passed in defending myself against those loathesome creatures.

So passed several weeks, and I was beginning to forget the date and the days of the week. What was happening in the wide world? Were my relatives and friends alive? One other prison regulation troubled me extremely: this was the fact that the sentry by the doors was continually raising a little piece of cloth that hung by the tiny window in my door, and glancing into the cell at me. If I stirred, or coughed, or prayed to God, the sentry's face incessantly appeared at the opening. In my youth I had read the adventures of Baron von Trenck,[49] who was imprisoned in Magdeburg and remained ten years in heavy irons on the orders of Frederick the Great. And there we see the actions of a philosopher who corresponded with Voltaire, who reasoned and made jokes with him—yet was a tyrant and a despot just like all crowned heads! Only give them power! It is for this reason that I asserted then, and still assert, that peoples *need* a constitution, a limiting of the prerogatives of individuals who rule. In his time the German Schnitzler did not understand us: he did not understand Russia. He did not show the *true aim* of our Society in his work, viewing us only as immoral persons and ambitious plotters.[50]

Sometimes at night when everything grew quiet, I would talk to the sentry; and frequently I managed to shake off my weariness and even take some snuff, which kind snuff-takers gave me. The strictest order that political prisoners were to be allowed no contact with a living soul was not issued only so that supervising them should be less dangerous; it also served as a method of weakening our intellectual capabilities, thus also weakening our steadfastness. But depite all this, tranquillity of spirit never left us. I even made an attempt to speak to my neighbour through the tiny window of my door, but this the sentries would not let us do. He who has not himself experienced the misfortune of being locked up in a casemate without books, tobacco, light, without the sounds of lively conversation, will not appreciate the measure of its burdensomeness.

It grew clear, in the last weeks of Lent, that the Committee was beginning to meet more frequently, and my comrades in the corridor were quite often taken to appear before it.[51] I, too, was taken out three times.

From beginning to end, the Commission of Enquiry was a biased one. The proceedings and the very questions were gross, being deceptive, deceitful and accompanied by threats. I am certain that if we had had lawyers half the members would have been found innocent and would not have been exiled to hard labour. When undergoing trial, many of us rattled chains on our feet; why should I not have been punished in that way? However, they very nearly did clap them on me during my last appearance before the judges, for the following reason.

The session was a full one—not a single empty chair. As usual, Chernyshev began:

'Major, you have refused to speak and have also refused to tell us where *Russkaya Pravda* is concealed. We ask you now for the last time: where is it? You understand that if you continue stubborn even now you will be bringing a grave punishment upon your head.'

'General,' I replied, 'an obligation of honour and an oath that I have given to a comrade did not, earlier, allow me to reveal the place where *Russkaya Pravda* is hidden, and those same reasons force me to be steadfast now in spite of any dreadful punishments that you may promise me. Let the author of *Russkaya Pravda* release me from my oath, even in writing, and I will tell you.'

Hardly had I said these words than from all sides I heard the shouts: 'Into the stocks with him! Into irons!' But Chernyshev seized some sheet or other from the table, gave it to me and said: 'Read it!' At once I recognized Pestel's hand, and read: '*Russkaya Pravda* was given to Lieutenant Kryukov and Staff-Captain Cherkasov of the General Staff in the presence of Major L[orer] and placed in a box to be buried in the Tul'chin Cemetery.' Having read these lines, I took a pen and wrote beneath them: 'This is, in fact, what happened.' I felt as if a mountain had slipped from my shoulders, and my judges all fell silent.[52]

Something else that Chernyshev did totally amazed me. This was when he rose from his seat and said:

'Gentlemen, I saw in the beginning and see now that Major Lorer could not have revealed another man's secret until he had leave to do so. I fully understand that sentiment.'

For this justness on his part I bowed to General Chernyshev, and went out accompanied by Podushkin who was kind enough to sit with me for a little time on the bed in my cell. The doors were not locked and it seemed to me that he was waiting for someone, so I asked him directly:

'Most likely you're not sitting here just for the conversation. Are you waiting for irons to put on me?'

'God bless you, not at all,' said he.

'Then why not? After all, they were shouting about it in the Committee, besides which criminals just like me — my comrades — are in stocks, aren't they? So why don't I wear irons?'

'That was only to alarm you.'

'Unsuccessfully! Irons don't frighten me. ... Just a little more unpleasantness to hear that noise continually, that's all.'

Here is another amusing episode from the proceedings of the Commission of Enquiry. When I was brought before the Commission for the last time, Chernyshev, putting his usual questions, did not receive the answers he expected, and grew angry. But the chairman, looking plump after a sumptuous meal, said to me, hardly moving his lips:

'Come now, Major, admit that you've got all this out of pernicious books. But I, you see, never read anything in all my life but the Church Calendar and have three stars as a result.'

Benkendorf conducted himself most honourably of all. Hearing some such nonsense as this, he would lower his eyes and say nothing, and when Cherny-shev began to shout and try to frighten me, even stopped him more than once, saying: 'Well, give him time to see reason and reflect a moment.' One of my comrades so lost all his patience with these gentlemen that he simply set the whole assembly laughing, saying: 'Gentlemen, why do you yell so? If *you* were all lieutenants now, you'd unfailingly be members of a secret society.'

On one occasion our good priest, Pyotr Nikolayevich, brought me in compli-ments from my kind sister-in-law,[53] but it struck me that he seemed somehow particularly sad now, often raising his eyes to the sky as if in prayer. Later I discovered that the good pastor had already learnt the decision concerning the fates of five of us — a decision that made all Russia shudder.

Slowly the subsequent days wore on. There is nothing harder than to wait, not knowing what one's fate will be. So we lived until the month of June. The Commission met more and more rarely and we were all waiting to be prosecuted, expecting then to defend ourselves. We should be tried in open court in the Senate, it was said; but how bitterly we were deceiving ourselves, how vainly lulling ourselves with that hope! Only the good under-officer who was my sen-try generally said to me: 'None of you gentlemen will escape Siberia. ...' 'Don't expect mercy from such men,' he once said, 'they're not the kind. Only yesterday one fellow was taken before them and brought back in irons and put in no. 7 on bread and water; but he's only smiling, the kind-hearted fellow! Your heart overflows to look at him.' This was Stepan Mikhaylovich, secretary of the Society.[54]

I well remember that morning when all our hopes were smashed, when the fate of every one of us was settled. I heard some sort of unusual noise and tramping in the Fortress at ten o'clock in the morning, as though on a car-riage-way. Probably disturbed by the same noise, my neighbour in the next cell managed to clamber up to his little window before I did and to rub off some of the chalk, for he said to me in French:

'Do you hear that strange noise, *voisin*? I just saw an extraordinary entry into the Fortress: a detachment of gendarmes, and Household cavalry, and masses of carriages, all moving at a walking pace as if they were in a funeral procession and all making for the Commandant's house. What do you make of that, neigh-bour?'

'I think our fate will be decided today and many of us won't see the sunset tomorrow, neighbour.'

Suddenly there was a terrific scurrying in the corridor. Podushkin could scarcely draw breath. Soon my doors were opened; my uniform was brought to me, and I was told to dress. They led us off to the Commandant's house. I pass-ed between a group of the public and many ladies on the way, and in the crowd

I caught sight of one of my acquaintances, who smiled at me sadly, inclining his head as if to say: everything's over for you.

For seven months the Commission of Enquiry had been sitting. Now the sorry drama was to start. At last I was conducted into a large room, and you may imagine my surprise when I found there many of my old acquaintances. The first who happened to greet me was my friend M. M. Naryshkin, of my old regiment. I was so glad to see him that I threw myself onto his neck. Then I caught sight of Fonvizin, and Abramov, a colonel in the same brigade as myself, and many others — some twenty of them. Not one of us knew why we had been brought together here, and no one suspected that similar groups or 'categories,' as they were later known, were assembled in adjoining rooms. Then I turned my attention to two young men in naval dress uniform, young men of about twenty, I would say, and asked their names. I was told they were the two Belyayev brothers, both warrant officers. During the terrible floods in St. Petersburg on November 9th, 1824, these two had saved many families from eventual death with the greatest selflessness, and the Emperor Alexander had with his own hand decorated them with Vladimir Crosses. But them nobody saved.[55]

Soon we were led off somewhere under an escort of sentries. Passing through several halls, I saw our serfs' priest, the doctor, and other officials. Many of them were crying. We all took our last farewell of them.

The Special Supreme Court had assembled early in the morning. We were all put in the Commandant's Hall, in Peter-and-Paul Fortress. The accused did not know that five of us had already been condemned to death without trial, the remainder to political death and to hard labour in various categories, one man to so many years, another to so many. The judges sat in their places, and we were led in by categories. We stood before them already indicted, and appeared sick and exhausted. But if the body suffers, the spirit animating a man may be filled with strength and energy, a fact that explained our calm, resolute air. Yes, we had the calm of men who know there will be no mercy for them, so are preparing themselves to sell their lives dearly. Confirmation of the charge against us continued only until six in the evening.

At last, we came to some locked doors guarded by an official of some kind. As we approached, this same official opened them wide, and an unusual spectacle revealed itself before our eyes. Across a chamber stood a huge table covered with red cloth. At its centre sat four metropolitans; along its sides, generals and the State Council. Around these, on chairs and benches as if in an amphitheatre, sat senators in red full-dress uniforms. Some enormous book or other lay on a pulpit, and by the book stood an official; by the official stood the Minister of Justice himself, Prince Lobanov-Rostovsky, wearing a ribbon of St. Andrew.

All were *en grand gala*, and we were placed in a line facing them.

With no warning, the official standing behind the pulpit started to read: 'General-Major Fonvizin, guilty by his own confession of this and that, is deprived of all the rights of his status, all ranks and all his orders, and is exiled for twelve years with hard labour, thereafter to remain in a settlement forever.' And so forth, to the end. Prince Odoyevsky came last. I was standing in the centre, and examined the faces of the members of the Special Supreme Court until my own turn came. I noticed N. S. Mordvinov's venerable grey head. He was sad, and had a white handkerchief on his knees.

When the reading was over Lobanov said, 'Right turn!' and we passed through some other rooms, accompanied by the same sentries and by police attendants. We were not taken to our former cells, however, but to the very bank of the Neva, in the Alekseyev Ravelin. Here, all eighteen of us were locked up in different rooms and made to pass that day sadly. But where were the laws, it may be asked? Where was the trial? We were sentenced to death on the findings of the Commission of Enquiry alone. And that same day the whole Imperial family left for Tsarskoye Selo.

Early next morning, when the sun had hardly risen, I was woken up and led with my companions in imprisonment onto the little bridge connecting the Alekseyev Ravelin with Peter-and-Paul Fortress. Here, we came upon comrades of another category, exiled for fifteen years: Nikita Murav'yov, his brother Aleksandr, the Kyukhel'bekers. ... We were all very wan, because of the early hour and our lack of sleep, and sadly dragged ourselves towards the Fortress gates; but here the whole scene altered: faces became animated and tongues were loosed because, quite unexpectedly, we encountered on the glacis the remainder of our comrades in misfortune. Hand-shaking and embracing started, and there was general delight. Never had I suspected that there were so many of us and, truth to tell, I even failed to recognize many by sight. This 'trial' was remarkable as much for the extreme variety of social elements comprising it as for the quantity of prisoners belonging to all classes of society, beginning with the very lowliest and ending with the very loftiest. Here I even saw the uniform of a Commissariat official, Mr. Ivanov, and caught sight of Lunin, who had been brought from Warsaw in a strange garb: he was wearing a frock-coat of the Grodnenskiy Hussars but had his prison slippers on his feet! Our crowd, in fact, presented a medly of black tail-coats, round hats, Georgian *papakhas*,[56] cuirassiers' white collars, plumes, and even shakos. But notwithstanding this extreme diversity of colours, we were happy to meet some of our comrades and, of course, pitied those men whose punishment was thought inevitable, but whom we still had in our midst.

Troops surrounded us. Finally Chernyshev galloped up, wearing a ribbon and dressed up as if attending some parade, surveyed us through his lorgnette and then, seeing that no one even glanced at him, went off again. Our column moved off, making its way through the Fortress gates. Soldiers of the Guards had half encircled the large square, and between them and ourselves gibbets stood out against the sky, with five ropes swaying from the fateful cross-beam. Bonfires had been lit, and the flames were being fed. Chernyshev rushed from group to group of prisoners with a preoccupied air; other general-adjutants rode about, too, but modestly. The only thing that surprises me is that the noble Benkendorf, who knew and liked many of us, did not manage to avoid that sorry duty. Hangmen[57] paced about in red shirts on the wooden scaffolding. Kept apart from the entire world since the previous evening, the five martyrs had spent the whole night with our priests, preparing themselves to appear in a pure state before the Court of the Eternal. Pastor Rengol'd had been with Pestel'.[58] They were not present now.

We were formed up in a little square. Under-officers brought up swords that had been sawn through; they told us to remove our epaulets, stars and dress uniforms, and started to cast them onto the fires. I had gold epaulets, and hoped to save them for my good under-officer Sokolov, but Chernyshev noticed this and ordered me to throw them on the fire. Aleksandr Murav'yov, a retired colonel on the General Staff, was standing beside me. Before the sword-breaking ceremony began, Kutuzov, the Governor-General of St. Petersburg, came up to him and asked: 'Are you Aleksandr Murav'yov?'

'I am.'

'Then step back.'

'General, I am not the only Aleksandr Murav'yov here; there is another.'

'You are a retired colonel of the General Staff?'

'I am.'

'Well, fall back then!' So he stood behind me.

An official of some kind came up, when everything seemed ready, and started to read what appeared to be a second sentence, but he was scarcely heeded by the greater part of us.

At a command, we were obliged to kneel, and they began to break our swords over our heads. The swords of Trubetskoy, Odoyevsky, Baryatinsky, Murav'yov and other Guardsmen they broke in front of regiments of Guards. As for the naval men, of whom there were many, they were dispatched to Kronstadt in closed launches and there the same sentence was carried out aboard a warship, and their uniforms were cast into the sea.[59]

After this sad ceremony, they dispersed us to various casemates and busied themselves with the hanging of our five comrades. All that follows below I reproduce from the words of our priest who, having accompanied the unfortunates on their journey to Eternity and remained with them until their last moment of earthly life, came in to me at five in the evening and gave me all the details. Pestel', Murav'yov-Apostol, Ryleyev, Bestuzhev-Ryumin and Kakhovsky, wearing white shrouds with black string and leather belts on which was written, in large letters, 'state criminal,'[60] said farewell to one another and stepped up onto the boards in calm spirits. When Murav'yov was standing on the bench he even called the priest across to him and said:

'Bless me for a last time. I part from this world without malice towards him who has sentenced me to this shameful death. I forgive him, if only he may make Russia happy.'

There were few onlookers, for the police had tricked them, spreading rumours that the execution would be carried out at another time and in another place.[61] It was said that couriers galloped with reports to Tsarskoye Selo every fifteen minutes starting at the moment we were led out of the cells, and that Benkendorf deliberately delayed the execution in the expectation of a pardon, for which reason he continually turned in the direction from which he expected a messenger to come. But alas, couriers rushed off to Tsarskoye Selo, but none returned. At six o'clock in the morning, the five men were no more.

As I have said already, our priest, Pyotr Nikolayevich, came into my cell in the evening. He was distraught, pale and his legs were trembling; he collapsed onto a chair and burst into tears at the sight of me, and I, one need hardly say, wept with him. ...

Next day, the roar of cannon announced some extraordinary festival. A public service was held on Senate Square; the clergy sprinkled holy water, and in the evening the Household Cavalry Regiment gave a fête for their Commander, the Empress Alexandra Fyodorovna, on Yelagin Island. They forgot that on the eve of that same day many of their own comrades had been sentenced to death, and that many were still languishing in cells! They forgot this! Eternal shame on the officers of the Household Cavalry!

Shortly after this sad event the whole court set out for Moscow, for the coronation; but the Sovereign had already gone.

Baron Rozen

I should certainly have slept on for twenty-four hours that day and night had the jailor not awoken me with his keys. Their terrific jangling was no sooner silent than the Town-Adjutant, Nikolayev, came in, followed by a tall man in a black coat and an artilleryman acting as prison warder. I sat down on my bed, supposing that another prisoner was coming in with them. But the Adjutant merely asked me how I was. The man in the black coat, also, who proved to be a doctor, enquired after my health. "Thank the Lord,' I replied to both, 'I've rested well.' 'Excuse our having disturbed you,' they said, 'but we must do our duty.' As quietly as they had entered the three men disappeared, and I at once dozed off again.

It was midday when I woke up, but the room was still dark—the window was cut in a deep embrasure and did not let the full light in. Never could I see either the sun or the moon, and scarcely a single star passed by the narrow window-pane. A lamp was brought in towards evening, but I had nothing to read because no one brought us any books in the first months of our imprisonment. Alone, confined in a narrow room, there was no exercise for the body, no distraction for the mind; thought alone was free. The future stretched before me, uncertain and drear; the present offered nothing; only the past remained to me.

On January 8th at nine o'clock in the evening the Town-Major came into my cell to conduct me before the Commission of Enquiry, which was meeting every day in the Commandant's house. This time he bound my eyes so well that my whole face was covered. I could hear talking by the steps of the Commandant's house, and through the handkerchief, made out the shining lamps of a carriage. The anteroom seemed full of servants. An adjutant made me sit down in an adjoining room, telling me to wait till he returned. Immediately I raised the bandage and saw great folding doors in front of me and, at the far end of the room, a large screen behind which were two lights. But there was nobody in the whole room. I do not know from where the idea came to me, but it struck me that the doors might open suddenly and that I might be shot. Probably it was the Town-Major's mysterious manner and the binding of my eyes that gave rise to the notion. For one hour I sat like this. At last, the Town-Major reappeared and led me, eyes still covered, through the next room, which seemed full of light. Though unable to make out the writers, I could hear a great number of pens scratching. There were more pens scratching in a third room, but still no word was spoken. Having eventually entered this third room, the Town-Major said to me *sotto voce:* 'Stay here.'

For thirty seconds there was neither sound nor movement. Then the words, 'Take off the handkerchief,' were heard. It was the voice of the Grand Duke Mikhail. I saw a long table before me; at the upper end of it sat the President of the Commission, the War Minister Tatishchev, and to his right the Grand Duke. Next came the renowned I. I. Dibich, S. V. Kutuzov, and General-Adjutant Count Benkendorf. To the left sat Prince A. Golitsyn (the only civilian there), General Chernyshev, V. V. Levashev, and Colonel V. Adlerberg, who discharged the function of a secretary. They were all, in some respects, distinguished men; but not one of them could lay claim to the qualifications necessary in experienced, competent, impartial judges. In no way did examinations held before this Commission of Enquiry differ from those held by the General-Adjutant in the Emperor's private chamber. Was this Commission meant to bring a court-martial? Then the whole affair could have been settled in twenty-four hours and without the help of anyone versed in the law, for the Articles of War would have immediately condemned all the accused to death! And this variety of court, in which only officers passed sentence and the plaintifs served as judges, was the customary method in Russia when important cases were to be decided!

The first question was put to me by the Grand Duke Mikhail:

'How could you, as commander of a unit of riflemen, keep back three whole companies standing partly in front of you?'

'When the battalion marched out of barracks,' I replied, 'it was in columns of companies, so that my section found itself in front of the three Jäger companies.'

'Pardon me, I was unaware of that,' said the Grand Duke in a friendly tone. At this, Dibich asked why I had kept my men in the middle of the long St. Isaac's Bridge. I replied that when I had myself observed that there was neither leader, unity nor order in arrangements on the Senate Square, it had seemed correct to me to remain quiet and to take no action whatsoever.

'I understand,' said Dibich, who was a tactician; 'you had it in mind to form a reliable reserve force.' Then he continued: 'Since when have you belonged to the Secret Society, and by whom were you received?'

'I have never been a member of any secret society.'

'Perhaps you mean us to infer that you consider that to be a member necessitates peculiar usages and ceremonies, signs and conditions, as in a fraternity of Freemasons; but to know the aims of a society suffices to make you a member of it at once.'

'I have already had the honour of telling Your Excellency that I have never been received into a secret society, and that I can appeal to all those who *were* members without fear of examination before witnesses or of confrontations with them.' I was interrupted at this point by Kutuzov:

'Yet you knew Ryleyev?'

'I know him — we were brought up together in the First Cadet Corps.'

'And didn't you know Obolensky too?'

'I know him very well. I served with him; he was senior adjutant in the Corps of Foot Guards. How could I not know him?'

'What further proof do we need?' remarked Kutuzov in his stupid way. I was silent, though I might easily have retorted that, since he too knew Prince Obolensky, he must himself have been a member of the Society.

After this the President, Tatishchev, told me I should receive written questions from the Commission the following day and would have to reply to each question, in writing, according to the headings. Before the session ended, Colonel Adlerberg said to me:

'You are accused of having wished to cut down the second sharpshooter on the right flank because he tried to persuade some of his comrades to follow the section of Carbineers.'

'My soldiers, M. le Colonel,' I replied, 'did not converse as they stood in rank and file. One of them — I don't know if he was the second or third from the flank — wanted to move forward. I held my sword in front of him and threatened anyone who tried to move without my orders.'

Colonel Adlerberg's remark at once made clear to me that they had been told of the most trifling circumstances connected with me. The Brigadier and another individual who had reason to fear my testimonies had given them this information.

With this, the first interrogation ended. The President rang a bell, the Town-Major bound my eyes and led me off. My face was covered by a handkerchief so that the clerks and secretaries should not recognize the prisoner. A few minutes later I found myself once more in cell no. 13.

After three days a sealed packet from the Commission was handed to me. The questions were almost the same as those put to me during the interrogation, but included new accusations and made mention of fresh names and information.

The Commission of Enquiry held daily sittings. The Grand Duke was rarely present, and Chernyshev seemed to be the principal person there. Often the Commission's law officers would sit up writing late into the night. All the special denunciations were collected in one document by D. N. Bludov; excluding all that was important or favourable to the accused, he inserted denunciations and private conversations, as any unbiased reader of the published report can see for himself.[62] The founders of the Secret Society and the leaders of the conspiracy were often called before the Commission. Pestel' was very frequently obliged to appear, and so tormented with questions that he lost his patience many times, especially as he was then ill. ... I still remember some of the questions as especially extraordinary. Chernyshev, for example (who was particularly zealous in the whole affair), asked my friend M. A. Nazimov what he would have done had he been present in St. Petersburg on December 14th! (He was on leave in Moscow at the time.) So manifestly unfair was this question that Benkendorf sprang from his chair and seized Chernyshev by the arm, exclainimg: 'Listen, you haven't the right to ask such a question: it's a matter of conscience.'[63]

The Town-Major inspected my prison every day, but was not talkative, so I was left to my own resources. I walked to and fro and moved about as much as possible in my narrow cell, in order to preserve my health. Sleep halved the weary hours. The food was wholesome, simple and adequate, not scanty, as in the Palace. Often, especially during the evenings, I would feel constrained to sing; singing strengthened my chest and made amends for lack of conversation, as well as giving expression to my feelings. I sang prose and verse of my own composition, arranged airs, and remembered numerous old songs. Once, late in the evening, I was singing the universal Russian song, 'In an Even Vale Stood a Shady Oak,'[64] when I heard another voice accompanying me throughout the second verse from behind the plank partitioning. I recognized the voice of my warder. 'A good sign,' I thought. 'If he sings with me, he'll talk to me, too.' I repeated the song once more from the beginning to the end; he knew the words better than I. When he brought me my food I thanked him for the accompaniment, and he finally made up his mind to speak:

'God be praised that you're not cast down and you still keep a cheerful heart!'

From that hour onwards he was more communicative, and readily answered my questions.

'Tell me, Sokolov,' I said (for so the artilleryman was called), 'what shall I do to get myself some books? I hear my neighbour over the way in no. 16 turning pages all night long.'

'God preserve you from such books! The fellow there reads and writes so much that he's already written fetters onto his hands.'

'And what does that mean?'

'I mean they've already fastened an iron chain weighing fifteen pounds to both his hands.'

This was Bestuzhev-Ryumin, a young man of twenty-one who was deeply implicated in the work of Polish as well as Russian conspirators. It was hoped to force him to make a full confession in this way. He could express himself better in French than in Russian, but as he had to write out his confession in Russian they had given him some dictionaries; this was the reason for the hasty and continual turning over of the pages of great folios.

Some days later, I heard chains clanking opposite me in no. 15.

'Have they brought a new prisoner in?' I asked Sokolov.

'No, he's been here for weeks, but they only put him in fetters yesterday.'

This aggravated punishment had been imposed on N. S. Bobrishchev-Pushkin, a staff-officer, from whom the Commission of Enquiry hoped to learn where Pestel''s constitutions were concealed. (They had been put in a small chest and buried in the ground, the spot being known only to Pushkin and to Zaikin. The latter was sent with a courier all over the place in question, and after a long search and much raking about under the snow the little box was found and immediately delivered into the Emperor's hands.)

'Are many of the prisoners in chains?' I asked.

'Oh yes; of my thirty, ten are loaded with them.'

The same proportion of prisoners in chains obtained in the other casemates and curtains of the Fortress. One youth, called Divov, a midshipman in the Guards Equipage whom the warders referred to as 'the little one,' was also in chains. His spirits were excited, his imagination was inflamed; he spoke of wonderful things to the Commission of Enquiry — things which existed only in his fancy. These were made subjects of an inquisition, and subsequently played a major part in Count Bludov's report. For this evidence, Divov was freed from hard labour after the verdict had been given, and sent to work in the fortress of Bobrovsk.[65]

The Town-Adjutant did not come to me as usual on March 6th, and Sokolov put on a mysterious air; he was in new clothes. My sentry, Shchibayev (a veteran of the Jäger Regiment of Bodyguards), who brought me my food every day, also appeared shaved and wearing a new cloak.

'What feast is it today?' I asked.

'It's no feast.'

'Then why are you wearing new clothes?'

'It's the day of Emperor Alexander's funeral.'

Everything around was quiet and monotonous as usual; the thick walls of the Fortress, with their earth- and grassworks, allowed no sound to penetrate. A carillon reached me only occasionally, through the window and embrasures. Suddenly, a cannon roared, and then another, then I heard the reports of innumerable guns. This was the end of the funeral ceremony.

Since every nook and cranny of the Fortress had been filled with prisoners, each one could get to the bath-house only rarely, because of the numbers. My turn came round for the first time in mid-April! The snow had disappeared and the weather was beautiful. I was led down by a guide, but my eyes were no longer bound. When I stepped over the threshold of the outer door from the dark corridor, the sun's rays so blinded me that I stood immobile and involuntarily covered my eyes with my hand. Little by little I withdrew the hand, and moved on; the ground appeared to rock under my feet, while the fresh air took my breath away. Though I passed by a long row of windows, I could see none of my comrades all along the inner wall of the Kronverk Curtain, for the window-panes were coated with chalk. Then, turning right along the other curtain, where the Fortress entrance stands, I saw a window just above a gate and recognized M. F. Orlov, who sat there writing. Not far from the gateway stood a subaltern's guard. I was delighted to recognize my own soldiers, and they at once hastened onto a platform and replied to my salute as loudly and as cheerfully as they used earlier to do. The bath-house was roomy, and the bath refreshed and invigorated me. As I returned I saw standing near the guard, my servant Mikhail, who was trying to attract my attention by strange gestures and movements.

'Is my wife Anna Vasil'yevna well?' I asked.

'She was here in the cathedral just now, and is coming down the path this minute.'

I quickened my step, and saw her walking slowly some 200 paces from me. I longed to hurry over to her, but remembered that she was nearing her confinement, and so might take fright. I also feared what my escort might say. So I could only wave to her with my hand, and walk on. Back in my cell, I found it even darker than before and was unable to make out the chair or table—indeed, I could only dimly discern the white border of a grey blanket.

In Passion Week, the Emperor permitted prisoners to have books of spiritual counsel, pipes, and tobacco. After so long a privation this was true luxury. I had given up smoking for the past four years, but now returned to it with all the greater zest, hoping the smell would overcome the damp, noisome, unwholesome air about me. My wife had sent me [Heinrich] Zschokke's *Hours of Devotion*, and three volumes on the wars of 1812–14 too, but these were kept back by the censorship of the Commission of Enquiry. Thanks to the acquaintance of my wife's uncle with Commandant Sukin, I also enjoyed the luxury of some snuff and a dozen pocket-handkerchiefs.

There was an unusual stir in the prison corridor on May 17th: warders and prisoners were continuously walking to and fro and talking loudly. Many of the latter called out, on passing by my cell, '*Bonjour, 13, portez-vous bien, 13!*' In the afternoon, the warder Sokolov told me that some of them had been taken before the Commission, where they had signed papers, then been brought back to their casemates.

'What do you think?' I asked. 'Will their being summoned there do them good or harm?'

'God knows,' was the reply. 'It seems to me that those left here in peace will be the best off.'

I fell asleep at last, still in a state of restless agitation, until the rattle of locks and bolts woke me up suddenly and the Town-Adjutant took me to the Commission. The walk to the Commandant's house showed me how beautiful the spring already was: the air was rich with the scent of elder-flowers and birds fluttered and sang in the Commandant's garden in which they had involuntarily congregated—for there were only bare walls on three sides, so they could not easily fly off.

I was led through the clerks' room, not to the chamber earlier used by the Commission but to another on the right, where Benkendorf and Senator Baranov were sitting at a writing-desk. The replies that I had written [earlier] to the Commission's questionings were handed to me and I was asked if the signature was my own. Also 'had I answered under pressure?' and 'had I anything to add?' I answered in the affirmative to the first two questions, in the negative to the last. I was then made to sign some papers. In Benkendorf's face I could read that all would not go well with me. Senator Baranov was not a member of the Commission of Enquiry, but as a member of the high criminal court appointed for our judgment he had to be quite certain that the signatures were genuine. That completed my case, the verdict having been already settled. ...

On my way back to the cells I avidly drank in the May air and picked some blades of grass as I passed by the garden hedge. Then I quickened my step in case my heart should grow soft (though feeling hearts will readily believe that I kissed and caressed the grass; when they were withered, I examined every blade and compared the variety of their beauty. Links with the natural world, they were the only things that gladdened my sight for months).

Voices and movement in the corridor became quieter and more rare from that day on. Monotonous tranquillity was broken only by the daily visits of the Town-Major, the Fortress adjutant and warder, or by occasional laments, declamations, or songs from some prison cell.

On Prince S. P. Trubetskoy's Imprisonment

No one, perhaps, behaved more inexplicably throughout December 14 and the following night than the proposed dictator of the state, Prince Sergey Petrovich Trubetskoy (1791–1860) – the man expected to command the troops gathered on Senate Square in revolt against the government and tsar. His conduct was a mixture of treason and apparent cowardliness; yet he was no coward, having proved himself a brave soldier during the war of 1812–14, from which he returned with honours. Nor can he justly be charged with deliberate betrayal, though he was one of the first of the arrested conspirators to provide a list of names of all the members of the Northern Society. Always he had 'striven to be an honest man and a true Christian.'[66] Later, in Siberian exile, his life bore out that statement.[67] But all this notwithstanding, the great blunders he committed on the day of the revolt stand as a massive and perpetual indictment against him. His failure to lead the revolutionary forces in their hour of greatest need placed a responsibility on him which, in his moments of remorse, he fully realized.[68]

Trubetskoy, whose ancient house could trace its lineage to the royal Lithuanian Gedymins of the early fourteenth century, was a brave subaltern who proved a cowardly general. While the Bestuzhevs were on Senate Square with the Moscow companies, Trubetskoy, who had declared that he would join them, took a cab and drove to the chief-of-staff's headquarters to enquire where he could take the oath to Nicholas. Having been told, he wandered aimlessly from place to place in St. Petersburg. He was informed that the insurgents were shouting for Constantine. Later, saying that he was ill, he entered a government office and remained there for three hours. He then asked if he could pass through Senate Square unnoticed. An official having told him that he could, he left and hastened to the house of his brother-in-law, Count Ludwig Loebzeltern. The count was the Austro-Hungarian ambassador, and his house the embassy. Trubetskoy was found there and arrested late at night.[69]

'His absence,' wrote A. A. Bestuzhev later, 'had a decisive influence upon us and upon the soldiers too, for with few epaulets and without military titles no one dared to take command.'[70] So the 'standing revolution' proceeded. Confusion reigned. By midday, the rebels numbered just 3000 men, precisely half the number Trubetskoy thought necessary to triumph. Finally, realizing the dictator was not coming, the weak-voiced and lisping Prince E. P. Obolensky proposed that Nikolay Bestuzhev be commander. Bestuzhev declined, pleading ingnorance of military tactics – he was a naval officer. Whereupon Obolensky took command or, rather, since he lacked initiative, conspicuously failed to do so.

Trubetskoy's epaulets were mentioned by another memoirist, in another context: because they were so heavy, it was said, he could not hang – it would have been extremely awkward for the government to proclaim that the 'state criminals' and 'rabble' had been headed by a member of an ancient and most eminent aristocratic Russian family.[71] Certainly Nicholas was shocked when he found Trubetskoy named with the rebels; certainly, too, the latter's surname saved his life. For if anyone deserved to mount the gallows with the five Decembrist martyrs (as they came to be regarded posthumously, especially under the influence of Herzen), it was Colonel Prince S. Trubetskoy.[72] Because he was a special prisoner, bearing a very special guilt, Trubetskoy received an individual treatment at the hands of Nicholas.

It is his treatment by the tsar and the commission of enquiry which, above all else, gives curious fascination to his memoirs. Like Lorer, Trubetskoy had the ability to recollect verbatim conversations held some twenty years before. And like Basargin, he omitted what was patently unflattering to himself. There is no mention in *his* memoirs of his kissing Nicholas's hands while on his knees and begging that his life be spared; for that, we must refer to Nicholas's private correspondence.[73] Still, much shines through the understatement and omissions that are prominent throughout his reminiscences.

It is apparent, for example, that a number of his judges, including Generals Tol' (Toll) and Levashev, experienced mixed feelings in his presence that left them ill at ease. He was a villain, but a nobleman of infinitely grander antecedents than themselves; he was a criminal and traitor, but a man of simple and direct manners, a winning smile and – so contemporaries emphasize – moving, expressive grey eyes. Fighting against these feelings, one suspects, his judges treated him more rigorously than they might otherwise have done: few prisoners were called more often from their cells than he, few had more gruelling 'confrontations.' Trubetskoy's brief memoirs are, in essence, a record, with a lengthy introduction, of his own experiences and various interrogations while held in Peter-and-Paul Fortress, That introduction deals, first, with events during the interregnum of November and December 1825 and, second, with the reasons that moved him and others in the capital to seize the opportunity thus offered and to stage a revolution (see Appendix C). The greater part of the memoirs, however, deal with his questionings by Nicholas, Generals Tol', Levashev, Benkendorf and Senator Baranov between December 1825 and July 1826. It is right that they be represented here by the well-known account of his encounter with the tsar, late in the night of December 14. That account casts useful light both on the new tsar's frame of mind after the day of drawn-out crisis and, especially, on the procedures used to round up those suspected of conspiring to provoke it.

One further point should be made concerning Trubetskoy's account of happenings in the Palace and the Fortress: he was not concerned with minor detail or, indeed, with any trivialities such as the actual mechanisms by which both buildings were to have been seized (by his own orders), the tsar deposed, and a new government installed. Trubetskoy was a prince and a leader. That he was motivated less by revolutionary ardour than by dubious considerations of prestige in accepting the nomination as dictator (December 10) made no difference to that fact. Being a prince, he issued orders that subordinates had then to execute – which was ironical, since it was stated in the manifesto that he had himself composed, and which the Senate was to issue once the rising had succeeded, that all classes were equal in Russia! Trubetskoy gave out the order, 'Seize the Palace.' Others had to carry it out. That attitude prevails throughout the memoirs. In vain we may examine them for details of conditions in the fortress, or of his attitude towards the individuals on the commission of enquiry. Trubetskoy was concerned with strategy, not concrete detail – broad vistas, not minutiae. The opening sentence sets the tone: 'Long ago the rumour circulated that the late Emperor Alexander Pavlovich had prepared his brother Nicholas as heir to the throne, and it was said that this was done with the consent of the Heir Apparent, Constantine Pavlovich, when he had wedded the Polish woman Grudzinska.'[74] By whom was such a rumour circulated? We are not informed. Was it true? We are not told. Comfortably couched in elegant, passive constructions, two emperors and other lofty members of the cast enter a prince's reminiscences. Personally, it was remarked, Trubetskoy was a direct and simple man, with no grandiose affectations; when he wrote, it was in the exalted tone of one raised far above the masses.

Perhaps that tone would have been modified, had Trubetskoy corrected or improved the draft used by his daughters and by Herzen in their respective editions. The former pair's note to *Zapiski Knyazya Trubetskago* (Berlin, 1903), however, repeated in the St. Petersburg edition four years later, is no less applicable to Herzen's London edition (in *Zapiski dekabristov;*

vypusk 1, 2) of 1862–63: 'The memoirs are preserved in a draft copy that received no finishing. ...' We must make the best we can of 'the repetitions and the scrappiness' of which the princesses speak frankly, and be grateful for the fact that their editions, at least, are less truncated than the Leipzig one of 1874.

S. P. Trubetskoy

The events of December 14th and the following days are well known. There were not cells enough in Peter-and-Paul Fortress to hold all those arrested, taken in the capital or brought from every corner of the massive Russian Empire.[75] Armed opposition once having been overwhelmed, the whole aristocracy, all servants of the government and all those in high office unconditionally accepted the man who had acceded — Nicholas. No one dared express the view that the irregularity of the sceptre's passing into new hands might in itself have caused that opposition. Everything was ascribed to the malicious intention of the Secret Society, whose members, and others, too, who had participated in the recent happenings, were brought to trial like criminals and malefactors.

All those of lower rank seized on the field of battle were committed to Peter-and-Paul Fortress. All others were brought to the Palace, and the new Emperor interrogated them in person. With many, his anger expressed itself as abuse. Prince Obolensky was led in, his hands tied; the Emperor swore at him, then, addressing the generals present in the room, cried: 'You cannot imagine what I've put up with from him!'[76] Prince Obolensky had been senior adjutant in the Foot Guards and Nicholas Pavlovich, when Grand Duke, had commanded one of the Foot Guard divisions.

Many loyal subjects hastened to bring their closest relatives before the Emperor of their own accord, not troubling to wait until those relatives were ordered to be seized. Thus D.S. Lanskoy gave his wife's nephew, Prince Odoyevsky, no chance to try to escape the fate awaiting him; giving him time neither to rest nor snatch a meal, he brought him to the Palace. Lanskoy's wife inherited 2000 serfs from Prince Odoyevsky when sentence was read over him. But there were some who showed great sympathy and great humanity. Hiding from his pursuers, Captain-Lieutenant Bestuzhev entered a strange house and, walking through a long series of empty rooms, found himself in the private study of a certain elderly noble. Startled by this unexpected apparition, N. asked Bestuzhev what he wanted, learnt that he was hungry and in hiding, locked him in that very study, brought him some food himself, offered him money and told him that he could not hide where he was because of his son in the Guards, who would unfailingly betray him. He then conducted Bestuzhev out of the house in secret. During their conversation they heard the son's voice in a nearby room; he had returned with several other officers and was curtly expressing his opinion of those who had revolted on that day. Without delay, the old man led Bestuzhev out, and he managed to reach Kronstadt.

Many officers and lower ranks who fled from Senate Square took refuge in my mother-in-law's house, which was surrounded on both sides. My mother-in-law's sister, Princess Belosel'skaya, suggested that she stay with her, while my wife's sister, Countess M., proposed that my wife and I stay in her home. This was later represented as an indication of my plan to hide in the house of a foreign envoy! On the night of the 14th, Mr. Lanskoy [77]came to wake me and told me that the Emperor was asking for me. Having dressed, I went into his study and there found Count Nesselrode in full uniform,[78] Count Aleksandr Gur'yev, his brother-in-law, who had come out of curiosity and whose hand I shook, and Fligel'-Adjutant Prince Andrey Mikhaylovich Golitsyn, who informed me that the Emperor wanted me. I sat in a sled with him. When we arrived at the Palace he informed me, in an antechamber, that the Emperor had ordered him to ask my sword of me; I gave it to him, and he led me to the General-Adjutant's room. He then went off to report. At every door stood three guards; everywhere about the Palace and all along the streets leading up to it stood troops and heavy armament. They summoned me. The Emperor came forward to meet me in full-dress uniform and ribbons and, raising his right forefinger directly to my forehead, said: 'And what was in that head when *you*, with *your* surname, your family, entered into such a business? Colonel of the Guards! Prince Trubetskoy! Are you not ashamed to be associated with such rabble? Your fate will be a terrible one.' Then turning to General Tol', who was the only other person in the room, he read, 'Read it!' Tol' took one sheet from among the papers lying on a table, and read from it a deposition: that the incident which had occurred was the work of a society which, besides having members in Petersburg, had a still larger branch in the Fourth Corps; and that the staff-officer of that corps on duty, Prince Trubetskoy, Colonel of the Preobrazhenskiy Life Guards, could give full information regarding the aforementioned society. 'That was Pushchin?' said the Emperor, when Tol' had read it through. 'Pushchin,' said Tol'. 'Pushchin is mistaken,' I said. 'Ah! So you think that Pushchin said that,' said Tol';

'But where does Pushchin live?' I saw that the handwriting was not Pushchin's but feared that, as I had repeated his name, they might make an informer of me. To Tol''s question I therefore answered, 'I don't know.'

Tol': 'Is he at his father's now?'

I: 'I don't know.'

Tol':   'I always used to tell the late Sovereign that the Fourth Corps was the nest of some secret society, Your Highness, and almost all the regimental commanders belong to it; but the late Sovereign did not choose to believe it.'

I: 'Your Excellency has highly inaccurate information.'

Tol':   'You do not have to tell me so, I know it.'

I: 'Enquiries will show that Your Excellency is mistaken. There is no secret society in the Fourth Corps, I can vouch for that.'

The Emperor interrupted our argument, handed me a sheet of paper and said: 'Write a deposition.' He pointed to a place on the divan on which I had been sitting before I had stood up; but before I could sit, he had begun another conversation. 'What a name! Prince Trubetskoy! And in an affair like this! A Colonel of the Guards! Such a sweet wife! You've ruined your wife! Do you have children?' I: 'No, I ... ' 'You are fortunate,' interrupted the Emperor. 'Your fate will be terrible, terrible!' Having continued some time in this vein, he concluded, 'Write down all you know,' and went out into another study. I remained alone, and found myself in a most difficult position. I did not wish to conceal my membership of the Secret Society, which would in any case have led to nothing good, since it was clear from the sheets read to me — sheets covered in various hands — that more was known than I might have wished. But neither did I wish to make it possible for me to reproach myself with having named a single person. For this reason I wrote in my reply that I belonged to the Secret Society, the aim of which was the improvement of our government; that circumstances following the late Emperor's death had seemed to the Society auspicious for the execution of its plans; and that, having resolved on action, its members chose me as director but I, finally seeing that my name was more needed than my person, had completely ceased to participate in it.

While I was writing, Mikhail Pavlovich came in and walked up to me; he stood a while opposite me, then went away. Meanwhile, others whom Tol' was interrogating were brought in and led away. The Emperor would come in for the questioning and then retire once more. When I had finished writing, I handed the paper to Tol' as he came in. He took it off to the Emperor. A little later Tol' called me into another study. Hardly had I crossed its threshold than the Emperor came up to me in great anger: 'What a mass of rubbish you write; and what should be said you don't say!' Moving away with rapid steps to a table, he seized a quarter-sheet of paper lying on it and came back to me with it. 'What's this? Is this your hand?' 'Mine.' The Emperor, shouting: 'Do you know I could shoot you immediately?' I, clenching my hands and also loudly: 'Then shoot, Sovereign! You have the right.' The Emperor, still loudly: 'I do not wish to! I wish your lot to be a terrible one.' Driving me back into the front study as he approached me, the Emperor repeated this several times, lowering his voice; then he gave Tol' a sheet of paper, ordering him to proceed with the case, and spoke to me once more of my lineage, of my wife's distinctions, of the awful fate awaiting me—but all this now in a sad voice. Finally, leading me to the table on which I had already written, he handed me a scrap of paper saying, 'Write to your wife.' I sat, he remained standing. I began to write: 'My dear friend, be calm and pray to God ... ' The Emperor interrupted. 'And what a lot you write! Just write, 'I shall live and be well.' I wrote: 'The Sovereign is standing by me, and orders me to write that I am alive and well.' I gave it to him. He read it through and said: 'I *shall* be alive and well; write 'shall' above it.' I did so. He took it and ordered me to go with Tol'. Tol', having led me out, handed me over to that same Prince Golitsyn who had brought me but who now, taking a section of Chevalier Guardsmen with him, took me away to Peter-and-Paul Fortress and handed me over to Sukin, the Commandant. My fur-coat had been stolen in the Palace; a colonel of field-engineers gave me his padded greatcoat in which to go to the Fortress. Here, I waited several hours in a hall, then in the Fortress church, until I was at last taken off to cell no. 7 in the Alekseyev Ravelin. In the church I prayed intensely, particularly at the thought that I should possibly never again be in a House of God.

On being brought to the cell allotted me in the Ravelin, I was ordered to undress. Leaving me only my shirt, underwear and stockings, they gave me a smock and low shoes, which they exchanged a few days later for a more tattered pair. My window was not puttied up like all the others, and I could never discover the reason for this. A little window in the door, curtained on the outside, made it quite possible for me to be observed at any time, while I was unable to see what was happening in the corridor. At night, they lit a lamp by my window which they lit again as soon as it went out. My furniture consisted of a very hard bed, a small table, a chair, and a bed-pan. In the evenings they would give me a candle and a pair of pincers the end of which had been snapped off. I was given no knives or forks, and the crockery was pewter. After a few days my wife sent me some linen, for which I exchanged what I had. They carefully inspected the cell to make sure that there was nothing sharp in it, not even a pin. They gave me food: tea with a white roll in the morning, clear or cabbage soup, beef and porridge or potatoes for lunch, tea and some kind of supper in the evening.

Throughout the first six weeks at least we were awoken in the night by loud knockings in the corridor. To our questions about the knocking they gave no reply; and to all questions in general they invariably gave no reply, or the reply was: I don't know, I haven't heard. ... During the day and in the evenings, underlings would creep up to our doors in felt boots or something of the sort, so that we could not hear their steps, and stealthily look through the Judas-hole. At first, we fairly often heard the wooden leg of the Commandant, too, as he escorted individuals with boots and spurs around, and voices among which many thought they heard 'one like the Emperor's.' And once I heard quite clearly as Sukin respectfully replied to questions and gave the cell numbers and names of those in them.

On the evening of the 17th, a town-adjutant came to fetch me, bringing me my full-dress coat. I dressed and was taken off to the Commandant's house, where I found General Levashev. Wearing nothing but a full-dress coat I grew extremely cold on the way. Levashev apparently took my trembling as a sign of cowardice — and therefore asked me why I was trembling. Having told me in French he had been sent by the Emperor to question me, he added: 'Ah, Prince! You have done Russia much harm; you have set her back fifty years.'[79] He then began to question me concerning the membership of the Southern Society and its formation. To my reply that I could give no information, because I did not have any myself, he read me out many details from which I saw, to my astonishment, that the Society's whole make-up and all its membership was known. (I did not know, of course, that Mayboroda had turned informer.)

'You know far more than I do, General,' I said; 'almost everything that you have read is new to me.'

He: 'That cannot be. You merely do not wish to speak.'

I: 'Even if I wished to, I could tell you nothing, since I know nothing about all this.'

He: 'You were in the south, and you saw Pestel'.'

I: 'I haven't seen Pestel' for several years now.[80] May I ask you about him?'

He: 'He has been arrested. If you do not wish to answer my questions, you may write directly to the Sovereign.' Then, having asked me if Colonel I. M. Bibikov [81] belonged to the Society and received a negative reply, General Levashev left me. My assertion that Bibikov was not a member of the Secret Society, it seemed to me then, had hardly convinced Levashev and I therefore, on returning to my cell, requested a piece of note-paper, a pen, and an inkwell. I wrote a letter to Levashev, asserting positively that Bibikov had not belonged to the Society and so knew nothing of its existence or of the 14th.

One day after this the Keeper of the Ravelin (old Lilien-Ankern)[82] came to my cell with a large envelope in his hand, and asked if I had written to the Sovereign. I said no; and he remarked that somebody had written from the Ravelin and he had probably come to the wrong cell. He went out. On the evening of the 23rd the Town-Adjutant came for me once again. I dressed, and was taken to the Commandant's house. ...

Questioning began concerning the 14th, its object and our means of attaining that object. I replied that its object was, taking advantage of unprecedented circumstances in Russia, to give Russia a sound form of government: that we had been convinced the troops would not believe a manifesto that had not been published in the name of the Emperor to whom they had already sworn allegiance; that we wished to turn their stubborness into a way of fixing the legality of changes that would spare our fatherland from future revolutions like the French Revolution; and that, when our opposition had proved strong, enough, the authorities would in all probability have entered into talks with us—and *then* we could have furnished the fatherland with what we had in mind.

The Grand Duke: 'Who would have entered into negotiations with you?'

I: 'The Sovereign.'

The Grand Duke (angrily): 'With you? With rebels!! This is a foreign-inspired business. Prince Schwartzenberg from the Austrian Embassy was on the Square.'

I: 'We would have allowed no foreigner to interfere in our affair. It was to have been completely Russian.'

The Grand Duke: 'What is the name of Count Loebzeltern's secretary?'

I: 'He has several.'

The Grand Duke: '*Son secrétaire particulier.*'

I: 'I don't know his name.'

The Grand Duke: 'How is it you don't know? Slumlauer.'

I: 'He is not a private secretary; he is secretary of the Embassy.'

The Grand Duke: 'It's all the same.'

Having detained me some considerable time, they let me leave. As I went out into another room I noticed that a sack was being thrust over the head of a small man so that I should not recognize him.

I was again asked for on the evening of the 24th, and once again found the same group. But this time the questions were numerous; two or three men would ask questions simultaneously, mockingly, bitingly, almost insultingly, one contradicting another when it was possible to contradict. Finally I said: 'Gentlemen, I cannot answer you all at once. Everyone asks something different. If you would be so good as to ask me questions in turn, I will reply.'

G. A. Golenishchev-Kutuzov (with a loud laugh): 'Ah no, it's better this way, he'll make a slip sooner!'

I: 'I trust that I shall not give Your Excellency that pleasure. And I repeat that I cannot reply when you question me as you are doing now. You all talk, interrupting one another. You fall on me like mad dogs, and demand a reply about matters that occurred several years ago. Can I remember everything in an instant? If you wish to have answers from me, give me written questions, and I will reply then.'

Almost all: 'What next! Answer verbally.'

I: 'I cannot reply.'

Grand Duke: 'Prince Trubetskoy's demand is just. Give him questions in written form and send them to him so that he can reply in writing.' The members agreed to this. All stood up. Then Prince Golitsyn came up to me and said: 'The Sovereign is most displeased with you. You will reply to nothing! But the Sovereign does not need your answers in order to find out about the affair—everything is known already! He merely wishes to see evidence of your frankness, and to see that you are sensible of his mercy. Do not force us to take measures that will be unpleasant for you.'

I: 'On the first day I told the Sovereign everything that bears upon *my* fate; and I am ready to answer everything else that you may wish to ask. But Your Highness will admit that I cannot turn informer.' The Minister of War approached me now and began, in a plaintive voice, to urge me to reveal all that I knew. At last I was released, and went back to my cell completely exhausted; I began to spit blood. The next day, which was Christmas Day, I was ill. The questions were sent in and I replied to them.

I do not recall which day it was when I received queries about a letter I had sent to Stepan Mikhaylovich Semyonov in Moscow,[83] and which had been delivered by Svistunov. I replied that [in it] I had told Semyonov of events in Petersburg. Then I was asked by whom Semyonov was received into the Society. I replied that I did not know. That evening I was summoned before the Committee. After various questions about my correspondence and acquaintance with Semyonov and his joining the Society—to which I answered that I supposed he *was* a member, though I could not say for certain—I was told to turn around, and asked if I would recognize Semyonov. I turned and saw him behind me. They repeated the question: 'Did this Semyonov belong to the Society?' I repeated my reply: that I could not positively say so. But at this point Semyonov burst out, 'Come, Prince! You *know* I wasn't a member! You didn't receive me into the Secret Society, and you know where I've been since I left Petersburg—and that I could have been received by no one.'

I: 'Mr. Semyonov is speaking the truth. *I* never received him, and I don't know that anyone else did.'

Question: 'You wrote to Semyonov through Svistunov. You wrote to him as to a member of the Secret Society.'

I: 'What I wrote to Semyonov I could have written to any other acquaintance, even if he were not a member of the Secret Society.'

Question: 'But still you supposed that Semyonov *was* a member, and wrote to him not only through Svistunov in Moscow, but earlier too.'

I: 'Our correspondence touched only upon Mr. Semyonov's personal affairs.'

Semyonov: 'Prince Trubetskoy knows I was not a member of the Secret Society the last time that we met: he can affirm that. Since then, I have lived for three years away from all my acquaintances.'

General Levashev

(addressing the Committee:) 'Prince Trubetskoy has no wish to tell us that Semyonov belongs to the Society, and I know why! Mr. Semyonov received his brother into it, and the Prince fears that he may reveal this.'

I: 'General Levashev's supposition is inaccurate; not one of my brothers belongs to the Society.'

Levashev: 'Your brother, now serving in the Chevalier Garde Regiment, is a member of the Secret Society.'

I: 'That's untrue!'

Levashev

(to the Committee): 'Mr. Semyonov educated Prince Trubetskoy's younger brother and received him into the Secret Society.'

I: 'Untrue! My brother, of whom General Levashev is speaking, does not belong to the Society, nor did any one of my brothers know of the existence of a secret society. Mr. Semyonov came from Moscow with my step-mother and lived in her house some six months, educating my younger brother; and even if Mr. Semyonov was a member of the Society, he couldn't have received my brother, who was not more than fifteen. But Mr. Semyonov was not a member of the Society then, and did not see my brother afterwards.'

After this, Semyonov went on demonstrating that he could not have belonged to the Secret Society. He further emphasized his separation from its members; the fact that of all the members he knew me best of all, and so could not have been received by anyone else; and the fact that *I* had not received him either; and in this last assertion he called me as a witness. Moreover, so skilfully did he make me his witness that I was bound in all justice to support him. Finally they released me, keeping Semyonov.

Next day I was called again before the Committee, which I found larger than before. Besides those I had seen already, Dibich and Potapov were present. But all the time Dibich alone spoke and interrogated me. Baten'kov was standing before the Committee. I was asked to give evidence that Baten'kov belonged to the Society, and was told that there were nineteen testimonies to that effect.[84] I retorted that I could not affirm Baten'kov's membership, because I did not know that anyone ever received him, because I myself had never spoken to him about the Society, and because I knew him only very slightly; that I had once, before the 14th, discussed with him the curious position in which our Fatherland then found itself (the interregnum); and that this conversation was fully justified by the prevailing circumstances—one did not need to belong to the Secret Society to discuss a topic occupying everyone so much.

Sitting in my cell in the Ravelin, I marveled that there had been no questions about members of the Society in the South. Only once had I received a sheet on which it was remarked that Colonel Pestel' had alluded to some circumstance which I was asked to explain; never, apart from this, was reference made to the Southern members. But I knew neither of Mayboroda's denunciation nor of Sherwood's and Vitt's, nor of the rising of the Chernigovskiy Regiment; I could not explain the silence. Yet I could only conclude that the Committee had more important information than any I might provide.

Until Shrovetide I was asked almost no questions, save those concerning the membership of several individuals, their sponsors, and the dates on which they were received. And to these questions I had pleaded ignorance. Finally, at the beginning of Lent, in the second week I think, the Town-Adjutant came for me. In the room where the Committee sat I found General Chernyshev and Colonel Adlerberg. The former had a notebook in his hand, from which he read me out various questions, stupid for the most part, about my stay abroad, my actions and acquaintance there—all this on the supposed basis of testimonies by numerous members of the Society. All the time, Adlerberg drew on a piece of paper that he had in front of him. As many have remarked to me, this was his only occupation throughout the interrogations. Chernyshev questioned me with a certain mockery. Having been kept a fair time, I was released. The next day I received an enormous notebook in which various details of events of the 14th and of our proposed actions that day were questioned. The points raised were mostly stupid. Among them was the following: 'Who, at my suggestion, had been chosen to deliver the blow against the reigning Emperor?' I should no doubt have answered simply to this question that there was no such suggestion and that no one had been chosen, which was the truth. But before replying to it I thought to allude to it in a letter to my wife. (I sent a letter to her every evening through the Town-Adjutant.) The next morning this Town-Adjutant brought me the letter back, saying that he was ordered to inform me that I should not write such things—for they might grieve my wife! I thereupon wrote in reply to the question that, in all probability, the Committee would not have put such an appalling question had someone not alleged that there was truth in this; in which case, it could ask the informer to name the volunteer—

I did not know him. My reasoning in making that reply was false; for it was based on the conviction that the Committee and all its actions were nothing but a comedy; that my fate and that of all imprisoned with me had been long before decided in the Emperor's mind; and that no matter how things went, I was to rot away in solitary confinement. If the Emperor concluded from my answers (I reasoned) that I was being stubborn in my disavowals, my confinement would be stricter still. I therefore decided, while not positively refuting these allegations, to oblige the Committee to address itself to its informer — who, having named a non-existent person, would be unable to substantiate his testimony. But it seems that I was quite mistaken in my suppositions.

Other questions I answered in detail, where my own acts or proposals were concerned, always trying to avoid confirming allegations against other individuals. But nonetheless they managed to squeeze a few careless words from me about Lieutenant Arbuzov of the Guards Equipage.

A few days after this, a priest visited me. He had already been to see me once and, so I felt, wished to make up to me; but he was not clever enough, and I remained doubtful as to his real thoughts and intentions. Now there seemed opportunity to learn both his thoughts and his intentions, and whether he was acting straightforwardly or slyly. So I told him of the question that concerned the Emperor's person and my answer to it. And I concluded, from the impression that this made on him, that he was a man of honourable feeling. He asked me to refute all lies decisively, then asked me if I wished to make a confession. I said I did, and he replied that he would come to hear it. I waited several weeks, however, and he came only when I had stopped expecting him. It was with a sincere feeling of my own unworthiness that I received the Body and Blood of Christ, and a pure joy took possession of my heart at that moment; hope in God's mercy took root in my heart. My confession, so it seemed, had attached the priest to me — he grew to like me and, beginning then, came to me fairly often, convinced that everything that he had heard about me earlier was a lie and that, though I might indeed have strayed from the path of righteousness, still I had never entertained evil intent. Evil intentions *had* to be ascribed to me, he saw, to justify that sentence it was meant to pass on me. All this time I received almost no questions. The Committee did not trouble me at all. But on March 28th, after lunch, the door of my cell was opened and General-Adjutant Benkendorf came in. Having dismissed the warder and first made a few insignificant remarks (about the dampness of my quarters), he sat on the chair and asked me to sit too. I sat down on the bed.

He: 'I have come to you on behalf of His Majesty the Emperor. You should speak as though to the Emperor himself; I am merely a necessary intermediary. Naturally, the Emperor cannot come to see you himself. He cannot come here, and it would be improper that he should have you summoned to his presence; there must therefore be an intermediary between him and you. The conversation that takes place between ourselves must thus be a secret to the whole world, as if it had taken place between the Emperor and you. His Majesty shows great goodness towards you, and is waiting for a sign of your gratitude.'

I: 'General, I am most grateful to His Majesty for all his favours, to which this bears witness,' (pointing to a pile of letters from my wife lying on my table, and which I received daily).

He: 'What is that? It isn't a question of that. Recollect that you are between life and death ...'

I: 'I know very well, General, that I am closer to the latter.'

He: 'Well, then! You don't know what the Emperor is doing for you. One can be kind, one can be clement, but there is a limit to everything. The law gives absolute power to the Emperor, yet there are things that he ought not to do, and I am not afraid to say that he exceeds even his right in sparing your life. But it is also necessary that you, for your part, give him some proof of your gratitude. I repeat to you that everything you say to me will be known only to the Emperor himself, and I am only the channel by which your words must pass.'

I: 'I have already told you, General, that I am most grateful to His Majesty for the goodness he has shown in allowing me to correspond with my wife. And I would like to know how I can show him my gratitude.'

He: 'The Emperor wishes to know what connections you have had with Mr. Speransky.'

I: 'I have had no special connection with Mr. Speransky.'

He: 'Forgive me. I must tell you, on behalf of His Majesty the Emperor, that he *assures* you, through me, that all that you tell me about Mr. Speransky will remain a secret between him and you. And that nothing will happen to Mr. Speransky because of it; he is above that. Mr. Speransky is needed, but the Emperor wishes only to know what degree of confidence he should show him.'

I: 'General, I can give you no documentary proof of my connections with Mr. Speransky, except of those that one ordinarily has in society.'

He: 'But you have recounted to someone a conversation that you had with Mr. Speransky. You even consulted him on the constitution to be given to Russia.'

I: 'That is untrue, General; His Majesty has been misinformed.'

He: 'Take care, Prince Trubetskoy! You know you are between life and death.'[85]

The Fortress

Aleksandr Mikhaylovich Murav'yov   1805–1853

Younger brother of Nikita, Aleksandr Mikhaylovich Murav'yov was a mere cornet in the Chevalier Garde at the time of the December rising. Received into the Northern Society at the tender age of twenty, he never attained importance in it; nor did he later distinguish himself in Siberia unless by his decision, made in 1832 when he might have left the prison of Petrovskiy Zavod, to remain there with his celebrated brother till the latter's term should end. Insofar as he is remembered at all, among the several Murav'yovs implicated in the rising, it is as the author of *Mon Journal*, written in the last part of his life (1847–50).[1]

The journal is ill-named. As I. D. Yakushkin justly noted, 'In the story of his life, Murav'yov says almost nothing of himself.'[2] The journal is, in fact, a monument to brotherly respect: unwilling that his notes on the Northern Society should fall into hostile hands, Nikita wrote them slyly on the margins of a dozen of his books. When, on his death, his library passed on to Aleksandr the latter gathered them, collated them and published them. They cast less light on Aleksandr himself than on his brother.

Mon Journal is not devoid of autobiographical content or interest, however, as the following brief extract shows. A latecomer to Peter-and-Paul Fortress, A. M. Murav'yov was shocked by its deliberately engineered grimness. It was, he saw, a large machine for breaking prisoners' spirits. Sobered and fortified by that objective realization, he fared better than many, and emerged mentally sharper than he had been when he first entered his cell. This extract is taken from Theodor Schiemann's *Zur Geschichte der Regierung Paul I und Nikolaus I* (Berlin, 1906). The text has been three times reprinted in the Soviet Union since the October Revolution, each time with minor alterations.[3]

Hideous monument to absolutism, the Fortress of St. Petersburg faces the Sovereign's palace like some fateful warning that the one can exist only because of the other. Of course the constant spectacle of dungeons in which moan victims of arbitrariness must, in the long run, necessarily dull pity for a neighbour's suffering. Great God! When will the day dawn when (at last) it will be *understood* that men were not created to be playthings for a few privileged families? When the sun of publicity shines upon Russia, how the evils hidden by those walls will make men shudder!

There were not sufficient cells for the great number of victims [in 1825]. Buildings that had been serving as barracks for garrison troops were transformed into jails. The window panes, covered with layers of chalky paste, stopped the invigorating sun from ever penetrating into *those* lairs. And in the long rooms of the barracks, cages were built with beams so spaced as to prevent any communication. A prisoner could make only two or three steps along his cell's diagonal. ...

We arrived from Reval', crossed the drawbridge and stopped by the door of the Commandant's house. The courier turned me over to a major who, not speaking a word to me, led me into a dirty, damp, narrow, dark cell. A broken chair, an ugly pallet and an iron chain sealed to the wall by one end were the only furniture. After months of confinement and a journey of 360 versts covered, I was exhausted by fatigue. Once the old major had withdrawn, I flung myself still fully dressed onto the awful pallet. ...

Here I was, alone and separated from the living. Lying down, I spent hours thinking of my mother and my brother who, I knew, was being held in the same fortress. Tears came to my eyes; I prayed to God, and praying comforted me. A feeling of joy invaded my heart—I felt proud to share the fate of my excellent brother. Taking courage, I stood up and paced my cell. Then suddenly I heard the noise of locks and doors again. The major reappeared, and conducted me to General Sukin, the Commandant of Petersburg Fortress, an old veteran whom I had known as a child. He received me sitting at his desk, pretending not to recognize me, and asked me my name. I replied that I was Murav'yov, an officer of the Chevalier Garde. To this he thought it civil to remark: 'I am quite sorry for the memory of your respected father, who has a criminal in you.' I shook on hearing this, but a feeling of pity seized me at the sight of this poor old man, so dulled by servility that he could remain wholly indifferent to the sight of another's sufferings, the sufferings of another man who did not share his views.

After this interview I found myself in my cell once more, but now I was content to be alone. I remained in my cell almost eight days, deprived of light and food. In the morning, a jailer accompanied by a sentry would bring me bread and water, but one morning the doors of my cell opened at an unusual hour. This time it was General Stukulov, whom I had also known before. He conducted himself like a gentleman, sighed to see me, and enquired after my health with tears in his eyes — and also asked if I had heard from my mother. Then he left me. Once a month the Emperor sent one of his general aides-de-camp to visit the prisoners, to show that he took 'a lively interest' in their fates. But this veil of sympathy hid a desire to seek out all the prisoners' beliefs and at the same time to bewitch our poor relatives.

The food was terrible, money provided for our upkeep being pilfered by the servants, encouraged by the major. Some of the prisoners were kept on bread and water; many had irons on their feet and hands. It was the Emperor himself who ... prescribed the diet, as well as these more painful aggravations of our grim captivity itself. Moral torture was also tried. Prisoners would occasionally receive heartrending letters from unhappy relatives who, utterly deceived by the appearances of the situation, would praise the magnanimity of one who had never shown it. A priest was obliged to bring the solace of religion and, more especially, to provoke confessions. When he had come to know us better, he admitted the error into which he had been led regarding us. The bloody dénouement of our trial surprised him and aroused his high indignation. Many of the prisoners grew ill, several losing their minds and some attempting suicide.

Nikolay Ivanovich Lorer 1795–1873

Far worse than the Kronverk Curtain in which A. M. Murav'yov suffered was the Alekseyev Ravelin, the place of ultimate confinement. With its own aged commandant, its own rules and procedures, the Ravelin was more than a special security block; it was a dark prison apart. The thick walls of its nineteen cells ensuring perfect silence, it was both physically and psychologically removed from General Sukin's little town. Here prisoners were placed to be forgotten. Here Nicholas sent those conspirators whom he most hated and least trusted: Bestuzhev, 'to be committed to the Ravelin under the strictest guard'; Svistunov, 'also to be committed there, and *treated with severity*'; Yakushkin, 'to be put in manacles and fetters and treated with that harshness that befits a wretch'; Lorer, Obolensky, and Ryleyev.

The bases of self-confidence eroded by the silence, as dampness from the river slowly ate into the walls, most prisoners in the Alekseyev Ravelin collapsed, gave 'full confessions,' or grew ill. Without books or company or any exercise, days fused with nights, winter with spring. And yet, although the half-starved, half-enraged Colonel Bulatov smashed his head against his wall, and S. Semyonov almost died of negligence and hunger, and Baten'kov had strange hallucinations and Falenberg indulged in riots of gratuitous self-accusation – many found great peace within the Alekseyev Ravelin.

Lorer, Obolensky, and Yakushkin were all incarcerated there. None suffered as did Aleksandr Murav'yov, Ivashev or Basargin, though their situation was, in fact, more desperate. Reflected in their memoirs, indeed, is a pervasive sense of, in the first two cases, reconciliation, and in the third, repose. (Yakushkin never modified his anti-tsarist views.) How did they come to terms with their positions? What was the source of their tranquility? The answers, which are different in each case, bespeak the whole range of emotional and psychological adaptability among the stronger prisoners. Of those who craved forgiveness or gave lists of all their friends without being asked, few left their memoirs – and fewer still even remotely honest ones. The strong survived with all their self-respect, and wrote memoirs to be trusted, more or less.

It will be noted from the following short extracts that, whereas Yakushkin was enabled to survive in solitary confinement *because* his attitudes towards the rising and the tsar remained unaltered, Obolensky found new strength for precisely the opposite reason. For him, peace came with true, christian repentance.

N. I. Lorer

I shall now proceed with a description of the Alekseyev Ravelin, which had fallen to my lot. I asked to be left in my former cell, in the hope of seeing the good Sokolov, but was refused permission. Many know Peter-and-Paul Fortress, but few of course have heard of this Alekseyev Ravelin, and hardly anyone can form a true conception of it. Such is this little spot that, once having arrived — and it may well be for your whole life — you will never see anything again except a scrap of sky and the tip of the cathedral spire, or perhaps only the angel on its top. On the left-hand extremity of the Fortress, over a fosse, there is a little bridge, on crossing which you come into a narrow corridor and find yourself staring at a triangular stone building with no windows. And this is the twelve-casemate Alekseyev Ravelin. In the centre of the triangle a tiny garden is concealed, just a few paces long, with two emaciated birch trees, a blackcurrant bush, and a few square feet of wretched grass. There are windows or, rather, embrasures in the cells' thick granite walls, with stout iron grilles, but these windows do not overlook the garden; they are set facing the lodging both of the commandant of the Ravelin and of his twelve assistants, who are veterans, and where they even have their own bath-house. The rooms are large and light, the ceilings whitewashed and the walls yellow. In each prisoner's cell there is a large bedframe with a straw-mattress, two large pillows and a woollen blanket, a table, and a chair not unlike an armchair. Dinner and supper are better than in the large fortress; the spoons are silver, but no knives or forks are issued. Twice a week they allow a prisoner to go out into the little garden (accompanied by a veteran, however), but at these times he can see and meet nobody. They suggested to me that I should breathe a little pure air, and I made haste to take advantage of that permission. The veteran accompanying me locked the door behind him, and sprawled unceremoniously in the middle of the patch, while I began to circle it like a beast inside a cage. All the corners and the walls here were covered with mould and cobwebs, and these walls rose up beside me like dark masses. A half-broken bench stood between two birches. How many tears had been shed there, I wondered, and how much thought over and felt? And where are those who once languished here now? Where are their bones?

On the very first day of my confinement in the Ravelin I made the acquaintance of its strange custodian, Commandant Lilien-Ankern,[4] a seventy-eight-year-old of German extraction. He went about in a green long-tailed frock-coat with a red collar and cuffs of the same colour, and visited us daily. His pace constantly steady, bent forward with his arms behind his back and with his mouth open — whence protruded two huge yellow teeth and no more — he would come straight up to one with the single question: 'How is your health?' and move away, waiting for no reply. Wishing to get to know him better, I once told him I was ill; but even then I heard no sound from him. He turned around rather more slowly and went off all the same. The veteran accompanying him told me he would not answer any question, and that all his assistants were bound by an oath of silence both when with the prisoners and in the city, into which one of the twelve would go for stores. Podushkin, in his kindness, afterwards allotted me a cell in the [main] Fortress with a view of the Neva and Petersburg in which my never-to-be-forgotten Pestel' had languished, and whence he had gone to hear his sentence read — and later to his execution. Entering this sanctuary, I found his bedding in disorder still. Hungrily I searched in every corner and all over the walls for any sign, some note scratched with a pencil or a pen, but all in vain: Pestel' left nothing behind him.

I soon grew used to my life and was content with my quarters. My cell was spacious; through the embrasure I could see the palace embankment and in the evening, having clambered up to my large window with its grille, I could breathe in the light wind from the river. The measured steps of a sentry resounded beneath my embrasure. My neighbours, it seemed, were family men, for I often glimpsed small boats scurrying about below our windows — boats filled with people of various ages and both sexes, and which stopped before our windows. Oarsmen looked up at the embrasures and, as it was impossible to talk, sang and so conveyed to their relations what they wished to say to them. The pitiless sentries would order a boat to move off; the rowers would pretend that they had struck a bank and were struggling to get off it, but meanwhile relatives managed to see as much of one another as they wished, and to exchange a word or two. ...[5]

How many times I sat at my window and admired the illuminations lit in honour of the Imperial family's return from Moscow! The sound of carriages, the murmur of the crowd, shouts of hurrah reached me; but for me it was a hundred times more pleasant when silence reigned about me, when the moon would emerge on the horizon and throw its silvery beams onto the smooth Neva, then quietly peep into my casemate, casting a grille across my floor and lighting up my gloomy cell. Then I would feel so well, so joyful in my heart, and hope for a better future would revive me.

Once the sentences had been read, relatives were allowed to visit us each week, in the presence of an officer, however. And on those days, the spacious Fortress courtyard was usually covered with carriages, while in the rooms of the Commandant's house it was difficult to thread one's way through crowds of relatives. Rarely would one come across cheerful faces; for the most part you would meet the tears and sorry countenances of individuals who sensed that soon even this last joy would be taken from them. Of course my sister-in-law visited me every week, and made herself ready to say farewell to me forever. Filling the place of a mother for me, this worthy woman waited for my leaving and prepared everything necessary for the long journey, making all the clothes that I should need. The Exchequer clothed and provisioned exiles who possessed no relatives or means.

Once, on a beautiful evening, I was sitting undressed by my window as was my custom, admiring the little craft that scurried over the Neva in all directions, when my good Sokolov came in to me with a suggestion that we go out for a stroll. The suggestion was unusual and not at the normal time, and I did not feel like dressing—besides which I felt somehow sad. But for some reason Sokolov was most insistent, so I finally agreed, not wishing to vex him, put on a greatcoat, and together we went out. We turned our steps towards the Fortress gates nearest the river, where boats and little barges generally put in. By the gates stood some twelve guardsmen in greatcoats and service caps. 'Who are these and why are they here?' I asked my guide who, smiling, asked me to draw nearer, which I did mechanically. But imagine my amazement when I recognized in that group privates of my company in the Moscow Regiment, which I had commanded when I served in the Guards! They recognized me too, for they met me with a friendly:

'We wish you health, Your Excellency! The company sent us to say farewell to you. They ask you to stand firm, and they themselves are praying God to give you strength to bear your misfortune and bring you safely to Siberia. We have a lamp burning before an icon of St. Nicholas,[6] and we'll place more candles in front of it and pray for you every day.' This simple, heartfelt speech moved me deeply, and I thanked them with tears in my eyes and asked them to convey my regards to the company.

Prince E. P. Obolensky

What shall I say of the days passed in confinement under the yoke of memories still fresh, of passions not yet stilled, of the Commission's incessantly renewed interrogation, of fears for those close to my heart and terror of bringing yet more grief, by one superfluous word, in a reply to that person whom the word might implicate? But all this was in the first days of confinement. Gradually, the questionings grew rarer, the summons to appear in person before the Commission ceased, and little by little peace established itself in my soul. A new light penetrated it, lighting it in its very darkest windings where the whole sum of the intellectual, emotional and active life is kept — a sum formed from one's days of thoughtless youth until the time when one becomes a thinking man. With what shall I compare that light, and how can I fittingly extol it? Its feeble image is the rising sun which, rising from the unseen heavenly depths, at first illuminates the mountain tops, touching the valley with its barely noticeable rays; rising gradually higher, its rays grow gradually brighter, and gradually all the mountains are illumined by it; so, too, more brightly and more warmly, are the valleys where the tender plants open themselves up to its life-imparting warmth, revealing their closed calyces to its beams and breathing in its animating force. In this manner the light of the Gospels' truth first illumined those features of my life and character sharply defined in the depth of my self-knowledge. Little by little penetrating further, the Gospels' light, with all its warm and animating rays of endless, full and perfect love, lit up, warmed and so brought to life all that was able to receive it in my self-knowledge — all that was able to breathe in its warmth, to open up and to accept its animating heat. So passed day after day, week after week. Spring came, and the beginning of the summer was upon us and we, the prisoners, were permitted to enjoy the air in a little garden in the Alekseyev Ravelin. The hours of walking were distributed among all prisoners equally; but there were many of us, so it was not every day that each of us enjoyed that pleasure.

Midnight came. A priest came out of Kondratiy Fyodorovich's cell bearing the Holy Sacraments; he also left Sergey Ivanovich Murav'yov-Apostol's, Pyotr Kakhovsky's and Mikhail Bestuzhev-Ryumin's. A pastor admonished Pavel Ivanovich Pestel'. I did not sleep; we were ordered to dress. I heard footsteps and whispering, but did not understand their import. Some time passed, and then I heard a sound of chains. A door was opened on the other side of the corridor; the chains began to jingle heavily. Then I heard the slow voice of my unfailing friend, Kondratiy Fyodorovich Ryleyev: 'Forgive me, forgive me, brothers!' and measured footsteps moved away to the far end of the corridor.

I threw myself against my little window. It was beginning to grow light. I saw a platoon of the Pavlovskiy grenadiers and a Lieutenant Pil'man, whom I knew; I saw all five men, encircled by grenadiers with fixed bayonets. A sign was given, and they moved away. We, too, were ordered out. And we were escorted by those same grenadiers and came onto the esplanade before the Fortress. All the Guards regiments were drawn up. In the distance I could see five gibbets; and I watched the five elected ones slowly approach the fateful spot. The words, 'Ratification-decoration'[7] were still ringing in my ears—still hope had not deserted me. They were soon finished with us: they broke our swords through, took our greatcoats off, and cast them on a fire; then, having put gowns on us, they led us back by the same route into the Fortress. Once more I occupied the same cell in the Kronverk Curtain. The chosen victims were prepared. The priest, Pyotr Nikolayevich, was with them. He went up to Kondratiy Fyodorovich and offered him some word of exhortation. Ryleyev took his hand, placed it against his heart and said: 'As you hear, father, it is not beating harder than before.' All five mounted the place of execution, and the execution was accomplished.

So fell the five victims, chosen from among us all as expiatory victims for our common sin; like ready, ripe clusters they fell upon the earth. But it was not the earth that received them, but the Heavenly Father, who found them worthy of His high, celestial mansions. They passed away into Eternity, purified of all terrestrial things both outwardly and inwardly in the crucible of suffering; having accepted death, they took with it the martyr's crown, which will not be removed from them throughout all coming ages. Glory to our Lord God!

On the evening of July 21st, 1826,[8] they brought to me in my cell in the Kronverk Curtain, a grey jacket and trousers of the same coarse soldier's cloth, and announced that we must get ourselves ready to set out on our journey. I had a meeting, the day before this, with my younger brothers who were pages and, on parting from them, asked them to send me all the clothing and the linen necessary. They carried out my wish; probably they found ready a frock-coat and a pair of trousers which, together with some linen, they put into a small suitcase which they forwarded to me. All this I received and, surprised by my new apparel, asked the Town-Major: 'But why have they sent me civilian clothes if I'm to wear a grey jacket?' The answer given to me was that the choice was up to me, and that I could make use of the official clothing if I wished to do so. Since I was ordered to prepare myself for a journey, however, I decided —having reflected that I had not one kopek in my pocket—that I was going to a far-off place, and that my only frock-coat would be utterly destroyed; so I resolved to wear the government-issue clothes. Though they did not look well, they were very comfortable because of their width. I waited for the time of my departure. Soon after midnight I was taken to the Commandant's house; going into a room, I saw Aleksandr Ivanovich Yakubovich, dressed like myself. ... Yakubovich was unable to stop himself exclaiming, when he saw me with a beard and in my strange apparel: 'Well! Obolensky'! (He led me up to a mirror.) 'If *I* look like Stenka Razin, *you* must resemble Van'ka Kain!'[9]

Shortly after this, the door was flung open and the Fortress Commandant, Infantry General Sukin, loudly announced: 'By the Sovereign's command, you are ordered to leave for Siberia in chains.' Having heard this order out, I turned to him and said that I had not one kopek on me and would ask one favour of him — that I be given back a rather valuable gold watch which had been taken from me when we came into the Fortress. He listened and ordered Trusov, the Town-Adjutant, to bring my watch to me at once. And this was done. Fetters were brought a little later; we were chained up, handed over to the state courier Sedov and four gendarmes, and went out onto the pre-arranged path. Accompanying us, the Town-Major of the Fortress, Yegor Mikhaylovich Podushkin, came up to me and pressed my hand mysteriously. I returned the handshake and heard him whisper barely audibly: 'Take it; it's from your brother.' I felt money in my hand, silently pressed *his* hand again, and inwardly thanked God for the unexpected aid. There were four troikas waiting by the porch.

I. D. Yakushkin

Ten days after this ceremony of disgracing we were transferred from the Ravelin to the Fortress, and I was brought into the Nevskaya Curtain. I left my first cell unwillingly. Of course, I had passed oppressive minutes there, but there had also been minutes flooded with such a light that everything within me had grown orderly, harmonious. At the beginning of a term of confinement one feels something weighing on one like the *fatum* of the ancients, and one's own insignificance before the mighty and inevitable; but little by little inner resources grow, and one starts to breathe more freely and even, now and then, to forget the darkness and the bolts. Complete and prolonged solitude, temporarily suspending us from all outside impressions, acts like animal magnetism in that it concentrates our whole being on the one object to which, at any given moment, we are giving our attention. Many questions I had asked myself when free, but which had earlier remained beyond my grasp, were settled—and sometimes wholly unexpectedly—while I was in the Ravelin. My dialogue with myself was rarely interrupted by anyone or anything, especially during my last days there. I grew accustomed to my first cell, and the putrid stains upon its walls, left by the flood of 1824, were not stains to me, but had become a picture of a new variety.

The cell to which I was transferred overlooked the Neva; and here the pattern of my life completely changed: instead of the profound silence to which I was accustomed in the Ravelin, I could hear almost continual movement in the corridor and the sound of voices and shouts in cells divided from each other only by timbered partitioning. When Town-Major Podushkin appeared, all would grow quiet for a little while. Sitting all day by my open window, I would give myself up to the pleasure of breathing in the fresh air and admiring the river which was covered with small craft scurrying from one bank to the other. These pleasant external sensations prevented me from long abandoning myself to any one feeling or thought; and such an animal existence did I lead during this time that I would swallow to the last morsel the appalling cabbage-soup and tough beef which they brought me in for lunch and dinner. And I grew so stout during my few days there that my own people could not approve when we met for the first time!

After the ceremony of disgracing, those of us who remained in the Fortress were allowed one weekly meeting with our close relations. These meetings always lasted for two hours, taking place in the presence of the Town-Adjutant; moreover we were forbidden to speak any language but Russian. At first, under the pretext of a meeting, relatives and non-relatives came, and every day the Fortress would be full of carriages.

I did not stay long in the cell with an open window facing the Neva. The imprudence of one of my neighbours resulted in our being taken from the cells which overlooked the river to cells in which the windows faced the cathedral; this character[10] had launched into a noisy conversation with his wife, who had come up to the very Fortress in a wherry.

In my new cell, at his invitation, I struck up a friendship with my neighbour. This was the more delightful since the wall dividing us did not make conversation quite impossible. This neighbour was Sutgof,[11] one of the main instigators of the 14th. I had not known him earlier, but now the circumstances in which we found ourselves immediately drew us close to one another. Having told me of his own affair with the Commission, Sutgof demanded the same frankness of me. He was sent off to Finland a few days later, and Aleksandr Murav'yov took his place. Murav'yov was a youth of barely twenty; I had known him earlier when he was still no more than a boy. Sentenced to twelve years' labour, he consoled himself with the idea that he would share his brother's fate and stay with him.

Just before dinner on August 5th, the priest came in to me with the news that I was to be sent to Finland that same night, and that he would be driving out to the first post-station with my relatives, to say farewell. Trusov came in at dusk and told me to prepare myself to leave; when it was completely dark he returned to my cell and, ordering me to follow him, led me to the Commandant. On the way he gave me various directions, advising me *inter alia* to beware of the courier and on no account to address him in French.[12] If I did so, he assured me, the courier had the right to deprive me of my supper. At this, I involuntarily recalled my childhood, when I was left without supper for speaking Russian to my sisters! Soon, my travelling companions also arrived at the Commandant's: Matvey Murav'yov, Aleksandr Bestuzhev, Arbuzov and Tyutchev.[13] Murav'yov I knew intimately, having served with him in the Semyonovskiy Regiment, (we were almost inseparable during the campaigns of 1812–14); the others I did not know.

Having announced the Sovereign's order to dispatch us to Finland, Commandant Sukin advised us to behave meekly during our journey, and to submit in all things to the courier. As we were leaving, Bestuzhev made a speech of gratitude to the Commandant for his conduct towards us, to which Sukin replied, very dryly, that we had nothing for which to thank him, since in all things concerning us he had merely fulfilled his strict duty. We came out of the Commandant's house to find our vehicles and gendarmes waiting at the steps.

We drove quite rapidly through the illuminated streets of Petersburg. When we had passed through the city gates, however, we went extremely slowly. There were forest fires in the vicinity of Petersburg just then, and at day-break the sun pierced through the smoke which was enveloping the city and environs with particles of smut. But at night it was pitch-black and our drivers were continually losing the way—often they would walk and lead the horses by the reins. We took three hours to reach Pargolovo.

The posting house, when we at last drove up to it, was brightly lit and full of people. Among them were my wife and two little sons, my wife's mother, Archpriest Myslovsky, and I. A. Fonvizin, who had also come to say farewell to me. We spent the whole night here, discussing our affairs; and it was agreed that my wife would follow me out to Siberia with the children, her mother accompanying her. After all the anxieties that we had lived through, such a future smiled on us.

Baron A. E. Rozen

In order to relieve the over-full Fortress in St. Petersburg, certain of the prisoners were removed, after some months, to Schlüsselburg, others to strongholds in Finland and on the Island of Åland. The rest stayed in their cells, where supervision was relaxed after the verdicts had been read. The improvements we enjoyed consisted, first, in our being taken one by one, in order, into a vestibule where the windows and the doors were opened, and where we could breathe in the fresh air daily for some twenty minutes. Besides this, we were taken out every ten days or fortnight for a walk along the ramparts. These measures were entirely necessary: the wan and yellow faces of most prisoners bore witness to the poisonous effect of the damp air in the prison. I myself suffered from scurvy; my gums were swollen and quite white. A third, and most important, alleviation of our situation consisted in our being allowed to receive books. I read all Walter Scott's novels with the greatest pleasure—the hours would pass so swiftly that I failed to hear the Fortress clock. Through Sokolov, I shared my books with a fellow-prisoner. Sometimes I would devour four volumes in a day, and spend those hours not in the Fortress but in Kenilworth Castle, in a cloister, in a Scottish tavern or the palaces of Louis XI, Edward, and Elizabeth. When evening came around I would take pleasure in the thought that I should start a new book in the morning. I could only manage light reading now; grave and learned tomes would have been out of the question, with the expectation of a speedy departure for Siberia always before me. Still, I should have liked some books about Siberia; but at this time few had been written on that country. Except for the travel accounts of Pallas, Martynov, and Martus, and of some individuals who had accompanied a mission through Kyakhta to China, no written information was to be had. ...[14]

On July 25th, my wife obtained permission to let me see her new-born son in the Commandant's house. Although in tears, she was composed and firm. My son, aged six weeks, lay on the Commandant's sofa, and his blue eyes and smiling mouth seemed to bring us messages of comfort. My wife asked me about the time and place of our reunion. I begged her not to follow me immediately to Siberia, but to wait until our son could run unaided. With her blessing, she gave me a picture of the Holy Virgin. I saw something sticking to the back of it—it was a thousand roubles in banknotes. This money I sent back, for it was unnecessary. Instead, I asked for a large cloak made of grey material, and lined with wax-cloth. This article of dress was subsequently of enormous use to me in the rain and cold that I had to endure.

When September came, we were allowed to see our relatives an hour a week until we should depart. My wife visited me each Wednesday and my brother, occasionally came too, one of them from Estonia. And in this way seven months passed, in daily expectation of departure for Siberia. A whole year of imprisonment in the casemate gone already, and still I was there waiting! In the winter, vacant cells were filled by Poles who had known of the Secret Society in Russia. So well did these Poles know how to manage their affairs and to conceal the holding of their Polish revolutionary meetings that only a few— Count Moszynski, Krzyzanowski and Janusch Kewitch[15]—were banished to Siberia. Opposite my cell a Colonel Worzel had replaced N. Bobrishchev-Pushkin. He did not know yet of the fate of the rest of those condemned, since, for many months, he had been held in another fortress; he asked me about his neighbours—those incarcerated opposite—and about former acquaintances of his, questions being disguised by being sung in French. He named Pestel', S. Murav'yov, and Volkonsky. I answered him by singing, 'Pendu, pendu, exilé à Nerchinsk.'

After the beginning of 1827 the departures recommenced. My valise was ready. My brother-in-law had come to Petersburg and brought me reindeer skins, out of which my wife made me a coat; the hair was turned towards the outside, and the coat was wadded inside with silk. This made light, warm, and comfortable clothing. As I had another fur besides, I could defy the January cold. On February 3rd, my wife's feast day, we met for the last time inside the Fortress. I was to start on the morrow. I knew this beforehand, for on that day M. M. Naryshkin, Lorer and the two Belyayev brothers were sent off, and after these it had to be my turn.

The Town-Adjutant remained sitting on my bed longer than usual on February 5th, and told me he would fetch me that night for my journey, (the departure of prisoners takes place at about midnight in winter). So I had time to prepare, that is, to commend myself and all those dear to me to the all-loving and Almighty Father. The clock struck eleven; the tune of 'God Save the Tsar' again rang in my ears—I was glad to have heard it for the last time. Sokolov then hastily unbolted the door. I managed to embrace him before the Town-Adjutant came in and took me to the Commandant. N. R. Repin, M. N. Glebov and M. K. Kyukhel'beker followed me, and we embraced. But our short conversation was interrupted by the entrance of Sukin himself. An artillery-man followed him, mysteriously holding up the ends of his cloak in his hands. The Commandant explained that, in accordance with the Sovereign's command, he had to dispatch us to Siberia and, he was grieved to say, in chains. At these last words, the artilleryman let fall the ends of his cloak and the chains meant for us rattled onto the floor. Sukin withdrew then, and the irons were clasped around our ankles, fastened with a lock, and the keys given to the courier who was to accompany us. After this we went out; it was not easy to go down the steps with chains on. I held firmly onto a rail, but one of my comrades stumbled and almost fell. The Town-Major then came up with some red cords used to tie up quills. One end of the cord was attached to a ring which joined the bars and links of the iron chain; the other end was fastened to our girdle, so that we could move quickly and take steps of half an ell. Gendarmes were waiting to place each of us in a sled; and so began our journey of 6,600 versts. The moon and twinkling stars lighted us on our way, and we passed over the Neva at a slow trot. My eyes were fixed on Vasil'yevskiy Island—I knew my wife was praying for me at that moment. We reached the opposite bank near the Marble Palace, turned into Liteynaya, down the officers' row by Nevskiy Prospect, then past Aleksandro-Nevskiy Monastery and on to the Schlüsselburg Gate. But few houses were lighted up; the streets were empty; we only heard the occasional call of the street watch as they walked to and fro, halberd in hand, or now and then met with a guest returning late from some convivial entertainment—it was Butter Week just then[16]. We halted at the bar. The courier entered the guardroom: the postilions meanwhile loosed the tongues of the post-bells, the sentry raised the bar, and the spirited horses rushed onwards. The cold, without a breath of wind, refreshed us. The postilions drove very fast.

6

The Journey

To many individual Decembrists, Siberia seemed a threatening land of endless cold and wilderness. They thought of the approaching journey from the capital to distant Chita, south-east of Lake Baikal, with dread; and for some it was horrific. Mikhail Bestuzhev was practically killed when the carriage in which he was sitting rolled, out of control, down a steep incline. He was caught by his chains in a wheel and dragged 'like Hector behind the chariot of Achilles.'[1] Others were filled with despair at the thought of spending the remainder of their days almost, as S. I. Krivtsov put it, 'at the frontier of an unpeopled realm, where ice and frost, like Herculean pillars, draw the line for man, declaring *non plus ultra.*'[2] And for a few it proved still worse than this: Artamon Murav'yov repeatedly reviled Yermak for ever 'conquering' Siberia, 'the source of anguish and of graves for exiles,' while others went insane.[3]

But very few of the Decembrists gave way to despair entirely. Even during their journey east, indeed, which was itself so great and welcome an improvement on their earlier wretched existence in a cell, much of the steadfastness and courage that would afterwards distinguish their Siberian sojourn was in evidence. On the whole, and notwithstanding the depressing circumstances in which many found themselves (those, for example, like Volkonsky, Rozen, and Yakushkin who had left behind young wives or infant children), the Decembrists did their best to put a good face on the journey. The handful who already knew Siberia, like Shteyngel', who had lived for years in Kamchatka and Irkutsk, or Zavalishin, who had visited the country more than once, kept up their comrades' spirits.

Confidence in the future, as the following three extracts show, was quickly justified. There were abysmal moments, certainly, with hard, corrupt, or pusillanimous officials, and lengthy periods of physical discomfort – sometimes repeated on the journeys from Petrovskiy to the various villages of settlement in 1832–37, as when poor Rozen tossed for days on Lake Baikal. But such unpleasantnesses were entirely compensated for by the impromptu hospitality of ordinary people and of some officials, such as Governor Stepanov of Krasnoyarsk. The impressive countryside, too, most especially by the steep shores of Lake Baikal and to the east, did much to occupy and soothe some exiles' jangled nerves. As the Decembrists came into immediate contact, for the first time, with the country and the people, having crossed the Urals and been parted from their first gendarmes, some of whom had proved most kindly, others hateful, early fears quickly melted away. Even while still within the Province of Tobol'sk, some were already looking on Siberia more favourably than would have seemed conceivable only a month before. As Basargin wrote, 'The further we moved into the country, the more it gained in my eyes. The common people seemed more free, more skilful, even better educated, than our Russian peasants. ... Here, they better appreciate human dignity.'[4]

Released after their long imprisonment, most men were bolstered physically and psychologically by the twin benefits of knowing their eventual destination and of being on their way.[5] Basargin was unwell on leaving St. Petersburg; by Tobol'sk, he had recovered all his strength. Naturally, such a change is well reflected in the tenor of the memoirs, most of which take on a brisker and more cheerful air in passages describing the long journey to Siberia. Once principally concerned with their own chances of survival and inclined, therefore, to dwell upon their private attitudes and secret hopes and dreads, the majority looked outwards on reaching Yaroslavl'. Natural description suddenly looms large in Baron Rozen's, in Basargin's, in the three Bestuzhevs' narratives; all found themselves confronted by wide plains, deep rivers and imposing mountain ranges. Knowledge that they would join their comrades, too, produced its beneficial impact on their mental health, which grew more stable in the winter of 1827 than, broadly speaking, it had been for two whole years. It is as if a gust of pure, fresh air were passing through the memoirs. Never lacking in objectivity where concrete realities are concerned – details of towns, buildings, officials' dress – both Basargin and Yakushkin seem to recover subtler faculties that have been dormant, in abeyance; they grow alive to atmosphere, to quick changes of mood in others, as they were earlier alive only to their own uncertain moods. Seeing different things, they also see them differently or, rather, sense them better.

Not all the Decembrists, however, had such relatively pleasant journeys out to Chita as did Rozen and Basargin. Two groups, in particular, suffered great hardship, one in Siberia, the other on the way. Both are frequently overlooked when the majority's fate is considered. Eight prisoners, whom Nicholas regarded (quite erroneously) as the most dangerous offenders still alive, set out from St. Petersburg on July 13, 1826 – the day of the hangings. These eight were Princes Trubetskoy, Volkonsky and Obolensky, Yakubovich, Artamon Murav'yov, V. L. Davydov and the two Borisov brothers. For them, there was no easy journey[6] and no warm reception: assigned to an iron-ore pit called 'Bliss' (Blagodatsk), they toiled from five to eleven A.M. each day to bring up fifty kilograms of ore. True, the mines of Akatuy where Lunin would expire were worse; but for men unused to hard physical labour, the régime in Blagodatsk was bad enough. Trubetskoy spat blood, Andrey Borisov went insane. Few could withstand what Lunin could endure.[7]

The second special group, which included Lunin and Yakushkin, was that which traveled to Siberia via Finland. Fort-Slava (Swedish: Svensksund), where the latter subsisted for a year, was similar to Sveaborg (Finnish: Suomenlinna) Fortress on Langörn (Susisaari) Island where Lunin and six others were imprisoned: it was silent but for an eternal dripping sound. Feeling that he should do so, the governor-general of Finland, Count A. A. Zakrevsky, visited both prisons. What he said to Yakushkin is not recorded; Lunin he asked if he had 'everything he needed.' 'I am quite satisfied with everything,' apparently came the reply; 'I lack only an umbrella.'[8] Two of the prisoners in Sveaborg, Poggio and P. A. Mukhanov, contracted virulent forms of caries because of the damp air and seeping walls. Both lost teeth and suffered from continual aches in the jaw.[9]

Yakushkin's account of his stay in Fort-Slava is a masterpiece of understatement. His greatest deprivation of all he does not choose to mention: the fact that he was separated from his wife, a beautiful girl of eighteen. Here first, however, are Rozen's recollections of the journey east:

Baron A. E. Rozen

No sooner had our verdict been pronounced than deportation of condemned men to Siberia began. For what reason I cannot say, those sentenced to hard labour were, contrary to the usual practice, put in irons for the journey. Such extra punishment was in general reserved for individuals who, either by some fresh offence or by escape attempts, had incurred a heavier penalty. But as those condemned for this rising were continually guarded by a gendarme, and were transported to Siberia by post-horses in groups of four, escape was quite out of the question. It was exceptional that we travelled by post, and the reasons for it were much questioned. Some thought that it might be to spare us the long march, others that it was to protect us from the people's rage. Many were of the opinion that it was to prevent the possibility of our spreading revolutionary ideas, and that the quickest means of transport was selected for that reason only.

The men were dispatched, as I said, by fours. The fate of the first eight to go,

Princes G. P. Trubetskoy, E. P. Obolensky, and S. G. Volkonsky and B. L. Davydov, A. Murav'yov, A. Yakubovich and the two Borisov brothers, was particularly harsh, for they were settled, one by one, in the northernmost region of Siberia, between Obdorsk and Kolymsk, in a country where the land will not support even corn. There they remained more than a year before being moved to the south, between Beryosov and Yakutsk. At first they were absolutely alone, with not a friendly voice, not a ray of sun to cheer them or to warm them. As might have been expected, such a life drove some of them insane, while others gave themselves up to despair which quickly put an end to their most miserable existence. Prince Shakhovskoy and N. S. Bobrishchev-Pushkin were among the former, while Furman and Shachirev fell victims to the latter fate within two years.[10] M. A. Nazimov lived a year in Nizhnye-Kolymsk. He was conveyed part of the way by pack-horse, part by a small sled drawn by dogs; his night-quarters on this journey must often have been in the open air with snow all around and thirty degrees of frost.[11] In August the dispatching of state prisoners ceased for some months, because it was thought unadvisable to bring all the men condemned to hard labour together in the Nerchinsk Mines, or in any mines, indeed, a rising being feared; nor was the precaution superfluous, as happenings in Nerchinsk have since then demonstrated.[12]

Like couriers, we sped along incessantly, by day and night: to sleep in the sled was almost impossible, nor was it comfortable to pass a night encumbered with fetters and clothing. Only while the horses were being put to could we snatch a few minutes — the swiftness of the journey became hourly more unbearable. Kostroma, Makeyev, Kotoluych, Volga, Glasov, Perin, Kungur, Yekaterinburg and Tyumen' passed before our eyes like apparitions. We spent a night in Glasov, and here, for the first time, our fetters were removed just for a moment while we changed our linen. Having reached this distance from the capital of European Russia, we began to learn the special ways of the courier accompanying us, and to see how splendidly he knew how to line his pocket. From Tikhvin he allowed only four sleds to be harnessed, inviting me to settle in a sled with him and placing my gendarmes in the sleds following us. Thus the posting money for the three horses that should have pulled a fifth sled for a full three thousand versts went straight to him. Nor was he satisfied with this profit: by various tricks the greedy and dishonest fellow brought things to such a pass that even on our journey to Tobol'sk seven horses fell dead to the ground. In vain I remonstrated and complained. And barely was I able to restrain myself when I saw the poor postilion losing his best and most spirited horse in this way, and sobbing as he had to cut the traces. ... However, when we reached the stations kept by Tartars, which became more numerous on the other side of Tyumen', the courier's power was at an end; *they* demanded the sum of money in full, and drove so fast he could say nothing to the drivers. When we approached a station, the drivers would immediately lift us from the sleds, so as not to keep the horses standing, then lead them round and round for an hour to get cool. We arrived at the house of the police-chief of Tobol'sk on the morning of February 22nd.

Now we were travelling along the great high-road which crosses Siberia diagonally. Everything was arranged with a view to the transporting of criminals; every posting-station was a barracks, too. The district to the south of this great road is the most densely populated in the whole country, though the population is so small that towns are from 100 to 400 versts apart from one another. ... Our way led through Tara, Kanish, Kokhylov, Tomsk, Achinsk, Krasnoyarsk, Kansk, Nizhniy Udinsk and Irkutsk—nine towns in a stretch of 3000 versts. From Krasnoyarsk on we were put on wheels, and so drove for several stages. The undulating hills of yellowish red chalk had finally cast off the snow, and now the road was tending to be dusty. The chief street of Krasnoyarsk consisted of well-built stone houses, many of them two stories high; we halted in the market place at the police office, where several local people argued for the right to lodge us.[13]

At length, on March 22nd, we reached Irkutsk. During these last 3000 versts we had travelled at only half the speed of our first 3000, between St. Petersburg and Tobol'sk—not a single horse had been killed by this second half of the journey, and we had stopped for the night, from once to five times a week. Our one day of rest in Irkutsk we were obliged to spend in an ordinary jail. And here we parted with our second guard and received a fresh one, in the person of a cossack under-officer. At the second station beyond Irkutsk we came upon Lake Baikal, which is called the Holy Sea here, and drove across it. The horses went sixty versts without a stop; the drivers had placed some boards on their sleds to form bridges over ice fissures if necessary, but the horses jumped those cracks, which were often several feet wide, with such dexterity that the long sleds barely touched water. Siberian horses are extraordinarily strong and hardy, though small and poorly formed. Without exertion they can cover eighty versts at a stretch.

On the other side of Lake Baikal was the monastery of Podol'skiy. Its wonderful surroundings, which I was afterwards to know so well, now lay beneath a thick cover of snow, the uniformity of which was only broken here by villages, hills, and trees. As we drew near to Chita, we saw Buriats' yurts[14] for the first time. At Klutshchay, the station before Chita, our sleds were changed for coaches; for here there is no snow upon the ground all the year round. The place stands at a great altitude, and so enjoys clear and unclouded skies; if snow does fall occasionally, the wind carries it down into the valleys straightaway. In a certain sense, in fact, it might be said that Chita is too cold for snow: the thermometer may stand at forty degrees of frost, so that quicksilver freezes and only spirit measures can be used.

Before arriving at our destination, however, we met with an adventure. On March 29, Glebov and I were driving in our stage-coach on the last stage of our journey into Chita. The driver was a non-believing Buriat who had very carelessly bound up the harness with string. When we had covered some ten versts, we found ourselves on a mountain top overlooking the small village for which we were then heading. We drove carefully and slowly down the slopes, but suddenly the harness rope snapped, as did the wooden pin securing the front wheels to the carriage. In an instant we were toppled over: Glebov was tossed over the off horse onto the road, while the driver threw himself off to one side. I was left with my right foot caught in the ropes of the side horse, and had to cling to the mane of the middle horse with both hands. The beasts went on at full speed for a good two versts, taking the front axle-tree of the broken carriage with them! Encumbered by my heavy irons, I managed to hold firm only with considerable difficulty until Repin and Kyukhel'beker, who had reached the foot of the mountain before us, saw my perilous situation, stopped the horses and extricated me. My chains prevented me from being able to assist myself in any way. Miraculously I was not hurt, nor were my clothes so much as torn. The carriage was repaired and finally, after an hour, we reached the object of our journey, the prison of Chita.

We were received by the captain of a line regiment, a town-adjutant, a clerk and a few sentries. The captain asked if we had any cash or valuables on us, as this was strictly forbidden. I removed from my neck a silken cord on which there hung a portrait of my wife, a locket containing my parents' hair, and a tiny packet of earth from my native land. When I had handed these things to the captain, he observed a gold ring on my finger and shouted in stentorian tones: 'What's that on your finger?'

'My wedding ring.'

'Off with it.'

I answered, civilly, that I had been allowed to wear it in the Winter Palace and the Fortress, and that wearing such a thing was not forbidden.

'Off with it, and now!' he shouted, still more roughly.

'Take the ring and the finger with it,' I answered calmly. I folded my arms and quietly leaned against a stove. The adjutant gave the captain no time to say a word, but whispered something in his ear, gathered our valuables together and went off.

I. D. Yakushkin

For us, the journey from Petersburg to our place of confinement was a pleasant drive. After our long incarceration we enjoyed ourselves, breathing fresh air all the day long and seeing before us the somewhat wild but also sublime Finnish countryside. On arrival at each station, lively conversation among ourselves also had its special charm. And here there were no bolts or walls dividing us, and neither town-majors nor adjutants to eavesdrop. Our courier, Vorob'yov, behaved splendidly towards us, and when we talked among ourselves too loudly in Russian, would say solemnly, 'Parlay fransay, moosyoo.' He feared we might be overheard and reported to Petersburg. At one station, where we were eating in a private room, a very warm discussion started up between myself and Bestuzhev[15] on the subject of our rising. I tried to prove to him that our unsoundness had arisen from impatience—that our true vocation had been to form the foundation of a great building, that is, to work underground and be seen by nobody; but that we had wanted to be in sight of everyone, and to comprise the cornice. 'So you fell off,' said our courier, who was standing behind me and whose presence we had totally forgotten. So pointed was his intervention that we all burst out laughing.

When we reached Rochensal'm,[16] Vorob'yov handed us over to the commandant, Colonel Kul'man [Kuhlmann]; within ninety minutes, we had set off for the shore escorted by a small detachment of soldiers and Kul'man himself. Lieutenant Khoruzhenko, in charge of this detachment, was in full-dress uniform. A six-oared launch was waiting for us at the shore, and we set out to sea in it. Our voyage lasted more than an hour, but at last we could make out in the distance a huge round tower that, as it were, sprang from the water. This was the fort known as Fort-Slava, which Field-Marshal Suvorov built[17] and in which cells had been prepared for us. Its aspect was a gloomy one and augured nothing good.

We were placed one to a cell, and locked in. Each cell, besides a Russian stove, had two small windows. In front of these, on the outside, boards had been placed to make a shield especially designed for us on the orders of Engineering General Opperman. By the wall stood a straw bed, a table and, to complete the cell's furnishing, a few chairs. It was dark and damp in my new abode.

At first we were kept strictly under lock and key and let out only for short intervals — and then singly — to walk in the courtyard. Vasiliy Gerasimovich Khoruzhenko, the garrison artillery lieutenant commanding the detachment that now formed our special guard, was also our immediate chief; and this he gave us to understand each time he visited us. It was at first as if he were afraid of us. Later, however, when he was sure that we were quiet characters, he grew more amenable. Sometimes he would bring us all together and drink tea with us and tell us various stories of his own past life.

When it grew colder and the stoves were stoked, it became obvious that they smoked and that, when the pipe was closed, the cells would fill with insufferable fumes. One night a sentinel heard an unusual noise in Bestuzhev's cell and, thinking that Bestuzhev was in communion with the powers of darkness, ran off in fright and told an under-officer that all was not well with his watch. The under-officer, in turn, informed an officer, and the officer, with a detachment, went up to the cell where the noise had been heard. For some time no one could bring himself to open the door, but when they did they saw Bestuzhev lying on the floor unconscious; he had been poisoned by the charcoal fumes. After this, we were practically never locked up during the day.

As to books, we had precious few. Murav'yov had brought with him a French Bible and Sallust in a French translation[18] and I had only managed to seize up a copy of Montaigne, but Bestuzhev, very fortunately, had two volumes of old English periodicals — one of *The Rambler*, the other of *Gertner*.[19]

Helped by Bestuzhev, Murav'yov and I began to study English. Khoruzhenko's library consisted of a part of *Chet'i-Miney* and *The Boy By The Stream*, both of which he decided to give us to read.[20] Never, however, did he resolve to get books for us from Rochensal'm. But to make up for this he handed over to us, wholly unexpectedly, a note book written in a beautiful French hand and containing the last part of *Childe-Harold*. This note book had been sent to us by two women living in Rochensal'm, Madame Chebysheva and her sister. Such a gesture on their part deeply affected us and we fully appreciated it. Only women, and women of true feeling, could so have understood our situation and so admirably found a way to express their sympathy for us.

Towards the year's end our supplies of tea, sugar, and tobacco were exhausted. Little remained of the 100 roubles given to me by my wife, and even that was needed for laundry and other necessary expenses. At this time they began occasionally to lock us up. More bustle than usual was apparent and our officer, summoning his detachment, began to drill it every day. We found out that Zakrevsky, the Governor-General of Finland, was expected soon.[21] And two weeks before the new year, he came. To Murav'yov he personally handed a parcel from his sister, Bibikova; to Bestuzhev he gave tea, sugar, and tobacco, in gratitude, one may suppose, for *Polyarnaya zvezda* which Ryleyev and Bestuzhev used to send him; and to me he gave a pair of bear–skin boots — a present from my mother-in-law. In short, he was most kind to us all. (I afterwards discovered that these boots had been sent as a hint that we should not be staying long in Fort-Slava; but we remained there another eleven months after Zakrevsky's first visit.) The visit itself was useful to us in several respects. Seeing Zakrevsky's own attentiveness towards us, our officer and Commandant Kul'man also grew somewhat more attentive. Kul'man was not an evil man, but a completely worthless one: obliged to visit us once or twice a month, he never made enquiries as to how we were treated — and as we never complained to him of anything, he was content with us.

Zakrevsky came again in the summer of 1827 and asked Kul'man to ascertain if we would care to remain in the fort for the whole term to which we had been sentenced. Not one of us thought of accepting such a proposal. True, we did not know what would await us in Siberia, but here we were experiencing all the bitterness of close confinement; the uncertainty of the future alarmed us not at all.

At last our turn came round. One fine evening in early November[22] we were ferried across Fort-Slava to Rochensal'm, to find, on our arrival there, that small carts with two horses, gendarmes and a courier were standing in front of the Commandant's house. Kul'man received us very civilly and read us the Sovereign's orders with tears in his eyes: he was to put us in irons and send us to Siberia. At this, fetters were placed on us, though by no means such heavy ones as I had worn in the Alekseyev Ravelin. Our courier, Miller, sat in a cart with me and gave me the good news that I would see my family in Yaroslavl'. As we were driving out of Rochensal'm we saw two ladies dressed in black, who were blessing us on our journey from a distance. These, I think, must have been those two good souls who had shown us such sympathy when we were in Fort-Slava.

We passed through Petersburg by night. At Schlüsselburg our courier was obliged to halt for several hours because Arbuzov had been so jolted about that he could barely stand on his legs. In the posting house one stage before Lake Ladoga we were met by two gentlemen; one of them wore an official's frock-coat and our courier, taking him for the district police officer, put us in a private room with a gendarme at the door; the other gentleman, so it transpired, was our Arbuzov's brother. The good Miller acceded to our requests and allowed the brothers to meet; and it was moving to see their mutual affection. Arbuzov the landowner had brought with him pasties, roast game and several bottles of wine. After dinner he went on exchanging kind words with his brother; but his kindness took no more concrete form and I decided, having taken him aside, to ask him if he had some money for his brother. He replied that he had brought nothing because he had no money at the time; to which I answered resolutely that if he really loved his brother he should go with us to Ladoga, borrow a couple of thousand there and give them to Arbuzov. The fellow started to assure me that most certainly he would catch up with us in Ladoga — but first he had to see his wife and ascertain whether or not they *did* have anything at home. All this together struck me as detestable. Now that his brother had been stripped of all status and rights by the Special Supreme Court, this individual held his estate; he had known in good time that his brother would be sent off to Siberia, and had come to meet him with nothing but tender embraces and a dutiful tear. He did not come to Ladoga, nor did he write or send assistance to his brother for ten years, though he then began to write him tender letters and to send him out a reasonable allowance.

On November 11th we reached Yaroslavl'. The courier presented me to the Governor, who informed me that I had permission to see my family. We went to them directly from the Governor's. Seeing me in chains, my wife, her mother, and everyone present met me in tears; but I managed to break through their melancholy mood by making some joke or other; there was no time for weeping, and we joyfully embraced after a long, burdensome separation. I found out that my wife and her mother and children had received permission to see me a year before, but that they had not been told when I should be taken through Yaroslavl'. Potapov, general on duty, always knew when couriers were wanted to convey us from our fortresses to Siberia and always told my mother-in-law; but which of us was to be taken off even he did not know in advance. For this reason my family had come to Yaroslavl' from Moscow several times, the first time spending a whole month there in wearisome waiting. Even this last time they had been waiting three weeks for me. Hardly had we entered a room and settled down than the Governor himself came in to tell my wife that I should be in Yaroslavl' for six hours. After this, he very kindly went off and left us alone. When we had all calmed down a little, I asked my wife's mother if she proposed to go with my wife and children to Sibera. Shedding tears, she told me she had had a definite refusal when she had sought permission to do so. My wife, also in tears, then told me that she would herself unfailingly follow me out, but that she would not be allowed to bring the children with her. All this, released on me so unexpectedly, so staggered me that for some minutes I could not say a word. But time was flying by, and I knew that some decision must be made. That a life for us together, that is, for my wife and myself, would always be marvellous

I could not doubt; I also understood that, left without me, even with her own family who loved her deeply, my wife would be in an embarrassing and awkward situation. Yet on the other hand, their mother's care was vital to our little children. I was convinced, moreover, that, despite her youthfulness, only my wife could properly direct our sons' upbringing; I resolved to ask her never, in any circumstance, to part with them. She resisted my request at length, but finally gave me her word to carry out my wish. I felt easier.

It was on November 22nd that we arrived in Irkutsk, which we saw, as we approached it, through a thick mist drifting over the river. There were thirty-two degrees of frost that day, we discovered, but still the Angara had not frozen over, so we crossed it by ferry. We were immediately taken to the city jail, where we were met by Pirozhkov, a special police officer acting as chief of the city police. For us, they had cleaned up a huge room in which women had been kept before.

And here it was that we first found out the place to which we were being sent: we were to be dispatched to the other side of Baikal, Pirozhkov told us, to Chita. In Chita, he attempted to convince us, all our possessions would be taken from us, and so we would be 'well advised' to dispose of them while in Irkutsk. We none of us believed him, and it was a good thing that we did not.

While our room was being cleaned, we saw Yushnevsky[23] going by under guard. So thin had he become that I could scarcely recognize him. We embraced warmly and were allowed to drink tea together that evening. Yushnevsky told me, among other things, that he had also been assured that all his things would be removed from him, to avoid which he had given many of them to his courier. His companions were Spiridov, Pestov and Andreyevich. They had been halted here to give the government a chance to organize their journey round the sea.[24]

Also in Irkutsk we came upon Matvey Murav'yov and Aleksandr Bestuzhev; both were at liberty, waiting to be sent down the Lena to Yakutsk. Bestuzhev sent me a copy of *The Gypsies*, and it was with real pleasure that I read that latest work by Pushkin. One evening we were taken to a bath-house, where we were courteously and dexterously attended to by men in chains. These were serious offenders with brands on their forehead — and some without nostrils — being held in the jail with us. Nor was such intimacy with them without benefit to me: instead of repugnance, which society endeavours to inspire towards those cast out from itself by its established institutions and its prejudices, I could not help feeling a certain sympathy with these unfortunates. Into this bath-house, to my absolute amazement, walked Aleksandr Bestuzhev, covered in soap; I leapt from a bench and embraced him.

Because there were heavy frosts it was hoped that Baikal would soon freeze over; in that case, we should be sent across on the ice. But then fairly mild weather set in, so Arbuzov, Tyutchev and I were dispatched, in the company of three cossacks and a cossack officer, down the road around the 'sea.' We arrived on the same day at Kultuk, a small settlement by the shore, and there we passed the night. Most of the inhabitants of this settlement live by hunting and fishing, and here it was that I ate roast *kabarga*[25] for the first time. The situation of Kultuk is delightful. The view of Baikal fringed by mountains is truly beautiful, and it struck me at the time that to be a settler here, and to live in that remote spot with one's family, would be the height of happiness.

Next day, the officer removed our fetters and we set off on our long journey on horseback. The officer staying behind to lay in a supply of vodka, the cossacks, too, were sent away from us, and for a while it was as though we were at liberty. The weather was not cold. After lengthy captivity, it is a specially delightful feeling to have a horse beneath one, which one can guide according to one's will, and not to have spies around one! As we went up a hill, the view of Baikal became wider, and stretched away into the distance. Just before dusk we reached the first station beyond Kultuk where, probably, we should have bedded down had our popular officer not exchanged angry words with a house servant of Burnashev, former head of the Nerchinsk mines. After this incident, our officer gave orders for the horses to be saddled, and we set off again. It was already night when we crossed over the pass of Khamar-Daban, and very late when, tired, we reached a station. Arbuzov was carried into a room. The journey on horseback had so broken him that he could not stand on his feet.

Next morning, we did not start on our way very early. In all, we covered some 200 versts on horseback, and over all that distance there was not a settlement of any kind. The horses, fodder for which had to be brought from far away, and the Buriat guides, too, remained at these stations only as long as there was no communication across Baikal by ice. The road through Khamar-Daban, and all across this mountainous and uninhabited terrain, was of remarkable construction. Wherever it passed by precipices, there were barriers; over every stream and torrent a bridge had been carefully built; even certain steep inclines had been levelled. The road was one of many monuments to Treskin's ad hoc but sometimes also reasonable administration.[26]

After this ride on horseback, our chains were put back on us and we travelled by sled, sometimes in areas where there was practically no snow. We were given a hearty welcome in Klyuchi, an Old Believers' settlement; while we drank tea and later had supper, many women and men came by to look at us and chat about what was going on in Russia at the time. That night we spent at Tarbagatay, also a settlement of Old Believers.

I had said to our officer earlier that I should like to see Aleksandr Murav'yov when we passed through Verkhnyeudinsk. During our night in Tarbagatay, this officer woke me, removed my irons and led me stealthily out of the room. Then he told me I should see Murav'yov and took me to Zaigrayev, whom numerous travellers describing Transbaikalia have mentioned. Zaigrayev was a smart and very well-to-do peasant. In his sitting-room there was mahogany furniture with an English clock in one corner, and on a table, when we entered, lay newspapers from Moscow; but instead of Murav'yov I found Princess Varvara Mikhaylovna Shakhovskaya.[27] She had come under the pretext of looking for a wet-nurse for her sister, but hoped to meet Mukhanov, to whom she was related and whom she knew extremely well. I had hardly known her before this, but now took up with her as if we had known one another for ages. She told me much that I did not know about my comrades.

Soon after the hearing of our case, Artamon Murav'yov, Davydov, Obolensky and Yakubovich had been sent to Siberia. Trubetskoy, Volkonsky and the two Borisovs were sent off after them. The day before his departure, Trubetskoy had been spitting blood in plate-fulls — a fact which did not, however, prevent his being dispatched. On arriving in Irkutsk, the group were placed in the factories. Trubetskoy's wife then came out to join him. Having settled with difficulty into the Nikolayevskiy distillery, Trubetskoy hoped that they would be left there to live for a while together; but they were not long left together. At the time of the coronation, Lavinsky sent a special messenger ordering all eight comrades to Irkutsk, from where they were immediately dispatched across Baikal and to the Nerchinsk mines. Every effort was made to detain Princess Trubetskaya in Irkutsk, and even to persuade her to return to Russia; but she, overcoming all obstacles by her decisiveness, followed her husband to the Blagodatskiy Mine, where they met; but still the pair were not to live together.[28] Burnashev, head of the Nerchinsk mines, treated our comrades tolerably brutally, regretting that his orders obliged him to care for the health of state prisoners; still, he sent them every day into the pits, to mine for ore with all the other convicts.

Princess Shakhovskaya's maid boiled up some coffee for my officer, and poured a little rum into it. So *beneficently* did this beverage act on the cossack that he several times failed to get up from his chair, a circumstance that made it possible for me to talk all through the night with the princess. But I waited in vain, when we passed through Verkhnyeudinsk, for Aleksandr Murav'yov to come out and greet us. From Verkhnyeudinsk we travelled on by sled, finally reaching Chita on December 24th. We were placed in a small casemate. Soon after those sent off to hard labour following their sentencing, all those reduced to the ranks and condemned to live in settlements were sent out to Siberia. Such were the places that had been allotted them to settle in that the situation of the latter was exceedingly unenviable—and for a few, evil in the extreme. For they were all sent to the northernmost regions of Siberia: Nikolay Bobrishchev-Pushkin and Shakhovskoy were sent off to Yeniseysk, where they both went mad. Chizhov was ordered to Gizhiga, and Nazimov to Srednye-Kolymsk, which consisted of a few cossacks' yurts. The cossacks, who had had instructions to keep Nazimov under strict surveillance, but at the same time to protect his health, did not know what to do with him; so they confined him in one of their yurts and sent a messenger into Yakutsk to say that Nazimov was ill and that they did not know what to feed him—they themselves ate dried fish all winter. Some time having elapsed, permission was accorded to transfer Nazimov to a certain modest settlement on the River Lena, where he was, in fact, a little better off; but in Srednye-Kolymsk he had contracted severe rheumatic pains in his arms and legs, of which he could never again entirely rid himself.[29] Chizhov was similarly moved from Gizhiga to another spot; and all the others sentenced in the eighth category were placed in regions most uncomfortable for human habitation.

The very day of our arrival in Chita was Christmas Eve, and in the evening we were all led from our small casemate, escorted by soldiers with rifles and bayonets, into a large one where a priest and his attendants conducted Vespers for us. And here I had the pleasure of embracing many old friends and acquaintances dear to me. Some sixty men were brought into the large casemate. All wore chains that were removed only when they went out to the bathhouse or to take Communion. Everything rattled and moved, but no one was depressed and it was somehow as though we were at a solemn feast. Only Nikita Murav'yov was ill and suffered cruelly in body and in soul: he had left three small children, a boy and two girls, at his mother's in Moscow, and had recently heard that the boy had died. In his grievous situation, poor Nikita could not even share his sorrow with his wife, who had set out for Siberia immediately after him. When I arrived in Chita, Princesses Trubetskaya and Volkonskaya and Mesdames Murav'yova, Naryshkina, Ental'tseva and Davydova were there already. All had left their relatives and all those near to them, but Murav'yova and Princess Volkonskaya had parted from their own small children, possibly forever, leaving for Siberia with the firm desire to share their husbands' fates and with the hope of living with them always. But for them even that modest hope was not to be realized: arriving in Chita they were allowed to see their husbands only twice a week, and never for more than a few hours on each occasion. Every time, they would walk stealthily up to the palisade, to see their husbands and exchange a few words with them; but even this solace was not always granted them, for the sentries had strict orders to allow no one to walk up to the jail, and it happened not infrequently that a sentry doing duty would chase a female visitor away, brandishing a rifle-butt.

Three days after us, Pushchin, Poggio, and Mukhanov arrived in Chita, and two days after that a courier brought in Vadkovsky. All four were put in the same room with us, and when we seven lay down on our plank-beds for the night, each one of us had less than an *arshin's* breadth; but this did not concern us then at all. We knew that the courier who had brought Vadkovsky in was to take someone away from Chita; but precisely whom, and to where, was unknown for several days. In the end he took Kornilovich away, it was said to Peter-and-Paul Fortress, whence he was sent off to the Caucasus and died.[30]

Prince Yevgeniy Petrovich Obolensky   1797–1865

Only on one occasion was exhausting and sustained physical toil demanded of the exiles. In Finnish fortresses, as in St. Petersburg, the prisoners' sufferings were first and foremost psychological; their physical discomfort was no more than that – discomfort. Although sometimes galling and acute, it was a consequence of deprivation, lack of space and evil air, not of exhausting labour. Many, indeed, would happily have worked; idleness proved no less debilitating and far more insidious than toil. In Chita and Petrovskiy Zavod also, after 1827, the exiles' sufferings proved to be principally emotional. Work on the 'Devil's Ditch' and with small hand-mills troubled only the least healthy; and their share was done by others. Still there was time enough for chess and conversation. But for the group of eight who left the capital in July 1826, and were hurried out directly to Siberia, matters were different. At Usol'ye, Nikolayevskiy and in the Aleksandrovskiy distillery, those pioneers of the Decembrist exiles found themselves required to work as they had never worked before. For one short period in particular, when General Burnashev's assistant, Rik (Rieck), arrived at Usol'ye to tighten surveillance over Yakubovich and Obolensky, the situation was a bleak one for that pair. They were locked in their rooms for eighteen hours each day. Protest having proved vain, they went on hunger strike, which Rik interpreted as mutiny. And but for the arrival of Burnashev, and the speedy and indignant intervention of Princesses Trubetskaya and Volkonskaya, the case might well have taken an extremely ugly turn. It was not until September 1827 that the eight men of the first party learnt of their imminent departure for the entrepôt and trading post of Chita, where some eighty of their comrades were already expiating earlier crimes.

Here, now, is Obolensky's fine account of life as a Siberian salt-miner.

E. P. Obolensky

Not for long did we enjoy cordial hospitality in Irkutsk; we—that is, Yakubovich and I—were appointed to a salt mine sixty versts out of that town, known as Usol'ye. Murav'yov and Davydov were sent to the Aleksandrovskiy distillery. We parted in the hope of meeting once again in the most auspicious circumstances; Yakubovich and I arrived in the place appointed for us on August 30th. Trubetskoy, Volkonsky and the two Borisov brothers, Pyotr and Andrey Ivanovich, came into Irkutsk after us; the former pair were sent to Nikolayevskiy, the latter to the Aleksandrovskiy distillery.

We were received in the mine office, on arriving there; the money that we had with us was taken, and we were led off to the dwelling of a widow in whose only little room we were to settle. She herself lived in a hut. The head of the salt mine, Colonel of Engineers Kryukov, was not at the mine at that time, so no special arrangements were made for us. We enjoyed our freedom, albeit freedom limited by police surveillance—at least it was untrammelled by any formal restrictions. From time to time we would be visited by the chief of police in the mine, constable Skuratov, who was the only person with whom we had official contact. With the ordinary folk living around the mine, our relations were confined to the buying of supplies and paying for the simple services which they performed for us. Unseen police surveillance followed us continuously and often, in the middle of a tête-à-tête with Yakubovich, I would hear the cautious steps of a police agent approaching the closed shutters, and through a chink in them not infrequently we would observe his eye. But in spite of all police measures, the news soon reached us that Princess Trubetskaya had arrived in Irkutsk; and there could be no doubting the veracity of this, for no one in Usol'ye even knew of the princess' existence, so to have invented the news of her arrival would have been impossible. This was, I think, two weeks after our arrival in the mine. Also towards this time arrived the long-awaited chief of mining, Kryukov, who was to make final arrangements with regard to our placement and work there. He received us not just kindly but with sympathy that deeply touched us. ... Dismissing us, the colonel told us he was setting us to work only for form's sake, that we could rest easy, and that we need fear no oppression whatsoever. We went home calm and happy on the score of the future awaiting us; sometimes we had involuntarily been troubled by the thought that we might be employed in that same work which simple exile-convicts performed. I myself saw them returning from their toil, covered from head to foot in saline crystals which had dried out in their hair, on their clothing, on their beards—they worked without shirts. Each pair of workers had to pour a certain quantity of tubs of salty liquid from a saline spring into the saltworks; it was not good to see. ... Skuratov brought us two state issue axes the day after our meeting with the chief, and announced that we were appointed woodcutters and that a place would be allotted to us where we could chop up firewood to the quantity fixed for each worker, according to mine regulations. This was said aloud. In a whisper he informed us we could go there for a stroll, and that our task would be performed without our help. ...

But now it is time to touch on the remarkable personality that was Princess Katerina Ivanova, *née* Countess Laval'. Princess Trubetskaya's father settled among us at the time of the French Revolution, having married Aleksandra Grigor'yevna Kozitskaya and, together with this latter's hand, received a rich inheritance which gave his house that lustre in which luxury serves only as a necessary appurtenance and embellishment to refined taste and high culture. Brought up amidst great luxury, Katerina Ivanovna found herself from her earliest years the object of the care and the attention both of her father, who loved her dearly, and of her mother and her other relatives. It was in 1820, I believe, and she was in Paris with her mother, when Prince Sergey Petrovich Trubetskoy arrived there, accompanying his ailing cousin the Princess Kurakina; when he had made the acquaintance of Countess Laval', he soon made friends with Katerina Ivanovna, and offered her his hand and heart; and so was fixed their fate which, afterwards, so markedly determined Katerina's lofty character, and which, among all the vicissitudes of fortune, established their family happiness on such durable foundations as nothing later could shake. Because of my dealings with the Society, I was close to Prince Sergey Petrovich. I saw Katerina Ivanovna for the first time in 1821, and never afterwards did my friendship or deep respect for her alter. ... The occurrence of December 14th and the sending of Prince Sergey Petrovich to Siberia merely occasioned a development of those inner forces with which she was endowed, and which she knew so well how to employ in reaching the exalted aim of executing her conjugal duty towards him, with whom she was united by eternal bonds that nothing could destroy. She asked, as a high favour, permission to follow her husband and to share his fate; she received the sovereign permission and, despite the urgings of her mother, who did not wish to let her go, set off on the far journey in the company of Count Laval''s secretary, the Frenchman M. Vaucher. She had not come to within a hundred versts of Krasnoyarsk before her carriage broke, and could not be repaired. The Princess did not hesitate for long, but mounted a stage-wagon and so arrived in Krasnoyarsk, from where she sent back a springless carriage that she purchased for her travelling companion, who could not bear travel by wagon and had stayed in a station. Finally reunited with her husband at Nikolayevskiy Zavod, she never left us thereafter and was, throughout our life together, our Guardian Angel. It is hard to express what the ladies, companions to their husbands, were for us; one might justly call them sisters of mercy. They cared for us like close relations, and always and everywhere their presence instilled in us courage and inner strength. It is not possible to state in words the solace for which we were indebted to them. Following Princess Trubetskaya came Princess

Mar'ya Nikolayevna Volkonskaya, a daughter of Nikolay Nikolayevich Rayevsky, celebrated in the patriotic wars. At the time of which I am speaking she was not yet in Irkutsk; but let us return to my interrupted tale.

Our days in the mine passed monotonously: every morning, Yakubovich and I went to our customary work, and I eventually acquired such skill in hewing that I could chop up a quarter of a *sazhen* in one day;[31] at three we would return to our room, have a substantial, though not sumptuous, dinner, and pass the evening either talking or in playing chess. In comparison with what I had expected we were then so comfortable that I was quite unable to believe that our position would not alter for the worse. My comrade was of the opposite opinion and lived in the firm conviction that, when the coronation occurred (it was fixed for August 22nd,) a manifesto would follow concerning our return to Russia. Each of us persisted in his view, and our discussions were enlivened both by my comrade's tales of his fighting life in the Caucasus and by our recollections of the recent past. In this way our days were flowing by when suddenly, on the evening of October 5th, as we were playing chess, in comes Constable Skuratov and tells us to get ready for a journey and announces that we are ordered to be brought into Irkutsk! My comrade's first thought was that a manifesto had been sent by courier, and that we were summoned to Irkutsk to be told of the sovereign pardon. I said nothing, but thought the opposite, and started to pack everything that could be put into our suitcases — in short, everything but the kitchen utensils of the house. My comrade had no wish at all to take anything with him, being quite sure that he could soon call in at Usol'ye on his return journey, and more conveniently and easily take everything that then seemed necessary for the journey. I went about my business silently. I packed our suitcases, but failed completely to persuade my comrade to take the twenty-five roubles in coins that were to stay in our landlady's hands until our supposed return. Troikas arrived; two cossacks sat with each of us and Constable Skuratov accompanied us in a third troika. I silently pointed out our escort to Yakubovich; but he waved his hand and, saying: 'Well, you'll hear, then you'll believe,' mounted the foremost troika and was off. So we continued on our journey to Irkutsk ... and there we learnt the real reason for our coming: *they were sending us to the Nerchinsk mines!*

We were treated to tea and breakfast; meanwhile, troikas for our further journey were already waiting. Looking out of a little window at this moment, I saw a lady whom I did not know who, having come into the courtyard, jumped off a droshky and was making enquiries of some kind of the cossacks who surrounded her. I knew from Sergey Petrovich that Katerina Ivanovna was in Irkutsk, and guessed that this unknown lady was asking about him. Having hurriedly run down a staircase, I ran up to her. It was Princess Shakhovskaya,[32] who had arrived with her sister, the wife of Aleksandr Nikolayevich Murav'yov; he had been sent to live in the town of Verkhnyeudinsk. Her first question was: 'Is Sergey Petrovich here?' On my affirmative reply, she said to me: 'Katerina Ivanovna is following me. She wants to see her husband without fail before he leaves; tell him that.' But the authorities did not mean to allow this meeting, and hurried us to leave; we lingered for as long as possible, but were obliged at last to mount the vehicles assigned to us. The horses started off; and in that instant I saw Katerina Ivanovna, who had arrived in a cab and managed to jump off and shout to her husband! In the twinkling of an eye, Sergey Petrovich leapt out of the vehicle and was in the arms of his wife; for a long time was this warm embrace prolonged, and tears flowed from the eyes of them both. Bustling around them, the chief of city police asked them to separate; but his requests were vain. His words came to their hearing, but their sense was quite incomprehensible to them. At last, however, the final 'farewell' was said, and the troikas whisked us off again with redoubled speed. Princess Trubetskaya remained in ignorance as to her husband's fate. No one had wanted to tell her the truth about our final destination; but once having firmly resolved to follow her husband and to share his fate no matter how bitter and hard, the princess approached the authorities with the request that she be given leave to do so. For a long time they wearied her with various evasive answers; and during this time Princess Mar'ya Nikolayevna Volkonskaya arrived in Irkutsk. The two were united in the thought of joining their husbands, and, drawing back before no threats or entreaties, acted in one and the same decisive spirit. Finally, the authorities represented to them the position of the wives of exile-convicts and the rules to which they would be subjecting themselves in the mines. First, they would have to relinquish those rights which were theirs by virtue of their station. Second, they could neither send nor receive letters or money, save through the mine authorities. Furthermore, meetings with their husbands would be granted them only at the discretion of those same authorities, and in that place that might be assigned to them. To these rules it was added orally that the mine authorities could even demand personal service of them— floor-washing, for example, or something like it. Having read through the conditions, Katerina Ivanovna and Mar'ya Nikolayevna did not hesitate to ratify them with their signatures; thus the authorities were finally obliged to give their consent and to allow them to proceed after their husbands without hindrance to the Nerchinsk mines.

But while *these* negotiations were continuing we had long before crossed over Lake Baikal on a little, low, two-masted vessel, the 'Yermak.' While by the lakeshore still, we were joined by our other comrades: Murav'yov, Davydov and the two Borisov brothers. And thus, in seven troikas, we were rushed from the Posol'skiy monastery[33] along the great Nerchinsk high road, accompanied by two cossack officers. ...

We soon arrived at the place allotted to us — the Blagodatskiy Mine, and the troikas stopped by the barrack that had been prepared for us to live in. This was a building seven *sazhens* wide. It was formed of two huts, the first one from the entrance being for our sentinels, the second one for us. In our hut, to the left as one went in, stood a massive Russian stove; to the right, along the whole length of the hut, had been built three store-rooms, separated from each other by partitions made of boards. Onto the wall facing the door a third room had been built, a room knocked together from planks. Two steps led to the first three store-rooms, each of which had a door. The first two store-rooms measured three and a little *arshins*[34] in length, and some two *arshins* in breadth; the last store-room was of the same length, but four *arshins* across. We quickly settled in: Davydov and Yakubovich each occupied a separate store-room, while Trubetskoy and I settled into the third. Trubetskoy had his plank-bed lengthwise; mine was arranged so that half of my body lay under his bed while the other half abutted on the door. Volkonsky occupied the other side of the building, opposite Trubetskoy. Murav'yov and the two Borisovs arranged themselves in similar style in their boarded room. Our guard was formed by an engineering under-officer and three privates, who kept watch over us continuously throughout the time that we spent in Blagodatskiy Mine. This guard was an internal one; the same sentries prepared our food, set the samovar, served us and shortly came to like us, becoming the most useful of assistants to us.

We were given three days' rest; the money that we had on us was taken, and arrangements were so made that we could buy all the provisions that we needed with money issued to us, and might be aware of what we spent. It turned out that there was very little money; each man gave up from his own funds what he chose, and nobody demanded more than had been indicated by us. In the course of these three days, the Head of the Nerchinsk mines, *Berg-Hauptmann*[35] Timofey Stepanovich Burnashev, arrived to look us over. In his words he was a little rough, but in his orders could be sensed his wish to improve our situation, burdening us with no extra load. Soon, the time arrived for us to start our work; we were informed, the day before, that we were to be ready for it early in the morning. At five o'clock next day the head miner arrived at our barrack, together with the miners who would be our comrades. A roll call began: 'Trubetskoy?' Answer: 'Here.' Yefim Vasil'yev?' And Trubetskoy went off with Yefim Vasil'yev. 'Obolensky?' 'Here.' 'Nikolay Belov?' And we two went off in the same direction. In this way, we were all distributed to different pits; each pair was issued with a tallow candle, a pick was placed in my hand, a hammer in my comrade's, and we descended into the pit and came to our place of work. The work was not onerous; it is generally fairly warm below ground, but when it did prove necessary to warm up I would take a hammer and quickly grow warm. A bell announced the end of work at eleven o'clock, and we returned to our barrack; then dinner preparations would begin. We elected Yakubovich our artel representative, since he had most experience in the military kitchen department. In general, we were completely at liberty inside our barrack. The doors were open; we had dinner, drank tea, and ate supper together. And a great comfort it proved for us to be together: that circle in which we had, for so many years, been used to exchange feelings and thoughts was now transferred from Petersburg mansions to our miserable barrack; we drew closer and yet closer to each other, and our common grief still further reinforced the ties of friendship that united us. ...

Soon, however, there arrived an order on the subject of our daily labours underground that put an end to our normal, comfortable situation, and was a cause of grave alarm — alarm which found an echo in the hearts of our female custodians. A special engineering officer, young Rik (Rieck), was appointed to us, probably to keep closer surveillance over us. We foresaw no change in our situation; but when dinner was over, or evening tea, we were ordered by Mr. Rik to go to our store-rooms; we were to remain locked up there all the time except when we were working, nor were we to presume to leave our room either for dinner or for supper; we should receive both meals, and tea, from sentries who would bring the food into our store-rooms! We showed Mr. Rik our store-rooms, and told him it would be impossible for us to endure the close malignant air, locked up in them for eighteen hours; nobody's health could stand that quite unnatural situation. No arguments produced any effect on Mr. Rik. Thinking our words signified our determination not to submit to his instructions, he shouted to the soldiers: 'Seize them!' And the soldiers were indeed prepared to carry out the order; but they knew us, so we went into our cells, obeying, without demur, the instruction given. And the soldiers looked at us in silence. When Mr. Rik had left, we began to consider what to do. What we had said to him we were convinced of fully: it seemed to us and, indeed, it *was* impossible to tolerate the evil air in the cramped space in which we found ourselves, where we could adopt no other position than that of sitting or lying. When Trubetskoy stood up he had to bend in order not to touch the ceiling with his head. After lengthy discussions, the idea occurred to one of us — I forget to whom — to take no food until the conditions of our confinement should be changed. It was unanimously decided to act on that proposal; and that same evening we refused the supper that was offered us. Next day we were sent off to work having drunk no tea; returning, we refused our dinner, and so passed our first twenty-four hours without food—nor did we even drink the water that was offered us. The same thing was repeated for the next twenty-four hours. I cannot recall if it was on this second day of our voluntary fast or on the third that we were not summoned to work. We were informed, instead, that the Chief, Mr. Burnashev, was expected. We prepared ourselves for a stormy meeting. ...

A stormy interview it proved: Burnashev charged the prisoners with mutiny (*bunt*). The prisoners calmly replied that a policy of abstinence was hardly rioting; that their grievance was against Rik, not himself; and that, in all events, to eat in such conditions was 'unnatural.' Burnashev spoke with all his well-born convicts , two by two. Finally, after two days, the store-room doors were all unlocked, and the earlier routine restored.

Our work went on in the same way, the only change occurring in the order of our days being that husbands now received permission to meet their wives in the wives' quarters, to which they were conducted by an escort who kept watch throughout the meeting. This change was a most pleasant one for our ladies. Spring came, and we received permission to take walks under an escort, on the days we did not work, over the rich meadows watered by the River Argun'. At first we went no more than two or three versts from our barrack, but gradually gaining more and more boldness, we were finally reaching the Argun' itself, which was at a distance of nine versts from us. The rich flora of that region drew our general attention and aroused our wonder at the beauties of Siberian nature—beauties so generously scattered and still so little known at that time. The two Borisov brothers, amateurs of the natural sciences, greatly occupied themselves with gathering flowers, as also with their zoological investigations; they collected quantities of insects of all different species and exceptional beauty, preserved them and took care of them, and so formed a quite sizable insect collection, which became an object of some curiosity for amateurs of natural science. Soon after this, however, there occurred a change in the work allotted to us; but this change, instead of lightening, increased the burden on us. An official came from Irkutsk to find out personally from each of us if our health was being ruined by our work beneath the ground, and if we would not rather work in the open air. We affirmed unanimously that the work below ground was not in the least burden-some to us—that in fact we preferred it to work in the open, because in the latter case we should be subject to all atmospheric changes, i.e., to rain and so forth, but our health would suffer from nothing as a result of the air below ground. Our representations were not respected. The very next day, we were sent off to begin some new task that had been assigned to us. Part of the reason why we preferred underground work we could not tell; we understood well that the burden on us must increase. In our work underground we had not had set tasks—we had worked and rested as much as we chose; on top of this, the work had ended at eleven o'clock and the rest of the time we had enjoyed complete freedom.

How, then, can one explain that sympathy that we were shown by exile-convicts underground who were engaged, a little way away, on the same work as ourselves, but whose toil was three times as great? *They* were in leg-irons, and on *them* lay all the wretchedness of mining underground. They it was who introduced the pits into new search areas and constructed galleries, which had to be supported by posts and linked arches. They it was who, as capable men, were employed as carpenters—and compactly and very well they built the subterranean passages. They, too, pumped out the water which from time to time accumulated in those places where a search was to be made; and carried out the ore, which they themselves and we had mined, to the shaft, where it was raised and taken off to a determined spot. Yet meeting us, these men, who were to all appearances hardened by crime, would show us an unspoken but quite obvious sympathy. More than once it happened that, as I was coming up from underground into the open air, to breathe it for a while, one of them, Orlov—a famous brigand, handsome, thick-set, and broad-shouldered and a perfect warrior in strength—had barely caught sight of me than he let his comrades know, and there and then he would begin a plaintive Russian song with his sonorous, silvery voice. With its familiar sounds, the song told on the heart, close and dear. And no, he did not start singing the song by chance; he said something by it that he could not put in words. Not with me alone, but with my comrades too, many of the convicts acted similarly, and more than once, in a fit of zeal, they took our hammers and in ten minutes finished off work that we could not have finished in an hour. All this was done without hope of reward. They watched over us, and we could only say in short words that we understood and valued their concern.

But an end was put to our underground work, and we went out to the new task next allotted us. It was a set task. The ore-carriers, usually juveniles, children of mine attendants, would break up the ore and separate that which was fit for melting from that which was not; we could not do this work, for it required great skill and knowledge in distinguishing and sorting ore according to its greater or its lesser suitability. So they gave us a barrow per pair, and our task was to transport 30 barrow-loads, each of five *poods*, from the place where the ore was sorted to another storage area. From one spot to the other was about 200 paces. The work began; we could not all complete our task; those who were slightly stronger substituted for their comrades, and in this way the assignment was fulfilled. At eleven o'clock a bell would announce the end of work, but another summoned us once more at one to the same toil, which finished at five or six o'clock in the evening. Thus, by the new arrangement the duration of our labouring *and* its burdensomeness were almost doubled. Our walks to the Argun' seemed less alluring; we were glad to rest on those days when we could. But for all this, our position was a fairly tolerable one, and the heavy burden of our work alternated with the freedom we enjoyed within our barrack and the consolations given to us by our guardians — who more than once witnessed our labours and alleviated them with friendly conversation.

Nikolay Vasil'yevich Basargin   1799–1861

Typical in various respects of the fates of those Decembrists 'fortunate' enough to remain in Peter-and-Paul Fortress while others were in Finland or Siberia was that of N. V. Basargin. The impatience, the slight illness, the increasing apprehension lest he not rejoin his comrades but be kept in another fortress, all were experienced by others in comparable situations. Basargin's mixed fortunes while travelling to Chita, too, reflect those of a large number of prisoners.

N. V. Basargin

Late autumn [1826] was approaching, and not one of us had yet been sent off. I had fallen ill, had almost lost the use of my legs and started to spit blood again. The Town-Major suggested to me that I go to the infirmary, but I would not agree to this, fearing that whilst I was recovering there all my comrades might be taken off to Siberia and I should be abandoned in the Fortress. For me, this fear was worse than illness, which I therefore attempted to conceal even from the doctor; when he visited me, I assured him I felt better and, given air, would soon recover completely.

Long autumn and winter evenings are particularly wearisome in confinement. I know this from experience. Given no exercise there could be no healthy sleep, the more so because chest pains and rheumatic aching in the legs did not permit one to stay long in any one position. Though I loved reading, one could not continually read all day and especially not in the evening by the dim light of a single tallow candle or a stinking night-lamp. Each man had talked over with his neighbours everything that could be said; and besides, I could not speak for long or loudly because of my weakness and my chest pains. Nor did chess amuse me now as once it had. In fact, it wearied me. In brief, I waited with impatience for some change and prayed to God that He might send me to Siberia soon. Of my relatives, I had no news whatever. None of them, I know, was allowed to come to Petersburg. Nor did I hope for letters from them; they could not know where I was, now that the sentence had been read, or even whether correspondence with us was permitted. I did not even want my brothers to write to me, fearing for them if they should show special concern.

It was winter already, and Christmas had passed. After Epiphany in 1827 I learnt that they had started to take some of us away, and impatiently awaited my turn—not without fear, however, that they might dispatch me to some fortress. Then one day, about January 20, the Town-Major came into my cell and asked if I had something warm to wear. 'Do they want to send me off, Yegor Mikhaylovich?' I asked. 'No, old fellow,' he exclaimed; 'where would they send you, if not home?' (I should add that he repeated this to every one of us on his visits—that we should unfailingly be pardoned, I mean.) 'I asked you because you need a warm coat for walking. You see how cold it is!' 'I've nothing at all,' I replied, 'except this jacket and two pillows.' 'Don't worry, you'll get everything you need.' Then I asked what I would pay for it all with, and if he had the money that was taken from me in the palace guardroom. 'Don't you worry about money,' said he. ...

I was certain they would soon be sending me off; and sure enough, he came again that evening with a guard carrying a small suitcase and one or two other things. 'Here's some linen and a sheepskin coat for you,' he said, pointing towards the guard. 'Dress up warmly.' I opened the case and in it found two pairs of woollen socks, warm boots, a cap, gloves, and three fairly thick shirts. A greasy sheepskin jacket covered with nankeen, another jacket, and trousers of thick army cloth completed the wardrobe. Helped by the guard (because I was extremely weak), I quickly put the warm footwear and clothing on, and the sheepskin coat on top, then set off with the Town-Major, supported by the guard, for the Commandant's house. Another sentry followed us with the suitcase that contained the other things. On entering the second room of the Commandant's house, a room leading off from the hallway, I found three of my comrades there: Fonvizin, Vol'f and Frolov. The first I had known even in Tul'chin; he had then commanded a brigade. With the second I was very friendly, and Frolov I did not know at all. Warmly but sadly we greeted one another. Soon General Sukin, the Commandant, came in with a sheet of paper; he had lost a leg and walked on a wooden stump. Turning deftly on this stump, he said in a loud voice: 'His Majesty the Emperor has ordained that the sentence of the Supreme Criminal Court be executed, and that you be sent to Siberia.' Then he quickly turned again and left. The Town-Major gave a signal to Lieutenant Glukhov of the garrison artillery, who was also standing there. Glukhov went out, but soon returned with a courier and a soldier who was carrying chains. We were obliged to sit, and the chains were put on us. Then we were handed over to the courier and led out onto the porch, where four gendarmes and five open post troikas were waiting. The night was dark.

So we left Petersburg, where all was plunged in blackness, coming to the first station in the night. We went in, to warm ourselves in the station-master's room. I, in particular, needed to do so, for my light sheepskin coat gave poor protection against the January frost. My comrades also went in. The courier (it turned out that I knew him—he had previously been my subordinate when I was senior adjutant, and he had come to Tul'chin with dispatches), treated us most civilly and was, in fact, as we later came to appreciate, a most kindly fellow. The fetters greatly hampered us, making it quite impossible to move freely. On his advice we tied them up and thus arranged them with as much comfort as possible for walking. Then I remembered a folded scrap of paper given to me by the Town-Major. You may imagine my amazement when I found in it, instead of my remaining money, ten silver 10-kopeck pieces. And this was all the wealth with which, feeble and ill, I was now setting out for the Siberian mines, 6000 versts and more from my family! One cannot say that such a situation promised well.

As we sat down to rest at a table, the courier going out to see to the horses, the station-master made a sign to Fonvizin, who immediately went out. His wife was waiting for him at the station. And before the return of the courier (who quite probably knew everything, but did not want it to be obvious), the pair managed to spend a few minutes together in the passage. When he did come in to announce that the horses were ready, we unhurriedly began to get ourselves ready, to give the Fonvizins a little more time; but finally we had to go. I sat in one sled with Fonvizin, to which the courier promptly agreed. He himself could see how poorly I was dressed for a winter journey. Fonvizin had a bearskin coat and a warm blanket covering his legs; sitting beside him, it was easy to protect oneself against the cold.

Fonvizin told me on the way that his wife had learnt and told him that we were to be taken to Irkutsk. She had given him 1000 roubles to serve us both for the journey and during our first weeks in Siberia.[36] The second station was Schlüsselburg; and I admit that I could not help wondering if it was *there* that we were being sent. Nor was I calm till we had passed the turning to the Fortress. At the station we again stepped from our sleds. It was still night. The courier was outside. I do not recollect why I went into a second room in this station, but hardly had I crossed the threshold of that room than I found myself in the embraces of three women who, weeping aloud, showered me with questions and offered me their services, their money, linen, clothing. I replied that I needed nothing, that I had sufficiency of everything, and thanked them cordially for their sympathy and their concern. This was some landowner or other traveling to Petersburg with her two daughters. We embraced warmly, and parted. They blessed me and saw us off with the most genuine good wishes.

Next day we passed through Tikhvin. In the afternoon, crowds gathered everywhere to look at us, and showed us the greatest sympathy. In Tikhvin itself several of the merchants and simple folk offered their services and help. Our courier, like a good man, acted towards us now only in such a way as not to bring upon himself the charge of supervising us slackly, and in no way went beyond his strict duty. I forget on what date we reached Yaroslavl' and put up at a hotel. While fresh horses were being harnessed we were given tea, and a man coming in with a tray made a sign towards the door of an adjoining room. We went across to it, and there found Nadezhda Nikolayevna Sheremeteva, mother-in-law of Yakushkin, one of our comrades, with her daughter, Yakushkin's wife. She was awaiting the arrival of her son-in-law. We exchanged a few words with her; as we went out to mount the sleds she and her daughter, who was carrying an infant in her arms, came out into the corridor, surrounded by a crowd of onlookers. They embraced and blessed us, and allowed their tears to flow. Yakushkin's wife was then a young woman of eighteen, remarkably beautiful. It was hard for us to see that young and lovely creature who experienced so early the misfortunes of this world, and who, perhaps, was doomed by her duty and attachment to her husband to live forever in Siberian mines, separated from society, relations, children, everything so dear to youth and to the heart.

We traveled to Tobol'sk from Yaroslavl' by way of Kostroma, Vyatka, Perm and Yekaterinburg. We traveled fast, but sometimes stopped overnight. Observing that our irons stopped us from sleeping, our courier was good enough to let us take them off at night. The gendarmes obeyed us; and the courier (as he himself observed) had orders to treat us politely and to show us every consideration, while not exceeding the limits of his duty. Arriving in Tobol'sk, we were quartered in the house of the police-master, where we rested for three days and nights. And here we parted company with our courier, who set off alone for Irkutsk having entrusted us to the Governor, Bantysh-Kamensky (a relation of Fonvizin). I do not know if it was because of this or simply out of humanity, but whatever the reason, Alekseyev, the police-master, received us with such warmth and was so hospitable throughout those three days that I felt it my duty, on returning from Transbaikalia ten years later to settle in Turinsk, to call on him — by now a retired official — and thank him for his sympathy and kindness. When we had rested three days, we set off once again for Irkutsk, this time accompanied by a Tobol'sk district police-officer, but with the same gendarmes. Fonvizin had bought a wagon in Tobol'sk, so we were spared the trouble of changing at each station. We had acquired another warm blanket, too, so I ran no danger from the cold. Movement and the fresh air had so beneficient an effect upon me now that even in Tobol'sk I was completely well, standing and walking as firmly as ever before.

We reached Irkutsk three weeks after our departure from Tobol'sk, having passed through Tara, Ishim, Kainsk, Kolyvan, Tomsk, Achinsk, Krasnoyarsk, Kansk and Nizhnyeudinsk. Everywhere along the way we met with unfeigned sympathy from both the populace and the officials. In Kainsk, for example, a policeman called Stepanov, an elderly man of enormous size and girth who had once been a courier, came up to us with two other men; the three dragged a basket holding wines and every kind of foodstuff. All this Stepanov made us eat or take with us, even offering us money that he had with him, with these amazing words: 'This money' (said he, taking out a thick sheaf of notes) 'I somehow or other scraped together *not altogether cleanly*, in bribes. In our line, gentlemen, you find yourself doing a lot of things that go against the conscience. Take the cash yourselves: it'll ease my conscience. I couldn't use it better—I haven't got a family. In fact, get rid of it for me, you'll be doing me a favour.' Although we would not accept his offer, the frankness and good nature of that rough character, unpolished by the touch of education, moved us deeply. On leaving him, we shook his hand sincerely and with gratitude.

In Krasnoyarsk the Governor, also called Stepanov, entertained us cordially. Indeed, in almost all the towns in which we stopped, officials visited us. At first, they would not dare to start a conversation; but always they would end by offering their services and showing sympathy. At posting stations, the officials from nearby halts would usually appear with comparable offers, while the common folk crowded around the sleds. Though they were visibly afraid of the gendarmes, it was not rare for some of the more bold spirits amongst them to approach us and to throw brass coins into the sled. To this day I have a brass coin given to me by a beggarly old woman; I guard it as something precious. She came into our hut, showed us a few small coins and said, 'That's all I have. Take it, masters, dear ones. You need it more than me.' We wept and I, taking the most worn coin from her, put it in my pocket.

The further we moved into Siberia, the more it improved in my sight. To me, the common folk seemed freer, brighter, even better educated that our Russian peasantry—especially more so that our estate serfs. They better understood the dignity of man, and valued their rights more highly. Afterwards, I several times [heard] from persons who had visited the United States and lived there that Siberians have many similarities with the Americans—in their manners, in their customs, and even in their way of life. Siberia, as a land of exile, has always taken in all men indulgently, without discrimination. When an exile has crossed her borders, she has not asked him why he undergoes the punishment of law; nor has it been anyone's business what crime he once committed. The word 'unfortunate,' which the Siberians apply to exiles, expresses very well that comprehension that they have of them. Of the exile, it is asked only that he behave himself in his new home, and that he work with diligence, making use of the resources offered by his new fatherland. Not only has sufficiency always awaited him within a few years, if he will do this; even wealth and the respect of individuals with whom he lives and deals may be attained.

There exists a custom in Eastern Siberia that [well] demonstrates in what a light the rural population looks on fugitives, who not infrequently desert their place of work or exile because of the oppressive toil, ill treatment by local authorities, or simply because they are barely sustained. In every settlement, under the windows of each house, you will see small shelves upon which rye bread, wheat rolls, curds, and milk in earthenware pots are left at night. Fugitives passing through by night take all this, as alms. The custom also serves to protect the inhabitants against theft — for lacking food, runaways must necessarily resort to breaking into private property.

We spent about a week in Irkutsk. And it was here that we learnt something of the government's plans for us. General Leparsky, we discovered, had been appointed special Commandant over us, and had already come to Chita with several other officials. We also found out that a building had been hurriedly prepared for us in Chita; it was surrounded by a stockade, and a number of our comrades who had left before us were already there. All this information was not wholly pleasant for us; still, it was comforting to know that we should all be there together — in company even dying's all right, as the saying goes.

From Irkutsk we were sent with a cossack *sotnik*[37] and four cossacks to Chita. And here we parted with the gendarmes who had accompanied us, as with the Tobol'sk police officer. So courteous had they been towards us, so unfailingly attentive, that we could not praise them enough or leave them without gratitude. (The police officer would call Fonvizin nothing but 'Your Excellency,' nor would he listen when we told him we had been deprived of all titles and rank.) But we had plenty of trouble with our *sotnik*, despite the fact that he was good to us. Unfortunately, he had a passion for fiery beverages and had a keg of vodka with him, from which he drank excessively at every station, constantly inviting us to follow his example. Neither advice nor our requests or exhortations helped. We were obliged to submit to necessity, and impatiently awaited our arrival in Chita.

We arrived there in the evening, fairly late, and found neither the Commandant nor even the Town-Major there; both were in the Nerchinsk factories where the first eight of our comrades were now living, having been sent there directly after hearing their sentences read out. A Lieutenant Stepanov received us, and quartered us in a small wooden building surrounded by a stockade. The whole building consisted of two small rooms divided by a corridor and a tiny third room, partitioned off in the corridor itself. We were put in one of these two rooms; in the other were our comrades who arrived before us, and we could hear them talking among themselves but were not allowed to see them that evening. The two Murav'yovs, Annenkov, Svistunov, Zavalishin, Torson, and the two Kryukov brothers were there. Stepanov examined our things, treating us tolerably rudely, set a guard and, going off himself, locked the door into the corridor, giving the guard the key. Never have I seen such an external likeness as existed between that officer and Count Arakcheyev—it was so striking that we subsequently called him nothing but Arakcheyev, and wondered if he was his natural son. Left alone without a fire, we somehow settled down onto the boards that had been placed in our room and tried to sleep, our heads full of by no means reassuring thoughts. Even here, we feared, we would not be allowed to talk freely with our comrades. How delighted we were when, the next morning, our door had barely been opened before all those comrades came in, greeting us joyfully and inviting us into their room for tea.

After us, others began to arrive. Every three days a new party of three or four would come. At first, they were all put in our little building. Later, when this had grown extremely cramped, they were placed in another one, built in the same style at the far end of the settlement. Towards the end of winter, that is, in April, more than seventy of us had assembled, half in one building, half in the other. Also towards this time several ladies arrived, too—first Murav'yov's wife, then Fonvizin's, Naryshkin's, and Ental'tsev's. These wives lived in rented rooms with the inhabitants of Chita settlement, and were allowed to see their husbands in their cells twice weekly—in the presence of an officer. The Commandant, too, soon arrived from Nerchinsk, called on us, and behaved towards us in a kindly, if formal, manner.

Chita

Even before the five supposed leaders of the Decembrist conspiracy were hanged, Nicholas had foreseen the need for special arrangements in Siberia: a strong prison, a prison guard, a commandant. On July 24, 1826, acting on Imperial orders, Dibich wrote to General S. R. Leparsky,[1] a russified Pole and former colonel of the Severskiy Dragoons, that the tsar had a special post for him. Although retired and seventy-two years of age, Leparsky was hale and healthy and, besides, unable to resist an offer couched in such flattering terms; moreover he was deeply in debt. He accepted the position of commandant of Nerchinsk, 'important ... because most state criminals held there require especially strict, but at the same time reasonable surveillance,' and was received by Nicholas in Moscow.

Leparsky had a reputation as a kindly officer, and also as a loyal and tactful one. Seeing that undisguisedly cruel treatment of the exiles would only prompt compassion for them among many Russians, and that his ends would certainly be better served if they could be forgotten by the mass of their compatriots, Nicholas may be thought to have hand-picked Leparsky, whom he had known for fifteen years.

At first, the government had planned to build a special prison for the Decembrists in Akatuy, a silver-mining centre nearer the Mongolian borderland. Although the foundations for this prison had already been laid, the future commandant succeeded in convincing the authorities that so bad was the air in Akatuy – no birds were to be found within a radius of a hundred miles, because of silver poisoning[2] – that to send the prisoners there would be tantamount to sentencing them to lingering death. Thus even before they arrived in Chita, Leparsky's chosen site, the Decembrists' lives had probably been saved by their new commandant.

Chita, a small frontier settlement and trading fort, had a motley population of 300 in 1827.[3] Thanks to the skill of Nikolay Bestuzhev, who could draw in ink as well as he could forge, and paint as well as he could make a violin, we have many splendid aquarelles and sketches of the fort as it was then; of the wide valley ringed with scrub-grown hills, the ten-foot high stockade of sharpened logs, and the River Ingoda in which the exiles bathed in summer.[4] It was, all in all, a healthy place. Winters were long and cold, but summers blazing: in June, several memoirists record, there was a veritable explosion of every kind of vegetation, and Chita became 'the garden of Siberia.'[5] As to the jail itself, Leparsky settled first on an abandoned cossack fort, which he ordered rebuilt to his specifications. He then immediately set about building another, larger prison. It was well that he wasted no time in doing so, for by December 1827 eighty-two prisoners had already arrived in Chita, not to mention several wives, and conditions, as Yakushkin emphasizes, were almost unbearably cramped.

Most aspects of the exiles' lives in Chita become clear enough in the four extracts that follow: none too demanding work on 'the Devil's Ditch' in the morning, correspondence through the ladies, an artel or cooperative, all have been well described elsewhere.[6] The extracts tell the tale more clearly, however, and in more convincing detail. Only two subjects need be mentioned here, to throw the extracts into sharper focus – the questions of money, and of the 'Academy of Chita.'

The right to receive financial aid, it should be understood, was strictly regulated by the government and limited to a specific sum. The law allowed the exile to receive not more than 2000 roubles for 'settlement purposes' and not more than 1000 annually.[7] These sums were paid out in instalments by Leparsky's nephew, the 'town-major' Osip Adamovich. Those who received no aid whatever from their relatives, and these numbered thirty-four, were granted a government subsidy of 114 roubles and 23½ kopeks, equal to that paid to a private in the army, and were also issued with clothing.[8] This allowance was too meagre, and many experienced hardship in their first two years of exile. Soon, however, programmes of mutual assistance were conceived and organized, and all privation disappeared in Chita, at least.[9] Many of the Decembrists were men of wealth, well able to contribute generously to an artel such as was later organized in Petrovskiy Zavod. Trubetskoy and Nikita Murav'yov both received between two and three thousand roubles annually from family estates, Volkonsky up to 2000, Ivashev, Naryshkin, and Fonvizin up to 1000.[10] In Chita, where goods and services were cheap, even allowing for the unforeseen inflation caused by the presence of the noble prisoners, such sums were very large indeed. In the ten years that they spent as state convicts, that is, until 1836, the Decembrists received from home almost 355,000 roubles in cash, and their wives another 778,000 roubles.[11] And this was through official channels only. This affluence, albeit most unevenly distributed, is not stressed in any memoirs.

A second point worthy of note is that the so-called 'Academy of Chita' was a very great achievement and had lasting consequences for the whole of Transbaikalia. It was significant that the majority of the Decembrists were willing, in 1827–30, to study subjects of which they knew little or nothing, even though they might never leave Siberia; intellectual vitality was by no means dimmed by exile. Nikita Murav'yov, who had a fine collection of maps with him, gave lectures on military history and strategy. Vol'f taught the basics of anatomy and physics, P. S. Bobrishchev-Pushkin mathematics, Prince Obolensky, literature. Mukhanov, friend of Pushkin and of other writers in the capital, gave lectures on Russian history, Torson on fiscal theory, N. A. Bestuzhev on seamanship. Through periodicals the exiles kept in touch, at a distance of three months and several thousand miles, with political events in Europe. On first hearing the news of the July Revolution in Paris, they formed a small impromptu choir and sang the Marseillaise.[12]

The influence of the 'Academy' was not confined to Chita itself. Outside, in the surrounding countryside, its presence was felt in a number of ways. The Decembrists' work in the fields of agriculture, medicine and education has been well covered by Soviet scholarship.[13] The group were quickly made aware of a shortage of fresh vegetables. As Father Myslovky apparently remarked, 'they led the lives of the ancient Apostles,' eating gruel and cabbage soup. Those horticulturally inclined tackled the problem which, two centuries before, had influenced the very pattern of Muscovite expansion in Siberia.[14] By means of artificial heating under glass, Poggio successfully grew melons and asparagus in Chita. Instructed by a patient Baron Rozen, the native population learnt the skills of cultivating buckweat, rye, and barley.[15]

Dr Vol'f's celebrity was widespread, and he saved numbers of lives outside the prison, possibly including Leparsky's; but he was not the only prisoner with a knowledge of medicine. Zavalishin, Naryshkin and Princess Trubetskaya also understood its elements, while M. K. Kyukhel'beker later opened up a small field-hospital.

Nikolay and Mikhail Bestuzhev sought permission to instruct the local children in reading, and were refused. They then requested permission to instruct the populace in church music and liturgy, for which a level of literacy was obviously necessary. Permission was eventually granted. Later, after the main body of exiles had left Chita, Zavalishin founded a school there. Others opened schools eleswhere.[16]

It would be wrong to think, however, that the Decembrists were concerned only with local problems; broader questions of regional and national significance also exercised their minds. While Basargin undertook a mighty general survey of Siberia's economic, social, and administrative problems,[17] the Borisov brothers gathered an enormous insect collection, classifying as they went along.[18] Nikolay Bestuzhev occupied himself with ethnographic studies and, influenced by the resident linguist, Zavalishin, compiled a Russian-Buriat dictionary. Then, as if to demonstrate his versatility, he made a series of precise seismological observations, using instruments that had been sent to him from Europe. So one might continue, but the point is clear: the presence of so many educated men, confined in a single settlement, could only produce a deep impact on Siberian life, and local life in particular. It is not only in the scholarly activities of Zavalishin, Shteyngel' and Murav'yov-Apostol throughout the 1840s that we see the influence of the 'Academy of Chita'; it is discernible in schools to which came hundreds of Siberian children for a basic education; in a new attitude towards agriculture adopted by progressive–minded settlers and petty bourgeois (*meshchane*) in the region; in the first glimmerings of enlightenment where earlier there were none. In their daily intercourse with the Siberian peasantry, and with youthful Siberians in particular, the exiles accomplished much in cultural and economic matters, although not in politics.

Leparsky's régime, it emerges from all this as from the extracts that will follow, was not oppressive. With the wives hovering by, it could not be; several had court connections. The majority of the Decembrist exiles, moreover, were young men and did not feel that all was ruined in their lives; that feeling did not come until the middle 'thirties. So long as they remained in Chita, where the native populace was favourably disposed towards them, most kept alive their hope of general amnesty on the occasion of a royal birth, or of a major victory over the Turks. Physical deprivation, and the absence of a future of significance for *all* their countrymen, blended, in the years 1827–30, with a certain youthful carefreeness. Stemming from the twenty-five-year-olds, that carefreeness sometimes affected even Colonel Tizengauzen, the doyen of the exiles.[19] There is, surprisingly perhaps, a more than faintly optimistic air about those parts of several memoirs that treat the Chita years. Only a few men were embittered, and unable to accept life and their comrades cheerfully. One of these was the unfortunate Sukhinov, Sergey Murav'yov-Apostol's former trusted lieutenant, who was to plan an abortive mass escape.[20] Another was the prickly Zavalishin.

Suddenly, in 1827, Chita had become the cultural centre of all the Russian territories east of the Urals. Irkutsk itself was eclipsed. In 1885, when the American George Kennan visited the town, matters had scarcely changed, although the two governors general of Siberia still kept their headquarters and staffs elsewhere. Kennan and his companion Frost passed several pleasant hours discussing politics with the shrewd, amiable and highly educated exiles then serving sentences in Chita. They gathered, in the evenings, in a building that had once been the Decembrists' carpentry and joining shop.[21] A. G. Murav'yova's grave was still tended, and her husband's memory fresh, like that of his companions.

Baron A. E. Rozen

Towards the end of May a tinge of green began to show on the fields and mountains around Chita. This little village lies on the great road between Lake Baikal and Nerchinsk, on an elevation surrounded by high mountains on two sides. The little river Chita falls near the village into the navigable River Ingoda, and forms a delightful valley. To the north lies Lake Onon, on whose shores Genghiz Khan held his court of justice. (He used to drown criminals in the seething waters. This was on his march into Rus'.) The descendants of his Mongols, the Buriats, still wander through this country with their felt tents—a country abounding in rivers and lakes; they appear now here, now there, but always on horseback and often armed with matchlocks, though generally only with bows and arrows so as to reserve their powder, the use of which they know well when it is necessary. Part of this tribe has abandoned its nomadic habit and has settled down. These Buriats practise agriculture, and their meadows and fields are as well irrigated as those of the Milanese. Its altitude considerably intensifies the winter cold in Chita, but it is a healthy place, with a fresh and bracing climate. Except in August, when the thunder is continual for days on end, the sky is almost clear. In August there are showers that start with massive single raindrops, then, after a few hours, flood the whole road—for the water quickly rushes down the slopes, gouging deep trenches as it goes. The great electricity of the air, too, is remarkable: the slightest movement of cloth or wool produces sparks or crackling. The climate, as I say, is healthy, and the speed with which things grow amazing: both corn and vegetables ripen within five weeks of the frosts' ending, that is, between mid-June and late July. Many varieties of vegetable, however, were then quite unknown in those parts. One of our comrades was the first to introduce the cultivation of cucumbers in the open, and of melons in hot-beds.

As to the Vale of Chita itself, it is renowned for its flora, for which reason the whole region is called the 'Garden of Siberia.' Never have I seen finer species of lily, iris and other bulbs than are to be met with here. The population of the village where we lived had reached 300. Like all miners, the inhabitants were poor, and lived in little houses on which a miserable church looked down. They lived by agriculture and by fishing, which is excellent in the River Ingoda and

Lake Onon. All the land belonged to the Crown, by whom it was allotted to the peasants; so they were greatly taken up with burning charcoal, which had to be shipped to the Nerchinsk mines by water. Until our arrival there, the place knew only one civil authority, in the person of the Superintendent of Mines, Smolyaninov, who boarded us at his own expense for the first four months of our sojourn.[22] The Crown gave us bread and, besides this, two copper kopeks daily for each man. In the three and a half years that we spent in Chita, the place took on an entirely fresh aspect, as much from the many new buildings as from the new guests, in whose suite came military authorities and guards. When we arrived, Chita consisted of twenty-six cabins and no more than three proper houses, in which lived the Commandant, the Superintendent of Mines, and the Town-Major.

At first, only thirty of us state convicts lived in Chita. But all the condemned joined us in August 1827, when the construction of a larger jail was finished. Till our reunion, we lived in two fortified cottages and only met at our work, when we dug foundations for our own new prison and deep ditches for the fence surrounding it. We were also ordered to fill with earth and sand a large hollow near the road. This hollow, down which foaming mountain torrents would occasionally rush, was threatening to destroy the road. In a few days the waters would wash away the work of a whole summer, and in 1828 we were obliged to build a log dam, merely to get a solid base for our dyke of earth and sand. We called this hollow The Devil's Ditch.

Life passed in cheerless monotony. At first, we had very few books indeed, writing was strictly forbidden, and neither paper nor ink could be obtained. When we were all together, we formed a choir from amongst ourselves, which shortened many a gloomy hour. Chess was our sole amusement in the spare time between work and sleep. Cards we could have procured through the warders, but we had passed the word to one another not to allow card-playing, so as to obviate any cause of dissention or unpleasantness. Our rooms were so small that we could not even keep them as clean as we wished. We had beds made of planks covered with furs or felt rugs. And at night, when the windows and doors were closed, the air grew intolerably oppressive. Still, the doors were always opened very early in the morning and I never missed the sunrise, but immediately went out to get some fresh air. The others bore the heavy atmosphere better than I, for they all smoked, and I had given up the habit.

As I mentioned earlier, about half of my comrades were not well off at all, many being totally neglected by their relatives, while others were extremely rich. Nikita and Aleksandr Muravyov alone received 60,000 roubles a year.[23] Every time a senior was chosen, at the end of a three-months period, a paper would be sent round on which every individual wrote down his contribution in proportion to our common costs. The money thus collected was spent by the senior on tea, sugar and other food, as well as on household necessities. Clothes and linen we had to obtain for ourselves. The rich bought all essential articles and divided them with the poorer brethren; and everything was shared in a truly brotherly way, money as well as suffering. So as not to spend money lavishly, our clothes were cut and made by our comrades themselves. The best tailors were Pavel Pushkin,[24] Prince Yevgeniy Obolensky and Anton Arbuzov. The best hats and shoes were made by Nikolay and Mikhail Bestuzhev and Pyotr Falenberg, who, by their work, saved a sum of money with which we were able to support other unhappy exiles. Thus our work continued as before — by now we were accustomed to our chains. Between May and September we filled in The Devil's Ditch, improved the broad road, planted and watered vegetables and potatoes. When, after Shveykovsky's return, I was chosen senior of the prison,[25] I salted down in brandy-casks 60,000 cucumbers out of our kitchen-garden. From September until May we were taken twice a day into a special building outside the prison courtyard, where hand-mills had been set; we were all required to grind eight pounds of rye a day. At first, of course, we found the going hard, until our arms and hands had grown accustomed to it. The healthiest and strongest helped the weaker ones to finish off their share. This work, that is, the turning of our millstones, was frequently accompanied by singing. One musically inclined comrade was appointed band-master. The church music of Bortnyanski[26] was particularly well rendered, I think. But we were taken to the church once a year only, during fasts, to take Communion. A priest would come to the prison to conduct divine service on the eve of major feasts. Never shall I forget how solemnly and how impressively this service was performed on the eve of Easter, 1828 when, before the tattoo was sounded, at about nine o'clock, there re-echoed from all sides the shout 'Christ is risen!' and the chains of prisoners clanked as they threw themselves into each other's arms in brotherly love. At the same moment, we embraced in thought our distant friends and relatives, who, as we knew, were joined with us in prayer.

Many of our comrades having had a scientific education, it was resolved that they enliven our long winter nights by giving lectures. Nikita Murav'yov, who possessed beautiful military maps and plans, expounded strategy and tactics to us; Vol'f gave talks on chemistry and anatomy; Pavel Pushkin explained the higher branches of mathematics, while Aleksandr Kornilovich and Pyotr Mukhanov read Russian history and Prince A. Odoyevsky, literature. I should add, in gratitude, that Odoyevsky had for years the real kindness to instruct me, a born Estonian, in Russian. Our doors were shut and lights extinguished at nine, but as we could not fall asleep so early we usually conversed for a while or listened to the tales of M. Kyukhel'beker, who had been on a voyage round the globe.[27] A. Kornilovich sometimes told us stories from the history of the fatherland, with which he had much occupied himself when editor of the paper, *Russia's Ancient Times*. For many years he and Professor Kunitsyn had had free access to the State Archives, and he had made a special study of the times of the Empresses Elizabeth and Anna. ...[28]

These long years of intimacy with such highly educated men had a considerable effect on those among us who had previously had neither time nor means to improve their mind. Some started to learn foreign languages, and of these D. I. Zavalishin was the most proficient; he learnt not only Latin and Greek, but also eight modern languages! (In every one of these languages he found an instructor among his comrades.)[29] Grammatical exercises often led to many comical scenes, but when anyone attempted English pronunciation, laughter was universal; and Mikhail Lunin, who was quite proficient in that language, would call out entreatingly: 'Read and write English as much as you like, gentlemen, only *please* don't try to speak it!'

It was about this time that I was chosen senior, in order to relieve Ja. P. Shveykovsky. I had, at times, occasion to transact business with Leparsky, in connection with the affairs of my companions in misfortune; and always he received me with marked courtesy. Often he said: 'What will be written about me in Europe? I shall be called a hard-hearted jailor, an executioner and an oppressor, while the truth is, gentlemen, that I only keep this post in order to protect you from the persecutions and injustice of unscrupulous officials.'

In the course of 1828, three more ladies joined us in Chita. Natal'ya Fonvizin, *née* Opytina,[30] had been unable to follow her husband out at once because of her two infant sons. In her early years, she was remarkable for her beauty and religious temperament; before her marriage, she had thought of withdrawing from the world and entering a convent. Later, sharing her husband's banishment and tribulations, she showed the most complete submission to God's will; but her nerves were so shaken that her health was broken.[31]

Alexandrine Davydova, wife of Vasiliy L'vovich, Colonel of Hussars, arrived at the same time. She had a numerous family and was obliged to leave them all with her relations before leaving. Unvarying sweetness, calm resignation and deep devotion were that charming woman's chief characteristics. Mlle. Pauline, the bride of P. A. Annenkov, also came to Chita that year; the betrothal had taken place secretly but the Emperor, openly and in a very marked manner, had granted her permission to go and join her bridegroom. She had addressed herself to him during some grand manoeuvres; it was a happy moment, for the Emperor received her with the greatest sympathy and gave her money for the journey, whereas every possible hindrance was thrown in the way of the other married ladies.[32] Now there were eight ladies in all at Chita. These conducted the whole correspondence with relations of all the state prisoners, forming a link between the living and the politically dead. As to their own lives, they showed utter self-denial; as I said before, only twice a week were they allowed to see their husbands for an hour and in the presence of a sentry and an orderly officer. This state of affairs lasted almost four years.

All prisoners are, of course, incessantly pre-occupied with thoughts of their release. Naturally, such an idea was often in our minds, while outside the prison walls it seemed that others were similarly employed. In the mines of Nerchinsk, where eight of my comrades had earlier worked together, there still remained some of the officers of the mutinous Chernigovskiy Regiment, who were not sentenced at the same time as ourselves but went before a special court-martial. Among them were Baron Solov'yov, Bystritsky, Mozalevsky, and a certain Sukhinov. This latter planned to stir up all the thousands of forced labourers in the mines there to assist in setting us free at Chita, and hoped then to arrange with us how the move should be followed up. Most in the mines agreed to this. It was decided to disarm the watch during the night and to set out the following morning; but the conspiracy was revealed by a traitor. Sukhinov and the other principals were thrown into jail in chains and condemned to death. The night before the execution of the sentence, Sukhinov hanged himself from the prison stove; the others were shot. ...

At Chita, we were guarded by an infantry company and fifty Siberian cossacks. Many among us were always taken up with thoughts of liberty and preparations for flight, but others saw the impossibility of success and declined to attempt it. As far as our guard was concerned, we could have overcome them easily; the soldiers were devoted to us and could willingly have been induced to lay down their arms; thus we might have escaped—but then what would have happened? We might flee southwards to China and reach the frontier, but the Chinese would no doubt surrender us. Besides this, once we reached the frontier fifty cossacks would be sufficient to harrass us day and night, preventing our resting for a moment and so exhausting us. Another road led to the south-east where, on the banks of the Amur, we might build a boat in one of the river creeks and sail down to the open sea,[33] making our way across to America. But how were we to reach the shores of the Amur? The nomad Buriats would not help us, and even at the river we would still be far from the sea. Our pursuers could easily destroy a vessel. A third road lay to the west, to the frontiers of European Russia, but that was a distance of 4000 versts: there would be countless difficulties to overcome in a journey of that length. The fourth road lay over the tundra, plains and bogs covered with moss. The easier way would be for each man to make his own escape—but the escape of some would cause the rest to be severely treated, and no one wished to be responsible for that, either to comrades or to wife. There was nothing left but to submit calmly to the law of necessity; and so we passed three years and seven months at Chita, until our new and spacious prison was completed by the ironworks of Petrovskiy—our ultimate destination.

M. A. Bestuzhev

At the time of our arrival there, Chita was merely a hamlet belonging to the Department of Mines and Factories and consisting of a few tumble-down huts. Mining engineer Smolyaninov managed it. The inhabitants, as is general among old Siberian settlers, were poor and idle, but our stay of almost three years there enriched those inhabitants, who sold both their poor produce and their meagre services at a high price. It also embellished Chita with dozens of fine houses, both the officials' and our ladies', that is, belonging to Trubetskaya, Volkonskaya, A. G. Murav'yova, Fonvizina, Annenkova and Davydova. The residents had a sufficiency, houses took on a more attractive appearance, dress a smarter one. Formerly in torn shirts, urchins now wore clean ones and, far from avoiding us, shouted on seeing us in the distance: 'Do you need any *spions?* (that is *champignons?*)'

An impression may easily be formed of the insignificant settlement of Chita. ... A large-scale plan was drawn up by Falenberg and my brother Nikolay. I say, 'and my brother,' not because Nikolay himself performed the actual surveying — we all took part in that in turn, each of us that is, who felt inclined to walk a little beyond the inviolable line of our agricultural work — but rather because Falenberg was indebted to my brother for making the necessary instruments.[34] To be in a position even to begin that serious piece of work, we had to go through a whole series of childish tricks and artifices, but little by little we earned the right, or at least the permission, to possess a few instruments. But to keep them in our casemates was not allowed. A special building was erected in the courtyard of the cell that served as an infirmary, and even there only a few men were permitted to engage in the work of locksmith, joiner, and turner. Wishing, first, to provide their comrades with a pleasant walk, second, to make a plan of the surroundings and, lastly, to draw sketches from them, my brother and Falenberg persuaded Leparsky to let them try their hand at making the instruments required for all of this. Counting on their failing, possibly, the Commandant gave his permission, and was mistaken in his expectation. The instruments were beautifully made, and all the accessories, too. Having inspected them himself, the Commandant found himself obliged to concede to their being used for the proposed purpose. But through what labyrinths of difficulties, labours, trials of patience, were the pair obliged to pass in order to achieve the end in view! You yourself must look into the history of each privilege granted to us if you wish to form a consistent impression of the struggle between, on the one hand, stubborn wills in captivity and, on the other, the kindly Commandant — a commandant responsible and liable for his indulgences and anxious to justify, by referring to the law, all the rigours disregarded by his orders (or at least, to leave himself loopholes when possible). My brother formed a splendid collection of views of Chita's beautiful surroundings; but he gave them almost all away to various people, so that he had only three of them in later years, and even those were copies of originals in the possession of Leparsky when he died in Petrovskiy Zavod.

Accustomed to make money easily, the inhabitants of Chita soon fell into penury after our leaving, and their poverty was greater than before.[35] Idleness went hand in hand with drunkenness and so, progressively degenerating, they lived until the time when their poor village was named the district town of the Transbaikal District; they themselves were then made cossacks and resettled in Atamanovka, twelve versts from Chita.[36] It must, however, be admitted that the choice of situation for the main centre of Regional administration was a most unhappy one. For the underlying notion that persuaded N. N. Murav'yov to choose this place was to make Chita into an entrepôt and trading town for the commerce between Irkutsk and the Amur.[37] At the time, he believed blindly in the possibility of traveling by water from Irkutsk to the settlement of Amur by means of the rivers Shilka, Onon, Chita, Khilok, Selenga, and so by Lake Baikal; nor was he halted by the smallness of the trails from the upper reaches of the Chita to the source of the Khilok. But time has demonstrated the unfeasability of the idea. Steamships scarcely get as far upstream as Sretensk, and only in the very latest years has the steamship 'Kozakevich' reached Nerchinsk, with no small difficulty. Only during the spring floods, in fact, has that waterway sufficient depth to render navigation possible; but to make up for that, the awful rapids in the most dangerous stretches are, and will remain, an insuperable obstacle. When we first met N. N. Murav'yov, we three (Torson was still alive then) tried at length, but unsuccessfully, to dissuade him from his object of making Chita the principal town of the district. A ukase was signed; but cities are not built by ukases, though Murav'yov's *idées arrêtées* triumphed. Significant privileges, the establishing of a fair, even personal persuasion by the Governor-General (directed at Siberian merchants), nothing helped. Destroy the district administration in Chita by ukase and in a year that town would show a picture of collapsed government buildings and collapsed officials' houses. And if the Amur commerce *does* develop with time, Shilinskiy Zavod or, still more probably, Sretensk will become the main entrepôt; in any event, the trade route will not run to Chita, the roads from which to Nerchinsk are appallingly mountainous, and to Verkhnyeudinsk swampy and desolate. In winter, the trade route will be along the river, upstream to the Khilotskiy trail and then by the Khilok, Selenga and Lake Baikal to Irkutsk, and it will probably be conducted with the aid of floating ice-drifts, as is done already in America and is now being tried on the Amur.

I. D. Yakushkin

We all ate together in our little cell, and took turns to be on duty. The functions of the man on duty were to prepare everything for dinner, and then to bring it in. For dinner, a warder would come in with a huge tureen of communal cabbage soup and another of minced beef; bread was brought in chunks. We were given neither knives nor forks, but each man had his own spoon made of bone, pewter or wood. A lack of plates was remedied by Chinese wooden saucers. At the end of every meal, a hateful duty would remain for the individual on duty: he had to wash up and bring everything back into order — but he did not have what was required to do so. There was neither laundering nor, often, even warm water with which to clean the plates. We also drank tea together; always the man who poured it was excused his turn of duty with the rest.

We lived so penned up that it was impossible to do anything intently; hardly could one manage to read through something in a day. Games of chess and the recounting of stories were our main pastime and relaxation. On weekdays, sixteen men would be appointed from all the casemates for work, to which we would set off behind an escort of armed soldiers. Four hand-mills had been set up in a small building, all in the same room. Our work lasted for three hours in the morning and three more after dinner. At this time, we were obliged to grind four *poods* of rye in all, to do which each man had to grind ten pounds;[38] but since no more than two men could be working at a given time at each of the four hand-mills, we changed places several times during the work session. Needless to say, this labour was not taxing, but a few who lacked the strength to do their share themselves hired a guard to grind it for them. The flour that we produced was, in the main, of no special distinction. Those who were not working smoked, played chess, or read and chatted in another room.

Very often in our conversations, we found ourselves discussing our common court case. And as we listened to parts of stories every day, verifying and comparing one story with another, all that related to our case grew daily clearer, as did the true significance of our Society which had existed for ten years despite all obstacles. The significance of December 14th, too, became clear. At the same time, we came to learn of the activities of the Committee during the interrogation of defendants, and of its subterfuges in preparing a report containing very little falsehood — but which was yet no more than a deception. It was not difficult (for the Committee) to choose a certain number of guilty individuals from among those held for questioning and sentence them to death; for every man caught uttering *unseemly* words against the government was already liable to all the law's severity. By far the hardest task of the Committee was, having offered seemingly unquestionable proof of honesty, to blacken the Secret Society's objective in the general public's sight, and so to defame the convictions of every member of that Society. In order to achieve that end, members of the Committee were obliged, while continually citing the defendant's own confessions and testimonies, to include in their report only those declarations and confessions that showed the Society in a poor light and represented its members as ridiculous or hateful, at the same time saying nothing that might evoke some sympathy for them.

For its part, the Special Supreme Court, understanding the activities of the Committee, destroyed the procedure determined by the law for all legal proceedings. The accused were never brought to trial to have charges against them read by the Committee; nor were they asked if they had anything to add to their own earlier testimonies, or anything to say in self-justification. On the contrary, indeed, they were summoned only days before the sentencing—to sign what they were told were their own statements, but which they were not given time to read and which, for the most part, were not written in their hand! But in all this, of course, neither the members of the Committee nor those of the Special Supreme Court deserve special censure; both in Russia and outside, such action is always taken in such cases, and there is no standing on ceremony in indicting individuals thought dangerous to a state's very existence. Certainly, it is hard to accuse members of the Committee of deliberate injustice towards any one of the defendants; indeed, only one example of obvious injustice can be adduced: while being prosecuted, Count Chernyshev was held in the Fortress and not once summoned before the Committee, nor did he even once receive a written question. Yet he was sentenced to hard labour. Chernyshev would, in time, have fallen heir to a considerable entailed estate which belonged to his family. Moreover he was an only son, so once he had been stripped of all his rights and all his fortune, the male line came to an end in the Chernyshevs. Chernyshev, who served so *zealously* on the Committee, took advantage of this circumstance to present his own claims to the whole estate. The Senate afterwards reviewed that case, found that the General's claims had not the least basis in law, and adjudged that the estate should go to the elder sister of the Count, who had been exiled to Siberia. This sister was married to a Kruglikov who, on receiving the estate, began to call himself Count Chernyshev-Kruglikov.[39]

All of us who were in Chita had much in common in our main convictions;

but while some of us were forty-year-olds, others had barely passed twenty. Such was our way of life then that no one in the prison was constrained by any social conventions in relationships with others. And every individual's personality showed itself very plainly in a great many respects, the views of some differing from those of others, so that gradually there were established little groups of individuals closer to one another in their inclinations and ideas than to the rest. One of these groups laughingly called 'The Congregation,' consisted of those men whose circumstances, during their confinement, had led them to piety. Among their various other occupations, these often met to read didactic works and to discuss the subject closest to their heart. Pushkin, formerly an officer in some dignitary's suite and a man of quite outstanding intellectual abilities, stood at the head of this group. Pushkin had appraised the Gospels' beauty at the time of his confinement and, at the same time, returned to the superstitions of his childhood; he tried in every way to give them meaning. The members of 'The Congregation' were mild, quiet men who bullied nobody and who were therefore on the best of terms with all our other comrades.[40]

Another and more remarkable group was that of the United Slavs. These gathered nowhere in particular but, having known each other even before their arrests, still had the closest of relationships one with another. All had served in the Army [i.e. not the Guards], having no brilliant positions in society, and many of them had been educated in cadet corps, which were not distinguished at that time for good organization. Broadly speaking, the degree of literacy of the Slavs was not remarkable; but as, on the other hand, they had the superstitions of their kind, they showed almost no vacillation whatsoever in their views. Observing them from closer quarters, one became convinced that for each one of *these*, to say and do a thing were the same — that in the decisive moment, not one of them would go back on his word.

The leading individual in this group was Pyotr Borisov, in whom the Slavs had almost endless trust. Some regarded him as the founder of the Society of United Slavs, but he would not confess to this and, knowing him, it was not easy to imagine him as the founder of any secret society.[41] Of an inquiring nature, he had been educated at home. Having entered the artillery as a junker at the age of eighteen, he was stationed with his company for some time on the estate of a wealthy Polish landowner who had a library. Knowing a certain amount of French, and taking advantage of such books as fell into his hands, Borisov now read Voltaire, Helvétius, Holbach and other eighteenth-century writers of that hue, and became a dogmatic atheist. Yet, though he preached unbelief to his comrades in the Slavs, many of whom took his word on the subject, he had the gentlest and most modest disposition; no one ever heard of his having raised his voice, or saw any trace of conceit in him. Benevolence towards everyone was plain in all his actions, and he would carry out the requests of anyone at all with a childlike obedience. He passionately loved to read, and could draw well; but should anyone ask him to dig a bed, he would at once desert his favourite occupations and take up a spade. Should anyone need water for the watering of that bed, Borisov would fetch it in a pail, without reserve. Watching all his actions very closely, it occurred to one involuntarily that *this* man, unreasonably by his own canon, was penetrated with the true spirit of Christianity.

Another man whom I later came to know was Kyukhel'beker,[42] who finished his term of labour in the summer of 1831. Kyukhel'beker had served in the Guards' Equipage, and took a zealous part in the events of December 14th. He had received a good education in a corps, and accompanied Lázarev on his voyage to Novaya Zemlya.[43] Energetic both by nature and by habit, he was a really excellent fellow and at the service of each and every one in Chita and Petrovskiy, being little burdened down by prison life. In Barguzina he found no society whatever and, having no external inducements to intellectual activity, settled down to the task of earning his bread. In his first years, he cleared and ploughed several *desyatins* with his own hands, and planted them with corn.[44] But such work did not preserve him from temptations. Kyukhel'beker became fond of a certain merchant-woman in Barguzina, first christened her child, then married the woman. The child died, but was recorded by no birth-certificate—and out of this, thanks to a deacon's denunciation, grew an affair that reached the Synod. The Synod pronounced Kyukhel'beker's marriage illegal and he, separated from his family, was taken off to Elatskaya *volost'*, some 500 versts from Barguzina. There he wrote a desperate letter to his sister, complaining of the cruelty with which he had been treated in being parted from his wife and little daughter. In consequence of the letter he was sent back to Barguzina, but was obliged not to cohabit with his illegal spouse. All this placed him in so awkward a position that it was easy for him to lose his presence of mind.

M. A. Bestuzhev

After our irons had been removed, on August 30 [1832], our confinement was itself no longer so strict. Husbands would walk over to see their wives each day, and because of the illness of one or other of the wives, a husband would spend the night with her. Finally, husbands did not live in the cells at all, but simply went to work from their wives' houses, as they had earlier, when their turns came round.

The surgeon sent [to treat] us from Irkutsk proved to be most unskilful. For this reason old Leparsky, who himself frequently suffered from various ailments, found himself obliged to have recourse to the advice of our comrade Vol'f, once a staff-surgeon at Second Army Headquarters. At first, Vol'f was not willing to leave his casemate, and would send Artamon Murav'yov, who loved to play the doctor, to Leparsky with prescriptions; but there were certain cases when Vol'f's presence was essential. Having sent for him for himself, it was not easy for the Commandant to forbid Vol'f to visit the ladies when they were ill; and finally Vol'f received permission to go out, accompanied by a sentry, whenever his assistance was required outside the casemate. Then we, too, were allowed to visit married couples, but only one household per man per day, and even then only if a special note was written by one of the ladies asking the Commandant to permit such-and-such a person to visit her under some pretext.

Pushkin was chosen senior in place of Rozen in 1829, and Kyukhel'beker was elected market-gardener. Both men tended the kitchen-garden with considerable attention. This garden was tilled by hired workers, and the total crop was so heavy that, having laid in enough supplies for the prison, Pushkin was able to provide some indigent inhabitants of Chita with potatoes, beetroot, and the like. Before our arrival in Chita, there had been precious few kitchen-gardens, and even those that did exist were in the most pitiable condition. Generally speaking, in fact, our presence there proved beneficial to a point to all in the mining department and to those men directed by mining officials also. Most of these were extremely poor; with us, they had every means of improving their condition. Every year, our ladies' expenditure and the expenses of the prison reached a hundred thousand in notes, a significant proportion of which vanished into Chita itself; within a couple of years, the circumstances of inhabitants of Chita had visibly improved: they bought new outer clothing and everything they needed, and many new houses were built and old structures repaired.

(On Nikolay Bestuzhev's Sketches)

In the whole (of Nikolay's) collection of aquarelle portraits of our fellow prisoners, there were only a few that were painted; nor could these be held the best, from an artistic viewpoint. There were many reasons for that: in the first place, lack of a studio and lighting, in the second, insufficiency of materials with which to paint and, lastly, lack of experience in painting aquarelles. Until now, Nikolay had drawn portraits in miniature, often on ivory, adhering to Isabey's[45] method of elaborate finishes in dots, and the switch to aquarelles of large dimensions, with features and strong tones, went badly for him until we received portraits by our celebrated portraitist Sokolov.[46] My brother was struck by the dash and boldness of Sokolov's brush and, taking him as his model and using his method, painted the remaining and larger part of his collection, as well as many portraits of our ladies, comrades and numerous acquaintances which did not form a part of it. But painting was not his only occupation. Soon indeed, he was completely drawn away from it by mechanical pastimes, so that he subsequently painted portraits only of those fellow prisoners whose groups had served their full sentences. And as some of these groups were very large, and time was pressing, one can but marvel at the speed with which he managed to throw off his portraits. But his best works apart from the portraits, and those which he himself liked best, were the views of Chita and Petrovskiy. It is a great pity indeed that he left not a single view of Selenginsk and of the places where we lived. It is the usual story. We make no haste to take what we can always have or what, so to speak, we have at hand; so my brother put it off from day to day, was unable to decide on a place, started work only to destroy it, and died, not leaving even his rough sketches of Selenginsk.

On Crafts Which Nikolay Bestuzhev Learnt

It was to me that the idea of the iron rings came first. At the time, cobbling and cartography had already wearied me. Naturally, I changed to the locksmith's and goldsmith's crafts all the more willingly for having an indulgent, skilful teacher in my brother, as well as all the necessary tools. But it is difficult to start with what is difficult, so I began with the simplest and easiest work: and the idea occurred to me to make rings out of our chains for our sisters and mother. When, by a gracious manifesto, our chains were removed, in Chita — chains which could not legally have been placed on us — I and several other prisoners gave a tip and a few gifts from our poor wardrobe to a soldier, and concealed the chains. These served me as my first raw material for rings. But five rings that we sent off did not reach their destination, but adorned the fingers of some postal official's daughters. So, aided by my brother and Gromnitsky, (his most keen, quick-witted pupil), I made another five, and this time set them not with silver but with gold from the rings of our ladies, who gave them up so that my brother and I would make *them* such iron rings. Soon, the craze for these rings had spread to such an extent that not only did our ladies and many friends desire them for themselves and their relations, but we received requests from [mere] acquaintances and strangers through acquaintances, so that the occupation, instead of being a pleasure, turned into hard labour, and we started to turn down requests! Then, just as in Rome there was counterfeiting of ancient works of art, so in Petrovskiy there emerged industrial counterfeiting — of Decembrist rings! The best smiths in Petrovskiy Zavod opened small shops to sell these sacred rings, while the dandies and the fashionable women of Kyakhta, Udinsk and Irkutsk came or sent to these improvised emporia, and proudly flaunted such a cheap distinction before others.

On Occupations in Chita and Petrovskiy Zavod

In Chita we were packed in cells like herring in a box. Constriction, stuffiness, filth and the concomitant delights, such were the conditions of our life throughout our whole stay there, and never did they change. Nor should it be forgotten that we were chained up, or that we were more restless, more talkative and younger then. So you must take into account the ceaseless chatter and the din of chains and voices. Also to be borne in mind is that, for all Leparsky's kindness, the administration had not yet become accustomed to all this; orders were strictly carried out, and our administration was completely bound by orders. Now, perhaps, you may see a pale shadow of our Chita life.

In Petrovskiy Zavod, all was quite different: here we almost all had separate rooms, which was the greatest luxury for us. But whether for good or for evil, our government goes the whole hog in nothing. Thus our new quarters were constructed in the style of horse-stables, and let in barely sufficient light to enable us to eat a piece of rye-bread and not miss our mouth with it. Through our ladies, we raised an uproar. We were ordered to knock windows through, but even then only a postage-stamp of God's light was admitted; and to make use of that light we were obliged to raise ourselves by means of trestles! In my brother's room, these trestles were built to last, and spaciously enough to support all his benches and machines; so they took up almost half the room. But mine were lightly made, with a view to comfort.

N. V. Basargin

Our quarters, then, were exceedingly confined. In the first room, eight *arshins* long and five wide, lived sixteen men; in the second, of practically the same dimensions, were another sixteen, and in the third tiny room, four. In the other building, it appears, it was more congested still. Each man had three quarters of an *arshin* on which to sleep on the boards, so that in turning over on one's side during the night one had necessarily to knock a neighbour— especially as we wore chains that were not taken off at night and which produced a quite extraordinary noise as well as perceptible pain with every careless movement. But to what cannot youth grow accustomed? What can it not endure? We all slept as well as in luxurious beds or on feather mattresses.

This tightness was even more obvious during the day. So little space was there for movement that it was impossible for all of us to step off the boards at once! Moreover, the noise of the irons was so great that one had to speak loudly even to be heard. At first, we were allowed to walk only around the courtyard of our building, but later we were not forbidden to go out when we so wished during the day. Permission to do *this* was almost unavoidable in such cramped conditions; to have withheld it, and the air and exercise, would have caused an epidemic. Still, the courtyard was small and surrounded by a stockade, at either end of which there stood a guard—and two at the gate; consequently, there was nothing to be feared.

When wives visited their husbands, everyone living in the room that had been designated for the meeting was led out. In fine weather, of course, we went and sat or strolled in the courtyard, but in bad weather we would all gather in the other room, and then we were like herring in a box! A common dinner was prepared for all. Usually it consisted of plain or cabbage soup and porridge with butter; all this was carried in in wooden vats, from which we took helpings onto our plates. At dinner time, trestles were brought into our room and planks then placed across them, covered with cloths or napkins; the food was set on this table, and we sat just wherever was possible—round the table, on the boards, in short, in total disorder. Supper, too, we ate anyhow, some standing, others walking about. Each man would take his piece of roast meat and consume it how and where he wished. Often it happened that, having lain down to sleep on a narrow bed made of thick felt, one suddenly felt something under one's ribs—something hard—and found a bone left there from dinner or supper.

The government allotted six brass kopeks a day for our upkeep and two pounds of flour a month, in accordance with the rule for all working exiles. Needless to say, we did not get that much, nor was the sum enough even for food, let alone maintenance. But as some of us had brought money which was entrusted to the Commandant—money to which the ladies, for their part, willingly added part of their own resources—there was formed a general fund sufficient to meet all our common needs. Besides this, the ladies sent us in coffee, chocolate, and various foodstuffs that served us as sweets. From the books brought by each individual we formed a tolerable library which all were free to use, and this proved one of our most pleasant occupations and most useful relaxations.

Working days were fixed for us; every day excepting feast days we were led out under escort to fill in a kind of ditch at the other end of the settlement, this for three hours in the morning and two hours after lunch. And very glad we were to have our work, since it allowed us to meet our friends from the other casemate. But we were not compelled to work; having first brought over a few wheelbarrows of earth, we generally sat down to talk or read a book which we had brought along, and so passed the hours of 'work.' One of us, I don't know who, named the ditch 'The Devil's Grave,' and they say that it still bears the name. Later, they thought up another task for us: they had a hand-mill built, with several mill-stones, and took us there to grind corn. But here, too, we did almost nothing, chatted, read, played chess, and only for the sake of form would we go in to the mill-stones for ten minutes—and grind two or three pounds of flour of worthless quality. Here, too, the Commandant must be given his due; in his kindness, he looked through his fingers at all this, and generally behaved towards us with indulgence and humanity.

We ourselves were forbidden to write to our relatives. In this respect as in many others where the limits of men's freedom were concerned, we were liable to the same rules as exiles of low birth. In other cases, indeed, we lost even the last scrap of freedom enjoyed by these. The arrival and the presence of our ladies greatly lightened our lot; for they could not be forbidden to write, and willingly took on the task of being secretaries for us, that is, they wrote to our relatives as from themselves but in the name of, and according to instructions from, each one of us, so establishing a correspondence and keeping up our contacts with our families.[47] Not three months had passed before most of us began to receive letters and aid from relatives.[48] Moreover, their presence was most beneficial to us even where our life in prison, upkeep, and treatment by officials were concerned. Through them, we could address the Commandant like free men not responsible for breaking that condition of dependence to which our sentence doomed us. Thus they became witnesses, even, one might say, participators in our lives, and *they* enjoyed all their rights; consequently, they could complain not only privately to their relations, but even to the government — which was obliged to spare them if only so as not to arouse public opinion against itself, earn the charge of cruelty and submit to the just condemnation of posterity and history. More than once, in their ignorance of criminal and civil law and not accepting that unbounded power which the government holds over the condemned, but standing only on their sentiments of justice and humanity, the ladies entered into disputes with the Commandant (as when some inconvenient measure was taken against ourselves), and uttered the most harsh and biting words right to his face. Calling him jailor, they would say that no *decent* man would have taken on his duty unless it were, despite the consequences and the Tsar's displeasure, to do all that he could to alleviate our lot — and that if he did act in this way, he would earn not only their respect but that of every man and of posterity as well. Otherwise (they said) they would regard him as a common jailor who had sold himself for money. Such words, needless to add, could not fail to produce an effect on the old man, the more so because he found them just in his heart. 'For heaven's sake,' he would reply, after one of these outbursts, 'do not get so heated, Madame! Be reasonable, I will do everything that depends on me, but you are demanding something that must compromise me in the government's sight. I'm sure you wouldn't want me to be made a private for not having followed my instructions.' 'Well,' they replied to this, 'be a private, General, but be a gentleman!'[49] What was he to do with them after that?

Both the situation and the climate of Chita were excellent. The luxuriance of the plant growth was extraordinary; everything that grew there reached amazing proportions. The air, moreover, was so good for me especially that nowhere else and never before had I enjoyed such health. Having, as I said earlier, a frail and feeble constitution, I seemed to gain new strength each day, and finally became so strong that I was practically another person. But in general we all became more healthy while in Chita. Having arrived exhausted by our solitary confinement and our moral trials, we were now spared all the consequences of those sufferings. Of course, our youth helped greatly in this, but the climate, too, was of no small assistance. Moreover, the absence of all physical ailments produced its necessary effect upon our spirits. We were cheerful, bore our situation easily and, living together like so many members of one family, gazed steadily and calmly towards the future awaiting us. To a greater or lesser extent, each one of us tried to keep busy doing something. Some, with the help of books and friends, studied languages they did not know: French, German,

English, Latin, Greek, and even Hebrew. Others took up mathematics, poetry, history, painting, music, and even manual skills. We constructed a tent in the courtyard, and would sit there days on end with a book and slate (to write on paper was forbidden), not seeing how the time passed. We usually strolled in small groups in the evenings, chatting about different things. But best of all was the fact that there was no question of reproaches amongst ourselves, nor were there even references to the trial. Though many of us had made careless statements, and had this or that 'lack of firmness' on one of our comrades' part to thank for our present state, no one allowed himself even a comment as to how others had behaved during the trial and enquiry. It was as though all hostile thoughts had been left behind us in the cells, and only mutual liking remained.

At the beginning of our time in Chita, I remember, we would frequently discuss the possibility of escaping our captivity. And I recall this all the more distinctly because our plan to sail down the Amur to Sakhalin has now been proven possible.[50] It was a question of disarming the guards and all officials and troops stationed in Chita, holding the Commandant and officers captive for a while and then, joining our forces, of getting guns, provisions, building a boat or barge and sailing down the Rivers Argun' and Shilka to the Amur and so to Sakhalin. We would have sailed down to the Amur's very mouth, then acted according to circumstances. The plan, I am convinced, could very well have been effected. There were seventy of us—young, healthy, determined men; to disarm the guards and walk out of our casemates would have caused no difficulty, the more so as most of the soldiers would then have stood with us. The whole garrison consisted of a little over a hundred men, and one might reasonably suppose that half of these would have joined us; the officers and Commandant would not have resisted us, and before news of our action could have reached Irkutsk and measures been taken against us, we could easily have built a craft, loaded up and sailed away—so taking ourselves beyond pursuit. In Chita, moreover, we should have found all that we needed: food, arms, and ammunition in sufficient quantities for our journey. As for the voyage down the Amur, it could have been accomplished with no special difficulties, as was later demonstrated by Governor-General Murav'yov's expedition. In short, there was a high probability of success. But difficulties did exist: unexpected resistance from the garrison, for example, and the consequent need to resort to force, perhaps killing several innocent men, would have charged our conciences with shedding blood simply and only for the sake of our own freedom. Then there were unforeseen eventualities, such as the accidental and premature discovery of our project by the Commandant or officers; and a lack of decisiveness by any one of us at the last moment. Finally, there was the question of the ladies: to leave them (to which they would most probably not have agreed) in the hands of an exasperated government or, taking them with us, to subject them to all the deprivations and dangers of our bold and disloyal undertaking. Thoroughly considering all this, and finding the objections of our more cautious comrades well grounded, ardent youth had to concur with prudence, and cease to think of its own liberation.

It was at this time that there occurred an incident in our casemate that might have had unhappy consequences for us all, and which showed the Commandant's good sense and kindliness towards us. It happened once that Madame Murav'yova came to see her husband in the presence of the officer on duty. This officer, Lieutenant Dubinin, was well named;[51] moreover he was not sober on this particular day. As usual, Murav'yov and his wife remained alone with this Dubinin in one of the rooms and we all dispersed, some to the courtyard, others to the other casemates. Madame Murav'yova was not well, and lay down on her husband's bed, discussing something with him and sometimes introducing French words and phrases into the conversation. But this displeased the officer, who roughly told her to speak Russian. She, glancing at him and not quite understanding, asked her husband (again in French), 'Qu'est-ce qu'il veut, mon ami?' Then Dubinin, who had lost all commonsense under the influence of wine, and who perhaps supposed that she was cursing him, suddenly seized her by the arm and shouted furiously: 'I order you to talk Russian!' Poor Murav'yova, not expecting such an outburst or such insolence, screamed in fright and ran from the room into the corridor. Despite her husband's efforts to restrain him, Dubinin ran after her. Most of us, including Murav'yova's brother, Count Chernyshev, heard the noise; we opened the door between our room and the corridor to find out what was happening. We saw the poor woman, in a near fit of hysterics and in tears, being pursued by Dubinin. In an instant we were on him, seized him — but he had already managed to reach the steps where, in a rage, he lost his head and shouted to the guards and sentries at the gate to fix bayonets and help him. We, in our turn, shouted to them to remain in their positions, that the officer was drunk, and that he did not know what orders he was giving. Fortunately they listened to us and not the officer, remained impassive onlookers and allowed Murav'yova to pass through the gates. We then asked the senior under-officer to run immediately to the Town-Adjutant and fetch him. Dubinin we released only when he was calm again and when the under-officer had set off to carry out our instruction. Then he ran off in the same direction. The Town-Major appeared, and at once relieved Dubinin from his duties. We told him all that had happened, and he asked us to calm ourselves. It was quite plain, however, that he feared that some serious issue might result from this, and that he might himself suffer some punishment for his excessive indulgence towards us. The Commandant was not in Chita then. He was expected the next day or the day after that. Until he did arrive, we were not taken out to work so that we might not communicate with our companions. Surveillance became generally stricter. On his return, the Commandant went straight to Aleksandra Grigor'yevna Murav'yova, apologized to her for Dubinin's rudeness and assured her that in future not one of the ladies would be subjected to such impertinence. Then he called on us, took out Murav'yov and Chernyshev, spoke for some time with them and asked us all, through them, to be as careful as possible in future. 'What', he asked, 'if the soldiers were not so sensible and obeyed the officer and not you? You might all have died. Then it would have been impossible to hide the affair. True, the officer gave grounds for offence first, and would have had to answer for himself; but of what use would that have been to you? You'd have been sentenced as rioters in any case, and in your situations exposed yourselves to God knows what. ...'

Meanwhile, in the summer of 1827, other temporary quarters were being built for us. I say temporary, because at the same time a large prison-fortress was being built in the Petrovskiy ironworks 600 versts from Chita, to which the government intended to transport us, and later did. These quarters in Chita were completed towards autumn, and we were all taken there. The building was of two parts divided by a wide corridor. Each half contained two large rooms which did not, however, communicate with one another.[52] Fifteen or twenty men could comfortably be given space in each; and each of us had his own bed and, beside it, a night table. Sufficient space remained in the middle of the room, even when we were all in it, for a large table with benches round it. Fifteen men were left in one of our former casemates, while the other was turned into an infirmary, should any of us fall sick. Also in this second (former) casemate, husbands had meetings with their wives. Soon, however, husbands were allowed to visit their wives in their apartments, under escort; nor, after the Dubinin incident, was there an officer present during these meetings.

In the autumn and winter of 1827, our remaining comrades started to arrive — those who had been in Finnish fortresses, as well as the eight who had been sent to the Nerchinsk mines immediately after their sentencing. Two came with their wives, the Princesses Trubetskaya and Volkonskaya. Having set out for Siberia with their husbands, these two ladies had been living with them all the time that they were in the mines. By winter's end, all of us who had been sentenced to hard labour were in Chita, excepting only Baten'kov, V. K. Kyukhel'beker and A. V. Poggio, who for some unknown reason had been left in fortresses. The first spent some twenty years in confinement, the other two about ten years each.

The arrival of our new comrades, the tales that each could tell of what had befallen him after his sentencing, of what he had suffered, how he had passed the recent months and so forth, quite naturally formed the topics of our conversation. Moreover, we had now begun, through our ladies, to receive journals and newspapers. A war was being fought with Persia then, and later, one with Turkey.[53] The progress of these wars could only interest us; we had not yet forgotten our military service, or grown indifferent to the triumphs of our arms — practically all the officers most active on our side, from the C.-in-C. to the last general, were known to us. Many of those who distinguished themselves in these campaigns, indeed, were our comrades, and some even our friends. Consequently we followed with the greatest interest every success of the Russian forces, every great deed by some acquaintance or some former friend of ours. Many are now statesmen, well-known generals or administrators — and I am certain that they still have warm memories of us. Those whom *I* have chanced to meet, at least, have not only not forgotten me, but have met me with the same warmth, the same frankness as before, as though there were no difference in our social standing. I thank them for this, and with all my heart! For it serves as proof to me that I was not mistaken in my choice of youthful attachments.

Soon we had organized a number of common pastimes and discussions of a general, instructive kind. Each Sunday morning, many of us met to read aloud religious passages — our own translations from distinguished English, French or German preachers, for example, or sermons by famous ecclesiastics of the Russian Church — and we would finish with a reading of several chapters from the Gospels, the Acts of the Apostles, or the Epistles. Twice a week we met for literary discussions, too. Then each of us would read something of his own composition or something that he had translated on a topic of his choice: history, geography, philosophy, political economy, poetry. ... There were even concerts, or musical evenings. Odoyevsky's fine, sonorous verses, which reflected well our situation and were consonant with our views and our love of the fatherland, were often sung by a choir and to the music of one of our musical comrades. It was at this time that Pushkin, our celebrated poet, sent us his epistle:

Deep in the Siberian mine,　　　　*Friendship and love shall come to you,*
Keep your patience proud;　　　　*Come through the gloomy doors,*
The bitter toil shall not be lost,　　*Even as round your galley-beds*
The rebel thought unbowed.　　　　*My free voice pours.*

The sister of misfortune, Hope,　　*The heavy-ringing irons shall fall,*
In the under-darkness dumb　　　　*The walls shall crumble at a word*
Speaks joyfully courage to your heart:　*And freedom greet you at the gates;*
The day desired shall come.　　　　*And brothers shall revenge you all.*[54]

It was in 1827, too, that the betrothed of one of our comrades, Annenkov, came out from Russia to join him. She was a French girl,[55] and had personally asked the Tsar's permission to travel to Siberia and join her fate to Annenkov's, having agreed already to every condition imposed. The Sovereign granted her request. She was given a sheet of paper to sign by which she renounced all her rights and subjected herself to all the restrictions, all the measures that could be taken in the event of her marrying a state prisoner. She arrived in Chita in the summer and was married three days later in the settlement church. It was a curious wedding, perhaps unique in the world. During the marriage ceremony Annenkov's irons were removed and then, the ceremony over, at once put on again, and he was led back to his casemate. Afterwards, the pair were treated like the other married couples, that is to say, they were allowed to meet twice weekly in Madame Annenkova's apartment.

By July 1830 we had been rather more than three years in Chita. For a long time we had known that a prison-fortress was being built to house us in Petrovskiy Zavod, and that we should all be taken there. Twice already the Commandant had gone there to supervise and hasten work.

Finally, the officers themselves told us that we should be transferred from Chita.

Though Chita prison had not been precisely comfortable for us, especially during the winter when there had been cruelly cold spells and we had had to sit whole days in rooms that were far from warm, the little windows frosted up so that light barely passed through them and so that candles had to be lit by 3 P.M. it was so dark; and though the noise made by the movement and the talk of twenty men gave little peace and kept one from all serious occupations, still we were now accustomed to that life—so accustomed that it was with regret that we thought of the impending change.

At last, the Commandant told us to prepare ourselves for the march to Petrovskiy Zavod. We were to walk there, covering the distance between two stations, twenty or thirty versts, each day, and resting one day in three. Those individuals whose health was poor, including me, were given permission to take a wagon with one other man, so that we could now and then sit down; and a lean horse was provided for this purpose. We were all split up into two parties, the first setting off three days ahead of the second. Both parties had an officer and escort, and the Commandant and Town-Major travelled independently, now visiting one party, now the other, at their own discretion. As to the ladies, they might go ahead to Petrovskiy Zavod or follow us in their own carriages and at their own expense.

While in Chita, I had had the solace of receiving letters and a little money from my relatives. One of my brothers, so his wife informed me, had been in the Turkish campaign; another, retired and living in the country, quickly replied to a letter from one of the ladies. I also received news from my late wife's relatives, and sorrowful it was: my five-month-old daughter, whom I had left with them and who was the sole token of my brief marriage, had died eighteen months earlier. This deeply affected me.

Just before we departed from Chita, an experience befell my friend Ivashev that clearly demonstrated the benevolence of Providence towards him. I have already mentioned, I think, that he, Mukhanov, and Zavalishin remained, at their request, in our first small casemate. It was freer and quieter for them there. I often visited them, with the Commandant's permission, sitting whole hours with them, and other comrades also came. In their turn, they often called on us. Besides all this, we saw each other almost every day at our work. Ivashev, as I earlier remarked, was quite unable to get used to his present situation, which visibly oppressed him. We would often speak of this among ourselves, and I did my best to support him and to give him more resolution. Nothing helped. He was gloomy, reflected, and depressed. Then once, at our work, Mukhanov took me aside to tell me that Ivashev was preparing to do something very foolish, which might cost him his life. He had decided to speak to me about it, he said, so that I, on my part, could try to dissuade Ivashev. Then he told me that Ivashev planned to flee.

This was the situation: Ivashev had established contact with some fugitive exile or other who was promising to conduct him across the Chinese frontier. This fugitive was to come the following night to the casemate stockade, which was already sawn through, a place from which to escape having been prepared. Leaving the prison, they would make for nearby woods where, in the fugitive's words, an underground shelter was ready; and there they would hide until the searching was over — sufficient supplies had already been laid in. When the searches were called off, the pair proposed to set out for the Chinese border and there act as the circumstances dictated. The project was so ill thought out, so stupid even, and its realization so impossible, that I wondered that Ivashev had agreed to it. There could be little doubt that the man who had tempted him to flee had some other motive: either to hand him over to the authorities in return for his own pardon, or to murder him and take the money on him—and I know that Ivashev had money. When he arrived in Chita, he did not declare to the Commandant the 1000 roubles he had brought with him, and on top of this he had secretly acquired another 500. He told me this himself.

Having heard Mukhanov out, I went immediately after our period of work to Ivashev, told him I knew of his intention and that I had come to discuss it. Very calmly he replied that it would be futile to try to dissuade him, that he was quite resolved to carry out his plan, and had not told me of it long before only because he had no wish to place me under any responsibility. To all my arguments, all my reasoning about the superficiality of his undertaking—and the danger threatening him—he merely repeated the same thing, that he could no longer stay in jail and that it was better to die than to live in such a fashion. My objections exhausted, I did not know what to do. Time was so short—the next day was already fixed for the escape and there remained only one way of stopping him—letting the Commandant know. But it is terrible to be an informer on one's colleague, one's friend. Finally, seeing that all persuasions were vain, I said decisively: 'Listen, Ivashev. I ask you in the name of our friendship to postpone your attempt one week. In that week we'll thoroughly discuss your project, weigh *le pour et le contre* objectively, and if you still feel the same way, then I promise you I'll make no difficulties.' 'And if I don't agree to put it off for a week?' he retorted heatedly. 'If you refuse,' I replied, 'you'll force me to do out of love what I loathe. I shall immediately request an interview with the Commandant and tell him everything. You know me well enough to be certain that I'll do it, if I think it's the only way of saving you.' Mukhanov supported me. At last, Ivashev gave us his word to wait one week. I did not fear that he would break it, the more so as Mukhanov lived with him and so could watch him.

Two days after this conversation, I again asked permission to see Ivashev, and we talked over his plans. I listed all the dangers, all the improbability of his succeeding; and he was still insisting on having his own way when suddenly there enters an under-officer and tells him that the Commandant wishes to see him. Ivashev glanced at me. 'Forgive me a momentary suspicion, friend Basargin,' he said, 'but what might *this* mean? I don't understand.' I told him I would wait till he returned, and remained with Mukhanov.

Ivashev did not return quickly—the Commandant kept him two hours, and we had no idea to what the long absence could be ascribed. We even feared that his ridiculous plan had somehow been discovered. But at last he came in, distraught, and told us, in disjointed phrases, news that stunned us too. The

Commandant had sent for him to give him two letters, one from his mother, the other from the mother of his future wife. Was he willing, the Commandant asked, to marry this girl whose mother had written a letter, which was addressed to Ivashev's own mother? In it, Madame Le Dentu told her of her daughter's love for her, Madame Ivasheva's, son; said that this love had caused a serious illness in her daughter during the course of which, expecting to die, she had revealed her affection. The mother had thereupon given her word to her daughter that, when she recovered, she would inform Madame Ivasheva of this and, if she and her son agreed, would allow her daughter to travel to Siberia to marry him. Madame Le Dentu also mentioned in the letter that never would her daughter have revealed her secret had Ivashev been in his former position—but that now that misfortune had struck him and she *knew* that her presence might afford him comfort, her daughter had not hesitated in breaking the conventions of society. Ivashev's mother had sent this letter, together with her own, to Count Benkendorf who, with the Tsar's permission, instructed the Commandant to ask Ivashev himself if he was willing to marry the girl Le Dentu.

Ivashev asked the Commandant to wait for a reply until the following day. We discussed this unexpected turn at length. Ivashev knew the girl very well; she had been educated with his sisters at his home, and he had liked her very well when he had gone there on leave— but he never thought of marrying her because of all the difference in their social standings, which would not let him entertain the thought. But now, recalling certain details of his earlier relationship with her, he found himself convinced that she had felt affection for him. He was much disturbed, however, by the questions of whether he would be able to repay her with his love for the sacrifice that she would make for him, whether she would be happy with him in his present situation, and whether he might not regret his action afterwards. Mukhanov and I knew his gentle nature and all his good qualities, and were sure they would be happy. And he at last agreed to accept the proposal. Needless to say, there was no talk of flight after this resolution.[56]

8

Petrovskiy Zavod

The move to the new prison of Petrovskiy Zavod, in August 1830, marked the first great watershed in the Decembrists' exile.[1] Already the compact, closeknit community of Chita was beginning to break up when, in the spring of 1828, state convicts in the seventh category were released and sent to scattered settlements in the far north of Siberia (where they suffered more than hitherto). The move away from Chita greatly speeded up that process. Soon after their arrival in Siberia, several Decembrists had expressed remorse for their participation in a plot against the tsar, and asked for pardon, which was speedily refused them; now, sensing that a change was in the air, other and prouder souls wrote to the tsar requesting that they serve as private soldiers in the Caucasus, where war was being waged as usual against Circassian tribesmen. 'The sufferings of a military man destined to rot in idleness,' wrote Aleksandr Bestuzhev piteously, 'especially when the glory of Russian arms thunders above Mohammed's grave, are comprehensible to noble hearts trained in battle. ...'[2] But still it was a handful who appealed, and an even tinier minority of the Decembrists who succeeded in winning a pardon from Nicholas, in whose memory December 14, 1825 retained an awful clarity. Most thought such an appeal humiliating. That feeling was expressed with mordant sarcasm by Lunin, perhaps the least conciliatory of all Decembrists, and one who actively opposed the tsarist government until his death: 'I hear (wrote Lunin) that some of our political exiles have expressed their wish to serve as privates in the Caucasian army, hoping to make their peace with the government. In my view, it is unwise of them to do so before subjecting themselves to some slight scrutiny – the first day one would ask to be flogged fifty times, the second day a hundred, the third two hundred. ... After this self-examination, one could declare: *dignus, dignus est intrare in isto docto corpore.*'[3] Few of the Decembrists showed such grim intransigence.

Many Decembrists viewed the coming march to Petrovskiy, 430 miles to the west, with the deepest consternation: the new prison was reported to be poorly built, windowless, and near a noisome swamp. In the event, it proved almost a holiday, a curious carnival full of unspoken hopes for freedom in the future. At last, after their long and dull confinement, the group was on the move again. One unforeseen result of the departure for Petrovskiy, however, was that a single group had soon become a cluster of small groups, of 'congregations,' married circles, trios and quartets. No less than inner change and stress, as exiles strove to come to terms with new faces and places, a sense of social dissolution is implicit in most memoirs that we have. There is another face to the coin, of course: new social balancings and rearrangements resulted in new friendships, some of which lasted until one of the pair, trio or quartet died or was killed. And there *was* still evidence of mutual aid on a material level – the Petrovskiy Zavod artel was infinitely better organized than its haphazard Chita predecessor, and assisted more men more effectively.[4] Yet one cannot help suspecting, having read appropriate passages in memoirs, that though hard *financial* problems were well handled in Petrovskiy, problems of an emotional kind were far less adequately handled than had earlier been the case. Weaker brethren are not mentioned by such competent and self-sufficient fellows as Basargin and Yakushkin, and even Baron Rozen only fleetingly alludes to them. How were the weaker brethren actually weaker than these three? One is reduced to making subtle suppositions on the evidence available.[5] Again, one is reminded, the closeknit, dense community of Chita, (to which the promenade west to Petrovskiy gave glorious but passing self-awareness), was, by the fall of 1833, a thing of memory. Of course, every Decembrist would be conscious all his life of belonging to a special group of comrades; nothing could alter that. But never would the consciousness of sheer fraternity experienced on the march of 1830 return at such a level of intensity. Never again would mutual tolerance be so wide.

Petrovskiy Zavod was a real prison, not a makeshift reinforced strongpoint like Chita. It looked forbidding and depressing. Moreover, its twelve identical sections, long corridors, and general, oppressive sense of order were continual reminders that this was a true convict jail. Unable to foregather casually for meals, or after meals for a long stroll or game of chess, as formerly, the exiles tended more and more to live their private lives. Each had a cell, which excellently suited Zavalishin, Nikita Murav'yov and several others. But not all the Decembrists were of scholarly inclination. Cards appeared, then, later, wine. Leparsky was, as earlier, accommodating beneath his stern exterior, and soon husbands were spending nights in their wives' homes in the settlement. (Women with children were forbidden to live in the prison.) Later still, the cells of wealthy, childless, married couples came to look like cramped hotel rooms, with soft furniture and rugs, paintings and porcelain dinner sets.

Nothing, perhaps, is more arresting in the passages of memoirs that deal with this period than the way in which, often unwittingly, they reveal deep differences of temperament and character; in this respect, the following brief extracts are typical. Now, in Petrovskiy, those with specialized interests could follow them, and did so. Others drank, played cards, and idled. Once blurred, the lines dividing individuals and sets from one another seem to grow sharper. Mikhail Bestuzhev, it emerges, *needed* books, journals, and intellectual conversation. To Yakushkin, these were pleasant things but of less moment. Gorbachevsky hardly mentions such trivia. Again, Basargin quickly took an interest in the convict-workers of Petrovskiy, in their honesty, well-being, past and future, that Trubetskoy would never share. For some, the move from Chita marked the dawning of a period of intellectual growth. Others, already highly educated, found interests that would sustain them in the lonelier years to come – Gorbachevsky in shamanism,[6] for example, and Yakushkin in meteorology. Others again declined in mind and body, growing physically and emotionally unstable.[7] It was, in short, a period of flowering individualism. With the forces and resources now acquired, some would be tolerably well equipped to face life in a solitary settlement on their release; others would be so ill-prepared that death would threaten them.[8] Most survived, but the fittest fared best.

One after the other, the Decembrists were released from prison and allowed to establish themselves as free settlers in Siberia. Most left Petrovskiy between 1835 and 1837. But though freedom was now closer – or, at least, a pseudo-freedom – middle age was even closer. Their lives, most realized by now, were damaged quite beyond repair. With this grim realization, psychological pressures mounted suddenly on men untroubled by them for the previous four years or, rather, happily unconscious of them.

Leparsky died in 1837. His successor, General Reybinder (Rehbinder), tried at first to stiffen the régime; but on meeting a sharp rebuff from those prisoners still left, he soon resigned himself to the existing lax conditions. Finally, in July 1839, the remaining group of convicts was released. 'I have the honour to announce,' wrote Vadkovsky to his sister on August 20, 'the happy delivery of Mme Petrovskiy prison. ... She has brought 23 children into the world at once, after a somewhat difficult pregnancy of 13 consecutive years! May the good Lord bless the mother! As for the little ones, they look pretty likely to live, though all are more or less asthmatic, or rickety, or valetudinary, or greying. ...'[9] Among those released were Trubetskoy, Obolensky, Pushchin and the two Borisov brothers, the elder of whom was growing insane.

Both because of its intrinsic interest and because most memoirists dwell on it pleasurably, the six-week promenade to Petrovskiy will be given prominence here; later passages are chosen to reflect the wide and varied interests of the Decembrists in the years 1830–36, as well as their material arrangements and their (subsequently much exaggerated) physical deprivations.

N. V. Basargin

In July—I do not remember the date—we set out from Chita.[10] I was in the first party. It was with regret that we left forever the place where we had lived more than three years, and which had left many pleasant impressions in my memory. A few of the inhabitants of Chita had so come to like us that they wept on parting from us, and accompanied us to a ferry more than three versts from the settlement. Especially had we won the affection of Madame Smol'-yaninova, the wife of the Chita mining engineer. Every day while we were working she sent us breakfasts of her own cooking and tried to be of use to everyone; but she was most devoted to Annenkov and Zavalishin. Annenkov's maternal grandfather, General Yakobi [Jacobi], had once been Governor-General in Siberia and of service to the father of Smol'yaninova. She could not forget this, and held it a sacred duty to repay the grandson for the grandfather's good deed. It was a beautiful trait in a simple, uneducated woman. Indeed, she suffered on Annenkov's account and did not regret it at all: a letter handed to her by Madame Annenkova, and which she sent in secret to a Moscow relative of Annenkov's, fell into the possession of the government. From the letter it was clear that it had come via Smol'yaninova. The Commandant was ordered to arrest her for a week. Zavalishin later married her daughter and lived with them in Chita when his term of close imprisonment was ended.[11]

Our march to Petrovskiy Zavod, which took just over a month in the most delightful summer weather, was more of a pleasant walk for us than an exhausting journey.[12] Even now I think of it with pleasure. We ourselves practically died of laughter on looking at our costumes and our comic procession, which almost always began with Zavalishin in a round hat with a monstrous brim and a kind of black coat of his own design that resembled a quaker's caftan.[12] Being small, he held a stick far taller than himself in one hand, and in the other a book which he read. Besides him came Yakushkin in a little jacket à l'enfant, then Volkonsky in a short, fur-trimmed jacket; then some in long-skirted sacristans' frock-coats, others in Spanish cloaks, others again in blouses—in such comically motley attire, in other words, that had we met some European fresh from the capital he would most certainly have thought that here was a mental asylum, and that the inmates were being taken for a walk. Setting out very early, at around 3 A.M. we would complete our stage for the day towards eight or nine o'clock, then settle down to rest. We did not stop in villages, of which there were very few on the Buriat steppe, but in a field where yurts had already been prepared. We would choose a place by a stream or spring and almost always in picturesque surroundings. So magnificent, so astoundingly beautiful is the countryside of Eastern Siberia, and of Transbaikalia in particular, that one cannot—and could not—help standing in wonder and rapture and gazing at the objects and scenery about one; so rich is that region in flora and in land-scapes pleasant to the eye. The air, too, was so good and steeped in the aromas of sweet-smelling flowers and herbs that one felt a special joy on breathing it.

Both parties had a 'host,' selected by his comrades, who usually set out ahead with helpers to the designated resting place and there prepared the samovars and luncheon. On arriving, we would choose yurts and settle into them, four or five men to a yurt. Having spent some half an hour making up beds and bringing order to our things, we generally set off to bathe and then sat down or, more precisely, lay down to drink tea, and so chatted until dinner. Ivashev, Mukhanov, the two Belyayev brothers and I always shared a yurt. Numbers of friends from other tents usually came over to ours. One of us five was generally on duty, i.e., would pour out tea, bring dinner and lay out the crockery. After dinner, we rested two or three hours then, as the heat diminished, strolled off to take a walk or to admire the surroundings. Then we drank tea and bathed again, and once more chatted until evening.

Our little campsite presented a fine picture in the evening, one worthy of a painter's brush. Around it stood a ring of guards, constantly hailing one another. In various places wood-fires were lit, around which sat our Buriat guides in various positions with their women amongst them, with their strange costumes and Asiatic faces. Fires gleamed in our yurts, too, and through the open entrances one could make out all the interiors and all going on in each of them. Almost always, at this time, most of us would stroll in groups inside the circle of the guards around the campfires, talking to the Buriats and among ourselves. A peerless sight this made in all, and often did I pass whole hours in sitting on some stump, admiring the spectacle around me. A rest day was particularly welcome to us all. Then, we would remain almost two days in the same place, so having time to admire the countryside, to converse and to take a good rest. ... During the march itself, many would go some distance to one side and make botanical investigations of the local flora, or collect insects. The Borisov brothers were particularly fond of this latter occupation and formed a huge and very curious insect collection in Transbaikalia, which, I believe, they sent to the distinguished Professor Fischer in Moscow.[14] Yakushkin was our botanist.

Lunin was in our party. By his original character and mind and education, as by a certain experience of life acquired in high society, he was a most remarkable and most agreeable man. Most of the favourites of that time — Chernyshev, Orlov, Benkendorf and others — were his service comrades. He had once been on the closest terms with Karamzin, Batyushkov and many more outstanding individuals; and we would listen with attention to his tales of behind-the-scenes events in the previous reign, as to his judgements on some statesmen of that era, placed on undeserved pedestals. Prince Volkonsky and Nikita Murav'yov, both also in our party, likewise entertained us highly with their conversation. The former, a member of the upper aristocracy of Russia, a former fligel'-adjutant and a general at the age of twenty-three, had distinguished himself in the campaign of 1812 and served either the Tsar himself or with commanders-in-chief. Many times had he been delegated to execute important missions and, therefore, had seen and learnt much. Murav'yov, the son of Alexander's and the Grand Duke Constantine's tutor, (the celebrated Mikhail Nikitich Murav'yov), was a man of great and diverse knowledge. The position he had occupied in Petersburg aristocratic circles was certainly not insignificant. To the house of his mother, widow of the late M. N., came all the remarkable men of that time: Karamzin, Uvarov, Olenin, Panin, and others.

At last we started to draw near to Petrovskiy Zavod. We had passed through the town of Verkhnyeudinsk and, moving on, were now already stopping in the settlements of Old Believers. In general, these Old Believers live most prosperously and freely in that region. Transported there from Russia in the reign of Catherine and being an industrious and sober people, they soon grew rich in their new homesteads; and several of their settlements amazed us by their size and build. They took us in most hospitably, and we were lodged with them most comfortably during our night stops.

One hundred versts from Petrovskiy Zavod, our ladies went on ahead to prepare rooms for themselves. Some of them had children already. Three of their daughters, born in Chita, are married now and live in Russia with their husbands. They have probably forgotten their birthplace and the circumstances which surrounded their appearance in the world and their childhood.

It was during our last night-camp before reaching Petrovskiy that we read of the July Revolution in Paris, and of the subsequent events.[15] This greatly excited our youthful minds; ecstatically we read every description of the barricades and of the three-day popular insurrection. That evening we all gathered and, having somewhere acquired two or three bottles of sparkling wine, each drank off a glass to the July Revolution. Then we sang the Marseillaise in a choir. Cheerful, and full of hope for a better future for Europe, we came into Petrovskiy.

I. D. Yakushkin

For a long time, old Leparsky pondered on the arrangement of our procession to Petrovskiy. Remembering the past, he organized us as he had conveyed parties of captive Poles during the time of the Confederation War.[16] In front went an advance guard formed of fully-armed soldiers, then came the state convicts, behind whom were dragged supply carts, and lastly came a rearguard. Buriats armed with bows and arrows walked to the sides and along the road. Mounted officers observed the procession in marching formation, while the Commandant himself sometimes dropped back from the first party in order to glance over the second with his own eyes. Naryshkina, Fonvizina and Princess Volkonskaya, not having children, followed us in their own carriages and saw their husbands when we halted for the night. ...

Fairly pleasant weather prevailing, this journey was, generally speaking, a delightful walk for us. During the whole time we were travelling, which was about a month and a half, we covered three stages of some thirty-five versts, all the rest being far shorter and not tiring in the least; but if anyone could not or did not want to go on foot, he could travel by cart, of which quantities were supplied for us and for our baggage at each night-stop. In the morning, hearing the tattoo, we would gather at a meeting place at seven, then, in our determined marching order, set off again. The Buriats were at our service, and carried our greatcoats, pipes and so forth. When we had covered ten versts or a little more, we would make a halt for a couple of hours; here, the married men always had breakfast provided for them, which they shared with single men. We usually arrived fairly early at our night resting place, where we were met by a billeting party, and settled into huts prepared for us. The individual playing the part of host in each party would set off with the billeters and make a dinner that was always pretty substantial; generally speaking, indeed, our rations were far better on the march than they had been in Chita. It was simply a pleasure for us, in comparison with our earlier life, to spend the greater part of the day in the open air—and then to spend the night not locked up in a stuffy cell.

We stood on no ceremony of any kind during our march, and every man went as he pleased; sometimes the good walkers would go two versts ahead of the advance-party, and only then would an officer approach them and ask them to wait for the rest of the group. At river crossings, General Leparsky was always present himself, and could not have been kinder to every one of us who approached him; one might have thought, on such occasions, that he still saw himself as the commander of the Severskiy Regiment.

On the Bratsk steppe, where there were few settlements large enough for us all to find room in them, Buriat yurts were erected for us at each night-rest, all in one line and equidistant from each other. The yurts at the ends were occupied by the authorities, while we settled into the remainder. These round yurts have a wooden base interlaced with narrow slats, the whole being wrapped round with thick felt. An opening is left at the top for smoke to escape through — when a teapot had to be heated up, a fire would be laid in the middle of the yurt. When it is calm, smoke rises freely through the opening; but when a wind blows, it swirls around and finally hangs by the ground. There was a Buriat with every yurt, to serve us.

On first meeting us, these Buriats pretended to understand no Russian at all; but later, when they had been fed, given tea and some tobacco, they grew talkative. Admonishing them, the district police officer had assured them that we were a dangerous crew, each one of us being a sorcerer capable of every kind of magic. Yurts were secured for us from nomads' encampments which were sometimes a hundred versts from the principal road, but they were already in position a month before our arrival. Such arrangements were undoubtedly wasteful for the district. To conform with them, many Buriats had roamed far.

M. K. Yushnevskaya and A. V. Rozen arrived to join their husbands on the way from Chita to Verkhnyeudinsk; they brought many letters and packets with them.

Rainy weather set in towards the end of September, water rose high in the Selenga, and the road which we were to have followed became impassable beyond Verkhnyeudinsk. So another was constructed for us, and the forest felled in places. So convenient was this road that Naryshkina could travel on it in her carriage. The banks of the Selenga River are very beautiful, but later our path lay through hills covered with woods which offered nothing remarkable. When we approached Tarbagatay, on the other hand, a wonderful view opened up before us: all the slopes of the hills facing southwards were cultivated with such thoroughness that one could only admire it. After a countryside that was completely wild, we were entering an area where lived a man whose energy and constant toil had overcome all obstacles presented by a hostile clime; with every step we bore witness to his powers.

The inhabitants of this Old Believers' settlement [of Tarbagatay] came out to meet us wearing festive costume. The men wore blue caftans, the women silk *sarafans* and *kokoshniks*[17] sewn with gold. But these, in their appearance and manners, were not Siberian women; rather did they resemble settlers of Moscow or Yaroslavl' Provinces. There are some 20,000 Old Believers in Transbaikalia, where the natives call them Poles. At the time of the First Partition of Poland, Count Chernyshev seized *raskol'niks*[18] in the Province of Mogilyov who were fleeing abroad, bringing them back to Russia. They were given the choice of joining the Orthodox Church (of the day) or going to Siberia. Many went over to Orthodoxy while others, more stubborn in their belief, were sent off to Eastern Siberia and settled in Transbaikalia. When we passed through Tarbagatay, there still lived there an old man whose own grandsons had turned grey-haired, and who remembered these events. According to his own account, he had come to Irkutsk with his mother and small brother when he had been sixteen; together with twenty-seven male serfs, his mother and his brother were dispatched to Tarbagatay. The place had been an impassable forest. He himself and all the single fellows fit for service had signed up as soldiers then, and he became the batman of a German doctor who, taking pity on his servant's disastrous situation, succeeded in arranging his 'retirement' within two years. In 1830, when we passed through Tarbagatay, there were more than 270 souls there according to the census. In general, most of the Old Believers of Transbaikalia are literate, industrious, and sober, and live in plenty. Twenty versts from Tarbagatay, we passed through a settlement of Little Russians. They had been there more than twenty years already, but those southerners live in nothing like the free style of their Old Believer neighbours.

A light snow fell a few stages before we reached Petrovskiy, and we spent our last night in the yurts.

M. A. Bestuzhev

Of our journey from Chita to Petrovskiy Zavod, it can only be said that it was extremely pleasant for us and beneficial for our health. Indeed, it gave us new reserves of strength for many future years. The weather was fine; the stages of the march were not exhausting, the more so as we rested in an encampment one day in three. We were divided into two parties. The first was commanded by a nephew of Leparsky who owed his life to Vol'f, and who was therefore grateful and amenable to all of us, almost to excess; the Commandant himself headed the second. Both parties were divided into yurts holding four or five men, who stayed together both in the actual yurts and on the Buriat steppe, as well as in houses in the villages through which we passed. My brother's tent and mine was also that of Rozen, Torson and Gromnitsky, my brother's apprentice in all conceivable crafts. Rozen was named the 'host' of our second party, and always he set out ahead of the group by horse and cart to prepare supper, so we found a supper ready on arrival and arrangements made already for the setting up of our yurts. Our yurt, comprised almost entirely of *mécaniciens*, was materially better equipped than any other one; it had every convenience for itinerant living. We had folding beds and a table and chairs all made by our own hands, as well as a travelling luncheon-basket which comfortably held everything required for the table and for tea. All our heavy equipment was carried in carts, on which we were allowed to sit and rest—a privilege of which few took advantage, however. Half-way through any stage of the journey, we made a stop for breakfast. This whole campaign was happily marked by the arrival of two of our ladies: Mar'ya Kazimirovna Yushnevskaya and Anna Vasil'yevna Rozen.

I ask you to judge of our situation when, after a life of such untrammelled freedom, we were locked up in the dark cells of Petrovskiy! I shall not repeat here the story of the *gracious* permission by which a few rays of light were let into our stables; nor shall I speak of our way of life in them. I will merely say a few words about Petrovskiy Zavod. It was a place that differed in no way from all the Siberian factories that were made into penal settlements for criminals—places in which the peasants assigned to a factory were doomed to a worse fate than forced labour. Do not think that I exaggerate—no, this is the truth. For a man doing hard labour and sentenced to so many years of toil, it is almost always possible, if he has behaved himself, to avoid work by the expedient of hiring himself out as a craftsman, or even as a simple artisan, to the factory officials. At the end of his term, he is registered as a settler in the *volost'*,[19] and, once he has lived five years or more without reproach, he has the right to register as a burgher in the town. Then, having received his guild ticket, he may trade on equal terms with any merchant. But the outcast tribe of mine workers and peasants is doomed, right from the cradle, to remain one of smiths, woodcutters, or foundry-hands, and that to the point of utter exhaustion. With my own eyes I saw a grey-haired man of seventy-five, a locksmith called Starchenko, die or, rather, die away while working at his press. And the fate of such men is the more grievous for their being hard-working and diligent. This particular old man was my teacher in casting and niello work. Notwithstanding all my intercessions with the factory authorities, with whom we were on an amicable footing, nothing could be done for him.

Still, our presence in the factory did have a beneficial effect by tempering the insolent arbitrariness of those in charge — an arbitrariness that here replaced all laws, divine and human, everywhere, and which punished the factory hand exactly as the criminal! Either directly or through our servants, all of whom were criminals, abuses that were hidden to Leparsky came to our hearing. And with what pure-hearted loyalty, what disinterested love did those outcasts from society repay us! In all our time at Petrovskiy, not one servant ever sinned against us in either word or deed; and though there were hundreds of criminals serving the first years of their prison sentences, never did we hear of property belonging to us missing — and there were thousands of opportunities for theft. Oh, what a telling psychological history of crime could one compose from all the unvarnished accounts that *we* heard — accounts all the more truthful for the teller's heart having been poured out to us. There was no need to play a part with *us*.[20] No doubt there are exceptions to every rule; but of the crimes of these prisoners, the greater part were necessary consequences of the vicious state of our society. Some were the victims of the inhumanity of landowners or bosses, others of the despair of an insulted father, husband or bridegroom, others again of a chance debauch or, far more commonly, of the arbitrariness of our senseless and unconscionable courts. Our cook, a Crimean Tartar named Salik (who was later returned to his homeland through the personal intercession of Princess Zinaida Volkonskaya with the Tsar), had been exiled for the crime of — happening to be present when a murder was committed! One of Ivashev's serfs, Malyshev, who had served in the gendarmerie and was exceptionally strong, had been sent off to perform hard labour because, when drunk and fast asleep, he had carelessly pushed away a sergeant who had come to wake him up for work. (To the very end of our stay in Petrovskiy, he worked for his master, Ivashev, like a ten-horse-power engine.) We also had in our service a criminal named Zhilkin, Stepan, who managed to wheedle his way to Selenginsk with us; he had been exiled and sentenced to hard labour because of a priest who had met him in a wood, robbed him, and taken his last rouble. Zhilkin had then begun to scold this priest for the greed that had led him to penury, and when the priest replied with oaths and crept up to him to fight, shoved him away with such force that the priest, banging his head against a stump, gave up the ghost. So devoted to us was Stepan that he vanished into thin air the day before it was time for him to return to Petrovskiy at last. Two years later my brother Nikolay, then in Irkutsk, met him on a street which he was levelling with a party of prisoners. Zhilkin recognized my brother, ran up to him and bowed down to the ground before him. Nikolay interceded on his behalf, and he was later given leave to join a house of peasant craftsmen, given the necessary implements, and soon became a well-to-do, diligent worker.

The first of the mining engineers appointed to direct Petrovskiy Zavod was A. I. Arsen'yev, an upright, disinterested, honest and well-intentioned man. We all grew very close to him — my brother and I especially. It was a rare day when he did not visit us in our casemate or when we did not visit him. Amongst us, he was one of us. He and we shared happiness on an equal basis. And he was a true father to the prisoners and hands. Introducing many improvements to the factory itself, he was the first to show that steel not inferior to the best produced in Russia could be made using the cast iron of Petrovskiy Zavod.

Kazimirsky, too, was soon on a friendly footing with us,[21] often visiting inmates and married couples, and inviting us to dinner almost daily. He was a noble man in the fullest sense of the word, and earned our general good-will despite his sky-blue uniform. Towards my brother and myself he was particularly well disposed, and we often visited him, keeping up our acquaintance even later, when we were in a settlement. In response to repeated requests on his part, my brother traveled to Irkutsk to meet him for a final time. This was when Kazimirsky, making his round as district general of gendarmerie, had three times tried to cross Baikal but had been stopped by storms. The journey cost my brother his life: he caught a chill in the spring winds of Irkutsk and thereupon made a 60-verst crossing of Baikal by ice — a crossing during which he gave up his cart to a poor family named Kirensky. For a long time he kept us in ignorance of his illness, which meanwhile advanced. He died still refusing to take medicine. It was as if, after his stoically stubborn fight with Nemesis our step-mother, he had grown weary of this life, and longed for death.[22]

I mentioned earlier, I seem to recollect, that we read almost no newspapers in Chita. In the boiler-room that was our prison society there bubbled steam kept under great pressure; but the stoker-jailors were not yet familiar with the working of such an engine, which every minute threatened them with a terrible explosion, and so they feared to add oil to the fire. A few issues of *Invalid* [The Veteran] did come to us as contraband, but even these were soon cut off after the hymns for the repose of Mariya Fyodorovna.[23] Correspondence with our relatives had just then been established through our ladies, and many of us had already begun to receive both money and parcels, but still very few books were sent. First it was necessary to satisfy the physical requirements: we needed clothes and shoes. Either there *were* no skilled workers in Chita or else, if there were some, they were bad, drunken and idle—so much so, indeed, that having given them our meagre supply of materials, we still remained without clothes! So we ourselves opened up workshops for the various crafts, such as the tailor's, the cobbler's, and the carpenter's. In this way, most of our time was swallowed up by physical pursuits. What with the poor lighting, the constant noise of rattling chains from a *perpetuum mobile* of living creatures and our exhaustion from a day's hard labour with the needle, as well as the hum of *vivos vocos*, it was difficult to indulge in reading, the more so because winter days were short and we were under lock and key from 9 p.m. till dawn. Nevertheless, our store of books, and sensible books at that, grew very large. This store was built up, and was given over to the use of everyone, from all that was sent out to each of us or was received by our ladies to their husbands' orders.

But now, in Petrovskiy Zavod, we started to lead very different lives. Our links with our relatives had already become strong, while continual correspondence through our ladies not only made it possible for us to receive constant financial aid, so improving our material existence, but also furnished ample mental sustenance.

Through our ladies, we of one accord subscribed to the most noteworthy political and literary works of the time, as to the finest periodicals, Russian and foreign alike. Everything at all remarkable then being written and published in Russia, everything printed abroad that was worth reading, whether in journals or in monographs, we received it all without exception. Petrovskiy Zavod spared us from physical pursuits by the great numbers of its craftsmen, and we could plunge with delight into the waves of an intellectual ocean that all but choked us.

I do not mean to enumerate the books in our extensive catalogue, and will mention only those periodicals that remain in my memory. We received the whole range—then limited, of course—of Russian weekly and monthly papers and journals, and among foreign ones: *Revue Britannique, Revue de Paris, Revue des deux mondes, Revue industrielle, Revue du mécanicien, Revue techno-*

logique, Mécanicien anglais, Cabinet de lecture, L'illustration française, Journal pour rire, Journal des débats, L'Indépendence belge, etc., etc. Also *The Times, Quarterly Review, Edinburgh Review, Morning Post, Punch, English Illustration,* etc., etc., *Journal de Francfort, Journal de Hambourg, Allgemeine Zeitung,* etc., etc., *Preussische Zeitung,* and several Polish[24] and Italian papers.

These are only some of the periodicals that have stayed in my memory—you may judge by them of the richness of our intellectual life in the field of current affairs. So that all should read the papers and the journals in good time and without causing offence to others, we elected a Director of Reading from among ourselves for a year. Having been given the post, the Director would allot the time for the reading of each item in the library, receive the mail, compile a list of readers and glue it to each issue of the journals and to the books. When the prescribed time had elapsed, each of us was obliged to hand the item on to the comrades indicated on the list. This system did more than a little to weaken our eyesight.

N. V. Basargin

Petrovskiy Zavod, a large settlement of 2000 inhabitants with government buildings for the manufacture of iron, a foundry, lake and dam, a wooden church and two or three hundred huts, seemed huge to us after sparsely-populated Chita. On entering it, we could easily spot the prison that had been prepared for us. An extensive rectangular building adorned with yellow paint, it occupied, together with the stockade which extended from its sides, a quite considerable area. We saw, too, that our living quarters, or casemates, occupied one side of the rectangle and a half of the two side wings.[25] The area enclosed in the stockade was to be for our walks; in the centre of the front facade was a guardroom and the entrance to the building's interior.

The whole building was divided into twelve sections; on each side there were three, and on the main facade (on each side of the guardroom), six. Each of these sections had its own door into the courtyard and was separate from the others; each section consisted of a corridor and five separate rooms, the exits from which were on that corridor, which was kept warm. Immediately before the exit from the guardroom to the courtyard stood another special building in which were a kitchen, a store-room, and a hall for communal meals. On our arrival, we were quartered in our casemates at once. Because there were not enough of them, some of us were obliged to share one room. As to the rooms, they were fairly high and spacious — but windowless. The light came in through the door, which was immediately opposite a window in the corridor. As a result, we had to place our table by the door and do our reading or other work sitting beside it. For this reason the door would remain open all day! At night, we were locked in, but not each man in his room — the whole section was locked up. Each section had a guard who was a retired soldier.

I spent six years in Petrovskiy Zavod, and always I recall that time with pleasure and a sense of gratitude to all my comrades. Nor can I fail to be grateful even to our good Commandant, old Leparsky, as to all the officers appointed to supervise us. ...

We were not taken out to work for some time after our arrival in Petrovskiy, but were allowed to rest from our journey and to settle into our new quarters. Husbands were allowed to spend several days with their wives, in their houses. I say 'in their houses' because each of the ladies, while still living in Chita, had either had built for herself, or had bought and trimmed, her own individual house in Petrovskiy Zavod. This they did not do themselves but, with the Commandant's consent, entrusted everything to one of the officials whom they knew, so that the houses were ready when they arrived. Only the two new arrivals, Yushnevskaya and Baroness Rozen, had no homes of their own and lived in rented rooms. Something like chaos reigned in our prison during the first days: we unpacked, ordered whatever furniture we needed, decided how best to arrange our rooms so as to get the benefit of the corridor light, ran from one room into another, sought out our friends, inspected all the sections and the whole prison interior, met in the hall for dinner or for supper, drank tea in various places (since not every man had his own samovar or his own sugar and tea). But this did not last long; and it gave rise to the idea of a communal artel. So well did this artel provide for our material lives throughout our stay in Petrovskiy Zavod that not one of us lacked anything or grew dependent upon anybody else in all that time. ...

With the organizing of our own artel, indeed, and with the steps taken to care, as much as possible, for those newly arrived, our lives in Petrovskiy Zavod or, rather, in the prison fortress, improved enormously from the material viewpoint. Each individual had his own resources, and could use them as he chose; each could even use his profits either to the common good — giving them up to the artel — or in accommodating certain habits of his earlier life which were now almost necessities. Now we did not all assemble to have dinner in the common hall, finding this inconvenient, but instead had section tables in the corridor. A guard would bring food from the kitchen, prepare and clear away dinner and supper (eating with us), wash up, set the samovars and stoke the stoves. For all this he received a monthly wage from us with which he was well satisfied.

In Dr. Vol'f we had our own physician, and a highly skilful one. In the event of serious illness, it was not only ourselves and our ladies who went to him, but also the Commandant, the officers and anyone who could, despite the fact that an official surgeon had been appointed to us by the government. This surgeon, a young man who had but recently left the academy, quickly perceived Vol'f's superiority over himself and had recourse at every step to his advice, experience and knowledge. So widely did the fame of Vol'f's skill spread that patients came to him from Nerchinsk, Kyakhta and even Irkutsk.[26] Seeing the benefits he wrought, the Commandant allowed him to leave the prison freely, with an escort. In a room specially designated for that purpose, and by Vol'f's own, was our drugstore, where were kept all necessary medicines and some fine surgical apparatus. All this, as well as well-known works and the best foreign and Russian medical journals, had been subscribed to and obtained in Vol'f's name by the ladies. In a word, we had nothing more to wish for as far as medical resources were concerned.[27]

In similar fashion we, too, subscribed to many Russian and non-Russian periodicals, also with the help of and by means of our ladies. From among French journals, we received *Journal des débats, Constitutionel, Journal de Francfort, Revue Encyclopédique, Revue britannique, Revue des deux mondes, Revue de Paris*; from among the German ones: *Preussische Staatszeitung, The Hamburg Correspondent, The Augsburg Gazette*; and almost every Russian newspaper and journal.

Here I may profitably mention a circumstance that greatly surprised me at one time, and which drew my attention to the high morality of the exiled workers in the factories of that region. I have already said that Petrovskiy had about 2000 inhabitants. A quarter of this population was comprised of officials, mining hands, serving and retired men of various classes, soldiers of the Department of Mines, old men who had served out their terms of labour, and so forth. The rest, that is, three quarters of the population, were exiled workers or convicts deported for serious crimes, who had been punished with the knout and bore brand-marks—people, in short, excluded from society forever by their crimes and, more especially, their punishment, and therefore society's natural foes. These worker-exiles were employed not only in producing iron and mining ores but also in other kinds of work: the blacksmith's, carpenter's, joiner's, and wheelwright's trades. Many of them were highly skilled, diligent craftsmen; they had dealings with ourselves because each of us needed a bedframe and a table and some furniture—in a word, their services. We paid them very well, helped them in their needs in some cases, and they were consequently highly satisfied with us. Our prison had been built by them, and when orders were given for small windows to be knocked through and for the walls to be plastered, it was they who were used for the work.[28] At least sixty men were employed on these operations in order to finish them more quickly, and when we were taken in turn out of our cells and into others, we took only our bedding with us, not wishing to drag our things about for just a short time; our remaining possessions we left in our cells, placing them in a pile in the middle of the room and covering them with sheets or carpets. Since none of us had either money or fine objects, we did not worry about losses. So for two months the workers had the opportunity to take from our belongings what they chose. And notwithstanding this, not one of us lost even a pin. How was this to be explained? I remember well how it surprised me; and starting at that time I paid particular attention to that class of factory dweller, and grew convinced by many proofs of their honesty and gratitude for good turns done to them. Before we had arrived, they had had as their supervisor some mining official or other, an unjust and evil individual who treated them in the most cruel fashion. In his time, we knew, neither he himself nor any of the Department of Mines' officials had dared to leave his own quarters by night. It had only to grow dark and everyone's windows were barred. All precautions were taken against the worker-exiles' evil designs. But in our time their supervisor was the mining officer Arsen'yev, a good, just man; he treated them humanely, issued them with everything prescribed and occupied himself with the improving of their way of life, although he was severe too, when this was necessary. Under his jurisdiction, anyone could walk with perfect safety through the factory at dead of night with no defensive weapon whatsoever. I myself more than once returned to the prison at night accompanied by a single escort, and met groups of five or ten worker-exiles on vacant lots, sometimes not even fully sober. They would pass us peacefully, removing their caps and greeting us politely. During all the time of my stay in Petrovskiy I never heard of theft. It was as if this crime did not exist, and more than once things were returned to us that we had left in the bath-house or on our walks. In short, I grew convinced then and am still convinced that those exiled to hard labour for serious crimes, murder, sacrilege and so forth, are far more moral than those individuals deported for theft or other, less serious misdemeanours. The former may have been incited to the crimes which they committed by strong passions, an inflexible character, vengeance or fanaticism, but they had not lost all moral principles. Consequently, I am sure that if only attention were paid to them, and if their correction were undertaken with skill, the greater part of them could be made not merely tolerable, but even highly useful citizens. Those individuals deported for deception, forgery, the stealing of the property of others and concealment of the stolen articles, on the other hand, cannot so easily be corrected, having been led up to these crimes by the continual development of evil tendencies by a constantly deteriorating level of morality. At all events, the government would be performing a supreme good deed—and, one might say, a moral feat—if it would but occupy itself with these lowest rungs of the social ladder; if it did not forever bar to them the path to their rehabilitation; if, in brief, it would act as a skilful physician, and not as an unbending and inexorable avenger.

In this connection I will give here, for consideration by the moralists, one striking example of iron will, firmness of character and indifference towards bodily torture in one of the worker-exiles. In Eastern Siberia there exists a custom among convicts to absent themselves from factories for about three months in the summer; they go into the neighbouring woods in order, as they say, to walk about in freedom for a bit and get a breath of free air. This is a crime on their part, of course, the more so as they now and then commit further illegal acts during these periods of absence. With the onset of cold weather, most of them come back to the factory, where they are punished for their flight and then used once again as workers. Lacking means sufficient to prevent these flights, mining authorities nevertheless take certain measures — and one of these is to pay ten roubles in notes to individuals who bring in captured convicts. In the event of a state convict's being killed during his capture, not only do the authorities not prosecute the individual who took his life, but they pay that person five roubles. Knowing of this decree, the Buriats have made a kind of business out of it. In summer, they set out on horses with weapons to capture fugitives and, spotting one or two in a wood, approach them to within a certain distance, prepare their bow and arrows and then shout to them to halt. If the fugitives obey, the Buriats order them to follow the track to the factory; they themselves go after them at a short distance with a rifle or an arrow trained on them—and in this fashion bring them in and receive the reward due to them. If the fugitives do not obey, and try to flee, they kill them and receive a recompense only a half as large. It is most natural that this serves as a cause of implacable hatred for the Buriats on the part of worker-exiles.

One of the latter, a former small trader from Orlov nicknamed Oily,[29] was so indignant with the Buriats that he decided to declare a war on them, and set out on campaign each year during the summer in order to destroy them in their turn. When the frosts set in, he would return to the factory and himself tell the authorities how many of the so-called enemy he had managed to annihilate. Often he even took the crimes of others on himself. They would chain him up, try him, whip him with a knout and hold him in jail for a while but, finally, release him—and come next summer he would do the very same again! Over a period of ten years he went on six of these campaigns, killed up to twenty men and was whipped mercilessly with the knout six times. Finally, such stubbornness and incorrigible spite forced the authorities to take decisive measures. The last time, when he was to have received a hundred and one blows for a punishment, the Commander, a severe and ruthless man, gave instructions to the flogger in advance to whip Oily to death. A day or two before the sentence was to be carried out, rumour of such a punishment leaked out, and reached a certain retired worker-exile, a devout old man, respected by all for his way of life. The old man went to the Commander and asked him to commute the sentence, promising to persuade Oily to give his word not to escape and to renounce his war against the Buriats and answering for it that, if Oily gave his word, he would keep it. For a long time the Commander would not agree but finally, convinced by the old man whom he himself respected, decided to cancel the punishment on these terms. The old man, coming to

Oily, tells him of the condition that may save his life and asks him for his word. For a long time the latter is unable to bring himself to give it. For one whole day, he struggles with himself. Finally, self-preservation gains the upper hand, and he gives the promise wanted. They punish him. His iron body withstands the punishment. He recovers, and after this lives an exemplary life in the factory. By his obedience and industriousness he earns the authorities' good will and becomes, I will not say a moral, but an honest man.

When we were in Petrovskiy Zavod he had already been living in freedom for some years, in his own house. With us, he always conducted himself well and once, when working in my cell, related to me how the Buriats still feared him. Not infrequently, he said, he would meet a Buriat and the Buriat, not knowing him, would ask him if their enemy Oily was alive, and then tell him of his own earlier escapades with them. Such characters as Oily may be both great villains and great men! All depends on upbringing and circumstance.

I. D. Yakushkin

On our arrival at Petrovskiy, the Commandant announced to the ladies that their husbands would not be allowed to meet them, but that they themselves might live with them in their cells. In consequence of this, Princess Volkonskaya, Yushnevskaya, Fonvizina, Naryshkina and Rozen, none of whom had children, moved into their husbands' cells; others who did have children—Princess Trubetskaya, Murav'yova, Annenkova and Davydova— slept at home and in the daytime came to visit their husbands. Because it was strictly forbidden to allow any outsiders in to them, the ladies who lived in our cells had no female servants; every morning, no matter what the weather, they would set out for their own homes to refresh themselves and see to everything necessary. Painful it was to see them going off to their homes or returning to the cells in bad weather or during hard frosts; without outside assistance they could not walk up the ice-covered cobblestones onto the embankment slopes, though afterwards they were allowed to have wooden steps constructed on these slopes—at their own expense. Strict instructions from Petersburg could not always be carried out precisely under such complex circumstances.

Naryshkina, who lived in a cell with her husband, fell ill with a chill and fever. Vol'f went to the Commandant and told him it was necessary that she have female attendants. For a long time the Commandant hesitated, but finally decided to allow Naryshkina's chambermaid to stay with her for as long as she was ill. Soon afterwards, Nikita Murav'yov fell into a putrid fever; day and night his poor wife was with him constantly, having already left to the mercy of Fate her little daughter Nonushka, whom she passionately loved and for whose life she was perpetually afraid.[30] In this case, too, Vol'f went to the Commandant and told him Murav'yov could not recover while he remained in his cell—but that he might spread his illness to others. And here, after some argument, the Commandant decided to allow Murav'yov to leave his cell for his wife's house for as long as his illness should last.

As to our cells, they had been built in haste and built so badly that they were continually being repaired; more than once, fires broke out in walls which nothing separated from stoves, while the walls of the corridor bulged out and had to be supported by stanchions and bolts. Even inside the cells it was not very warm, but in the corridor it was sometimes positively cold, so that it was not always possible to open one's door onto the corridor to let in a little light. Consequently we sat with a candle during the day. While repairs were being made to cell no. 11, I was transferred to no. 16, and here, in the third section of the prison, I found Obolensky, Shteyngel', Pushchin and Lorer. We all had dinner and lunch together in the corridor, and each section had a sentry — a foot-soldier — to act as servant. In the daytime, we were left to wander freely from our section into any other that we chose; but at ten in the evening all the cells were locked, as was the section as a unit. Next, the gates of each separate courtyard were locked up and, finally, the outside barrack gates, so that each of us always slept behind four locks.

Under the same arrangement as at Chita, we went to work in a mill, and the flour that we produced was good only to feed the local oxen. All day long on Saturdays and until lunch on Sundays we were taken, one by one, out to the bath-house. For our common exercise, a spacious courtyard was provided, enclosed by a high palisade and adjoining the prison barracks from which the palisade divided it. There were a few small trees in this courtyard, and we made paths along which we could stroll at any time. Animal lovers brought in roe-bucks, hares and cranes and tumbler-pigeons; and in winter, hillocks were made and an area was flooded for those who liked to skate. The ladies living with us came to watch our common amusements, and occasionally took part in them themselves, allowing themselves to slide downhill.[31] Many of us had beds of flowers, melons and cucumber in the separate courtyards. In the summer, we assiduously attempted to cultivate fruit — an exercise entailing major difficulties because of the unfavourable climate in Petrovskiy.

Poggio, Vadkovsky and Pushchin settled down to working out the functioning of an artel. In accordance with their plan, three chief administrators, a host, a buyer, and a treasurer, were elected to manage the artel in all its aspects. After these, we elected a market-gardener and the members of a provisional committee. Every person taking part in the artel had a voice in these elections; first, candidates were chosen for the posts, then ballots held to choose from amongst them. The host managed all aspects of the economy of the artel. On him depended purchases of food, the kitchen, and so forth. Several times a week the buyer would leave the prison to purchase all that was needed. And the treasurer kept the accounts, noting down private expenses. The three often had meetings to decide how to assign funds that belonged to the artel. The kitchen-gardener looked after our allotment, in which there was never an abundant crop since the climate of Petrovskiy was most unkind to vegetation: it was a rare year when potatoes even were not killed by morning frosts. However, the local inhabitants supplied us with vegetables in plenty. Twenty-five versts from Petrovskiy, corn and everything in the market-garden were grown successfully. The members of the provisional committee, three in number, would check the accounts of the host, buyer, and treasurer from time to time. Besides the artel's permanent officers, duty officers would be appointed from among us to supervise the organising and distributing of food. In Petrovskiy, the general fund greatly increased; all that had earlier been spent on private aid was now subscribed to the artel, and more than 500 roubles from these common funds fell to the portion of each individual participating in that same artel, each year. Coming together, host, buyer, and treasurer would determine what amount should be allotted, per man per month, for tea, sugar, and supper.

By such an arrangement, the dependence of some individuals on others ended, nor was there any further cause for the unpleasant, but inevitable, clashes that had earlier occurred. So that each man participating in the artel should have as much money as possible at his disposal, expenditures on tea, sugar, and supper were very much controlled: for one month, each individual was provided with a third of a pound of tea, two pounds of sugar, and two small wheaten rolls a day. Lunch consisted of a plate of cabbage soup and a tiny piece of beef; and part even of these supplies had to be spared for the warder, who was fed on our leavings. Supper was even scantier than lunch, and often we would finish a meal and still be hungry — but this was not without advantages for many of us, given our way of life. ...

Completely unexpectedly, Sosnowycz was sent out to join us in Petrovskiy. He was a Pole who had been sentenced in Grodno in connection with the affair of Wolowicz and the other emissaries. Of those sentenced with him, he alone was condemned to hard labour, but because of his advanced age and because he was completely blind, he was spared hard labour and sent into confinement in 'one of the fortresses' of Eastern Siberia. But there is not a single fortress in Eastern Siberia! Governor-General Sulima[32] was much troubled, not knowing what to do with this Sosnowycz. Finally, he decided to send him to Petrovskiy, to be placed in a casemate with us. Sosnowycz was a thorough Pole; one could infer from what he said that his subtle answers had long troubled his awful judges — which, of course, did not dispose them in his favour. His 15-year-old son had been tried with him. This boy had been beaten with birch rods, to make him testify against his father. In a confrontation with his son, old Sosnowycz had admitted that one of the emissaries had called on him, and that he had given him a guide for his return journey across the border. His son had been sent to the Caucasus to serve as a private soldier; his wife and daughter remained without a crust of bread. Yet despite all this, Sosnowycz was not cast down. Having joined us, he entered into the artel, making no payment whatsoever, and enjoyed our common advantages.

By now, we were being kept nothing like as strictly as we had been when we first arrived at Petrovskiy, and for fear of fire our cell doors were not locked at night, as they had earlier been. Should their wives fall ill, the married men were allowed to go to their homes, but usually they lived in their cells, as did even some of the ladies.

Aleksandra Grigor'yevna Murav'yova was coming once, in September 1832, to see her husband in his casemate. The day was warm; she was lightly dressed and, going home that evening, she caught a heavy chill. After suffering for three months, she died. Her death produced a powerful impression not only upon us, but also in Petrovskiy generally and even in the barracks where the convicts lived.[33] An order came from Petersburg, when news of Murav'yova's death had reached there, that the wives of prisoners were not to live in cells — their husbands were to be released to see them every day. Later, we were all allowed out every day in groups, as had been done at Chita. For all these privileges, however, the awkwardness of our situation, and that of the married couples in particular, was incessantly being made plain. A little while after his wife's decease, Nikita Murav'yov received an order from the Commandant to transfer into a cell, and he was forced to leave his little daughter, Nonushka, without even a nurse in whom he could place confidence. His daughter was in sickly health, and he continually worried over her. Hearing of this sorry situation, and knowing that he himself would not approach the Commandant, I asked the duty officer to tell the General that I had to speak to him. One hour later, I was summoned to the Commandant in the guard-house. When we were alone, I asked him to change his instructions regarding Nikita Murav'yov and not to separate a father from his little daughter. To this, Leparsky replied rather severely with his usual formula: 'I cannot,' alluding to his orders as they touched upon our upkeep, infraction of which would result in his being strictly punished. But to this I remarked that, in that case, he would be acting *most* inconsistently if he wished to execute his orders *without fail*, for he had broken them before when he had found them too severe! Finally, he agreed to leave Nikita Murav'yov at home, saying to me: 'Mark you, if any unpleasantness comes out of this for me I shall complain about you to your friend Grabbe!'[34] Leparsky had good reason to be always nervous that some carelessness of his would be reported to St. Petersburg: he knew his every action was observed from Irkutsk and that, besides, there were sometimes visitors to Petrovskiy of *another kind*, many of whom came as spies. All the time of our confinement in Chita and Petrovskiy, we had only one death among us — that of Pestov, who had belonged to the United Slavs. His illness lasted no more than forty-eight hours, and all Vol'f's efforts were inadequate to save our comrade.[35]

Our very way of life, plainly enough, was the reason for the low mortality rate. In general, we were far less subject to those hazards to which people of our age are liable when they are free; and if we did fall ill, we had every kind of medical supply, and were surrounded by our comrades' warm concern. If our way of life had a beneficial effect in preserving us physically, however, it had a highly deleterious effect upon our intellectual capabilities. Out of fifty men, two went insane in Petrovskiy — Andreyevich and Andrey Borisov. However, settlements proved even more harmful in this respect than actual imprisonment. Of thirty men living in settlements, five went insane: Shakhovskoy and Nikolay Bobrishchev-Pushkin in Yeniseysk, Furman in Surgut, and Vranitsky and Ental'tsev in Yalutorovsk.

Their way of life told plainly on our ladies, too: being almost daily in a state of agitation, they were often liable to unhappy accidents in pregnancy, and many births were unsuccessful. Of twenty-five babies born in Chita and Petrovskiy, seven miscarried; on the other hand, of the eighteen live births only four died — the rest grew up. Nowhere could children have been more surrounded with unwearying solicitude than in Chita and Petroskiy; for parents were constrained there by no social obligations and, undistracted by diversions of that kind, could give constant attention to their children.

As a result of the reduction of our terms of labour, fifteen men set off for settlements in 1833 and 1834, only three of whom, Rozen, Naryshkin, and Lorer, were sent to Western Siberia, where they settled in Kurgan. Fonvizin was settled in Yeniseysk, from where he was later transferred to Krasnoyarsk; the remaining twelve were scattered over villages of Eastern Siberia. Subsequently Pavel Bobrishchev-Pushkin, too, was transferred to Krasnoyarsk to join his insane brother. In 1835, Petrovskiy was visited by Bronevsky, the new Governor-General, appointed to replace Sulima. As Bronevsky was Leparsky's junior in service, the Town-Major accompanied him when he came to us.

Left alone with us, General Bronevsky asked, in the accepted fashion, if we wished to make any complaints. Having been told, also in the accepted fashion, that we were satisfied with everything, he was most amiable towards us. Then all the corridor doors were unlocked for him, the doors of all the cells opened wide, and each of us was required to be in his cell for the occasion. Passing along the corridors with the Town-Major, General Bronevsky called in at some cells, merely glancing into others with that curiosity with which a visitor commonly looks through iron bars at a menagerie that he has never seen before.

Many of us finished our terms of hard labour in 1836, and in June, instructions were received to send eighteen men to settlements — but to which places we did not know. The Murav'yov brothers, Vol'f and I agreed to stay together in one settlement if possible, and letters we received from our families gave us reason to believe that things might be arranged as we desired. Nikita Murav'yov, Volkonsky, Ivashev and Annenkov, as family men, were obliged to get some money together before leaving on a distant journey, so they could not be sent away at once. Aleksandr Murav'yov stayed with his brother and Vol'f, as a physician, had the Imperial permission to accompany the Murav'yovs to their settlement. Basargin and Mit'kov, pretending sickness, also stayed a little longer in Petrovskiy. Thereupon ten individuals: Tyutchev, Gromnitsky, Kireyev, the two Kryukov brothers, Lunin, Svistunov, Frolov, Torson and I, were dispatched to Irkutsk, with an officer and several under-officers, on reversible carts.

Not without sadness did we say farewell to our remaining comrades, with whom we had shared almost nine years of imprisonment. Twenty-two men in the first category; the two Bestuzhevs in the second; three Chernigovskiy Regiment men, Ippolit Zavalishin, the Pole Sosnowycz and Kuchevsky (who turned up in Chita for God knows what reason), were to remain in Petrovskiy another three years. The two Bestuzhev brothers, according to the sentence of the Special Supreme Court, were prisoners in the second category, as I say, and it is hard to see why, by Imperial ukase, they were punished equally with those in the first. Mikhaylo, the younger brother, who served in the Moscow Regiment, had led his company onto the Square on December 14th, but he was found more guilty than Shchepin-Rostovsky, who also went onto the Square with his company, and who cut down two generals and a colonel besides! Nikolay, the oldest of the Bestuzhevs, was with the Guards Equipage on December 14th together with Torson. Both men were found less guilty by the Special Supreme Court than Zavalishin, Arbuzov, and Divov!

The main fault of Nikolay Bestuzhev in the sight of the supreme authority was, it appears, that he spoke very boldly before members of the Commission of Enquiry, and acted just as boldly when he was brought into the Palace. He had been seized beyond Kronstadt three days after the 14th; in those three days he had been wandering on foot without a break, and had met with every kind of adventure. When he was led into the Palace for interrogation, he announced to General Levashev that he would answer no questions until his hands had been untied. Now, in the *first* days after the 14th, almost *all* those who had taken part in the revolt had had their hands tied behind their back with rope, in the main guardroom, and had then been brought before the Emperor. But General Levashev did not dare comply with Bestuzhev's demand without first seeking permission from the Tsar himself, who was usually in the apartments nearest to that hall in the Hermitage where questioning was carried out. Next, when General Levashev untied Bestuzhev's hands, Bestuzhev told him that, as he had eaten nothing for three days and nights, he would answer no questions whatsoever until he had been fed! General Levashev rang and ordered that Bestuzhev be provided with a supper; and at supper, judge and defendant clinked glasses full of champagne!

Heavy rain fell on the day of our departure. Princess Trubetskaya, with her husband and her little daughter Sasha, accompanied me and said farewell by the chapel in which Aleksandra Murav'yova lay buried.[36]

Baron A. E. Rozen

Petrovskiy is one of the iron-foundries belonging to the Crown, where iron vessels are cast, iron hoops and wire forged and drawn. There was also a saw-mill in the works which had been out of gear for years, its machinery having been damaged beyond repair—so it was thought. The manager of these works discovered from the Town-Adjutant that some of us were familiar with machinery. He asked the Commandant to allow 'those gentlemen' to inspect the parts and offer an opinion as to the feasibility of their being repaired. N. Bestuzhev and Torson went off to the place and, to the wonder of officials, master workers, and workmen, the machinery and saw-mill were set going within hours. N. Bestuzhev had in mind then a design for a new chronometer of cheaper construction (than the present one). This idea he carried out twenty years later, when he was sent to Selenginsk to live. His new clock was set up in a hall during the winter. In spite of a frost of twenty-five degrees, it went perfectly. When we had the sorrow of losing our much-loved and honoured Alexandrine Murav'yova by an early death, Bestuzhev, with his own hands, made a wooden coffin and all the ornaments and fittings, then cast one in lead, in which the wooden shell was placed. He was an artist too. He painted all our portraits, and made some very fine sketches of Chita and Petrovskiy. Torson kept himself busy by making models of threshing, reaping and sowing machines. N. A. Zagutsky,[37] for his part, contrived to make a splendid wooden clock, his only tool being an ordinary dinner knife.

In our joiners' room, we all made tables, chairs, armchairs, benches and cupboards that were needed. The best joiners were N. Bestuzhev, Frolov, P. S. Pushkin and A. Borisov. Repin and Andreyevich spent a good deal of their time painting, the latter devoting himself to a large altar-piece in oils for the church in Chita. Music, too, had its disciples: F. F. Vadkovsky and N. A. Kryukov played the violin, P. N. Svistunov the 'cello, A. P. Yushnevsky the piano, M. M. Naryshkin, Lunin, and I. F. Shimkov[38] the guitar, and Count Igelstrom the flute. Prince Odoyevsky and V. P. Ivashev were devotees of poetry. Pushkin wrote subtle fables, and rendered the *Psalms* into Russian verse. Ivashev composed an epic poem entitled 'Stenka Razin.' The reading and newspaper room was besieged at all hours that we had at liberty, while on Sundays we assembled to read from the Holy Scriptures and from edifying works. Save once a year for

Communion, we were never taken to church. We held to a resolution made at Chita not to play cards, allowing ourselves paper and ink, however, despite the fact that both were strictly banned.

M. S. Lunin lived in the most curious manner. He lived in No. 1, a totally dark cell in which no windows had been pierced — a guardroom had been built beside it. Nor did he share our common table, keeping his fasts after the custom of the Roman Church, which he had joined some years before when in Warsaw.[39] A third of his cell was shut off by a curtain behind which, elevated on some steps, was a large crucifix blessed by the Pope, which his sister had sent him from Rome. All day long, loud prayers in Latin would be audible from his cell. In his ways, however, he was no ascetic; and when he strolled among us he was always both agreeable and witty. Whenever we called on him in his cell we always found him ready to converse in a secular, often a jocular strain. Lunin was much provoked by Victor Hugo's *Notre-Dame de Paris*, which penetrated even to our wilds and was read avidly: he had the patience, indeed, to burn the whole work with a candle! Lunin always painted our future (that is, the time of our settlement) in the darkest colours, declaring that only three courses would be open to us — marriage, a monastery, or the bottle. He himself came to a sad end. ...[40]

A. P. Yushnevsky, too, was a particularly noteworthy man: he had formerly been General Intendant of the Second Army.[41] He was a stoic in the strictest sense of the word, and had been closely associated with Pestel', who never hid a thought from him but consulted him about his every action. Yushnevsky was a married man; his wife followed him out after a little while, and they lived in Petrovskiy in the barest circumstances, his property still being in the hands of the sequestrators. Even his brother, the lawful heir, was not allowed to enjoy this property until the revision of papers in the office of the Second Army's Intendant was completed. This enquiry was long and gave grave annoyance to Yushnevsky for, being a prisoner, he was deprived of every means of clearing himself of certain accusations that were being made against him. The delight of the old man may be imagined when, after eight years, he heard the verdict of the commission of enquiry, in which it was expressly stated that the former General Intendant had not only caused the government no injury but had, quite to the contrary, been instrumental in significantly benefiting it by his wise and timely measures.

We had been one year in the new prison when I was obliged to part with my wife, as the time of her confinement was approaching. She hired a house in which Princess Trubetskaya had lived until her own was finished. One week before the confinement, I was allowed to leave the prison and remain with her; a sentry was posted in front of our house and did nothing but accompany me when I had to go to work or to the mill. On September 5th, 1831, my second son, Konrad, was born. I embraced him with deep love and thankfulness. But when, subsequently, three sons and a daughter were all born to me, the thought of their futures almost weighed me down to the ground. At such moments, when my courage failed, it was not easy to rejoice over even the most promising of children. I resolved, after my second son was born, to do my very best to qualify myself to educate them. At least I would be giving those deprived of not just property but also of the rights of citizenship some chance of making their own way in the world. As soon as my wife could leave her bed, I was obliged to leave her by herself and return to my prison. ...

I should mention, in conclusion, that seven of my comrades were engaged men whose brides did not follow them out, and that eight of our married men, whose wives had stayed behind, had to support the awful extra grief of hearing that their wives had married others. The impression made by this news was deepened by the spectacle of ladies who had followed their husbands through misery and exile, and who were not only models of conjugal devotion but the greatest blessings to their husbands and to all of us.

9

Settlement

As early as 1828, a few Decembrists had left Chita to settle in Siberian villages as free men – free, that was, within the bounds of close police surveillance. In 1831, the trickle turned into a flow; in July of that year, all prisoners with five-year terms (after two commutations) were released; those of the fifth category, including Rozen, followed twelve months later; and in November 1832, those of the fourth, including Lorer and Fonvizin, Odoyevsky and the two Belyayev brothers. But it was not a life of luxury that awaited all these men, most of whom were now approaching middle age. Their every move was watched, their correspondence checked, their very churchgoing observed.[1] Most, having settled down in a remote village or town, simply attempted to live out their latter years as uneventfully and comfortably as possible within the neighbouring circle of their relatives or friends. (Some twenty-one Decembrists settled in or near Irkutsk, nine in the settlement of Minusinsk and eight more in Kurgan, in the Province of Tobol'sk. There were groups of four or more men in Tobol'sk itself, Turinsk, and Yalutorovsk.)[2] A few, including Lunin, Gorbachevsky, Obolensky and Yakushkin, remained faithful to their earlier ideals, and so became the living, walking conscience of the group, engaging in a periodic roll-call of long letters which, together with the memoirs of Rozen and Lorer, Shteyngel' and Gorbachevsky, provide a good impression of the exiles' life as 'free settlers.'

Lunin remarked forebodingly, we have just seen, that three possible fates awaited the new settlers: marriage, the bottle or a monastery. In the event, only the first proved dangerous.[3] Though many matches with Siberian girls of humble origins brought happiness, as for example, to Prince Obolensky, some brought distress, as to V. K. Kyukhel'beker. The greatest danger of all, however, had not been well foreseen: material want. A few of the Decembrists, including the Volkonskys, the Murav'yovs, the Trubetskoys, were rich; but the majority worked on the fifteen *desyatins* of land granted to every settler by the government simply because they had no money. Nor did their manual labour always help the situation. Some had wretched soil or next to no equipment, while others had no knowledge of the land. Most, proving neither as adept as Baron Rozen nor as totally incompetent as Igel'strom, managed to eke out a living.[4] Financial help from home, or from the wealthier of their comrades, saw most Decembrists out of desperate straits – though Prince A. I. Baryatinsky died, of syphilis and in the greatest poverty, in a stinking wooden shack outside Tobol'sk.

Even in Petrovskiy, the process of dispersal had begun, and something of the (sometimes stifling) intimacy of Chita days had long before been lost. Predictably, that process was still more accelerated after 1832. Excellent studies have been written on the medical, social and other contributions to Siberian life of *the* Decembrists.[5] The very obvious fact remains, however, that the various small groups scattered in different areas deserve separate study: for what would *the* Decembrist contribution to, say, medical hygiene have been, were it not for Dr. Vol'f and Trubetskaya in Irkutsk? Or to the theory of public education, but for efforts by specific groups and persons – Obolensky in Nerchinsk, Zavalishin in Chita, Yakushkin in Yalutorovsk? By the same token, no selection of accounts of the Decembrists' later lives can ever do full justice to the group's experience. For each individual's experience was unique.

It is bearing this in mind that two short extracts are included here from the memoirs of, first, Lorer, then of Rozen, to give at least a general idea of problems facing most of the new settlers. Lorer, like Rozen, left Petrovskiy for Kurgan in 1833, and four years later moved on to the Caucasus. But here, all similarities between their tales are at an end.

N. I. Lorer

Monotonously, our term of imprisonment passed, and for some, the time of leaving was approaching. I was among the earliest to leave Petrovskiy. On the very day our group finished its term of penal servitude, a courier brought orders to Secret Councillor Lavinsky to dispatch us to Irkutsk, and from there on to a settlement, as organized by the Governor of Irkutsk, Tseydler [Zeidler].[8] We were granted two weeks for rest and preparations; and I must say that our joy was great and wholly unexpected—we had thought we should be sent away only after another year, and did not know that our sentence had been further shortened on the occasion of the birth of the Grand Duke Mikhail Nikolayevich.[9] I was visiting my comrade Lunin on this last day, and there learned of the change in store for me.

When the day of our departure for a settlement arrived, we went to say farewell to Leparsky; he was extremely moved. Parting from us, he despaired of ever seeing us again and apologized at length for not having been able to alleviate our lot still more. A good old man! We left the walls of our incarceration in several sleds, accompanied by our comrades who were staying. An inexpressible melancholy drained my heart.

At our first night's lodging, just before we set off on our distant journey, I came out of the house which we were occupying and saw a crowd of peasants wearing festive dress. It was morning. I went up to the crowd, and the men congratulated me on some feast or other and for having happily completed my term of servitude. They also asked: 'Will Trubichikha and Narynzhikha be passing by soon?', mangling the names of Trubetskaya and Naryshkina. I was struck by the long, thin face of a man in a short nankeen frock-coat in this crowd of healthy faces. I went up to him to ask him who he was and, to my surprise, received a reply in perfect French:

'Je suis français, monsieur.'

'Your name?'

'Champagne de Normandie, sir. The Emperor Paul sent me here, forty years ago. Be kind, sir, give me a few sous!'

With the help of my comrades, I collected a small sum and handed it to the unhappy foreigner. But my assistance did not benefit him. The peasants told me there and then that he would drink it; and sure enough, I saw that same gentleman when we set out. He was running somewhere, his hands in his overcoat. To my question: 'How goes it, Monsieur Champagne?' he replied: 'Quite nicely, sir! I'm off to the *kabachok!*'[10] 'Adieu, Monsieur Champagne de Normandie!' Wretched man left to the mercy of fate.

We had soon galloped the distance that separated us from Irkutsk, crossing the frozen surface of Baikal, passing the [city] gates and so finding ourselves, not in a jail now, but in warm quarters that had been prepared for us. The town governor informed us that Governor-General Lavinsky would be visiting us soon, and we, expecting him, somewhat adjusted our appearance and began to look a little more like gentlemen. Lavinsky, whom I now saw for the first time, was a fine figure of a man, large in stature, with an open physiognomy that inspired confidence.

'Gentlemen,' he said to us after we had made each other's acquaintance slightly, 'I have been obliged to cast lots amongst you to determine who shall live where. Had the government entrusted these arrangements to me I should, of course, have settled you in towns and villages, but places are indicated in my instructions from Petersburg. There, they do not know Siberia in the slightest and are content to spread a map, seek out a spot beside which are the words, 'Demoted town,'[11] and think it is in fact a town—when in reality it does not even exist. Waste land and snow! Besides this, I am forbidden to settle you together, even in pairs, and brothers must be separated. And in Siberia, where is one to find so many convenient places for settlement? Which of you gentlemen is Lorer?' I stepped forward. 'You have drawn a bad spot—Myortvyy Kultuk, beyond Baikal. Only Tungus and Samoyeds live there, and if you find a log cabin there you may count yourself lucky. However, I'll say this by way of consolation: if you're a lover of nature, the situation is entrancing and of the most romantic kind.'

'Your Excellency,' I replied, alarmed by the fate awaiting me, 'the beauties of nature may engross and solace a free traveller, or a tourist, but I'm to finish my days there, and never leave.'

Lavinsky assured me that he had already written to Petersburg, asking permission to settle me in another place, and advised me in the meanwhile not to frown, not to despair, but to depart. Since there was nothing else to do, we submitted to our fate and merely asked the Governor-General if he would not stay longer in the town and inspect its points of interest, to which he agreed. Nowhere had I ever had occasion to hear such a pure sound of bells as in Irkutsk, and I believe this is because, with 39 degrees of frost, the air itself is very pure; the heavenly vault was of a bright blue colour. We visited the churches, and equipped ourselves with necessary things.

Soon, the time drew near for me to part with my comrades in exile. Particularly pitiful was the situation of the two Belyayev brothers, who had grown up together, served together, never parted from each another and were bound by the closest of friendships. Where you saw Aleksandr, there, most likely, you would see Pyotr as well. But these brothers and friends had now to part. One was dispatched 1000 versts in one direction, the other more than 600 in the other. I accompanied them to the gates where, hugging for the last time in this life perhaps,[12] the brothers threw themselves down, each onto his own sled, and were borne off by the inexorable cossacks.

Next day I called upon the Civil Governor, Tseydler, with a request not to dispatch me to Myortvyy Kultuk until Naryshkin and his wife,[13] whom I expected, should arrive. This was conceded; I remained, quite alone. From boredom, I wandered aimlessly through the town and would go to look at the Angara, which is a very rapid river but so pure that one can see every small reed on its bottom. Once I ran up against an old man in a coat of raw sheepskin who wanted me to buy some snuff. I pressed him to come into my room, and making the purchase, asked him:

'Are you a retired soldier?'

'No, my good sir, I am not a soldier—I am Count Kakhovsky, and often used to play cards with our mother Catherine; but I was exiled here long ago thanks to the most august Potyomkin. And now I must hang about with a snuff-box for my upkeep.'

Subsequently I found out that everything the old man told me was the truth, but that he now and then talked nonsense, for which reason he had not been returned to Russia by any one of the all-gracious manifestos of which there had been plenty since Potyomkin's time!

The Naryshkins finally arrived and charmed my solitude somewhat, though not for long, for before them and before me lay different paths. Selenginsk had been determined as their place of settlement, some thousand versts from me. Lavinsky called on them, for he had known Pyotr Petrovich Konovnitsyn in 1812, when he himself was acting as Governor of Vil'no.[14]

The day of my departure came. On the Governor's advice, I had completed all the necessary purchases, furnishing myself with tea, sugar, flour, candles, pots, an axe, and rope, all of which cost me more than 200 roubles in notes. My friends the Naryshkins even furnished me with articles of luxury. I remember that they gave me a pair of silver candlesticks and even a box of scented candles; nor did they forget to provide me with books. Wandering through the town, I had another happy meeting. In one of the shops a man approached me who, by his accent, had to be German. When he found out that I was about to leave on a journey, he offered to hire himself out to me as a servant. I discovered that he was a native of Riga, a church caretaker once, and that, having been long ago sent to a settlement for some trifling affair, he had remained permanently in Siberia. Delighted with this find, I asked permission of Lavinsky to take the fellow with me, to which the Governor replied that, though we were forbidden to have servants, he would make an exception in my case and allow me to retain the German as a yard-keeper; he ordered papers to be issued to him. The German and I came to terms, and I went to say farewell to my friends the Naryshkins, possibly forever. Elizaveta Petrovna blessed me and hung an image round my neck. Then, in tears, I kissed them, took a seat in the sled with the young cossack who was to take me to Myortvyy Kultuk, piled my German on another sled together with my things, and rushed off into a wild, uninhabited land.

The cossack escorting me was a good fellow, and very talkative. Almost at once he told me he was very glad that he was managing to make *this* trip during the winter, since in summertime the road became intolerable or, rather, impossible. Quite frequently, he had me understand, bears lay across the road. Once, he told me, these uninvited guests had obliged the Kyakhta mail to turn back to Irkutsk, and so forth.

'Have you ever been in Kultuk?' I asked.

'No, I haven't, but some comrades of mine have and they tell me there's only one log-cabin there, belonging to a trapper and manufacturer; I don't know if it's there now, but it was at one time. ...'

Soon we were passing through a wretched little hamlet where we changed horses. Even this, my cossack told me, had been fixed as the place of residence of one of our number. 'So there are happy fellows who end up in places like this,' I thought, imagining my awful Kultuk. Almost everywhere we went, we found dense, centuries-old forest, with a narrow, barely noticeable track running through it. At one quite unexpected turning, I caught sight of a little white house enclosed by a caved-in stockade, its window-frames and windows knocked out, and obviously of European construction. Some exile, I was told, was brought here once, but had been seized one night and taken off; since then, the little house had been tumbling down, uncared for.

While still in these woods we began to ascend a hill. The frost was terrible, and I grew rather afraid for my German servant. At dawn, in one of the passes, I caught sight ahead of a high ridge of mountains and learned that these mountains were called Khamar-Daban and formed our frontier with China.[15] We began to descend, and the woods thinned out. To the right gleamed frozen Lake Baikal, while at our feet, far down below, Myortvyy Kultuk came into view, that is, about a dozen huts that served as homes for the Tungus, the Samoyeds, and settlers. We drove up noisily to the one log cabin in the place, and its owner came out onto the little porch to meet us. A hale old man, he placed his hands in his belt and watched the newcomers with wonder. Having said how do you do to him, I asked his permission to rent lodgings with him.

'If you please, I can let you have half the cabin, sir. I myself live in the other half with my old woman.'

'What'll you take a month?'

'5 roubles.'

I was so chilled that I was glad to hear such an honest price. We came to an agreement. I went into the warm little cottage, thanking my stars that I should not spend a single night in the open — or, worse still, in a filthy yurt. The little room allotted to me, though extremely small, was very clean. A little table had been covered by a clean towel, and round it stood red benches; there were sacred images in one corner. The windows, too, were small and, like almost all windows in this region, made not of glass but of mica or animal bladder — brittle glass will not withstand forty degrees of frost. When my bag and baggage were brought in, the little room was so encumbered that it was not easy to turn round in it! I began to unpack and organize myself; on the small table appeared the silver candlesticks with candles, an inkwell, papers, and books. A field samovar was soon on the boil, some sugar had been broken up and my host, the cossack, the German and I warmed up our bones a little. Then I wrapped myself in my greatcoat and committed myself to slumber. So (I thought), I'm to live out my whole life in this God-forsaken hole, alone and separated from my country, my friends and my acquaintances by 7000 versts. I despaired; but my Karl, 'poor Richard' though he was, busied himself with my belongings and put them all in order. 'Well, he's separated from his family and homeland too,' I thought, 'yet *he* doesn't lose heart.' Thereupon I asked him: 'Tell me please, Karl, why you are working while I lie here, when we are equal? Both you and I have been exiled.'

'Ja, Herr, ich weiss nicht.'

'Well, I'll tell you a German proverb: You have the purse, I have the cash.[16] I think that's why.'

Karl laughed at my proverb and most likely agreed with it, thinking to himself, 'Yes, if I had the cash and you the purse, we'd change rôles, and the former major would be cleaning *my* boots and putting on the samovar, whilst I was lying down. ...' Weariness soon had its way with us, and we all fell sound asleep.

In the morning, gloomy thoughts again possessed me, despite the fact that, on comparing myself with Robinson Crusoe, I found myself more fortunate than he—for at least I had a German with me, a living creature with whom I could share my time, whereas the dweller on the desert island had to be satisfied with nothing but a goat. But in the morning, nonetheless, I crawled out of my nook and tried to give myself some reckoning, from the porch, of that spot of earth on which my fate had cast me.

Kultuk is encircled by hills and rocks. The colossal mass of Khamar-Daban towers sullenly above the peaks at the foot of which, by the shore of Lake Baikal, sheltered our modest little retreat. You will not find Myortvyy Kultuk in any calendar whatever, or on any map of Asia, or in any *Annales de voyages:* it is an abandoned and forgotten scrap of earth. Only the Tungus found it, God knows how, and for *that* they vegetate in it, again God knows how, without grain.

I do not know for what reason—perhaps because of carbon fumes—but my head began to ache badly and I fell into a high fever. Still, on returning to my bench I was soon cheered up by the arrival of my loquacious host, who took a seat beside me, obviously wanting to chat with me a little.

'What do you have to say, granddad?' I began.

'Well, this: my old woman's very upset about you, master, and she's sorry for you. Such a good and affectionate gentleman, she says; for what faults could they have sent *him* out here? We've been living here forty-four years—the Emperor Paul was a strict Tsar and exiled plenty to Siberia, but he never sent anyone to Kultuk. My old woman doesn't want to believe that you're some kind of *serious* criminal. But that's not the point, anyway: she's *worried* about you, how's he going to spend the summer here all alone, she says. We go off into the woods for sable, you see, and we always leave the cottage empty. We just leave some flour and a bit of bread for the *varnaks*, (that's what convicts are called in

Siberia); in spring they go about in crowds like wild beasts, burning villages, robbing and killing people. The government sends Buriats out against them and pays them ten roubles a head, but you can't exterminate them all. So how can you stay here alone with your German? They'll kill you when they find out you're rich, you know!'

'But why leave bread in your houses for these robbers?'

'So as to propitiate 'em. If we do, they don't burn down our houses, master.'

'Well in that case, my excellent host, I'll go sable hunting with you and help you; anything's better than being slit like a ram!'

'My old woman and I have been thinking about that, but that'ld be *really* bad for you—even worse than here. There's midges and flies and gadflies all over the swamps. We're used to it all, but even we wear masks, otherwise we'd be eaten up. That's how we pass the summer and autumn, then we come home towards winter. The cottage is still intact and the old woman cleans it out, washes it, and scrapes it—those robbers are for ever making it foul. During the winter, when I go down to Irkutsk with the furs, I pay a tax to the Tsar, get in provisions for the winter—and the little cottage is all ready. That's how we've been living year by year for forty years now.'

This simple tale showed me my future life in all its dreadful nakedness. And how was I to defend myself when I had no weapon with me but a pen-knife? And was it possible for a single individual to defend himself against a crowd? The Buriats, it was true, waged regular war on convict packs, rounding them up and killing many with arrows; but I could not even count on this. I was mightily preoccupied with my future.

Next morning my cossack was to go back to Irkutsk. I gave him a letter for Naryshkin and ten roubles in token of my gratitude for the trouble he had taken over me. With his leaving, I remained even more orphaned. Soon, I had lost my appetite. No book interested me, and only the whispering and rumbling of the samovar distracted me. So passed three days and nights. One evening I was sitting at my little table, pensive and sad as usual. Outside it was frosty but calm, and my host's dogs barked only occasionally, on sensing a wild animal. It was nine o'clock by my watch when suddenly my ear was struck by the overflowing sound of a bell and the shout of a coachman driving horses. My host came into my room to say that someone was bowling down from the hill. 'Surely it isn't an assessor come to make sure I'm here, in order to report to the authorities?' I thought. But just then a sleigh stopped by our cottage. I hear the knock of a sabre, the doors open, and my escort, the young cossack who recently left me, runs in to me!

'Get ready, Nikolay Ivanovich, here's a letter for you. We're going to Irkutsk.'

What? How? I had lost my senses for joy and for surprise. With trembling hand I unsealed the note, which was written in pencil. It was from Elizaveta Petrovna Naryshkina. I have kept it, and it reads as follows:

'Dear N., come as quickly as possible; we are going to live in peace at Kurgan, in the Province of Tobol'sk, 4000 versts closer to our Fatherland!'[17]

Though it was night, still I gave orders that the packing should proceed immediately and, in my joy, gave all my stores, crockery, and utensils, to my hosts, saying to the old woman that God had evidently heard her prayers and was delivering me from out of this captivity. 'Here are my other two wax candles for you,' I added to her. 'May they burn low before an image in your cottage to the glory of our Saviour!' Then I paid my host five roubles for the coming month, embraced the old woman and, having said my farewells to those good people, left Myortvyy Kultuk that very night. God grant that I may be the last to be exiled there!

All along the way I puzzled as to who my intercessor and deliverer could be. Who had arranged things so that I should join my best friends, the Naryshkins? Then I did not know; but all the way I prayed to God for the health of my unknown benefactor.

At nine o'clock in the morning I was already embracing my friends in a warm, comfortable room, and there I learned to whom I was indebted for my happiness. Elizaveta Petrovna's mother, Anna Ivanovna, wrote from Petersburg that my niece, A. O. Rosset,[18] who was then a favourite fraülein of the Empress Aleksandra Fyodorovna, had decided to take advantage of a good mood of the Emperor's when she was in attendance, and to lighten my destiny by having me dispatched to the same place as the Naryshkins, to whom, as I have said, we were related. The court sycophants were very much afraid even to speak of us, but my niece, who was possessed of a lovely appearance, intellect, and some alertness, ignored court etiquette, and gained her end.

After a few days we left Irkutsk and set out for Kurgan, which was in the Province of Tobol'sk, 4000 versts closer to Russia. In Krasnoyarsk we called on our comrade in exile, Krasnokutsky,[19] who was lying there ill; his legs were useless. He had been *Ober-Prokurator* of the Senate and deported to Siberia. He was a nephew of Count V. P. Kochubey who, in spite of their close relationship, uttered not a single word on behalf of a man whom everyone liked and respected. We found our comrade, who had not enjoyed the proper use of his legs for several years already, lying on a bed; his legs resembled sticks, and it was sad to see the wretched and unhappy man. His mother had submitted a petition to the Tsar, entreating him to pardon one now only half-alive, but the merciful Tsar refused, saying only that Krasnokutsky could travel where he pleased throughout Siberia. The sufferer preferred, of course, to stay in Krasnoyarsk, where he soon died.

In Tobol'sk we even found one of our comrades and a founder of the Secret Society, A. N. Murav'yov, but not as an exile and not living there as in a settlement, but in the distinguished position of Governor! Of course, such a bizarre thing can occur only in autocratic states. The criminal court had sentenced Murav'yov to hard labour—I forget how many years; the Tsar, in his absolute power, sent him to live in Yakutsk, and stripped him neither of his colonel's rank nor of his orders. Soon, Murav'yov was appointed Chief of Police in Irkutsk and, finally, Governor of Tobol'sk.[20] But here he failed to get along with Governor-General Vel'yaminov,[21] so was transferred to Archangel. We rejoiced in our heart that the worthy Murav'yov had been spared from penal servitude by happy chance—though in a *moral* sense there would have been more honour to him had he expiated his offence, if an offence it was, through the same punishment as his companions. For he should not have received any mercy or any commutation. Here is what Schnitzler says about him in his book: 'Colonel Alexander Murav'yov, in view of the sincerity of his repentance, was to be merely deported to Siberia—it was not said for how many years—being neither stripped of his rank nor losing his noble station.'[22] After Archangel, Murav'yov was appointed President of the Provincial Administration in Simferopol' and, when the Sovereign was there, was enquired after during a presentation of officials. Nicholas Pavlovich asked the Governor 'how Murav'yov was serving.' Such a humiliating appraisal was in itself enough to change one's destiny into hard labour!

The next day, we presented ourselves to Governor-General Vel'yaminov, who received us very amiably having informed us that we should be living in the town of Kurgan, that this spot was the Italy of Siberia, that grapes ripen and cherries blossom there, and so forth. Vel'yaminov was a decent old man who occupied himself with literature a good deal, read widely and was in correspondence with Humboldt, but who governed badly the immense district entrusted to him.

At last, we set off for Kurgan, the place where we should settle permanently. Kurgan is a small and pretty district town, with a stone church and 3000 inhabitants, on the left and slightly elevated bank of the River Tobol'. Around it is a flat plain that reminded me of my native Ukraine, but not of Italy, as Vel'yaminov had artlessly informed us. Kurgan was famous because Kotzebue,[23] exiled by Paul, had lived there. They say he used to love to stroll along the bank of the Tobol'—I don't know if he had Zimmerman's 'Solitude'[24] with him then. I found his house intact still, and also sought out the old man, a contemporary of his, who used to send Kotzebue fresh butter of which, apparently, he was extremely fond.

The good Rozen, also our comrade and sent here one year earlier, met us like a relative in his own house, which had cost him 4½ thousand roubles. The Naryshkins settled, for the time being, in a peaceful and convenient apartment which, together with a garden and a vacant plot, they intended to acquire by purchase, while I rented two rooms not far away from them. My landlady was a stout and quarrelsome merchant-woman, the widow of a clock-maker's apprentice. In Siberia, as in Germany, all the cares of housekeeping lie on the female sex, and my landlady invariably managed her own rooms, and mine too, by herself.

Soon, our other comrades started visiting us, too, and a small circle was formed. People of high rank in Kurgan, however, avoided us, and we associated with only our own immediate superior, the Town Governor, who fortunately proved to be a splendid individual and did his best to make our odd position easier. Through him passed our correspondence with the cultured world—but for all that, it did not escape the hands of the Third Department and the Governor-General of [Western] Siberia. Yet despite this, we began to breathe more freely. We could walk and drive now where our fancy took us, provided that it was not more than twenty-five versts from Kurgan and that we always slept in our homes. But even this was adequate for us after twelve years of wearisome seclusion.

I was in correspondence at this time with my good friend A. F. Briggen, who was living in Pelym. I tried continually to persuade him to ask permission to join us in Kurgan; after living in Pelym two years, he managed to do so, and very glad we were at his arrival, for we gained a new, intelligent and amiable comrade in him.[25] Briggen had formerly served as a colonel in the Izmaylovskiy Regiment and, having married a Miklashevskaya, a sister of the famous Caucasian hero[26] who was killed down there, had retired and lived on his father-in-law's estate in the Province of Chernigov. In his solitude, Briggen busied himself with a translation from the Latin of the life of Julius Caesar, which he dedicated to his friend V. A. Zhukovsky.

Strangely incomprehensible is the Emperor Nicholas's vengeance against all those whom he knew personally and intimately. It was not by the court's sentence, but by his personal instruction, that all those individuals well known to him and, as luck would have it, less guilty than others—such as Briggen, Norov, Nazimov and Naryshkin—were punished more severely than were others. Briggen's arrest in 1825, in fact, is especially remarkable. Residing in his village, as I said, Briggen was preparing to leave the country at the end of 1825, had already received a passport and had sent off to a banker for 15,000 roubles on credit. A carriage was made ready for the journey and his things were all arranged. A service was held, and Briggen went out from his own house.

Twenty versts from the house his carriage breaks, and Briggen returns home. After twenty-four hours all is repaired once more, and Briggen and his wife and children once again make their adieus to their relatives staying behind. Suddenly, a district police officer flies into the courtyard with a courier, and they seize Briggen and take him off to Peter-and-Paul Fortress!

At the time of the coronation in 1856, Briggen was pardoned by Imperial manifesto. His wife and son, already an officer, and other relatives waited for him in that same house and that same village from which, thirty years earlier, he had been wrenched so unexpectedly. They were all waiting for him in a fever of impatience, thinking to meet a sick and decrepit old man, when suddenly there entered a brisk and cheerful individual with high colour in his cheeks and the words: 'Ladies and gentlemen, be so good as to tell me which person among you is my wife; I am Briggen.' The old woman and the son threw themselves on his neck while Briggen, embracing his former friend, his former companion in life, suggested to her jokingly that they once again get married.

Baron A. E. Rozen

On our way to Petrovskiy Zavod, in August 1830, we had passed through the town of Verkhnyeudinsk. The nights outside that town we passed in our felt tents, which were well made and which let no wind through. Buriat families would sit on felt rugs round the fire in the middle of the yurt, naked children tumbling about among their elders, who spend their time tearing and cutting animal skins with their teeth, fashioning arrows, casting bullets or milling felt. The chief luxury of every class among them, and a principal support of those who can afford it, is a special kind of tea—a mixture of decayed and spoilt tea-leaves, which is pressed into cakes, and cherry-gum or some other sticky substance; these cakes look like smooth bricks one or two feet long, seven inches wide, and three inches thick. From this resemblance, the tea is called in Siberia 'brick tea.' With their hatchets, Buriats would break off little pieces from these lumps, ground or pound them in mortars, boil the resultant powder in a kettle, add some flour, milk or butter, and fat, and drink this brew with great relish from wooden lacquered bowls rather deeper and larger than our Western saucers. The Buriats also have a passion for tobacco, which they smoke in little copper pipes. They inhale all the smoke.

These nomad Buriats subsist on the product of the chase, on fish, and even on carrion. Descendants of the Mongols, they have as few wants as had earlier their forefathers of the time of Genghiz Khan, who marched his innumerable armies prodigious distances without stores or provisions. Our Buriat drivers and escort took neither bread nor any other foodstuff with them; twice a day, they would leave the encampment in groups and spend half an hour in the woods satisfying their appetite with bilberries. By degrees, they grew accustomed to us. Some of them spoke Russian and served as interpreters (whom they called *Tolmeshchen*) for the rest. A group of them assembled regularly round the table at which Vadkovsky and Trubetskoy played chess. By exclamations and signs of approval, they gave us to understand that they were well acquainted with the game. One of them was invited to play; he did, and beat our best player. He also told us that the game had long been known to them, having reached them from China.

The curiosity of these nomads was greatly pricked by my comrade, M. S. Lunin, whose wounds had secured him permission to be driven in a carriage, which he covered with an oil-cloth. He slept in it by night and lived in it by day. For many days this carriage would be encircled by a crowd of Buriats the moment that we stopped for our night's lodging—Buriats who waited most impatiently until the prisoner should show himself; but the oil-cloth curtains remained steadily closed, the mysterious individual whom they held to be the chief criminal amongst us remaining invisible. Finally, it occurred to Lunin to emerge and ask them what they wanted. The Tolmeshchen explained, in the name of the spectators, that they wished to see him and find out for what specific reason he was banished to Siberia.

'Do you know your *Taisha?*' (*Taisha* means a chief of the highest rank in Buriat).

'We know him.'

'And do you know the *Taisha* over your *Taisha*, who can put him in a carriage and send him away to destruction [*Ugey*]?'

'We have heard of him.'

'Well, I wished to put an end to his power, so I am banished.'

'Oh! Oh! Oh!' echoed the wondering group and, bowing deeply, the curious crowd drew back from the carriage and its mysterious occupant.

A small number of this nomadic race have turned to Christianity, live in houses and practise agriculture; the remainder are heathens and are led by their priests, the Shamans, who purposely keep up their superstitions, occasionally reducing themselves to a state of full unconsciousness by extravagant bodily exercises. In this state, they utter prophesies and curses. The Buriats are uncleanly to the highest degree. They have no linen, wear furs next to the bare body and boots of chamois skin, and little fur caps both in summer and in winter. Their heads are shaved, all except for one tuft, which crowns the top. Small eyes, low and flat foreheads, square faces with prominent cheek-bones, and pale yellow complexions, such are the distinguishing marks of their race. Among themselves they are called *Mendu*.

After some days, we reached the banks of the Selenga, the grandest and most beautiful part of Siberia. Imagine a broad river, whose right bank was composed of high rocks of various-coloured strata, red, yellow, grey and black granite, mixed with spar, slate, sand, lime, gravel, and chalk; this bank was sixty feet in height! In clear weather, the perpendicular wall of rock shone with a thousand lovely hues. The country around is broken by hills, which are crowned with massive blocks of stone resembling fortresses and castles; these are probably the result of some earthquake, a theory confirmed by the appearance of the shores of Lake Baikal. This lake, which in Siberia is called the Holy Sea, is of unfathomable depth. Nature on the Selenga, in short, is very beautiful, yet it lacks animation. The population is extremely small in proportion to the vastness of the country.

Near the town of Verkhnyeudinsk we turned off the road to the left and, after a three-day march, arrived at a large village called Tarbagatay. Its houses and inhabitants give it the aspect of a village in Great Russia. Here, on a tract fifty versts long, live the so-called *Semeyskiye*, a people whose forefathers were exiled to Siberia from Dorogobush and Gornel,[27] chiefly because of their sectarianism, both under Empress Anna, in 1733, and under Catherine, in 1767. They were allowed to sell their goods and property and to settle in Siberia with their wives and families. When these exiles crossed Baikal and arrived at Verkhnyeudinsk, they were ordered by the local authorities to settle in empty places, far from other settlements. The government commissary took them to an ancient forest by the little river Tarbagatay, and allowed them to select their own site for a hamlet; they were exempted from the payment of Crown taxes. How great was the surprise of these officials when, returning one year later, they discovered a fine and well-built village, kitchen-gardens and fields on a spot which twelve months earlier had been covered by dense forest! This wondrous change was the result of diligence, combined with the ready money that the exiles had brought with them, having sold all their property at home.

My wife and I were quartered in a peasant's house. These houses had several rooms and a covered staircase, large windows, and roofs made out of boards. On one side of the entrance was a large room for workmen, and a huge Russian baking-oven; on the other were two to five rooms, with Dutch ovens.[28] Here the floor was covered with carpets made expressly for the purpose, and the tables and chairs were polished. Even mirrors, bought at the yearly fair in Irbit, adorned the walls. Our hostess regaled us most hospitably with ham, sturgeon, and cakes of various kinds. In the courtyard we saw carriages bound with iron, good harnesses, strong, well-fed horses and healthy, well-built men. The whole gave an impression of great prosperity. Like all those of their creed, these people have no use for wine, tobacco, tea or medicine, nor are they inoculated, considering such things sinful. Yet I did not see a single person marked with smallpox there. They are a God-fearing people, too, and read the Scriptures diligently.

Many of them are capitalists: some possess capital to the amount of 100,000 roubles, do a great trade in corn and have considerable dealings with the Chinese, to whom they sell wheat and sheepskins at a profit. 'Why are your neighbours so poor?' I asked my host.

'Can they be anything else?' was his reply; 'before the cock crows, we are out in the fields and ploughing in the cold morning air, whereas the native peasants are hardly up and boiling their brick-tea; the sun is high before *they* get into the field. We've finished our first work while the Siberians and their draught cattle are still toiling in the midday sun: neither they nor their horses have the strength to plough the land decently. And on top of that, the earlier settlers love their brandy. They waste every kopek on it and can amass no capital.'

Bestuzhev asked one of these farmers why they did not import machines, which would lighten and speed up their farm-work, in threshing and cleaning the seed, at least.

'Our corn is mostly dried,' answered the farmer. 'We often store it for five years, when prices are low and harvests good. A broad shovel is all we need for winnowing. How much can a machine winnow in a day?' We told him. 'My shovel and hand will do as much,' said our host, extending his sinewy hand with its wrist more than four inches wide. The whole existence of these people testified to their contentment and prosperity. ... The soil grows excellent wheat, which can be exported to great advantage. Indeed, the riches of these peasants made me feel as if I were looking at Russians at work in America, rather than in Siberia. Here they are quite as well off as in America; they have a large and fertile territory, an industrious population, and they govern themselves.

Now, [July 1832] I drove as fast as possible without halting for a moment. The charms of the Selenga passed by my eyes unheeded, their beauty lit up now by the brilliant light of day, now by the pale moonlight. But my thoughts were far away, with my wife and child in Irkutsk, or in the prison I had left so recently, and I scarcely saw what passed before me. Instead of going to Posol'skiy Monastery, where the ships generally lie in harbour, I drove (on the advice of my companion) along the bank of the Selenga to the little river port of Chertov-kino, from where heavy fishing smacks go to Irkutsk when they descend the river to Baikal. But I had hardly reached this village than I saw, a verst away, a boat that had just then put out; there was no other vessel in the port, so there was only one course open to me — to drive along the shore till I drew level with the boat. ...

We drove on and on along the shore, flying over field and meadow to catch the boat. In half an hour we reached the next stage, where the sailing vessels called. I shouted to the helmsman with all my strength: 'Stop, take me aboard!'

'Will you give me twenty-five roubles?'

'Willingly.'

'Give me thirty?'

'All right.'

'Thirty-five roubles?'

'Done.'

'Forty roubles, then?'

'Anything for a boat, at once!'

Two fishermen jumped into a little boat and put off to the shore. I and my companions stepped in. With me I had only a portmanteau, a basket containing some bread, and a bottle of wine which Princess Trubetskaya had given me for the journey. I had had no time to get myself any other provisions. The wind was favourable, and we were hoping to get across Baikal in five hours.

The boat was dragged down the river by three men with a rope, and slowly did they pull it along. But the skipper had only six men to work his vessel. A springless carriage stood in the middle of the boat; in it there sat a grey-haired man wrapped in a military cloak. Now our little boat was gliding swiftly down the Selenga's clear waters. Having greeted my unknown travelling-companion, I asked the sub-officer to pay the skipper the promised money for our passage immediately, and asked him earnestly to do his utmost to hasten that same passage. I promised a handsome reward for his men, if we made a speedy crossing. The boatmen, however, who pass their whole lives on the water, proved more sluggish and more difficult to move than amphibious creatures; they seemed not to understand the meaning of the word haste. It was three in the afternoon, and we were still a mere sixteen versts from the river-mouth, when they began to fasten the rope to a tree, in order to sit down and get some food and rest! 'We've time enough,' they said; 'wind's favourable—we'll be on the other side early tomorrow, if we can just get down the Selenga. ...' So the boat stayed on the bank. I persuaded my companions to jump out and pull on the rope themselves till the fishermen had rested and eaten. The indefatigable soldiers immediately followed my lead, and we tugged the boat forward a little; but on jumping out I sprained my foot, and every step became more and more painful. Still, I hardly felt it, as I thought with high anxiety of my wife and child, who were expecting me. ...

When I woke up next morning, I saw that the river bank was far away. We were on the lake now, with the sails hoisted; but the wind was falling rapidly; and finally the sails were flapping idly. The gaff creaked on the mast, swaying slowly from side to side, and in the end came to a state of perfect rest. And there we lay, some twenty versts from the mouth of the Selenga. My impatience and anxiety may be imagined. The fishermen lay down to sleep, saying: 'If we don't get there today, we shall tomorrow.' So I had time enough to study Lake Baikal. Its shores are sometimes high and steep, here and there with bare rugged rocks of granite and flint which alternate with greensward and small woods. There are traces of volcanic activity on all sides, and it may be supposed that Lake Baikal, the Selenga and the Angora once formed a single river. In some places, the lake is fathomless.

Though I bathed it ceaselessly with water, the pain in my foot became intolerable; I had to ask the skipper to demand his payment from my companions. They had provisions for seven days aboard; indeed, they never set out on a voyage on Baikal without stores of that kind, the weather there being so fickle.

Thus we lay for two days, motionless in the middle of the lake. On the third day a storm blew up. The vessel, though secured by an anchor, rocked like a candle moved by an impatient hand. Still the wind was contrary. My situation was becoming more intolerable each hour. Night and day we were tossed on the waves, while the reflection of the sun on the water and the high wind caused such inflammation of my eyes that I could barely read a few lines at a time from Goethe's 'Genius,'[29] which happened to be in my pocket. To add to all this, I was sea-sick.

Almost joyfully, in spite of the new form of imprisonment to which we were hastening, my wife and child and I continued our journey to Kurgan.[30] We drove very fast, hurrying so as to reach Kurgan early — it was no less than 4200 versts from Petrovskiy to our new destination, and an unforeseen delay in my departure from the prison and the hindrances on Lake Baikal had robbed us of three weeks of the best time of the year. It was already early August, and the night frosts had set in. But at least this spared us from the little flies which so torment both man and beast during the short Siberian summer that it is quite impossible for them to work during the daytime, and even common labourers have to cover their face with a linen veil.

I have already described the extraordinary speed of the Siberian horses. We drove on, night and day, without a break. In the evening, I got onto the box beside the driver and attempted to induce him to go slower and more carefully by promising him a good tip; but promises and threats were equally futile, and the horses were not to be checked. While they were being put to at a posting-station, a crowd of men always surrounded the unmanageable creatures, holding them firmly by the halter. As soon as the travellers were seated, the driver would shout: 'Let go!' The men thereupon flung themselves to right and left to get out of the way, and the carriage would shoot past them like, without exaggeration, a cannon-ball. ...

Wherever the climate permits, agriculture and the breeding of cattle are carried on here with the greatest success. The commerce is conducted by means of the great high-road from Tyumen' and Nerchinsk; this road is the channel by which the produce of those vast, rich plains will be made available to future generations. Even during the reign of Catherine II, Siberia was called the golden territory because of the abundance of precious metals there; but though the river-beds and mountains of Siberia do, indeed, contain rich gold-fields, the chief wealth of the land is in the fruitfulness of the soil. Many places in the Provinces of Tomsk, Yeniseysk and Irkutsk produce abundant harvests; and the land needs as little dressing as the plains of the Ukraine.

In 1835, we were each given the right to fifteen acres of arable land in the vicinity of Kurgan. My plot was bounded on the town side by the shore of little Bosinakov Lake. I fertilized the sandy and unfruitful shores of the lake with ashes, which could be had gratis from a large soap-boiling house nearby, and in two years the land was fruitful. For agricultural implements, I used two-horse Siberian ploughs, like the Belgian plough, which were well adapted to the soil there. When I had introduced the use of extirpators, rollers and iron harrows, I turned my three-field husbandry into a four-field alternate husbandry. And some of my experiments answered well. Himalayan barley and potatoes were the only crops that would not thrive. I also started a little stud. The work could easily be got through with the help of one labourer — two in the summer. The harvesting and threshing was done either by extra hired help or else by an 'invitation to the feast.' The population being so sparse, it was difficult to get any work done for cash; the only chance was to offer a feast as well as wages — to suit the tastes of the pleasure-loving Siberians. The required number of men, women, and girls would soon assemble then, each bringing holiday clothes and implements as well. From early morning till late evening they would work diligently, while my wife had pies baked, cabbage soup and porridge made, and she herself prepared a table in the middle of our courtyard. Work stopped at seven, and the people gathered to the sound of a fiddle and two flutes, in order to wash and dress. When the meal was over dancing started, and it lasted practically without a break till sunrise. I simply could not see how they found the strength for it, for even while the musicians were resting there was no halt: the men and women then took it in turn to sing; beer and brandy were freely handed round; and the girls refreshed themselves with gingerbread and nuts.

The sums of money that our relatives had sent us were not limited, so long as we had lived in prison or as forced labourers; but now, in our settlement, a bachelor was allowed only 300 silver roubles a year, and a married man not more than 600. This sum was quite adequate here, however, for living was very cheap. A *pood* of rye-meal cost seven kopeks, and wheat-meal fourteen kopeks; meat was a half to one kopek a pound, and a cartload of hay, thirty kopeks.

The monotony of life in Kurgan was broken by three fairs each year, which took place on March 18, October 27, and December 20. Merchants from Irbit, Tobol'sk, Shadrinsk, Tyumen' and even Kazan' would come to these. From early morning till late evening, everything would be in movement; almost every buyer was a seller at the same time, and throughout the great, unbroken holiday to which the fair gave rise, the streets, so empty as a rule, would be filled with a gay bustle that lasted until late at night. Samovars were set up on the streets, and numbers of customers gathered around them. Close by, other groups would assemble round some wandering musician who played songs and dances on his accordion. Many carried their own handiwork to sell — boots, gloves, wooden vessels, woven baskets, and so forth. One prominent figure was the seller of chamois and reindeer leather breeches, of which he carried many pairs over his shoulders. Meanwhile, horses and riders would be swarming by the banks of the River Tobol', where Russians, Kirghiz and Gypsies haggled over little, mettlesome Siberian horses. The reply to an enquiry about the price of a horse was invariably: 'Oh, two or three sacks.' There is so little gold and silver coinage in Siberia that all the money circulating is either in the form of paper or in copper coins. These last are counted out ready in bags of twenty-five roubles, and the honesty of the people is such that one can rely on the contents of the bags. After sunset, the booths are closed and the peasants retire into the neighbouring villages for the night, returning to the town at sunrise; but some prefer to pass the night under the open sky, lying beside a watchfire.

There are always thirteen officials in each Siberian district town: the inspector of police, the police officer and three assessors, the judge and three assessors, the district fiscal inspector, the postmaster, the tax-collector, and the doctor. These form the aristocracy, but are often divided by family quarrels or by business matters. The isolation from all other society, however, together with the immense distances between the towns and the necessity of intercourse, force them to make swift reconciliations, which generally occur on feast-days. Everyone celebrates his own name-day and those of every member of his family. Two days before, the host sends out invitations: 'M.N. greets you and hopes you will come to breakfast, tea and dinner with your wife on such and such a day.' These social gatherings are heavy to a degree that can hardly be imagined. In the morning, the guests assemble for breakfast; at two o'clock they return for a well-served dinner, after which they drive home for a sleep. Then, in the evening, they meet again at eight for tea, dancing, and supper. They disperse at last at two in the morning. Lemonade and dried and preserved fruits are handed round during the dance. The ladies are very well dressed, and have most attractive jewellery; the Urals being so near, it is easy to obtain precious stones. ...

Besides their name-days, the Kurgan officials kept a common festival each year on the last Sunday of Carnival week.[31] On this occasion, a huge sled made of six ordinary peasants' sleds would appear; at the four corners, supports were laid and fastened on the top by laths placed crosswise. In the middle of the cross so made was a horizontal wheel, on which a grimacing harlequin would play antics and pull faces while a banner floated over the whole thing. The officials and musicians sat on benches on a platform. Six horses drew this vehicle, an outrider going before. They would drive through the streets in procession, from one acquaintance to another. At every door, the hostess would receive them with pancakes and wine, and in every house they would embrace and kiss each other while, in preparation for Lent, they asked each other's pardon for offences they had possibly committed. Countless sleds with one, two, or three horses followed this giant sled, to the accompaniment of songs and ringing bells, until late evening. The Siberians, it may be said, take the greatest delight in sled-driving: there are races on the River Tobol' without a break throughout the winter. At the consecration of the river in the spring and on Twelfth-day, too, there are large meetings of riders. In the spring they swim the horses into the consecrated water, while in January they merely drink and splash themselves with it; then the races start. So powerful is their belief in the blessing of the water that often, when it has been done, numbers of men undress and plunge several times through a hole hewn through the ice, and this in 25 degrees of frost! I saw it more than once.

The rumour circulated, long ago, that the late Emperor Alexander Pavlovich had prepared his brother Nicholas Pavlovich as heir to the throne, and it was said that this was done with the consent of the heir apparent, Constantine Pavlovich, on his marriage to the Polish woman Grudzinska.[1] Alexander, it was said, had made a testament on that occasion, but there was no positive evidence on the subject. In the Prussian Court Calendar for 1825, however, Nicholas Pavlovich was shown as heir to the Russian throne, in accordance with an agreement reached when Constantine had married. It was said that the Emperor expressed displeasure to the Prussian court over this publication. But all this, as is commonly the case in autocratic states where the government's every action is a state secret, was known only to a few, and produced only faint echoes in society.

The Emperor Alexander Pavlovich, it is well known, died in an almost abrupt fashion. News of his death reached Petersburg at about the same time as news of his illness: the first courier from Taganrog, on November 24, brought tidings of the illness, the third, of November 26, of the decease — and this at the very time when the entire Imperial family was attending a thanksgiving service for his improved condition, news of which had come that same day in the morning by the second courier (sent off a few hours before the death).[2] The service was broken off. The State Council assembled. All its members were silent, and the lips of those whose voices were habitually attended to in counsel remained sealed. Only Count Miloradovich's voice was heard;[3] and he called for an oath of allegiance to be sworn to the heir-at-law, Constantine Pavlovich. Prince Golitsyn demanded that the former Sovereign's testament be read, and Count Miloradovich agreed to this, on condition that the testament be held binding on no one. It should be read, he said, only out of respect for the deceased. The testament was brought and read. The members rose and went to inform the Grand Duke Nicholas Pavlovich that an oath was to be sworn to Constantine; and with him they proceeded to Mariya Fyodorovna, and from her chambers to the court chapel for the swearing of allegiance.

Count Miloradovich, as Military Governor of St. Petersburg, instructed the Commandant to send an order to the guard posts that the sentries should immediately be brought to swear allegiance to Constantine. Meanwhile, a lectern was erected before which the inner watch, then formed of troops of the First Battalion of the Preobrazhenskiy Regiment, might do the same.[4] On hearing the reply to his enquiry as to why this preparation was now being made, the senior grenadier[5] came out and said that they had not so much as heard of the Sovereign's illness. Together with the other grenadiers, moreover, he showed his mistrust of the truth of this news of His Majesty's death. Not one of the generals would convince them of its truth, they said, until the Grand Duke Nicholas Pavlovich should himself come and announce that he had already sworn allegiance to the new Sovereign, Constantine Pavlovich. *Then* the grenadiers on guard duty would agree to take an oath to Constantine.

The senators, however, took the oath to Constantine on hearing the news of Alexander's death announced by the Minister of Justice, (Prince Lobanov-Rostovsky)[6]. As to the sealed envelope entrusted to the Senate by the late Emperor with the instruction that, taking no action on his death, the senators should first unseal and read it in full session, the matter was not even raised. A question being put to the Minister concerning the envelope (by one of the *Ober-Prokurators*),[7] His Excellency ordered that it should be sent to him at home!

The Senate's ukase on the matter having been made public, a general swearing of allegiance followed. Returning to his palace,[8] the Grand Duke Nicholas Pavlovich sent for Opochinin,[9] a councillor then in retirement, and asked him to go to Constantine Pavlovich and remind him that he had himself, of his own will, renounced rights of inheritance even before his marriage — as long before as in 1822. Nicholas kept Opochinin with him several hours, dismissing him only when evening came and having furnished him with letters and instructions to return at once. Opochinin rode off in the night. And the Grand Duke sent to make sure that he had, indeed, departed.

Opochinin returned the following evening with the Grand Duke Mikhail Pavlovich, whom he had met coming from Warsaw with the news that Constantine had received no allegiances whatever in the Kingdom of Poland but, the day he had heard news of Alexander's death, had locked himself up and would see no one. Once more, a few hours later, Opochinin was dispatched with new letters — and returned when an oath was already being taken to serve Nicholas.

Constantine Pavlovich made no reply at all to the letters Opochinin brought, and certainly, therefore, gave no proof to the populace that he was *voluntarily* renouncing the throne in favour of the next in line of succession. More, it was said that the reply in which he granted the throne to whoever wanted it was couched in the most indecorous terms — a possibility substantiated to a point by the fact that it was not published together with the manifesto announcing the accession of Nicholas Pavlovich. In order to be certain of the rightness of Nicholas's accession, indeed, it was found necessary to make public letters which Constantine had written to the late Emperor in 1822 when he was marrying Princess Lowicz.

This interregnum lasted exactly two weeks. No other circumstance could have been more propitious to the execution of the aims of the Secret Society,[10] had that Society been strong enough to realize them. But its members, alas, were scattered over the immense expanse of the Russian Empire; and some were abroad. Only a few were in the capital, where the main action was to occur. But all this notwithstanding, those few resolved to use the opportunity presented to them, the moreso because the thinking public now firmly expected that Constantine Pavlovich would not accept the throne that was legally his. Reasons that prompted them to use the proffered opportunity were as follows:

1. Never once was there a precedent in Russia of a legitimate heir's voluntarily giving up his throne; it was to be expected that such a renunciation would be believed only with difficulty now.

2. The young Grand Dukes were unpopular, particularly among the military. Only a certain part of the Court would have preferred Nicholas as Emperor — the ladies of the Court considered it would be an affront to them to have a Pole as Empress, and a Pole not even of noble lineage.

3. Vexation with the strange position in which the state now found itself[11] had started to manifest itself in all the houses forming part of the capital's most aristocratic society. Not one exalted personage had raised his voice, however, in these days when to have done so might well have produced a strong response. Whether it was lack of spirit, or love of the Fatherland, or even a concern for personal advantage that sealed all lips is difficult to say; but no one dared express ideas regarding the possible and necessary improvement of our system of government. Only in stupid mockery did the capital's highest society find some expression. There were wagers as to who would get the throne; it was asked whether or not the rams would be sold. There was laughter because an official once at an *ober-prokurator*'s desk and well-known as a cardsharp was sent from the Senate to the Emperor Constantine to inform him that an oath was sworn to him. His being a cardsharp was applied jokingly to the situation in hand.

4. Finally, the members of the Secret Society were certain of collaboration on the part of several of the state's highest dignitaries — men who, while fearing to act openly now that the Society had yet to show its strength, would join us just as soon as they perceived that a sufficient military force could lend them aid.

The Secret Society's first action was to make sure that all its members would further its aims with equal diligence; but here, too, there was found what is found generally in all human affairs. Many members had joined the Society at a time when its ultimate objectives were seen as in the unknown, distant future. Being members, as they knew, they would always enjoy the Society's support, something that might help them to advancement. Now they had reached significant positions but, the latest circumstances growing clear, they saw no personal advantage in their acting in complete conformity with the objectives of such a society, the members of which, having no private aim, strove to sacrifice themselves for the good of the Fatherland alone.* Many who had been ardent members in their youth had cooled over the years. Now we were faced with decisive action which, in the event of success, offered no personal advantages, but which, in the case of failure, could threaten ruin. It was more advantageous, as they saw, to support the man who had good hope of securing the throne—to place themselves and all their talent and resources at the feet of him from whom rewards might be expected, and to whom all estimates promised success. So the Society found itself weakened by the defection of such members as would certainly, by virtue of the power placed in their hands, through high rank in the Guards, have changed the general balance. But at the same time it was seen that a majority among the Guards officers did not accept the possibility of Constantine's renouncing the succession; and their dislike of the young Grand Dukes was evident enough from their discussions. Once the Society revealed its plans to them, they showed enthusiastic willingness to act under its supervision. All these officers were young men; not one of them held a rank higher than company commander.

It was necessary to find a staff officer known to the soldiers of the Guards to take the place of the battalion and regimental commanders who had passed over to the authorities. This leader was needed only at the outset of our action, to take command over all the assembled troops. Colonel Bulatov[12] was in the capital, an officer but recently transferred from the Life-Grenadier Regiment to

---

*Many of the Society's members who have remained in Russia later occupied, and occupy still, important positions in the government: Grabbe commanded a division on the Caucasian lines; Gurko replaced him and was later Chief-of-Staff of the Caucasian Corps—and now of reserve forces; Prince Mikhail Gorchakov was Chief-of-Staff of the army in the field; N. N. Murav'yov commanded a corps; M. N. Murav'yov became a senator, Pjotr Koloshin the head of a department; Il'ya Bibikov served with the Grand Duke Mikhail Pavlovich; Kovelin was Military Governor-General of Petersburg; L. V. Perovsky, Minister of Internal Affairs; Prince Menshikov a member of the Society of Russian Knights and head of the Naval Staff; Val'kovskoy was Chief-of-Staff in Georgia; Litke tutor to the Grand Duke Constantine Nikolayevich. I do not recall other, less significant posts occupied by members, nor are we counting here Shipov, Rostovtsev or Moller, who betrayed the Society, or Prince Dolgoruky who left it from fright.

the field army; the Life-Grenadiers remembered and liked Bulatov, and this was one of the regiments on which we counted most. Bulatov agreed to take command over the troops that would assemble at the rallying position.

It had been learnt, meanwhile, that the Emperor Constantine himself would not be coming, and did not wish to make public in his own name the manifesto announcing his renunciation and the transferal of power to Nicholas Pavlovich —a most embarrassing circumstance for the latter. Nicholas therefore had to publish it in *his* name; but how could he convince others that Constantine had in fact renounced the throne, and by what right could he establish his own accession? Would it not bear all the signs of theft? To publish the manifesto in the Senate's name would, of course, be a quite lawful, popular act, and the populace was well used to receiving all ukases in its name; however, it was thought that this would be to arrogate to the Senate such power as could belong to the Emperor alone, and that a precedent of such a kind might, in the future, serve as pretext for the Senate's taking even the supreme authority under its jurisdiction. It was therefore decided, in the circumstances, to publish the manifesto in the name of the Emperor acceding to the throne; to make public Constantine Pavlovich's letters to the late Tsar; to begin the receiving of oaths from the army; and to bind the commanders of Guards regiments with personal responsibility, should they not overcome their regiments' expected stubbornness. Seeing Constantine's strange conduct, Count Miloradovich, who had persuaded Nicholas of the necessity of ceding the throne to the lawful heir, resolved to cooperate in overcoming all obstacles to the proclamation of Nicholas as Emperor.

The Secret Society, which was well informed of every action taken by the Grand Duke and the military command, as of the thoughts expressed in their discussions by both officers and men, ordered its actions in accordance with that knowledge. It was known it would be difficult, if not wholly impossible, to persuade many officers and all the troops that Constantine Pavlovich had indeed renounced the throne of his own will; even among the common people, Mikhail, not Nicholas, was acknowledged lawful heir (as having been born when his father was the Emperor). Only the habit of blind obedience, and coercion, would make the soldiers swear as their leaders demanded; but as the regimental commanders were themselves but little loved by their subordinates and did not have their confidence, it would be easy to cause that obedience to waver. And indeed, when the troops were marched out by regiments on the morning of December 14th for the swearing of allegiance, they showed bewilderment and indecision which, at the first words of the officers who questioned the legality of the demanded oath, turned into open stubbornness. So accustomed to blind obedience is the Russian soldier, however, that most commanders succeeded in restraining their subordinates, although Fridrikhs and Styurler,[13] being even more unpopular than others, and Kartsov, whom his own subordinates did not respect at all, were unable to secure the men entrusted to their authority.

As is well known, high military command is accustomed to think of the Russian soldier as a blockhead who will swivel about and go where his chief may order. Count Miloradovich, however, who had been gathering information about the disposition and morale of men and officers alike throughout the interregnum, was convinced that it would not be easy to make them swear allegiance by simply publishing a manifesto in the name of a man who wished to take the throne. In vain he struggled to arrange that it be issued in the name of the Emperor to whom allegiance had been sworn already. Only in that eventuality, he said, could he give an assurance that tranquility would not be shattered in the city. The Count's feelings shook the confidence of Nicholas all the more because he, too, was warned by his followers of the Guards' mood, and of the existence of a secret society that meant to utilize that mood. On the night of December 13th/14th, the Commander of the Preobrazhenskiy Regiment[14] did his best to swing his men over to Nicholas's side. To do so seemed the more essential (to him) since, when on the inner watch on the day of the oath-giving, the Grenadiers' platoon in His Majesty's own company had shown a tendency to hesitate, and that so soon. As well as promises, large sums of money were distributed from artel funds. So it was brought about that, when the First Battalion was marched out on the actual morning and approached by Nicholas Pavlovich, and when he asked the men if they wanted him as Sovereign, an affirmative answer was given. Thereupon, he ordered them to load rifles and follow him.

B

Extracts from Correspondence   Appendix

Extract from a Letter of P. G. Kakhovsky to General V. V. Levashev[1]

Your Excellency,

The rising of December 14 was the result of causes already given. I see, Your Excellency, that the Committee established by His Majesty is making a great effort to discover all the members of the Secret Society. The government will derive no significant benefit from that, however. We were not trained in the Society, but were already prepared to work when we joined it. It is in the spirit of the time and in our state of mind that the origin and root of the Society are to be sought. I am acquainted with a few who belong to the Secret Society, but am inclined to think that the membership is not very large. Among my acquaintances who do not adhere to secret societies, however, very few are opposed to my views. Frankly I tell you that among thousands of young men there are barely a hundred who do not long passionately for freedom. These youths, striving with pure, strong love for the good of their Fatherland and for true enlightenment, are becoming mature.

The people have conceived a sacred truth: that they do not exist for governments, but that governments must be organized for them. This is a cause of struggle in all countries: peoples, having once tasted the sweetness of enlightenment and freedom, strive towards both: and governments, surrounded by millions of bayonets, make efforts to drive off these peoples, back into the gloom of ignorance. But these attempts will all prove vain. Impressions once received can never be erased. Liberty, that torch of intellect and warmth of life, was always and everywhere the attribute of peoples who have left behind primitive ignorance. We cannot live like our forebears, like barbarians or slaves.

But even our ancestors, although less educated than ourselves, enjoyed civil liberty. In the time of Tsar Alexis Mikhaylovich, the National Assembly,[2] including representatives of various classes of the people, still functioned and participated in affairs of moment in the state. Five such assemblies were summoned in his reign. Peter I, who killed everything national in the state, also stamped out our feeble liberty. Outwardly, that liberty then vanished; but it lived on in the hearts of true citizens. Its advancement has been slow in our country. Wise Catherine II expanded it a little. Her Majesty made enquiries of the Petersburg Free Economic Society regarding the value and consequences of the emancipation of the peasants in Russia. This great, beneficial idea lived in the heart of the Empress, whom the people loved. Who, among Russians of her time, could have read her *Nakaz* [Instruction] without emotion? The *Nakaz* alone redeems all the shortcomings of that time, characteristic of the century.

Emperor Alexander promised us much; it may be said that he stirred the minds of the people, alerting them to the sacred rights of humanity. Later, he changed his principles and his intentions. The people grew alarmed, but the seed had sprouted, and the roots grew deep. So rich with revolutions are the latter part of the last century and the events of our own time that we have no need to refer to distant ones. We are witnesses to great events. ... The United States, by virtue of their form of government, have forced Europe into rivalry. Even to distant generations the United States will shine as an example, and the name of Washington, the friend and benefactor of the people, will pass from age to age. Memories of his devotion to the welfare of the Fatherland will move citizens' hearts.[3] In France, the Revolution that had started so auspiciously finally turned, alas, from a lawful into a criminal one. But it was not the people, but court intrigues and politics, that proved responsible for that. The Revolution in France shook every throne in Europe, and had a greater influence on governments and peoples than had the establishment of the United States.

Napoleon's dominance, and the war of 1813–14, united all the nations of Europe, summoned to action by their monarchs and fired by the call to freedom and to citizenship. By what means were countless sums collected among citizens? What guided the armies? They preached *freedom* to us, in manifestos and appeals and orders! We were lured and, kindly by our nature, believed all this, sparing neither our blood nor property. Napoleon was overthrown. The Bourbons were recalled to the French throne and, bowing to the circumstances, granted a constitution to that brave, magnanimous nation, pledging themselves to forget the past. The monarchs united in a Holy Alliance. Congresses sprang into existence, informing nations that they were assembled to reconcile all classes and to introduce political freedom. But the object of those congresses was soon revealed, and nations learned how greatly they had been deceived. The Monarchs thought only of how to keep their boundless power, how to support their shattered thrones, and how to extinguish the last spark of enlightenment and freedom.

Offending nations started to demand what belonged to them and had been promised to them. Prisons and chains were their lot! Crowns broke their pledges, and the constitution of France was violated at its very base. Manuel, representative of the people, was dragged by gendarmes from the Chamber of Deputies! The freedom of the press was limited, the army of France, against its will, sent to destroy the lawful liberty of Spain. Forgetful of the oath given by Louis XVIII, Charles X compensates *émigrés*—and lays new taxes on the people for that purpose! The government interferes with the election of deputies, and in the last elections only thirty-three of those chosen are not in the king's service and pay, the rest being sold to ministers. The firm, courageous Spanish people rise for their country's liberty at the cost of blood, saving the King, the Monarchy, and their country's honour. Of their own will, the people received Ferdinand as King, who swore an oath to safeguard their rights. As early as 1812, Alexander I had recognized the constitution of Spain. Then the Alliance itself assisted France by sending troops to her, so helping to dishonour her army in the invasion of Spain. Arrested in Cadiz, Ferdinand was sentenced to death. He summoned Riego, swore to be once more loyal to the constitution and to expel French forces from the country, and begged Riego to spare his life. Honest men are apt to be trustful. Riego gave guaranty to the Cortes for the King; Ferdinand was released. And what was the King's first step? By his order Riego was arrested, seized, poisoned and, half-alive, that martyr, saint, and hero, who renounced the throne offered to him, friend of the people and saviour of the King's life, was taken by the King's order through the streets of Madrid in a shameful cart pulled by a donkey, and hanged like a criminal. What an act! Whose heart would not shudder at it! Instead of the promised liberty, the European nations found themselves oppressed. The prisons of Piedmont, Sardinia, Naples, and of the whole of Germany and Italy in general were filled with citizens in chains. So oppressive has the people's lot become that they have started to regret the past and bless the memory of Napoleon the conqueror! And *these* are the events that have enlightened them, and made them understand the impossibility of coming to accords with sovereigns. ...

The events of December are calamitous for us and, of course, must be distressing to the Emperor. Yet the happenings of that day should also be fortunate for His Imperial Highness. After all, it was necessary that the Society begin its activity at some time, but hardly could it have been as precipitate as in this instance. I swear to God that I wish the good Sovereign prosperity! May God aid him in healing the wounds of our Fatherland, and to become a friend and benefactor of the people. ...

Most obedient and devoted servant of Your Excellency,
Pyotr Kakhovsky
1826/ February 24.

Extract from a Letter of Baron V. I. Shteyngel' to Nicholas I[4].

... No matter how many members of the Secret Society, or of those who had merely known about it, may be found; no matter how many may be deprived of freedom on account of it, still there will remain a great number of people who share their sentiments and their ideas. Already Russia is so educated that even shopkeepers read newspapers; and newspapers report what is said in the Chamber of Deputies in Paris. Is not the first thought to occur in everybody's mind, 'Why can't *we* discuss our rights?' The majority of our professors, literary men, and journalists certainly adhere wholeheartedly to those who want a constitutional government, for freedom of the press is to their advantage. So do booksellers and merchants. Finally, everyone who has been abroad, and some who have been educated there, and all who have served or who now serve in the Guards, hold the same views. What young man, even if he is only partly educated, has not read and been entranced by the works of Pushkin, which breathe freedom? And who has not quoted from the fables of Denis Davydov, such as his 'Head and Feet?'[5] Perhaps there are such among those who are honoured to attend upon Your Majesty. Sovereign! There is no other way to eradicate free thinking than to destroy an entire generation born and educated in the last reign. But if that is impossible, there remains one thing: to win over hearts by kindness and to draw minds by decisive, open steps for the advancement of the state's future prosperity.

Your most devoted
Baron Vladimir Ivanovich Shteyngel'
1826, January 11.

Letter from Nicholas I to Constantine Pavlovich[6]

December 23, 1825
St. Petersburg
Cher Constantin! Je commence par Vous assurer, qu'avec l'aide de Dieu, tout est rentré ici dans l'ordre habituel. L'esprit est très bon et le deviendra encore plus, quand on Vous verra ici.

Depuis ma dernière, Komarovsky,[7] que j'avais envoyé à Moscou, est revenu porteur ou plutôt pour confirmer toutes les excellentes nouvelles que j'avais déjà. Un semblable rapport m'est déjà parvenu de Finlande et de Mohilew; j'en attends de la 2de armée.

Nos enquêtes vont parfaitement, ainsi que les arrestations de tous les individus apportés, membres de cet horrible et extraordinaire complot: un extrait de ce qui se passe sous ce rapport Vous est envoyé par ce courier. Vous y verrez des noms bien connus, et j'ai les soupçons les plus fondés pour être persuadé que cela remonte jusqu'au Conseil d'Etat, nommément jusqu'à Mordvinoff, mais comme j'ai pour règle de ne mettre la main que sur ceux qui sont dévoilés ou trop fortement soupçonnés pour pouvoir les laisser libres, je ne presse rien.

Lounine est positivement de la bande, et quant à moi, j'y vois l'énigme de sa rentrée au service chez Vous et de tout le zèle qu'il a fait voir. Il est de fait, qu'il est chargé de se faire un parti là-bas; mon opinion, si j'ose en avoir, serait de ne pas l'arrêter, mais de tâcher de le prendre sur le fait, ce qui ne peut ni tarder, ni manquer. Ici l'on est tout zèle pour m'aider à cette affreuse besogne; *des pères m'amènent leurs fils*; tous désirent des exemples et surtout voir leur famille purgée de pareils êtres et même de soupçons de ce genre.

J'attends *Michel Orloff* et *Lopouchin* qui doivent déjà être arrêtés.[8] Ceux de la 2de armée sont les plus importants, ce que Vadkofsky, amené hier, ainsi que tous les autres confirment. C'est surtout Pestel et Serge Volkonsky, qu'il m'importe d'avoir; j'attends aussi Mouravieff et Tchernischeff. Voilà où nous en sommes.

Je suis abîmé de besogne, Vous le comprendrez, me plaindra et ne m'en voudrez pas du désordre de ce ligne; mais la tête me tourne, et l'essentiel est que Vous sachiez tout. J'ai écrit au prince-lieutenant—j'ai cru bien faire. Grabowsky,[9] que j'ai chargé au sujet de l'armée: sur cela dictez ce que Vous voulez. Michel m'a parlé de l'événement du Corps de Lithuanie, j'attends Vos ordres et la forme pour cela que Vous désirez. Adieu, adieu, à Vous pour la vie de toute mon âme et de tout mon coeur.

Nicholas

Je baise les pieds à ma soeur, que Dieu nous la conserve; j'embrasse Paul et Kourouta.

Letter from Nicholas I to Constantine Pavlovich[10]

July 14, 1826
Yelagin Island

Le bon Dieu a permis, cher et excellent Constantin, que nous voyons la fin du terrible procès; hier l'exécution a eu lieu. Cinq des plus coupables d'après la décision du tribunal suprême ont été pendus; les reste [sic] dégradé, cassé et condamné à vie ou à des termes plus ou moins longs, aux travaux forcés et à perpétuité. Que Dieu soit mille fois béni de nous avoir sauvés et qu'Il daigne faire en sorte que ni nous, ni nos petits enfants n'ayons plus de scènes pareilles. Tout s'est passé avec le plus grand calme, ordre et indignation.

Aujourd'hui à la même place, où le 14 le pauvre Miloradowitch est tombé, nous avons servi un Te Deum et des prières funèbres pour lui et ceux qui ont péri ce jour. La garnison était sous les armes et il n'y a pas eu un spectateur, qui n'ait pas été vivement ému, en commençant par Votre serviteur. Que Dieu en soit encore mille et mille fois béni. N'allez pas croire cependant que je croie que l'on puisse s'endormir à cette heure—bien au contraire, je prêche à chacun de redoubler d'attention, pour éviter des esclandres ou des contre-coups, et il faut constamment avoir l'oeil au guêt.

Nicholas

Earlier Western Translations of
Decembrist Memoirs   Appendix

C

It is a pardonable curiosity on the part of the translator to wonder who, if anyone, earlier toiled in his own vineyard. Happily, in one sense, regrettably in another, some brief account of previous translations into Western languages of whole Decembrist memoirs, or of large extracts from them, (of odd translated paragraphs, or pages, a massive list might be compiled), may be given very simply; such translations have been few. This resumé, it should be stressed, takes no account of those memoirs originally published in languages other than Russian, most notably Baron A. E. Rozen's *Aus den Memoiren eines russischen Dekabristen; Beiträge zur Geschichte des St.-Peterburger Militär Aufstandes vom 14/26/ December 1825, und seiner Theilnehmer* (Leipzig, 1869), or, axiomatically, of those published in Russian by Herzen's émigré Free Russian Press (London, 1862–65; *Zapiski Dekabristov*; pts. 1–3).

The first translated volume of memoirs to appear by one who actively participated in events of December 1825, and who paid the price of exile – Herzen's own reminiscences, *My Exile to Siberia* (London, 1855; 2 vols.) are obviously disqualified by their author's absence from the conspiratorial scene in that year, as are Nikolay Turgenev's in *La Russie et les Russes* (Paris, 1848; 3 vols.), though that book throws fascinating light on the preparatory phases of nineteenth century Russian radicalism – the first volume, it would appear, was that of Prince E. P. Obolensky. *Souvenirs d'un exilé en Sibérie; le Prince E. Obolenski: traduits du Russe par le Prince A. Galitzin* were published, as the eighth volume of a 'Bibliothèque Russe et Polonaise; nouvelle série', in the spring of 1862. Eighty-eight pages long, the book, or large booklet, went to press simultaneously in Paris and in Leipzig. For decades, there had been strong cultural ties between St. Petersburg and Leipzig – ties strengthened by the presence of Vladimir Orlov, Radishchev and many other youthful Russian nobles at the German university, and doubly reinforced by a continual stream of Russian travellers. Saxony, after all, lay between East Prussia and France; and Leipzig was a major staging-post on the coach road from Frankfurt to both Weimar and the Rhine. As if to consolidate its position as the centre for translation and dissemination of Decembrist narratives in Germany, if not throughout the West, a second volume of memoirs by Prince Obolensky appeared, in the same year, in that same city. Headed simply *Mon exil en Sibérie*, it was the work of the grammarian Paul Fuchs, and very different, both in point of style, and in its format, from the (no less accurate) offering of Prince Avgustin Petrovich Golitsyn (1824–75). It would be difficult to imagine two more sharply contrasted translators of a single text. Fuchs was a diligent, painstaking, admirably organized North German Protestant; Golitsyn, a passionate adherent to Roman Catholicism, a polemicist, and gifted amateur historian. As it is inconceivable that Fuchs should have produced an academic squib such as 'L'Eglise Russe est-elle libre?' (Paris, 1862), or such a work of spotty scholarship as 'La Russie au XVIII siècle; memoirs inédits sur le règne de Pierre le Grand, Catherine I, Pierre II' (Paris, 1863), so it was hardly possible that Golitsyn see fit to waste his time writing grammatical *aides-mémoire*. Golitsyn laboured erratically, sometimes producing much, more often nothing. Fuchs published year by year, occasionally publishing three works within twelve months! His *New Method to Learn a Language in Six Months; An English Grammar for Russians* (Frankfurt-am-Rein, Jügels Verlag, 1867) was written for a broad market, Golitsyn's books for the connoisseur and scholar. But in the memoirs of Obolensky the two found common ground. While Golitsyn found Prince Yevgeniy's inner moral battles and deep preoccupation with the church most sympathetic, Fuchs was no less powerfully drawn by his horrible experiences and attitude towards them. Linked, too, by their command of Russian, their interests met geographically in St. Petersburg, Siberia and – Leipzig. In August 1869 Prince A. P. Golitsyn published there a short historical study, *Pyotr I, chlen parizhskoy Akademii Nauk (Peter I, Member of the Parisian Academy of Sciences)*. Golitsyn's contribution to the speedy propagation in French literary circles of knowledge of the harsh realities of exile in Siberia deserves a separate study.

The first Decembrists known *as such* in Germany and France, then, (N. V. Basargin's little book *Die Schüle der Kolonnen* perhaps made an impression, but its author was not seen as a Decembrist first and foremost), were N. I. Turgenev and Prince Obolensky. Next came Baron Rozen.

No doubt because of the accessability of German as opposed to Russian prose to most would-be translators at the time, Rozen's memoirs were translated speedily. In Evelyn St. John Mildmay the Baron found a gifted intermediary, and the first English translator of Decembrist memoirs. *Russian Conspirators in Siberia; A Personal Narrative by Baron R., A Russian Dekabrist* was published in London, by Smith, Elder and Co., in 1872. It is, occasional stylistic tics and over-loose renderings apart, the work of a competent translator. St. John Mildmay, it appears, was a one-book man,[1] and a reticent one at that: *Russian Conspirators* ... has no translator's note or foreword. Nor, indeed, can an idea be formed of its author's character by carefully perusing it, though it contains 272 pages, including a 21-page appendix, 'Sketch of the Secret Societies of Russia, 1815–1825.' For all the care that plainly went into its making, St. John Mildmay remains a faint, shadowy presence.

It remains only to mention the work of Adda Goldschmidt and, *en passant*, of the compiler of *Une Histoire de la maison ducale et princière des Trubetzskoi* (Paris, 1887). Of the latter, the least said the better: those parts of Sergey Trubetskoy's memoirs which *are* included are indifferently translated. To Adda Goldschmidt, some credit is due.

At the invitation of Dr Ernst Schultze, philologist and publisher of a series entitled 'Bibliothek wertvoller Memoiren' (Hamburg 1906–12), Goldschmidt translated lengthy extracts from the reminiscences of three Decembrists: Obolensky, Volkonsky and Yakushkin. The versions, bound in a single volume entitled, somewhat weightily, *Verbannung nach Sibirien; aus der Dekabristenzeit: Erinnerungen hoher russischer Offiziere (Jakuschkin, Obolenski und Wolkonski) von der Militär-Revolution des Jahres 1825*, appeared as Bd. 3 of Schutze's series, in 1908 (dated 1907). The memoirs, Schultze informed the public, were intended 'to edify readers of both sexes.' Apparently they did so; the edition sold out.

But was the curiosity of Western European readers quite exhausted by these long extracts by Goldschmidt? Had the rising of December 1825 and its long aftermath become too dim a memory to European publishers by 1910 to tempt them to commission more translations? Certainly there was no dearth of competent translators in the first third of this century; indeed, there were more individuals able to do credit to a Russian book then than at any time during the nineteenth century. The time of lonely pioneers was over. But it was Russian literature that drew English and French translators, the novels of Turgenev and, especially, Tolstoy, not literary-cum-historical memoirs, that most attracted Germans and Italians. As literary translation flourished, in the first part of this century, historical translation waned and died. Perhaps the explanation is a partial one; but it is difficult to know how otherwise one can account for the cessation of translations of Decembrist memoirs into any tongue whatever. Once lost, it was a taste never regained; never, that is, until today.

A Chronological Bibliography of
Decembrist Memoirs Readily Available in
North America   Appendix

(Editions used as bases for translation here are marked*)

The following bibliography has no pretensions to exhaustiveness. There are already adequate bibliographies of works on the Decembrist movement and of Decembrist texts that students may consult: those given, for example, in A. G. Mazour's *The First Russian Revolution, 1825* (Stanford, 1961; 2nd printing), pp. 300–20; in S. Ya. Shtraykh's *Zapiski, stat'i, pis'ma dekabrista I. D. Yakushkina* (Moscow, 1951), pp. 696–705; and in *Russkaya literatura XIX-ogo veka: bibliograficheskiy ukazatel'*, edited by K. Muratova (Moscow, 1962). It is hoped here merely to indicate, by placing memoirs in the order of their chronological appearance, whether as monographs or articles, in Russia or in Western Europe, which individual Decembrists first became familiar to a wide public; which memoirs have been once or several times reprinted, for whatsoever reasons; and which have been republished (or first published) in the Soviet Union since 1917.

1847–48   N. I. Turgenev
    La Russie et les russes. Mémoires d'un proscrit. (3 vols., vol. 1 trans. into Russian by A. A. Kizevetter; Moscow, 1915).

*1862   E. P. Obolensky
    Souvenirs d'un exilé en Siberie ... (Paris; trans. Prince A. Golitsyn; *see Appendix C).*

1862   E. P. Obolensky
    Mon exil en Sibérie (Leipzig; trans. P. Fuchs; *see* Appendix C).

*1869   A. E. Rozen
    Aus den Memoiren eines russischen Dekabristen ... (Leipzig; *see* Appendix C).

1873   F. F. Vadkovsky
    'Zapiski polkovnika Vadkovskogo,' *Russkaya starina,* V, 635–50.

1874   S. P. Trubetskoy
    Zapiski knyazya Trubetskago (St. Petersburg).

1877   M. F. Orlov
'Kapitulyatsiya Parizha v 1814 godu,' ibid., XII, 633–62.

1882   A. P. Belyayev
'Vospominaniya,' ibid., XXIX, 1–76 ff. (Also published in a booklet, St. Petersburg)

1882   A. F. Frolov
'Vospominaniya,' ibid., V, 564–82 ff.

1886   A. S. Gangeblov
'Vospominaniya,' *Russkiy arkhiv,* VI, 181–268.

1901   S. G. Volkonsky
Zapiski (St. Petersburg; 2nd ed., 1902).

*1903   S. P. Trubetskoy
Zapiski knyazya Trubetskago (Berlin, Hugo Steinitz verlag; Russian ed., St. Petersburg, 1907).

1904   D. I. Zavalishin
Zapiski dekabrista (Müuchen, 2 vols.; reprinted in St. Petersburg, 1906).
Vospominaniya knyazya E. P. Obolenskago (Leipzig, 1861) is a rarity in North America.

*1905   V. I. Shteyngel'
'Zapiski,' *Obshchestvennyye dvizheniya v Rossii* ... (St. Petersburg), vol. I, 321–75.

*1905   E. P. Obolensky
'Vospominaniya,' ibid., I, 232–81.

1905   M. A. Fonvizin
'Obozreniye proyavleniy politicheskoy zhizni v Rossii,' ibid., I, 97–203.

1907   A. E. Rozen
Zapiski dekabrista (St. Petersburg).

1909   M. K. Gribovsky
'Zapiska o Taynom Obshchestve,' in M. Lemke's *Nikolayevskie zhandarmy i literatura,* 1826–1855 (St. Petersburg) pp. 575–628.

*1917   N. V. Basargin
Zapiski (Petrograd; ed. P. E. Shchegolev).

1922   A. M. Murav'yov
Zapiski (Petrograd; ed. S. Ya. Shtraykh).

1922 M. I. Murav'yov-Apostol
Vospominaniya i pis'ma (Petrograd).

1923 M. S. Lunin
Sochineniya i pis'ma (Petrograd; ed. Shtraykh).

1924 M. N. Volkonskaya
Zapiski (Leningrad; ed. P. E. Shchegolev).

1925 I. D. Yakushkin
Zapiski (Moscow).

1925 I. I. Gorbachevsky
Zapiski i pis'ma (Moscow; ed. B. E. Syroyechkovsky).

1925 I. I. Pushchin
Zapiski o Pushine i pis'ma iz Sibiri (Moscow; ed. Shtraykh).

1925 V. I. Shteyngel'
'Dnevnik dostopamyatnogo nashego puteshestviya iz Chity v Petrov-
skiy Zavod 1830 goda,' in *Dekabristy: neizdannyye materialy i stat'i*
(Moscow) pp. 128–48.

1926 V. F. Rayevsky
'Zapiski,' in P. E. Shchegolev's *Dekabristy* (Moscow).

1929 V. K. Kyukhel'beker
Dnevnik (Leningrad; intro. Yu. N. Tynyanov).

1929 P. E. Annenkova
Vospominaniya (Moscow; 2nd ed. 1932).

1930 A. V. Poggio
Zapiski dekabrista (Moscow-Leningrad).

*1931 N. I. Lorer
Zapiski dekabrista (Moscow; ed. M. N. Pokrovsky).

1931 F. F. Vadkovsky, A. M. Murav'yov, A. V. Poggio, P. I. Falenberg, N. R.
Tsebrikov, and I. D. Yakushkin; extracts from their memoirs in
*Vospominaniya i rasskazy deyatelyey taynykh obshchestv 1820-kh
godov* (Moscow; ed. Yu. Oksman and others).

1931 G. S. Baten'kov, S. V. Maksimov, A. E. Rozen, P. N. Svistunov,
V. N. Solov'yov, A. F. Frolov and others; extracts from their memoirs;
ibid., vol. 2.

*1931 A. A. Bestuzhev, M. A. Bestuzhev and N. A. Bestuzhev.
Vospominaniya Bestuzhevykh (Moscow; ed. M. K. Azadovsky and
I. M. Trotsky; enlarged ed., 1951).

1934 A. I. Odoyevsky
Polnoye sobraniye stikhotvoreniy I pisem (Moscow-Leningrad; ed. D. D. Blagoy and I. A. Kubasov).

1955 A. N. Murav'yov
'Avtobiograficheskiye zapiski,' in *Dekabristy; novyye materialy* (Moscow; intro. Yu. I. Gerasimovaya).

1955 V. S. Tolstoy
'Vospominaniya,' ibid. (Intro. S. Zhitomirskaya).

1956 V. F. Rayevsky
'Vospominaniya,' intro. M. K. Azadovsky, in *Literaturnoye nasledstvo*, vol. 60, 57–128.

Notes 1

1 On Obolensky's case, see *Vosstaniye dekabristov; materialy po istorii vosstaniya dekabristov. Dela verkhovnogo ugolovnogo suda i sledstvennoy kommissii ...*, II vols., ed. M. N. Pokrovsky (Moscow: 1925–39), I: 220–50. Hereafter referred to as *Materialy*.

2 See Appendix C.

3 For a brief biographical sketch, see V. Bogucharsky, 'Knyaz' Yevgeniy Petrovich Obolensky,' in *Obshchestvennyye dvizheniya v Rossii v pervuyu polovinu XIX-ogo veka*, comp. V. I. Semevsky, P. E. Shchegolev and Bogucharsky (St. Petersburg: 1905), pp. 205–30. Hereafter referred to as *Obshchestvennyye dvizheniya v Rossii ...*

4 On Pestel''s visit to the capital and his impact on Obolensky, see A. G. Mazour, *The First Russian Revolution, 1825* (Stanford: 2nd printing, 1961), pp. 120–26.

5 The prince was, in the words of A. E. Rozen, 'certainly no tactician'; see pp. 000-00 for Rozen's account of events.

6 *Mezhdutsarstviye 1825 goda i vosstaniye dekabristov v memuarakh i perepiske chlenov tsarskoy sem'i*, comp. B. E. Syroyechkovsky (Moscow: 1926), pp. 32–33. Hereafter referred to as *Mezhdutsarstviye*.

7 This translation is based on M. Zetlin, whose study *Dekabristy* (trans. as *The Decembrists* by George Panin, New York, 1958) is essentially a colourful reconstruction of events. It is readable and, in the main, reliable; regrettably, however, no sources whatsoever are provided.

8 *Sibir' i dekabristy*, ed. M. K. Azadovsky and others. (Irkutsk, 1925), p. 28; also Mazour, *First Russian Revolution*, p. 240 and Zetlin, *Decembrists*, pp. 320–21.

9 See Mazour, *First Russian Revolution*, p. 130.

10 See Appendix D.

11 See Bogucharsky, in *Obshchestvennyye dvizheniya v Rossii* ... p. 228.

12 The Finland Foot Guards *(Finlyandskiy Pekhotnyy Polk)* were on manoeuvres in White Russia in the early summer of 1821. Besenkovichi is 5½ miles west of Vitebsk. Obolensky alludes to the Naples revolt of mid-July 1820; at Troppau, three months later, Alexander had been well disposed towards the Neapolitan constitutionalists, but was swayed by Metternich.

13 Further evidence of Obolensky's faulty memory for dates: *Dumy (Meditations)*, twenty-one patriotic poems on historical themes written in 1821–23, appeared in 1824. The separate edition of *Voynarovsky* appeared in mid-March 1825.

14 i.e., the Northern Society.

15 i.e., *Korennaya duma*. Obolensky borrows Nikita Murav'yov's phrase.

16 The estate adjoining the hamlet, both of which once belonged to Alexis, son of Peter I, is described (in terms of bitter-sweet nostalgia) by a later owner, Vladimir Nabokov, in *Eugene Onegin*, 4 vols. (New York, 1964), 2:433.

17 72 Moyka; now rebuilt.

18 Pyotr Bestuzhev was never a member of the Society, though he did appear on Senate Square on December 14,

1825, against his brothers' wishes.

19 A reference, apparently, to *Russkaya starina: karmannaya knizhka dlya lyubiteley otechestvennogo, na 1825 god* (St. Petersburg: Departament Narodnogo Prosveshcheniya, 1825), edited and published by Kornilovich, which was, however, a collection of tales and articles, not 'a simple tale.'

20 For an admirable resumé of the history and decline of Fort Ross (iya), see H. H. Bancroft, *History of California,* 7 vols. (San Francisco, 1885), II.

21 See Mazour, *First Russian Revolution,* pp. 118–25.

22 Ibid., pp. 99–109.

23 i.e., not the Guards.

24 Further on this duel, see K. F. Ryleyev, *Polnoye sobraniye sochineniy,* ed. A. G. Tseytlin (Moscow, 1934; reprinted by 'Academia,' The Hague, 1967), pp. 650–57, where a full bibliography is also provided. The duel occurred at 5 a.m. on September 8, 1825.

25 See *Polyarnaya zvezda, izdannaya A. Bestuzhevym i K. Ryleyevym* (Moscow-Leningrad, 1960), where the full text, 1823–25, is given together with that of *Zvezdochka.* On Obolensky's points, see V. A. Arkhipov, 'Literaturno-esteticheskiye pozitsii Polyarnoy zvezdy,' ibid., pp. 811-12.

26 Karl-Louis Sand (1795–1819), an enthusiastic German student, assassinated the writer-diplomat August Kotzebue (1761–1819) in Mannheim on March 23, 1819, and became a popular hero among other students. On P. Kakhovsky, see Mazour, *First Russian Revolution,* pp. 132–37.

27 The revolt of the First Company of the regiment occurred on October 17, 1820. Mazour gives brief details, *First Russian Revolution,* pp. 58–60.

28 As Bogucharsky notes in *Obshchestvennyye dvizheniya v Rossii* ... (p. 246), Mikhail Bestuzhev-Ryumin also served

in it, later transferring to the **Poltava Foot Regiment.** I. D. Yakushkin *had* served in it.

29 Alexander died painlessly on the morning of November 19 of 'bilious remittent fever': R. Lee, *The Last Days of Alexander and the First Days of Nicholas* ... (London, 1854) p. 55; news of his death reached Warsaw on Nov. 25, St. Petersburg two days later. According to Prince Trubetskoy (see Appendix A), the service in the Winter Palace was broken off, not modified.

30 Perhaps the best readily available biography of Shteyngel' is V. I. Semevsky's 'Baron Vladimir Ivanovich Shteyngel'' in *Obshchestvennyye dvizheniya v Rossii* ... (St. Petersburg, 1905), 1, pp. 281–320.

31 See M. Dovnar-Zapolsky, *Idealy dekabristov* (Moscow, 1907), pp. 157, 164.

32 Also, 'Dissertation on the Reason for the Decay of Trade', 'An Essay on the Calendar' (1819); and a biographical sketch of Count A. P. Tormasov (1820).

33 M. N. Pokrovsky, *Dekabristy: sbornik statey* (Moscow, 1927), pp. 78–79.

34 See Mazour, *First Russian Revolution,* p. 96.

35 *Vospominaniya Bestuzhevykh,* ed. M. K. Azadovsky (Moscow-Leningrad, 1951), p. 301.

36 'Statisticheskoye opisaniye Ishimskogo okruga Tobol'skoy gubernii,' *Zhurnal Ministerstva Vnutrennykh Del,* II (1843), pp. 3-48, 200–55.

37 A characteristic of all early Soviet editions of Decembrists texts.

38 Mikhail Romanov (tsar, 1613–45).

39 Tsar Aleksey (Alexis).

40 January 14, 1823; see Baron M. A. Korff, *Vosshestviye na prestol Imperatora Nikolaya I* (St. Petersburg, 1857), pp. 29–30. (Published simultaneously, under the title, *The Accession of Nicholas I* in London by John Murray.)

41 Signed by Alexander on August 16.

42 Aleksandr Fyodorovich Labzin (1766–1825), a mystic with great influence over the tsar, was exiled to Simbirsk in 1823 as a result of intrigue by, among others, Phoetius, whose 'victory' over the Bible Society was also that of Count A. A. Arakcheyev.

43 In St. Petersburg, November 19–21, 1824 (N. S.)

44 Alexander was very fond of Sof'ya, daughter of M. A. Naryshkina, who died of consumption on June 23, 1824; see N. K. Shil'der, *Aleksandr 1, yego zhizn' i tsarstvovaniye* (St. Petersburg, 1898), 4:322–23. Hereafter referred to as *Aleksandr I.*

45 Nastas'ya Fyodorovna Minkina was Arakcheyev's housekeeper and mistress. She was knifed on September 10, 1825, by the brother of a chambermaid whom she had tortured with hot pincers; the brother was knouted to death after his 'trial.'

46 An error: the service was held in the Winter Palace.

47 That hymn with which the third part of mass by the Orthodox rite begins – the 'Liturgy of the Faithful.'

48 'On November 19, exactly 12 months and 12 days after the prophetic flood; it may in general be remarked that the number twelve had, as it were, a fateful significance in Alexander's life': Shteyngel''s comment.

49 A man totally deaf, the prince was named chief justice in June 1826.

50 See Trubetskoy's remarks; Appendix A.

51 *Ober-prokuratory,* officers of the Senate, assisted the *general-prokurator,* head of the Senate chancery, in supervising the working of the Senate and of other central administrative organs.

52 'The name of this man, who was enthused with love of the Fatherland, should not be forgotten in Russia. His day of commemoration is Sept. 21': Shteyngel''s note.

53 Shteyngel'alludes to himself.

54 That is, reigning empress; Elizaveta Alekseyevna (Louisa-Maria-Augusta, 1779–1826) was already empress, as wife of Alexander.

55 Both her daughters, Mariya (b. 1799) and Elizaveta (b. 1806), died in infancy.

56 Nikolay Longinov, state secretary, father of the great bibliographer, M. N. Longinov (1823–75).

57 On P. Kakhovsky, see Mazour, *First Russian Revolution,* pp. 132–37.

58 Literally, Islamic leaders descended from Husain, the brother of the Prophet. Shteyngel' clearly has a regicide in mind.

59 'This was Yakov Ivanovich, now General-Adjutant and Head of Staff of the military educational institutions; he was then one of those who adored freedom ecstatically. He wrote a tragedy, *Pozharsky,* filled with bold expressions of his love for his Fatherland, and did not hide his scorn, if not his hatred, of the state of affairs in Russia then': Shteyngel''s note.

60 'When the insurrection occurred on the 14th, Rostovtsev, sent by a general to the Finland Regiment, was incautious enough to cross between the Senate and the rebels' column. Someone shouted 'Traitor!' They threw themselves on him and beat him unconscious with rifle-butts': Shteyngel''s note.

61 I. D. Yakushkin, *Zapiski* (Moscow, 1925), pp. 12–13.

62 Semevsky et al, *Obshchestvennyye dvizheniya v Rossii ...,* I, 183.

63 See Zetlin, *Decembrists,* p. 118.

64 Nikolay Ivanovich Grech (1787–1867), journalist and literary historian, allied himself with F. V. Bulgarin and the reactionary party in Russian literature after 1817.

65 Formerly a Swedish ship, part of the 'Navy of the Army' formed in 1756 to

defend the Aland Islands. Other Swedish ships seized by the Russians, the 'Retvisan,' for example, similarly kept their original names.

66 See C. de Grunwald, *Tsar Nicholas I* (trans. B. Patmore, London, 1954), p. 31.

67 Anton Vasil'yevich Moller (Müller, 1764–1848), naval minister and father of the painter Fyodor Antonovich.

68 Vice-Admiral Mikhail Nikolayevich Vasil'yev sailed north from the Bering Straits in May 1820, only to meet impassable ice at 76°6' Latitude.

69 Count M. S. Vorontsov (1782–1856) was appointed governor-general of Novorossiya, Russia's southern territories, in May 1823; see Nabokov, *Eugene Onegin*, III, 193.

70 The writings of Herzen are available in English, trans. by Constance Garnett (London, 1924).

71 'The officer, Count Samoilov if I am not mistaken, had left the army and was living quietly in Moscow. Nicholas recognized him at a theatre, fancied that he was dressed with rather elaborate originality, and expressed the royal desire that such costumes should be ridiculed on the stage. The theatre director and patriot, Zagoskin, commissioned one of his actors to impersonate S. in some vaudeville ... 'You acted me very well,' said the Count to him later, 'and the only thing wanting to complete the likeness is this diamond which I always wear; allow me to hand it to you.': Herzen's note. (abbr.)

72 Mirovich, a young adventurer and gambler in the Guards, in 1764 attempted to rescue from Schlüsselburg Fortress Ivan IV, the legitimate heir to the throne, who perished in the process. Mirovich was beheaded.

73 Leader of the great cossack and serf rising of 1773–74.

74 'Nicholas's victory over the five was celebrated by a religious service in Moscow. In the Kremlin, the Metropolitan Filaret thanked God for the murders. ... I was present at that service, a boy of fourteen lost in the crowd, and on the spot, before the altar defiled by bloody rites, I swore to avenge the murdered men, dedicating myself to a struggle with that throne and that altar and those cannon': Herzen's note.

75 Further on this, see de Grunwald, *La vie de Nicholas 1-er* (Paris, 1946), pp. 156–57: 'With his height of more than six feet, his head always held high, a slightly aquiline nose, a firm and well-formed mouth, an imposing, domineering, set face, monumental rather than human, he had something of an Apollo about him.'; 'The habit of repressing feelings has become so inseparable from his very being,' remarked Prince A. Kozlovsky, (cited by de Grunwald, ibid., p. 35), 'that you see no awkwardness and no embarrassment in him; nothing is studied yet all his words, like his movements, follow a cadence as if he had a sheet of music before him.' But such harshness sprang from apprehension, not from confidence.

76 Also known as Princess Gagarina; Paul's mistress.

2

1 For details, see the bibliography provided by A. G. Mazour, *The First Russian Revolution, 1825* (Stanford, 2nd printing, 1961) pp. 300–20.

2 On A. I. Yakubovich (1792–1845), ibid., p. 132.

3 An employee of the Russian-American Company, Ryleyev had lodgings on the ground floor of the gaunt Company building (72 Moikà) for a nominal sum.

4   'Departing, we were so firmly deter-
    mined either to succeed or to die that
    we came to no agreement whatever as
    to action, should we fail'; A. A. Bestuz-
    hev in *Materialy,* I: 187, 452. 'We shall
    die, oh, how gloriously we shall die!'
    exclaimed Prince A. I. Odoyevsky
    (cited by Kotlyarevsky, *Dekabristy:
    Odoyevsky i Bestuzhev* (St. Peters-
    burg, 1909), p. 17.

5   See Mazour, *First Russian Revolution,*
    pp. 170–71.

6   Prince D. A. Shchepin-Rostovsky
    1798–1859), staff-captain in the Mos-
    cow (*Moskovskiy*) Regiment, was
    never officially a member of the North-
    ern Society. Nonetheless, he received
    a sentence of twenty years' hard
    labour.

7   A. N. Sutgof (1801–72), lieutenant,
    Grenadier Guards; also sentenced to
    twenty years' hard labour; served as a
    private in the Caucasus, 1848–56.

8   i.e., to Constantine.

9   Kornilovich was arrested, tried and
    sentenced to eight years' labour, of
    which he served only two in Chita
    before being sent to the Caucasus.

10 See Mazour, *First Russian Revolution,*
    pp. 164–66. Sergey Shipov's desertion
    of Trubetskoy meant the loss of the
    newly reconstituted Semyonovskiy
    Regiment; Moller's and Tulubyev's, the
    loss of the Finland Foot, despite all
    Rozen's efforts.

11 i.e., of the regimental barracks.

12 Not, as is commonly thought, Pea
    Street or *Erbsenstrasse* (from *Gorokh),*
    but Harrach Street, after a member of
    that ancient Austrian house. See also
    chap. 2, note 48.

13 See *Materialy,* I: 232, 248. It was now
    between 8.30 and 9 A.M.

14 Prince D. I. Lobanov-Rostovsky, gen-
    eral-of-infantry turned minister of
    justice, was appointed attorney
    general on June 1, 1826. But even the

tsar had doubts as to his mental capabilities; see *Mezhdutsarstviye,* p. 207.

15 In their barracks, between 11 and 12
    A.M. On Ya. I. Rostovtsev's attempt
    first to warn Nicholas of a revolt, then
    to warn the plotters of his warning, see
    M. Zetlin, *The Decembrists,* trans.
    George Perin (New York, 1958) pp.
    161–66.

16 Rinaldi's cathedral, begun under Cath-
    erine, was unhappily finished in brick
    in 1802. Rebuilding to Ricard de Mon-
    ferrand's design began in 1818, ending
    in 1858.

17 The horses were not shod and could
    not be galloped on icy cobbled streets;
    the retreat took place amidst laughter;
    see Nicholas's *Zapiski,* given in part
    in *Dekabristy: sbornik otryvok iz isto-
    chnikov,* comp. by Yu. G. Oksman and
    B. L. Modzalevsky (Moscow, 1926),
    p. 329.

18 Like Arbuzov, Kakhovsky, P. Belyayev
    and Ryleyev (but few others in the
    North), I. I. (Jeannot) Pushchin (1798–
    1859) was a convinced republican in
    1825, and remained one.

19 Mikhail Karlovich (1798–1859),
    younger brother of the poet.

20 i.e., N. S. Bobrishchev-Pushkin.

21 Prince A. I. Odoyevsky had recently
    celebrated his twenty-second birthday.
    He was sentenced to fifteen years'
    labour, but was sent to Kar-Agach in
    the Caucasus in 1837; there, he died
    of malaria.

22 On Kakhovsky's murder of Count
    Miloradovich and Colonel Styurler
    (Stürler) see *Materialy,* I: 369–70, 377.

23 Bestuzhev, like several leading Decem-
    brists, had had a sound classical
    education and could quote the Latin
    classics appositely. The allusion here
    is Virgilian: *Durate, et vosmet rebus
    servate secundis (Aeneid,* I, 207).

24 see Mazour, *First Russian Revolution,*
    pp. 171–75.

25 In the Eastern Church, the bride and bridegroom step beneath two crowns, held by the best man, before walking three times round the lectern (*analoy*) in token of an eternal contract. The crowns are commonly of metal, painted gold.

26 At first, it was supposed that General Sukhozanet had brought a draft constitution with him; see *Russ. star.*, VII (1873), 368.

27 'The firing lasted an hour. No distinction was made between participants in the rebellion and mere spectators, all being shot down. Many were trodden to death by the panic-stricken masses, assisted (on their way) by cannon-balls and canister shot'; eyewitness, cited by Mazour, *First Russian Revolution*, p. 179.

28 The Bestuzhev family connection with the Academy of Arts was strong; A. F. Bestuzhev, father of the Decembrists, was closely associated with its President, Count A. S. Stroganov, and Nikolay received early training there; see *Literaturnoye nasledstvo*, 60 vols. (1956), 2: 20–24. Hereafter referred to as *Lit. nasl.*

29 Vasil'yevskiy Ostrov, 7th line, Gur'yev's house; now (1974) an empty site, by no. 18, 7th line.

30 Ryleyev and the two Bestuzhevs, A. A. and N. A., passed two sleepless nights on 'promenades,' visiting as many regimental barracks as possible, telling the troops how the army had been deceived, that Alexander's will was being hidden, and that the shorter terms of military service promised by him were being denied; see *Materialy*, I: 160–61.

31 N. A. Bestuzhev (1791–1855) acted as a father to Mikhail after A. F.'s death in 1810. Serving at naval headquarters in St. Petersburg and later in Kronstadt, three hours' sail away, Nikolay would have had a ready supply of naval coats on leaving port in 1823.

32 An incomplete list of the killed and wounded was published in *Byloye*, III (1907), 194–99.

33 Captain K. P. Torson (1796–1851), an intimate of the Bestuzhevs, was a most competent naval officer; in Chita he gave lectures on the national finance system, as well as on his voyage round the world with Golovnin.

34 i.e., the eighth unit of the Guards' Equipage, the exclusive naval detachment responsible, until the Revolution, for manning the Imperial yacht, forming the bodyguard in the Winter Palace, and for certain other ceremonial duties.

35 See Appendix C.

36 No bibliography exists of Western Europeans' accounts of the rising.

37 See my study, *M. S. Lunin: Catholic Decembrist* (The Hague, Mouton, 1974).

38 See Zetlin, *Decembrists*, pp. 348–49.

39 On Rozen and his publications, see F. Brokgauz and I. Yefron, *Entsiklopedicheskiy slovar'* (St. Petersburg, 1899), 27: 13.

40 Rozen's Siberian descriptions may be compared, both in range and in tone, with those of Baron A. Haxthausen-Abbenburg, trans. R. Farie, *The Russian Empire, its People, Institutions, and Resources* (London, 1856; reprinted by Cass, 1968).

41 General K. I. Bistrom, honorary colonel of the Finland Foot Regiment.

42 Moller (Müller), a former member of the Union of Salvation (and no relation of the naval minister – see chap. I, note 67), lost enthusiasm for rebellion as soon as it became a real possibility.

43 By 3 P.M., however, loyal artillery units had forced a way onto the bridge.

44 Several hundred curious onlookers assembled by the Senate and the west face of the Admiralty, to the vexation of Nicholas and his suite. Obolensky, *de facto* leader of the insurgents from

noon until 3 P.M., lost a golden opportunity of bringing these crowds over to his cause; many were sympathetic; see *Krasnyy arkhiv*, XII, 286–87 and *Vospominaniya Bestuzhevykh*, p. 147.

45 The Cross of St. Vladimir was awarded for 'civic services' (*za zaslugi grazhdanskiye*); because there was no war, Belyayev could not have received the higher St. Catherine or St. Andrew Crosses.

46 Rozen underestimates. By 2 P.M. the rebels numbered 3000 – but the government had mustered 9000 men; see *Materialy*, I: 98.

47 A. M. Bulatov (1793–1826) was lured into the conspiracy by Ryleyev (see Appendix A), and later committed suicide by smashing his head on the stone wall of his cell in Peter-and-Paul Fortress (January 18); for details, see S. Shtraykh's notes to *Zapiski, stat'i, pis'ma dekabrista I. D. Yakushkina* (Moscow, 1951), p. 570.

48 Now Ulitsa Dzerzhinskaya.

49 'What seems most inconceivable in this story,' recorded Prince Eugene of Württemberg, who was in the suite, 'is the fact that both the Emperor and I were not shot down'; *Zapiski Nikolaya*, cited in part in *Dekabristy: sbornik otryvok iz istochnikov*, pp. 328–29; also *Russkiy arkhiv*, III (1878), 351. Hereafter referred to as *Russ. arkh.*

50 Imperial aides-de-camp, when full generals, were called general-adjutants, when of lower rank, flügel- or fligel'-adjutants.

51 Nennal; see Baron M. A. Korff, *The Accession of Nicholas I* (London, 1857; 3rd impression), pp. 129, 179.

52 See *Russ. star.* XXX (1881), 498–99.

53 See *Mezhdutsarstviye*, 27. Nicholas hesitated, then ordered three cannon to be brought forward.

54 See note 34.

55 N. A. Panov (1803–50) 'persuaded the Life-Grenadiers to follow him, even after they had sworn allegiance to Nicholas, telling them that 'their lads' were not swearing and had occupied the Palace. And he actually led them towards the Palace; but seeing that there were Lifeguard – chasseurs already in the courtyard, he joined the Moscow men': Shteyngel''s note.

56 See note 16.

57 'He took the first horse standing saddled by the rooms of one of the Horseguards officers': Shteyngel''s note.

58 'One could well believe that the Count was speaking the truth: he was exceedingly extravagant and always in debt, despite frequent presents of money from the sovereign. But Constantine's generosity was known to all. The Count might have expected to *do even better* under him': Shteyngel''s note.

59 'The whole Army knew the Count's saying: 'God, the bullet to kill *me* hasn't been cast yet' ': Shteyngel''s note. Miloradovich stole the remark from Napoleon, of course, who silenced the King of Spain with it in 1814.

60 See Rozen's account of this; pp. 73–74.

61 From the present University Embankment; the bridge, like its replacement, the temporary Dvortsovyy or Palace Bridge, no longer exists.

62 'This was Yakubovich, who had arrived from the Caucasus, had the gift of eloquence and succeeded in interesting Petersburg *salons* with tales of his own heroic deeds. Among liberals, he did not hide his dissatisfaction with, and personal hatred for, the late Emperor [i.e., Nicholas]. Throughout the seventeen day interregnum, the members of the Secret Society were convinced that he 'would show himself' when it was possible': Shteyngel''s note. Yakusovich had received a bullet in the head while on service in the Caucasus –

hence the kerchief (which, apparently, he did not need at other times).

63 See M. A. Bestuzhev's comments on Styurler, pp. 000–00.

64 'These words were later given in evidence during the interrogations, in the Committee, with the members of which Sukhozanet already shared the honour of wearing General-Adjutant's aiglets. But this was nothing – he was afterwards Director-in-Chief of the Cadet Corps and President of the Military Academy. However, one must give him his due: he lost a leg in the Polish campaign': Shteyngel''s note.

65 On this, see N. K. Shil'der, *Nikolay I* (St. Petersburg, 1903), I: 514–15, where the papers of M. M. Popov of the Third Department are adduced as evidence of much theft and savagery; also Mazour, *First Russian Revolution*, p. 180.

3

1 P. I. Falenberg (1791–1873), for example; see A. G. Mazour, *The First Russian Revolution, 1825* (Stanford, 2nd printing, 1961), pp. 217–19.

2 See Yakushkin, *Zapiski*, p. 80.

3 See note 30 to chap. 2.

4 A. Boretsky–Pustoshkin, family friend of the Bestuzhevs since 1815.

5 A district, literally 'Goat's Bog.'

6 See note 47, chap. 2.

7 Standard army greeting until 1917, subordinate to officer.

8 General K. I. Bistrom, who also held a divisional post of commander of Foot Guards. Prince E. P. Obolensky was adjutant to Bistrom, not 'the Regimental adjutant.'

9 Nikolay Petrovich Repin (1796–1831), a Guards artilleryman with a fine knowl-edge of eighteenth-century French philosophy; burned to death in his cabin by the River Lena in Siberia.

10 Nicholas did not sleep on the night of December 14–15; see Mazour, *First Russian Revolution*, pp. 204–207.

11 The feldjägers were used as state couriers. The corps consisted, in 1825, of four officers and seventy-seven men, most under the age of twenty-one.

12 Vasiliy Vasil'yevich Levashev (1783–1848), general-adjutant and president of the state council, made a brilliant career under Nicholas, becoming a count in 1833.

13 i.e., December 27.

14 Rozen means Mikhail Aleksandrovich (1799–1888).

15 Not Vladimir Fedoseyevich but Aleksandr Nikolayevich (1795–1868), elder son of the hero of 1812. Brought to St. Petersburg on January 5, on a suspicion of 'infecting the Black Sea fleet with revolutionary notions,' he and his brother Nikolay were released 12½ days later.

16 All three men were shortly afterwards released. Andreyev was second cousin to the civilian A. N. Andreyev who died with N. P. Repin in the cabin fire of 1831.

17 General Aleksandr Yakovlevich.

18 i.e., the chief executive officer of the fortress. Edinburgh had a town-major until the late nineteenth century.

19 Nicholas's orders to Sukin of 1825–26 are cited extensively by P. E. Shchego-lev, *Dekabristy: sbornik statey* (Lenin-grad, 1926), pp. 266–69.

20 See Mazour, *First Russian Revolution*, p. 245.

21 Orders for Yakushkin's arrest were issued on January 4, and he was ar-rested in Moscow on January 9.

22 Shul'gin was rapidly losing favour with Nicholas during this week, having

begun to drink heavily; see *Mezhdut-sarstviye*, p. 170.

23 Prince D. V. Golitsyn, C.-in-C. of the army, Moscow.

24 A.–D. Teyer (1752–1828), the author of a work on agronomy, *Istoriya moyego khozyaystva* (1816); Rozen and Poggio later successfully applied the rotatory system expounded in it in Siberia.

25 Appointment to the Commission of Enquiry materially assisted General A. L. Potapov in his career; he became head of the Third Department and so director of all secret police work.

26 See note 12.

27 'Pour cette fois je ne vous parle pas comme votre juge, mais comme un gentilhomme votre égal, et je ne con- çois pas pourquoi vous voulez être martyr pour des gens qui vous ont trahi et vous ont nommé!'
'Je ne suis pas ici pour juger la con- duite de mes camarades, et je ne dois penser qu'à remplir les engagements que j'ai pris en entrant dans la Société.'

28 Southern HQ of the Second Army (twenty miles east of the Moldavian border), and operations base for Pestel'. Disappointed that he could not carry out the regicide, which the majority of members at the 1817 'con- ference' saw as too extreme, Yakushkin remained aloof from the Unions of Salvation and Welfare for three years; *Materialy*, 3: 53, 122; also Mazour, *First Russian Revolution*, pp. 71, 131.

29 By 1825, Russia was, in fact, bankrupt; the foreign debt had reached 106,000,000 roubles (see A. Gur'yev, *Ocherki razvitiya gosudarstvennogo dolga v Rossii*, St. Petersburg, 1903, pp. 22–24). The value of one rouble (1810) had dropped to 25 kopeks by 1825, and internal tax arrears exceeded 80,000,000 roubles.

30 'The Holy Family,' by Domenichino Zampieri (1581–1641) still hangs in The Hermitage; so does 'The Prodigal Son'

of Salvator Rosa (1615–76), together with eight others of his paintings, all of panoramic battle scenes.

31 'From all corners of Russia, one after another, there were brought to St. Petersburg those implicated in the affair. Tensely, the Tsar waited in his study, selecting masks, every time a new one for a new person. For one he was a strict monarch offended by a loyal subject; for another – a citizen of the fatherland equal to the arrested man before him; for a third – an old soldier ...'; Shchegolev, *Dekabristy: sbornik statey*, 200.

32 For Alexander I.

33 The Alekseyev Ravelin was physically separate from the main part of the fortress.

34 Colonel A. Lilien-Ankern was, in fact, nearer eighty. For a readable though sometimes melodramatic, account of the fortress's history, *see* P. Payne, *The Fortress* (New York, 1967).

35 The flood of Pushkin's *The Bronze Horseman,* which, rising on the night of Nov. 18, ended on Nov. 21.

36 Archpriests fulfilled much the same functions in nineteenth century Ortho- dox cathedrals as residential canons in England.

37 Schiller's drama was exceedingly popular in St. Petersburg in 1811–13, when Yakushkin was a subaltern there.

38 i.e., of Our Lady of Kazan'.

39 On P. N. Myslovsky's mixed motives and uncertain attitude towards the prisoners, see A. M. Murav'yov's journal, given by T. Schiemann in *Zur Geschichte der Regierung Paul I und Nikolaus I* (Berlin, 1906), pp. 171–87; also D. I. Zavalishin, *Zapiski dekabrista* (Müchen, 1904), 1: 362–64, and pp. 103–105 here.

40 'Celui-ci a les fers aux bras et aux pieds.'

41 Apocryphal: Pelageya, aged four, and

Anna, aged three, were in Kerensk, far from St. Petersburg.

42 Literally, 'something empty.'

43 Yevgeniy, born on January 20, was Yakushkin's second son.

44 See note 14, chap. 2.

45 From Skalozub, a character in Griboyedov's *Gorye ot uma (Woe From Wit)*.

46 Lieutenant-General Fabian Shteyngel', former governor general of Finland; made a count in 1812.

47 A village by the Lena, twelve miles downstream from Irkutsk.

48 M. N. Zagoskin, author of *Yuriy Miloslavsky* (1829) and *Roslavlev* (1831), who was not destined, incidentally, to live to such a meeting.

49 For part of that letter, see Appendix B.

50 An outbreak of violence.

51 Paul I was murdered on the night of March 11, 1801 (O.S.).

52 *Ochnaya stavka*: an essential part of Russian juridicial procedure until the Revolution, and, in modified form, to – day.

53 10 km. east of Loviysa, by the coastal village of Bernaya; only ruins remain.

54 *Zapiski N. I. Lorera* (Moscow, 1931), p. 9.

55 Count Pyotr Khristianovich Wittgenstein (1768–1842).

56 I.e., in 1825.

57 See Mazour, *First Russian Revolution*, pp. 99–109.

58 Literally, 'virtues.'

59 Courland, of which Mitau was the capital, had effectively become a Russian suzerainty when Peter I married his niece Anna to the last of the hereditary dukes, the Kettlers, in 1720.

60 March 11, 1801, in the Mikhaylovskiy Castle, later occupied by the School of Engineering (and the youthful Dostoyevsky, who detested it.)

61 'Ecoutez, jeune homme! Si vous voulez faire quelque chose par une société secrète, c'est une bêtise. Car si vous êtes douze, le douzième sera invariablement un traitre! J'ai de l'experience et je connais le monde et les hommes.'

62 Count Ivan Osipovich Vitt (Witte) proved a heavy liability. Through one of his agents, Komarov, the denunciation made by A. Mayboroda was substantiated, leading to the uncovering of the entire Southern Society.

63 Aleksey Petrovich Yushnevsky (1786–1844), general-intendant of the Second Army and director of the Southern Society in 1824–25.

64 Prince Aleksandr Ivanovich Baryatinsky (1798–1844), mathematician and deist, one of the most active members in the south.

65 Kiselyov did more for the Russian peasantry as minister of Imperial Domains (responsible for the welfare of Crown serfs) than Yushnevsky ever could; appointed to the post in 1834, he founded schools for them, withdrew them from local police jurisdiction, and advanced their economic interests.

66 Count Chodkiewicz owned land in Berdichev, fifteen miles south of Zhitomir, where Count Moszynski was living in 1825.

67 i.e., Sergey Murav'yov-Apostol.

68 Lorer meant Dashkova.

69 A. I. Mayboroda was, with Ivan Sherwood and Count Vitt, one of the main traitors among the members of the Southern Society. He was trusted absolutely by Pestel', and betrayed him coolly.

70 Both were attached to the Quartermaster's Department, having passed through the school for such officers (*kolonnovozhaty*) run by the father of the Murav'yov brothers. N. A. Kryukov (1800–54) had an English mother; he should not be confused with his brother

Aleksandr (1794–1867), aide-de-camp to Count Wittgenstein. 'Cherkassky' is an error for Baron A. I. Cherkasov (1799–1855).

71 Lorer's wording here (*zhidy* ...) bespeaks his anti-semitism.

72 'La société est découverte: si un seul membre sera pris, je commence l'affaire.'

73 The fault was not that of Sir James; the Emperor refused medical aid; see R. Lee, *The Last Days of Alexander and the First Days of Nicholas* (London, 1854), pp. 41–47.

74 Mikhail-Kasimir Oginsky (1729–1800), Lithuanian-Russian noble, harpist, canal builder and composer of songs based on national airs.

75 Lorer adhered to the faith of his French forebears, who settled in northern Germany during the eighteenth century as a result of religious persecution.

76 Ivan Semyonovich Povalo-Shveykovsky (1791–1845) was colonel of the Saratov Foot Regiment, Vasiliy Karlovich Tizen-gauzen (1779–1853), colonel of the Poltava Foot Regiment. Both were active in the Southern Society. In 1825, the Russian army was organized in regiments of three or four battalions, each comprising 800 to 1000 men in four companies; thus, each full colonel adhering to Pestel' brought a thousand men onto the side of the Society.

77 A. I. Lorer, an unlucky officer. Captured at Austerlitz and held captive in Brno for two years, he was again wounded at Eylau; though he fought again in Sweden (1809), he died young.

78 i.e., a trail over packed snow and ice.

79 A hooded carriage or sled; see Byron, *Don Juan*, canto IX, 30.

80 The St. Petersburg season lasted until early April, entertainments being given almost nightly.

81 Chernyshev's neighbour on Pod'ya-cheskaya (Scrivener) Street was Prince A. A. Shakhovskoy, poetaster; on the 'gay-dog parties' given there, see V. Nabokov, *Eugene Onegin*, 4 vols, (New York, 1964) II, 426.

82 Ney was sentenced to death by a Royalist tribunal in August 1815. Lorer was probably familiar with Léon Jérome's painting.

83 Lorer appears to recollect here that Pestel''s eyes were jet-black.

84 The invitation to M. M. Speransky, the ardent constitutionalist, to take part in the prosecution of Decembrists was, of course, a test of his loyalty to Nicholas. It was also a political humiliation.

85 N. V. Basargin, *Zapiski*, intro. P. E. Shchegolev (Petrograd, 'Ogni', 1917), xi.

86 Ibid., iii–iv.

87 Series 'Biblioteka memuarov Izdatel'stva 'Ogni'.'

88 As senior adjutant at Second Army HQ, Basargin's duties centred on his desk.

89 General A. I. Tatishchev.

90 Ferdinand Bogdanovich Vol'f (1796–1854) was a staff-surgeon attached to Second Army HQ. He became *de facto* camp doctor at Chita in 1827–30, in Petrovskiy in 1830–33, and saved many lives.

91 See note 18.

92 In the event, July 10, 1826.

93 Pavel Khristoforovich Grabbe (1789–1875) escaped with a mere four month prison sentence and continued a successful career thereafter, becoming general-adjutant in 1839, and count in 1866.

94 A reference to Nicholas's remark: 'My successor must do as he pleases; for myself, I cannot change.' It was not addressed to the tsarevich, however.

4

1 See P. E. Shchegolev, *Dekabristy: sbornik statyey* (Leningrad, 1926), pp. 266–67.

2 *Mezhdutsarstviye*, pp. 32–34.

3 See *Materialy*, III, 60; also I. K. Luppol, *Istoriko-filosofskiye etyudy* (Moscow, 1935), pp. 252-54.

4 The memoirs of General-Major Mikhail Aleksandrovich Fonvizin (1788–1854) are included in *Obshchestvennyye dvizheniya v Possii* ... see Appendix D.

5 Zavalishin, *Zapiski dekabrista*, I, 365

6 See Shil'der, *Aleksandr I*, 1, 544.

7 V. S. Ikonnikov, *Graf N. S. Mordvinov* (St. Petersburg, 1873), pp. 382–3, 444.

8 From *Materialy*, I, 8–9.

9 Karl Theodor Hermann (Russian-German), statistician and political economist; elected to the Russian Academy of Sciences.

10 The serfs of the Baltic Provinces were 'freed,' without land, in 1816 and 1819.

11 From *Materialy*, I, 156.

12 Louis Bignon (1771–1841), French diplomat and author of various political and historical works, was known to Russians as the signatory of the convention of July 3, 1815, allowing the Allies to enter Paris. Constant was known as the author of *Adolphe* and as an *idéologue* during the first years of the Napoleonic régime. Other prisoners, in answer to questions 6 or 7, mentioned Adam Smith, de Lolme, Condorcet, Say, Tracy, Franklin, Byron, and Filangieri.

13 From *Materialy*, I, 226.

14 A. P. Kunitsyn (1783–1840), jurist, exponent of natural law at St. Petersburg University and other institutions in the capital.

15 Heinrich Storch (in Russia, Andrey Karlovich Shtorkh) was vice-president of the Imperial Academy of Sciences. Jean-Baptiste Say (1767–1832), French political economist.

16 From *Materialy*, I, 294. Nikita Murav'yov (1796–1843) was a founder of the Union of Welfare and author of the Northern Society's Constitutional Project.

17 From *Materialy*, I, 343.

18 Many Decembrists found heroes in the works of Cicero, Tacitus, Titus Livy, and Polybius; Brutus, especially, was idealized: Yakushkin kept a copy of his letters to Cicero by his bedside table; See Yakushkin, *Zapiski dekabrista*, p. 20.

19 from *Materialy*, I, 430.

20 Arnold Hermann Heeren (1760–1842), German historian; author of the popular *Handbuch der Geschichte des Europaischen Staatensystems und seinen Colonien*. Jeremy Bentham (1748–1832) was revered, in Russian liberal circles, as the founder of utilitarianism.

21 Denis Ivanovich Fonvizin (1745–92), playwright. His incidental treatise on the desirability of 'fundamental laws' for the Empire (1783) was circulated in manuscript form in St. Petersburg. General-Major Mikhail Orlov (1788–1842) was an active member of the Union of Welfare, but played no part in the events of December 1825, and escaped scot-free. Dmitriy Petrovich Buturlin (1790–1849), soldier and military historian, became president of the Censorship Committee in 1848.

22 from *Materialy*, I, 481–82.

23 Ibid., III, 8.

24 Ibid., III, 44.

25 Ibid., III, 128.

26 Ibid., IV, 89–92.

27 Antoine Louis Destutt de Tracy (1754–1836), philosopher; his ideas based on sensualism provided an ideological

foundation for French liberalism; author of *Eléments d'idéologie* 4 vols., 1817–18).

28 Mikhail Nikolayevich Novikov (1777–1822), a leading Freemason of the 1780s and '90s.

29 Novgorod, an independent and quasi-democratic city-state during the twelfth and thirteenth centuries, had been ruled by an elected prince, a *posadnik* or mayor and a *veche* or city assembly, at which, in theory, all free citizens could vote.

30 i.e., in 1820–21.

31 *Materialy*, V, 22. Pyotr Ivanovich Borisov (1800–54) was co-founder of the Society of United Slavs.

32 Ibid., V, 117–18. Mikhail Matveyevich Spiridov (1796–1854) also belonged to the United Slavs.

33 Prince A. N. Golitsyn was Minister of Public Education, P. Golenishchev–Kutuzov a member of the conspiracy against Paul I in 1801, General I. I. Dibich not, at the outset, even a member of the Commission of Enquiry, although high in Nicholas's favour – a curiously qualified trio to investigate Basargin's crimes. Adlerberg was present as the tsar's special representative, or eye. Here is a much later description of the group by the Grand Duke Nikolay Mikhaylovich, published in *Istoricheskiy vestnik*, VII (1916), 108: 'The chairman of the Commission was Minister for War Tatishchev, a totally obscure figure. Of the members, Chernyshev, Levashev, Golenishchev-Kutuzov, and Potapov were known for their heartlessness and servility, D. N. Bludov for his liberalism in theory and cowardliness in practice. Only one, Benkendorf, was thought more independent, and constantly attempted to soften the Emperor.'

34 'The Moscow conference' of January 1821; see A. G. Mazour, *The First Russian Revolution, 1825* (Stanford 2nd printing 1961) pp. 80–85.

35 Ivan Grigor'yevich Burtsev (1794–1829), aide-de-camp to Kiselyov, was chosen together with Lieutenant-Colonel P. N. Komarov to represent the Southern group at that conference. Both were conservatives in 1821, and approved the dissolving of the Union of Welfare; Pestel' did not. Most of the Southern members agreed with him and were vexed with Burtsev; Mazour, *First Russian Revolution*, pp. 83–84.

36 This was July 9 1826.

37 There were, in fact, 72 judges, hand-picked by Speransky; they included 36 Senators, 17 Councillors of State, 15 special appointees and three representatives of the Holy Synod.

38 Vasiliy Petrovich Ivashev (1794–1840), aide to Count Wittgenstein and N. V. Basargin's closest friend until his death. Basargin's relationship with Ivashev and his wife while in Siberia closely resembled that between Lorer and the Naryshkins. Other single men attached themselves to married couples to the comfort of all three.

39 Town-Adjutant, assistant to Major E. M. Podushkin.

40 Yakushkin's note: 'It is stated in the report [drafted by Bludov on the basis of A. Borovkov's summaries and conclusions, and presented to the tsar on May 30] that I volunteered to make the attempt, being tormented by the passion of unhappy love. I have every reason for thinking that this was the testimony of Nikita Murav'yov, who hoped to decrease my guilt in the Commission's eyes by this sentimental phrase. When I asked him about it later, he would always laugh and shrug it off instead of replying.'

41 Trubetskoy's letter from St. Petersburg (September 1817) reported rumours that Alexander favoured an autonomous Poland, was thinking of moving his capital to Warsaw, and planned to annex some adjoining Russian provinces to Poland; see *Materialy*, I,

51–52; III, 6–10. The news caused such indignation among the members of the Union of Salvation then in Moscow that Yakushkin, Lunin, and A. N. Murav'yov offered to assassinate the tsar; ibid., III, 53, 73; IX, 256.

42 General-major P. P. Passek, a close friend of Yakushkin, died of natural causes; Chaadayev was in France and returned to Russia only in August 1826.

43 In 1826 numerous Decembrists were sceptical of the conduct of Myslovsky; see note 38, chap. 3.

44 Countess Sheremeteva was Yakushkin's mother-in-law and supported him materially and morally throughout his exile.

45 The Princess Avgusta Tarakanova (1744–1810), daughter of Elizabeth, became a nun in Ivanovskiy Convent, Moscow, in 1785, and remained there until her death. Her father was A. G. Razumovsky. Another Tarakanova was a pretender, probably of German, possibly of Polish origin. She claimed to be 'Princess of Vladimir' (1772), then daughter of the empress (1774), who saw in her a possible threat and had her abducted by Grigoriy Orlov May 1775). She was found dead in her cell that December 4; but the Neva did not, contrary to later belief, rise more than two feet that winter: see *Mémoires de feu le prince Pierre Dolgoroukov*, 2 vols. (Génève, 1821, 2: 113–15.

46 V. K. Kyukhel'beker (1797–1846), poet, intimate of Pushkin and joint editor of the radical almanac *Mnemozina*, was a brave idealist yet a pathetic figure. It was typical that the bullet from his pistol failed to strike the Grand Duke Mikhail Pavlovich on December 14 from a range of 5 yards; see *Russ. star.* XXX (1881), 498–99. The Grand Duke pardoned him, and saved his life by having him placed in the second category of criminals.

47 As arranged by Nicholas on July 10.

48 Established in 1310 to, in effect, police the patrician order and defend the Venetian régime. Condemned men were said to have been cast from the *Ponte dei Sospiri* into the water, where they sank without trace.

49 Friedrich von der Trenck (1726–94), was imprisoned by Frederick II of Prussia for conducting an affair with the king's sister, Amelia. He escaped, but was re-arrested (1754) in Austria and held captive for nine years. He was executed in Paris as a spy.

50 Johann-Heinrich Schnitzler (1802–69), historian and statistician, was a private tutor in Russia in 1823–28, and thereafter wrote various works on the country. Lorer refers to his *Histoire intime de la Russie sous les Empereurs Alexandre et Nicolas* (Paris, 1847). Rozen was apparently familiar with his *Essai d'un statistique générale de l'Empire de la Russie* (Paris, 1829), A. O. Kornilovich with his biographies of Paul I and the Counts Razumovsky. His celebrity faded in the early '60s.

51 Before dispersing on June 17, it met 147 times.

52 See *Materialy*, IV, 121–22, 127–34. Once the box was exhumed in 1826, its contents were hurried to a secret hiding place. *Russkaya Pravda* was first published by P. E. Shchegolev in 1906, in a highly careless edition.

53 Varvara, wife of Lorer's younger brother Dmitriy.

54 S. M. Semyonov (1789–1852); an expert on Hobbes and Spinoza.

55 On the same day, P. P. Belyayev saved Benkendorf from possible drowning; Benkendorf was attempting to reach an inundated cabin, visible from the Winter Palace, but failed to control the launch in heavy waters. Belyayev took command, and all reached the Vyborg Side in safety.

56 A tall Caucasian hat made of sheepskin.

57 i.e., assistants to the specially imported hangman, a middle-aged Finn who spoke no Russian.

58 An error for Rheinboth; an old family friend of the Pestel''s and Lutheran pastor in the fortress (for 1826).

59 During the ceremony, the warship 'Knyaz' Vladimir' ('Prince Vladimir') flew a black flag, not the double-headed eagle.

60 According to other accounts, the words were the prisoner's surname plus 'regicide.' The belts became mixed up.

61 8 a.m., on Wolf's Field (*Volkovoye Polye*).

62 Rozen does not exaggerate the infamous part played by Dmitriy Niko-layevich Bludov (1785–1869) in this affair. Bludov was a joint-founder of the Society of Arzamas in 1815, the friend of many radicals now implicated in the rising, and a minor writer. His report, which stressed the 'blood-thirstiness' of the insurgents and made extensive use of vivid similes and striking scenes, was a well-drafted political pamphlet. It paved the way to his fortune.

63 'Ecoutez, vous n'avez pas le droit d'adresser une pareille question: c'est une affaire de conscience.' Nazimov was later still more grateful to Ben-kendorf for this action: the window of his cell looked out onto the glacis, and he was one of the handful of Decem-brists to witness the hangings of July 13.

64 'Sredi doliny rovnyye, na gladkoy vysote'; lyric by A. Merzlyakov.

65 *Materialy*, I, 34.

66 See Mazour, *First Russian Revolution*, p. 247.

67 *Materialy*, I, 38–39, 152.

68 Ibid., I, 43–44, 71–72.

69 Ibid., I, 443.

70 Ibid., I, ix.

71 Z. Borovkov, 'Zapiski', *Russ. star.*, XI (1898), 351–52.

72 *Mezhdutsarstviye*, p. 62.

73 Ibid., pp. 62–64.

74 The Countess Joan Grudzinska, later Princess Lowicz, was Constantine's second wife, for which reason the empress dowager and the conservative element at court strongly opposed his accession to the Russian throne.

75 Literally true: adjacent barracks were converted into temporary jails; see A. M. Murav'yov, *Zapiski* (Petrograd, 1922), pp. 19–20.

76 See *Mezhdutsarstviye*, 32–33.

77 Secretary of the navy.

78 Count Karl Robert Nesselrode (1780–1862), minister of foreign affairs, was sent to arrest Trubetskoy because of the latter's having sheltered in the Austro-Hungarian embassy. Count Loebzeltern himself was suspected of complicity with the rebels or, at least, of foreknowledge of the rising.

79 'Ah, mon Prince! Vous avez fait bien du mal à la Russie: vous l'avez reculée de cinquante ans.'

80 An exaggeration; the two met in St. Petersburg in March 1824, and again in the South twelve months later.

81 Colonel I. M. Bibikov was crushed and almost trampled by hostile onlookers near Senate Square on December 14; he was taken for a government official, but Mikhail Kyukhel'beker saved him. Thus he was suspect.

82 Lilien-Ankern was a russified Swede who had entered the Russian service in the 1760s. Small, withered and deaf, he embodied an earlier age. His uniform, a long-skirted green coat with red tabs, was twenty years out of date by 1825.

83 Semyonov, who took his master's degree in ethical and political sciences at Moscow University (1816) and might have expected a post there (1819), entered the civil service instead, but

also gave private tuition. He later taught in I. D. Yakushkin's school in Yalutorovsk.

84 The ordeal of Gavriil Stepanovich Baten'kov (1793–1863), who was not on Senate Square on the 14th, was unique: he spent twenty years of solitary confinement in Peter-and Paul Fortress. It has been suggested that Speransky, whose protégé Baten'kov was, actually brought about his close confinement; this is highly arguable; see B. L. Modzalevsky, 'Dekabrist Baten'kov', *Russkiy istoricheskiy zhurnal*, V (1918).

85 He: 'Je suis venu chez vous de la part de Sa Majesté l'Empereur. Vous devez considérer comme si vous parliez avec l'Empereur lui-même; je ne suis qu'un intermédiaire nécessaire. L'Empereur, comme de raison, ne peut pas venir vous voir lui-même. Il ne peut pas venir ici, il serait inconvenable qu'il vous fasse appeler chez lui; il faut donc qu'il y ait un intermédiaire entre lui et vous. La conversation qui aura lieu entre vous et moi doit donc être un secret pour tout le monde, comme si elle avait lieu entre l'Empereur et vous. Sa Majesté a de grandes bontés pour vous, et elle attend un témoignage de votre reconnaissance.'

I: 'General, je suis très reconnaissant à Sa Majesté pour toutes ses bontés, dont voici le témoignage.'

He: 'Qu'est-ce que c'est que cela? Il ne s'agit pas de cela. Rappelez vous, que vous êtes entre la vie et la mort ...'

I: 'Je le sais bien, général, que je suis plus près de la dernière.'

He: 'Eh bien! Vous ne savez pas ce que l'Empereur fait pour vous. On peut être clément, mais il y a une mesure à tout. La loi donne un pouvoir absolu à l'Empereur, cependant il y a des choses qu'il ne devrait pas faire, et je ne crains pas de dire, qu'il outrepasse même son droit de faire grâce en votre faveur. Mais il faut aussi que de votre côté vous lui donniez une preuve de votre reconnaissance. Je vous répète de nouveau, que tout ce que vous me direz ne sera connu que de la personne de l'Empereur, et que je ne suis que le canal par lequel vos paroles devront passer.'

I: 'Je vous ai déjà dit, général, que je suis très reconnaissant à Sa Majesté pour la bonté qu'elle a eu de me permettre de correspondre avec ma femme. Et je voudrais savoir comment je puis lui témoigner ma reconnaissance.'

He: 'L'Empereur voudrait savoir quelles sont les relations que vous avez eues avec M. Speranski.'

I: 'Je n'ai eu aucune relation particulière avec M. Speranski.'

He: 'Permettez. Je dois vous dire, de la part de Sa Majesté l'Empereur, qu'elle vous certifie par ma bouche, que tout ce que vous me direz sur M. Speranski restera un secret entre lui et vous. Qu'il n'en arrivera rien à M. Speranski; il est au-dessus de cela. On a besoin de lui, mais l'Empereur veut seulement savoir quel degré de confiance il doit lui accorder.'

I: 'Général, je ne puis rien vous citer de mes relations avec M. Speranski, excepté des relations qu'on a ordinairement en société.'

He: 'Mais vous avez raconté à quelqu'un une conversation que vous avez eue avec M. Speranski. Vous l'avez même consulté sur la constitution à donner à la Russie.'

I: 'C'est faux, général; on a induit Sa Majesté en erreur.'

He: 'Prenez garde, prince Troubetskoï! Vous savez que vous êtes entre la vie et la mort.'

5

1 I. D. Yakushkin, 'Zamechaniya na Zapiski A. Murav'yova,' *Zapiski dekabrista,* p. 160.

2 Ibid., 2nd ed., pp. 171–76.

3 By S. Shtraykh as *Zapiski A. Murav'yova* (Petrograd, 'Byloye,' 1922); by E. E. Yakushkin in the journal *Byloye* (1924, no. 25, 273–81); and again with the same basic text, in 1931.

4 Swedish; see note 82, chap. 4.

5 Here Lorer inserts a 112-line poem by Prince A. P. Baryatinsky entitled 'Stances dans un cachot,' which I omit. The iambic tetrameters are fluid, but the sum effect is hackneyed.

6 Lorer's patron saint.

7 Myslovsky's enigmatic reply to Obolensky's earlier enquiry as to the ultimate fate of the five condemned to die.

8 Apparently an error: Obolensky left for Siberia on July 13 (O.S.).

9 Figure in Russian folk-tales; a robber or brigand.

10 Fonvizin (?).

11 Aleksandr Nikolayevich Sutgof, lieutenant, Grenadier Guards.

12 It was supposed that the courier would be the notorious Zheldybin. In fact, it was the more humane Vorob'yov.

13 Aleksey Ivanovich Tyutchev (1800–56); of the United Slavs.

14 Peter Simon Pallas (1741–1811), German naturalist, was appointed Professor of Natural History at St. Petersburg University in 1768. That year he left for Siberia, returning in 1774. *Reise durch verschiedene Provinzen des russischen Reichs* appeared in 1774–76. Rozen also refers to the *Tagebuch zwoer Reisen von Kjachta und Zuruchaitu nach Peking ...* (1781). The painter A. E. Martynov (1768–1826) published his *Zhivopisnoye puteshestviye ot Moskvy do kitayskoy granitsy* (St. Petersburg, 1819). The Siberian letters *(Pis'ma ot vostochnoy Sibiri)* of A. I. Martos (1790–1842) were not published until 1827. Rozen could not have known them in 1826, on leaving for the East.

15 Moszynski, Kryzanowski and Janusz-Kiewicz were members of the Polish Secret Patriotic Society and associates of Lukasinski and Chodkiewicz.

16 Shrovetide, a time of carnival and gaiety in pre-Revolutionary Russia.

6

1 *Vospominaniya Bestuzhevykh,* pp. 205–06.

2 See M. O. Gershenzon, *Dekabrist Krivtsov* (Berlin, 1923; 2nd ed.), p. 244.

3 P. E. Shchegolev, *Istoricheskiye etyudy* (Moscow, 1913), pp. 392–94.

4 N. V. Basargin, *Zapiski,* p. 94.

5 The government's decision to keep all the Decembrists together was, as N. A. Bestuzhev remarks, a grave error which 'allowed the exiles to survive politically beyond political death'; *Vosp. Bestuzhevykh,* pp. 145–46. The prospect of solace and companionship was especially vital to those in Finnish fortresses who, left alone, would certainly have broken down.

6 The group was in Irkutsk within thirty-six days.

7 See my study, *M. S. Lunin: Catholic Decembrist* (The Hague, Mouton, 1974).

8 Herzen's version of the reply, "Dekabrist Lunin,' *Kolokol,* no. 36 (1859), 296; there are others.

9 P. N. Svistunov, 'Otpoved',' *Russ. arkhiv.* (1871), bk. 1, 367.

10 Prince F. P. Shakhovskoy (1796–1829) went partially insane in Siberia and

was locked up, on Nicholas's orders, in Spaso-Yevfim'yevskiy Monastery, Suzdal'; he died there within two months. N. S. Bobrishchev-Pushkin was committed to Tobol'sk asylum in 1840 but emerged in 1856 and lived with his brother. A. F. Furman went mad in Surgut, in the far north; there was no Decembrist named Shachirev.

11   Nazimov spent more than a year in Srednye-Kolymsk, 180 miles north-east of Yakutsk, becoming the furthest-flung Decembrist from St. Petersburg.

12   An allusion to the mass escape of exiles and convicts planned by I. I. Sukhinov (1795–1828) from Zerentuy-skiy Mine. Sukhinov hanged himself.

13   On the hospitable reception given to the Decembrists by most Siberians, see A. G. Mazour, *The First Russian Revolution, 1825* (Stanford, 2nd printing, 1961) p. 228.

14   Circular domed tents of skins or furs stretched over a collapsible lattice frame; used by the Kirghiz and various Mongol nomadic tribes.

15   Aleksandr.

16   Finnish, Kotka; eighteen miles west of Vyborg.

17   Apparently an error: Suvorov built no such fort in the 1760s, nor did Rochen-sal'm and Sveaborg capitulate to Rus-sian arms until March 1808 (when 24,000 occupying troops were com-manded by Buxhoewden).

18   For obvious reasons, Sallust's *Cata-linae Coriuratio* was popular in Rus-sian liberal circles; see note 18, chap. 4.

19   Possibly *(The) Guardian,* edited by Steele, 1712–14, but more probably a reference to John Gardnor (1729–1808), author of *Views Taken on the Rhine ...* 1792). This was not a periodi-cal, however.

20   *Chet'i-Miney,* a menalogion compiled by the Metropolitan Makariy of Moscow

in 1542–63, remained the official cal-andar of the Russian Orthodox Church for 150 years, and was reprinted more than seventy times. *Mal'chik u ruch'ya* was a popular eighteenth-century prose tale.

21   Count A. A. Zakrevsky (1783–1865) was a man of (expediently) liberal sympathies, and a great enemy of Arakcheyev.

22   An error for 'early October,' according to E. E. Yakushkin; see I. D. Yakushkin, *Zapiski dekabrista,* p. 580.

23   General A. P. Yushnevsky; see note 60, chap. 3.

24   i.e., the Holy Sea, or Lake Baikal.

25   *Moschus moschiferus,* a small, thick-furred, ruminant quadraped, like a small deer in appearance.

26   On N. I. Treskin, appointed civil gov-ernor of Irkutsk by Governor-General I. B. Pestel' in 1806 and effective ruler of Siberia for a decade, see M. Raeff, *Siberia and the Reforms of 1822* (Washington, 1955), pp. 22–23.

27   Princess Shakovskaya was A. N. Murav'yov's sister-in-law and Muk-hanov's fiancée. Nicholas forbade the marriage, and the provocateur R. Medoks later made her his victim.

28   See Zetlin, *Decembrists,* pp. 290–92.

29   Worse than the climate was the lone-liness of Srednye-Kolymsk, with a total population of 250. But even Yakutsk, main administrative centre of the region, counted less than 2500 inhabitants in 1828; *Sbornik trudov Irkutskogo Universiteta,* otdel 1, vypusk 2 (Irkutsk, 1921), 111.

30   A. O. Kornilovich (1800–34), soldier and historian (see note 19, chap. 1), was indeed placed in Peter-and-Paul Fortress in February 1828, as a result of a denunciation by Faddey Bulgarin, journalist-cum-spy. Sent to the Cau-casus in November 1832, he died there of a 'bilious fever.'

31 One *sazhen* = 2.13 metres.

32 See note 27.

33 Posol'skiy-Preobrazhenskiy Monastery, founded in 1681 and one of the most flourishing in Siberia in the nineteenth century; see N. Abramov, 'Materialy dlya istorii khristianskogo prosveshcheniya Sibiri', *Zhurnal Ministerstva Narodnogo Prosveshcheniya,* 147 vols., (1854), 81: 33–35.

34 One *arshin* = 28 inches.

35 For details of the Prussian *Bergbeamte,* on which the Russian service was modelled, see *Mejers grosses konversations-Lexikon* (Leipzig, Wien, 1907, 2; 670).

36 N. D. Fonvizina later joined her husband; they had children but they died; after Fonvizin's death (1854) she married I. I. Pushchin.

37 Lieutenant; literally, 'centurian.'

7

1 For a concise sketch of Leparsky's career, see M. N. Kuchayev, 'S. R. Leparsky, Kommandant Nerchinskikh rudnikov,' *Russ. star.* (1880), 708–24.

2 P. Annenkova, *Vospominaniya* (Moscow, 1929), pp. 166-67.

3 In 1956, its population was 162,000 and growing quickly; *Bol'shaya Sovetskaya entsiklopediya* (Moscow, 1949–58), pp. 47, 407. As an entrepôt for fur-trappers, it was of more significance in 1725 than a century later.

4 See my article, 'A Note on N. A. Bestuzhev and the Academy of Chita,' *Canadian Slavonic Papers,* XII (1970), 47–59; also *Dekabristy-literatory; Literaturnoye nasledstvo,* vol. 60 (1956), bk. 2., passim.

5 N. A. Bestuzhev imagined that Switzerland looked like the region round Udinsk; *Pis'ma iz Sibiri dekabristov M.*

i N. Bestuzhevykh (Irkutsk, 1929), bk. 1, 16–17.

6 A. G. Mazour, *The First Russian Revolution 1825* (Stanford: 2nd printing, 1961), pp. 222–48.

7 *Sibir' i dekabristy,* ed. M. K. Azadovsky and others. (Irkutsk, 1925), p. 141.

8 A. I. Dmitriyev-Mamonov, 'Dekabristy v zapadnoy Sibiri,' *Chteniya v Imperatorskom Obshchestve Istorii i Drevnostey Rossiyskikh,* IV (1895), 13.

9 Some, however, always viewed co-operatives askance or even chose not to participate in them; Zavalishin typified the first group, Lunin the latter.

10 Figures taken from N. V. Basargin, *Zapiski,* p. 138.

11 Figures given by M. Zetlin, *Dekabristy* (trans. as *The Decembrists* by George Panin, New York, 1958), p. 298, which tally with those provided by M. N. Kuchayev; *see* note 1.

12 See N. I. Lorer, *Zapiski,* pp. 145–46.

13 For a basic bibliography, see K. Muratova (ed.), *Istoriya russkoy literatury XIX-ogo veka; bibliograficheskiy ukazatel'* (Moscow, 1962), pp. 27–28.

14 See R. J. Kerner, 'Russian Expansion to America,' *Papers of the Bibliographical Society of America,* XXV (1931), 114–16.

15 Further on this, see *Russ. star.* VII (1881), 346–48; also *Dekabristy v Zabaykale; neizdannyye materialy,* ed. A. V. Kharchevnikov (Chita, 1925), 26.

16 See my article (note 4), 57–58.

17 N. V. Basargin, *Zapiski,* 178–85.

18 Mazour, *First Russian Revolution,* p. 255.

19 V. K. Tizengauzen was fifty-one in 1830; Lunin and Shteyngel' were both forty-seven. On the ages of the 121 'most dangerous criminals,' see Mazour, *First Russian Revolution,* p. 221.

20 Zetlin tells the tale in broad outline; *The Decembrists,* p. 303–04.

21 George Kennan, *Siberia and the Exile System,* 2 vols. (N.Y., 1891); see 2: 335–42 for impressions of Chita in 1885; 2: 278–318 for a survey of conditions in the Nerchinsk mines and, in particular, Akatuy.

22 This he did on the instances of his wife, an illegitimate daughter of the former Governor General I. V. Yakobi, whose nephew, I. A. Annenkov, was one of the prisoners.

23 An exaggeration; see note 10.

24 i.e., Bobrishchev-Pushkin.

25 Colonel I. S. Povalo-Shveykovsky was not a great success as prison senior, being thought by some to feed the exiles poorly; I. D. Yakushkin, *Zapiski,* 117.

26 Dmitriy Bortnyansky (1751–1825), composer of church music, trained in Italy.

27 Kyukhel'beker sailed with Tulubyev on the 'Apollon' in 1821–24, visiting the Kamchatka settlements of the Russian-American Company on the return voyage.

28 *Russkaya starina,* jointly edited with Sukhorukov in 1824–25. A. P. Kunitsyn (1783–1841), distinguished jurist.

29 Like Yushnevsky and Poggio, the dyspeptic Zavalishin later eked out a living by teaching foreign languages to the children of the wealthy.

30 Apukhtina.

31 Nonetheless, she survived Fonvizin; see note 36, chap. 6.

32 Like Princess Trubetskaya, Polina Guebel (1800–76), officially known as Mlle. Pol' for some reason, was French by birth. She had lived with Annenkov for some years before the rising, and had a son by him.

33 A voyage successfully made by Captain Perry Collins (1814–1900) in 1856, and by at least two Russians before him; see *A Siberian Journey; Down the Amur to the Pacific* (Madison, 1962).

34 In hoping that Nikolay's 'golden hands' might be given to one of his three sons when the former 'migrated to a better world,' Rozen expressed a general admiration for the handiman's great skills; *Vosp. Bestuzhevykh,* 591–92 (letter of December 21, 1833).

35 There are many later impressions of the region in accounts by Western European travellers; see especially Charles Cottrell, *Recollections of Siberia in the Years 1840–1841* (London, 1842) and S. S. Hill, *Travels in Siberia* (London, 1854). For more scholarly approaches, see the works of G.-A. Erman and Baron A. Haxthausen-Abbenburg (bibliography in Mazour).

36 In 1851.

37 N. N. Murav'yov-Amur'sky (1809–81), governor general of Eastern Siberia in 1847–59.

38 One *pood* $=$ 36 lbs. Thus 9 lbs. per man would have sufficed.

39 Several memoirists mention General A. I. Chernyshev's base conduct during the 1826 enquiry and his attempt to seize the estates of Zakhar Grigor'-yevich Chernyshev (1796–1862), which were in the highly profitable 'black earth' region, and held some 9000 serfs; see Yakushkin, *Zapiski,* 588–89.

40 Others in P. S. Bobrishchev-Pushkin's group were Prince Baryatinsky and N. A. Kryukov, formerly an agnostic; ibid., p. 590.

41 He and his brother were, indeed, its founders, as of its predecessors, Primeval Concord and The Friends of Nature; see Mazour, *First Russian Revolution,* pp. 142–45.

42 Mikhail Karlovich (1799–1859).

43 1819.

44 One *desyatina* $=$ 2.7 acres. After 1835, all Decembrists were allowed fifteen *desyatins* of land in order to gain a livelihood. 'So I am required to plough the soil,' remarked K. G. Igel'strom

(*Sibir' i dekabristy*, Irkutsk, 1925, 142); 'the question is, where could I have learnt agriculture?'; see pp. 000-00.

45 Louis-Gabriel Eugène Isabey (1803–86), Parisian painter influenced (for the worse) by Delacroix.

46 Pyotr Fyodorovich Sokolov (1791–1847), portraitist.

47 All letters had to be mailed unsealed, however, and passed through the hands of the authorities in Irkutsk as well as in St. Petersburg; *Dekabristy v Zabaykal'e*, pp. 40–44.

48 'But even correspondence with our close relations was brief and circumspect; every phrase was considered ten times before it was set down, so that when it passed the first censorship, Leparsky's, our kind ladies would not be compelled to rewrite our letters. *Vosp. Bestuzhevykh*, p. 254.

49 'Au nom de Dieu, ..., ne vous échauffez pas, Madame! Soyez raisonable, je ferai tout ce que dépend de moi, mais vous exigez une chose qui doit me compromettre aux yeux du gouvernement. Je suis sûr que vous ne voulez pas qu'on me fasse soldat pour n'avoir pas suivi mes instructions.' 'Eh bien, soyez soldat, général, mais soyez honnête homme!'

50 See note 33.

51 *Dub* is 'an oak,' with the suggestion of a wooden head; *dubina* is 'a bludgeon' or 'a blockhead.'

52 The eight Nerchinsk veterans settled in one room, all the Moscow Decembrists in another (called 'Moscow'), while a third was called 'Vyatka' after Pestel''s regiment.

53 In the former war (1826–28), Russian forces under I. F. Paskevich took Armenia from the Persians; in the latter, Dibich took Adrianople and threatened Constantinople.

54 Pushkin sent the piece with A. G. Murav'yova, in January 1827.

55 See note 32.

56 Camille Le Dentu (1804–39), the daughter of an émigré, lived with her mother in the Ivashevs' house for many years; her mother was governess to V. P. Ivashev's female cousins. Camille arrived in Petrovskiy on September 9, 1831 and was married on the 16th. V. P. died only a year after his wife, in 1840; she of puerperal fever, he of an apoplectic fit. On the tragedy, see O. K. Bulanova, *Roman dekabrista ...* (Moscow, 1933; 3rd ed.); also, for a cooler and more sceptical appraisal, Yakushkin, *Zapiski*, 172–74. In Yakushkin's view, Camille did not love and, indeed, hardly knew Ivashev when she first came to Petrovskiy.

1 Two groups left Chita on August 7 and 9. Shteyngel''s diary of the move was published by B. L. Modzalevsky in *Dekabristy: neizdannyye materialy i stat'i* (Moscow, 1925), pp. 128–48.

2 *Russ. star.* XII (1881), 886, letter dated February 10, 1829.

3 M. S. Lunin, *Sochineniya i pis'ma*, ed. S. Shtraykh (St. Petersburg, 1923), p. 32.

4 For fullest details, see N. V. Basargin, *Zapiski*, pp. 138–56.

5 In particular, we know little of the Siberian lives of middle-ranking members of the United Slavs – Spiridov, for example, V. A. Bechasnov, P. D. Mozgan and N. O. Mozgalevsky.

6 Several wives, too, took an interest in the pantomimic dances and religious rituals of the Tungus and Buriats, and assisted G.-A. Erman during his visit of 1829; see Erman, *Reise um die Erde*, 2 vols., trans. as *Travels in Siberia* (London, 1848), 2: 180–81.

7 Of the seventh category prisoners sent to northern outposts in 1828, some, like N. F. Lisovsky, never fully recovered. The solitude was absolute.

8 Some, moreover, were deprived by the government of even hunting rifles, making them apprehensive of wandering criminals; *Sibir' i dekabristy,* p. 142.

9 'J'ai l'honneur d'annoncer ... l'heureuse délivrance de Mme la prison de Pétroffsky ... Elle a mis au monde 23 enfants à la fois après une grossesse assez pénible de 13 années consécutives! Que le bon Dieu bénisse la maman. Quant aux petits, ils ont l'air assez viable bien que tous soient plus ou moins: qui asthmatique, qui rachitique, qui valétudinaire, qui grisonant ...' Cited by B. L. Modzalevsky in *Dekabristy: neizdannyye materialy ...,* p. 217–18.

10 August 7.

11 The pair were obliged 'to leave for a milder climate' in August 1863, Zavalishin having enraged the Governor-General, M. S. Korsakov; see A. G. Mazour, *The First Russian Revolution, 1825,* (Stanford, 2nd printing, 1961) pp. 250–51.

12 Other parallel accounts of the walk are those of P. Annenkova, *Vospominaniya,* 190–94; N. I. Lorer, *Zapiski,* 151–53; and A. P. Belyayev, *Vospominaniya dekabrista o perezhitom ...* (St. Petersburg, 1882), pp. 233–35. All are strikingly similar in detail, though varied in tone.

13 i.e., a long tunic with a waist-girdle.

14 Friedrich-Ernst-Ludwig von Fischer (1782–1854); Junior Professor of Natural Science at Moscow University from 1812, first Director of the Imperial Botanical Gardens from 1823.

15 i.e., Charles X's flight to England and his reception there; see also N. I. Lorer, *Zapiski,* p. 145.

16 1794. The Severskiy Dragoons went with Suvorov to Praga (November 3–4), the fortress defending Warsaw on the east. The storming was followed by a massacre; but hundreds of captives were taken.

17 High head-dress in old Russia.

18 Old Believers; this in 1772.

19 A small rural district.

20 Zavalishin echoes this: 'We were the first to appear in Siberia as members of the upper class who were entirely approachable and kept, besides, rules quite the opposite of those which the inhabitants were used to see followed by superiors and officials. ... For this reason, no one kept a secret from us, be he Russian, cossack or sectarian ...': *Sibir' i dekabristy,* p. 96.

21 Ya. D. Kazimirsky was town-major of the Chita, then of Petrovskiy Zavod Fortress, and well liked by most exiles.

22 This in 1855.

23 *Russkiy invalid,* a government-owned periodical then edited by A. F. Voyeykov, survived until the Revolution. Mariya Fyodorovna, widow of Paul I, died on November 12, 1828. The anonymous 'hymns' expressed unsuitably radical hopes for the future.

24 A group of Polish revolutionaries, participants in the Warsaw rising of November 28–30, 1830, arrived in Petrovskiy early in 1831; see my paper, 'M. S. Lunin and the Question of Polish Sovereignty,' *East European Quarterly,* V (1970), no. 1, 1–13.

25 i.e., the building formed a 'U,' the fourth wing being formed by the stockade.

26 According to Rozen, *Aus den memoiren eines russischen Dekabristen,* p. 197, Siberia had one doctor for every 40,000 inhabitants, 'dispersed over 500 versts of country.'

27 See Mazour, *First Russian Revolution,* p. 246.

28 In July 1831.

29 Literally, *Maslennik;* suggesting greasy wealth and, possibly, unctuousness.

30 Born on March 15, 1826, Sof'ya Niki-tishna (Nonushka) lived her whole life in Decembrist circles, marrying a nephew of Sergey Murav'yov-Apostol.

31 Here Yakushkin added, but later struck out: 'But all these amusements terribly reminded one of the amusements of the fallen angels on the bank of the fiery river, so splendidly portrayed by Milton.'

32 Nikolay Semyonovich, governor general of Eastern Siberia in 1834–36.

33 See also N. I. Lorer, *Zapiski*, p. 155–56.

34 See note 89, chap. 3.

35 Pestov died on December 25, 1833 of a carbuncle and gangrene of the spine; N. V. Basargin, *Zapiski*, p. 168.

36 The chapel, of stone, was built by Nikita Murav'yov; see I. D. Yakushkin, 'Vospominaniya ob A. G. Murav'yovoy,' *Zapiski dekabrista,* p. 171.

37 Error for N. A. Zagoretsky (1796–1885).

38 Here and elsewhere, I correct Rozen's initialing, which is unreliable.

39 See my article, 'The Catholicism of M. S. Lunin,' *The Slavonic and East European Review*, 1971, pp. 255–71.

40 He died in Akatuy in 1845; see note 7, chap. 6.

41 Officer responsible for stores and distributing provisions; see also note 60, chap. 3.

9

1 See A. G. Mazour, *The First Russian Revolution, 1825* (Stanford, 2nd printing, 1961), pp. 231–33.

2 For details, N. V. Basargin, *Zapiski*, p. 214.

3 See Mazour, *First Russian Revolution*, p. 240.

4 Ibid., p. 234 and M. Zetlin, *Dekabristy* (trans. as *The Decembrists* by George Panin, New York, 1958), pp. 322–23.

5 For bibliography, see Mazour, *First Russian Revolution*, pp. 306–18.

6 Early in 1833.

7 The rank of Mikhail Vasil'yevich Lavinsky, governor general of Eastern Siberia until the appointment of Murav'yov-Amursky, was equivalent to general lieutenant; he was the last civilian governor general.

8 Ivan Bogdanovich Tseydler, also a civilian governor.

9 October 13, 1832.

10 'Votre nom?' 'Champagne de Nor-mandie, monsieur. L'Empereur Paul m'a envoyé ici, il y a 40 ans. Soyez bon, monsieur, donnez-moi quelques sous!' ... 'Comment ça va, Monsieur Champagne? Tout doucement, mon-sieur; je m'en vais au kabachok! [drinking-house]'.

11 *Zastatnyy gorod*; a provincial town that had lost its status as an administrative centre.

12 It was not; the brothers were reunited in the Caucasus.

13 The wife of Mikhail Mikhaylovich Naryshkin (1795–1863), Elizaveta Petrovna, joined him in Chita in April 1827.

14 Count P. P. Konovnitsyn, member of the Northern Society, Naryshkina's father.

15 i.e., Mongolia.

16 'Ich hab' das Geld und du hast den Beutel.'

17 'Cher N., venez au plus vite possible, nous allons vivre tranquillement à Kourghane dans le gouvernement de Tobolsk, 4 mille verstes plus près de notre Patrie!'

18 Aleksandra Osipovna Rosset, later Smirnova, wrote her memoirs (*Zapiski, dnevnik, vospominaniya, pis'ma A. O. Smirnovoy*, Moscow, 1929), in which

are many details of Lorer's life on his brother's estate of Vodyanoye, in Kherson Province, during the '50s.

19 Semyon Grigor'yevich Krasnokutsky died in 1840, outliving Kochubey by a comfortable six years.

20 And, after 1856, civil governor of Nizhniy Novgorod.

21 Ivan Aleksandrovich Vel'yaminov (1771–1837), governor general in 1827–33.

22 'Le colonel Alexandre Mouravieff, en considération de la sincérité de son repentir, devait être simplement déporté on ne dit pas pour combien d'anneés en Sibérie, sans être dégradé ni privé de la noblesse.' Johann-Heinrich Schnitzler, *Histoire intime de la Russie sous les Empereurs Alexandre et Nicholas* (Paris, 1874), vol. 1, 200.

23 August-Friedrich-Ferdinand von Kotzebue (1761–1819), the dramatist, was arrested at the Russian frontier in 1800 en route from Vienna to St. Petersburg where his sons were studying. He was sent to Siberia for offending Paul I with his play, 'Der alte Leibkutscher Peters des Dritten' (in Russian translation), but soon brought to the capital and showered with honours; see also chap. I, note 26.

24 Johann Georg Zimmerman (1728–95), physician, wrote his four-volume treatise on solitude in 1784–85. Lorer would have known Marmier's free translation (Paris, 1845).

25 Aleksandr Fyodorovich (von der) Briggen (1792–1859) was allowed to serve on the Kurgan circuit court in a minor capacity in 1838.

26 Apparently a reference to Mikhail Pavlovich Miklashevsky (1756–1847), famed for commanding the *Ekaterinoslavskaya druzhina* at his own expense in 1806–07 and preserving it as a military force; but he retired later to Chernigov estate, alive and well.

27 I.e., the region east of Smolensk. Rozen is surely mistaken in claiming to have reached Tarbagatay in three days. Following the River Selenga, the distance is 115 miles.

28 Tiled stoves.

29 That is, 'Wandrers Sturmlied' (c. 1771). Rozen perhaps had Cotta's Stuttgart ed. of Goethe's works (2 vols., 1815), which A. F. Smirdin imported to St. Petersburg.

30 30 miles south of Tobol'sk.

31 Shrovetide.

Appendix

1 Countess Grudzinska became Princess Lowicz; see *Russ. star.* XX (1877), 379.

2 See A. Mazour, *The First Russian Revolution, 1825* (Stanford, 2nd printing, 1961) pp. 131, 156–7.

3 General–Adjutant Mikhail Andreyevich, governor general of St. Petersburg (1771–1825), was generally admitted to be a decisive officer; see *Vospominaniya i rasskazy deyateley taynykh obshchestv 1820–kh godov*, ed. Yu. G. Oksman (Moscow, 1933), 199–200. Now, decisiveness became rashness.

4 Trubetskoy's own regiment.

5 The Grenadier Guards were sharing watch duty in the Palace with the Preobrazhenskiy Regiment and units of the Chevalier Garde on December 13–14. Their colonel, N. K. Styurler, was shortly to lose control of his command to Sutgof and Panov; see pp. 59 ff.

6 See *Mezhdutsarstviye,* p. 207.

7 S. G. Krasnokutsky.

8 The Anichov Palace, on Moyka.

9 F. P. Opochinin (1778–1852), *Ober–gofmeyster.*

10 The Northern Society.

11 '... in the strange predicament of having two self-denying Emperors and no active ruler:' *The Times,* (January 7, 1826), p. 2., col. 3.

12 On the wretched Colonel Aleksandr Bulatov (1793–1826), who took his own life, see I. D. Yakushkin, *Zapiski dekabrista,* pp. 570–71.

13 On their unpopularity, see p. 56

14 Trubetskoy himself.

Appendix B

1 Based on the text of A. K. Borozdin's *Iz pisem i pokazaniy dekabristov* (St. Petersburg, 1906), pp. 3–18.

2 *Zemskiy Sobor.*

3 Many other radicals admired Washington; see *Materialy,* III, 90–91.

4 Based on Borozdin, *Iz pisem i pokazaniy,* pp. 69–70.

5 "Golova i nogi" (1803). So liberal was the idea that the feet might object to being led through the mire by the (autocratic) head that it was not published in Russia until 1872 (*Russ. star.* V).

6 From *Sbornik Imperatorskogo Istoricheskogo Obshchestva,* CXXXI, 12–13.

7 General–Adjutant Count Yevgraf Fedotovich (1769–1843).

8 Both Mikhail Orlov and Prince P. V. Lopukhin were acquitted by the Commission on Nicholas's personal instructions.

9 Presumably Stepan Fomich, later secretary of state for the Kingdom of Poland.

10 From S.I.R.I.O. (see note 6), CXXXI, 85–86.

Appendix C

1 The identity of Rozen's English translator is arguable, however; for, as a glance at Burke's *Peerage and Baronetage* (London, 1967, p. 1708) shows, Evelyn Augusta St. John Mildmay (1868–1927) was four years old in 1872. Nor, according to family sources, were there any other Evelyns. All in all, it seems quite probable that Evelyn's father, Colonel Edmond St. John Mildmay (1815–1905), was in fact the translator, and that for unknown reasons he chose to publish under his own daughter's name. Born in Württemberg, where *his* father lived, having married a deceased wife's sister and been banned from England, Edmond was fluent in German, served in Radetzky's hussars of the Austro-Hungarian service, where perhaps he gained an interest in recent European military history; and, having moved to England in his late twenties, became equerry to H.R.H. Prince George, Duke of Cambridge (1850–1904) — in which capacity he would have had more time and opportunity than most contemporaries on active duty for a long work of translation. There were other St. John Mildmay links with Austria: Edmond's younger brother Horace Osborne (1817–66) was also in the Austrian service (Fifth Hussars), and married a Fraülein Dornbach. Regrettably, the original correspondence with Smith and Elder, publishers, which passed into the hands of John Murray when the latter acquired that house in 1917, cannot be found, although the Smith, Elder files survived the 1940 blitz in London. If and why Edmond St. John Mildmay published his translation under the (quite ineffectual) *nom-de-plume* of Evelyn thus remains, at present, a mystery.

Index

Abramov, N.E. 363
Abramov, S., Col. 168
Academy of Arts, The 62, 75, 80
Achinsk 213, 238
Adlerberg, V.F. 152, 157, 173, 190, 357
Admiralty, The 57, 68
Adrianople 365
Akatuy 211, 241, 364, 367
Aland, Island(s) of 206, 348
Aleksandra Fyodorovna,
  Empress 171, 311
Aleksandrovskiy Zavod 224
Alekseyev, police-master
  of Tobol'sk 237
Alekseyev Ravelin, The 12, 102–05,
  139–40, 162, 169, 197–98, 200–03,
  217, 353
Alexander I, Emperor 1, 5, 14, 28–29, 45,
  115, 117, 145, 168, 184, 325, 332, 346
Alexis Mikhaylovich, Tsar 34, 331, 346
Alexis Petrovich, Tsarevich 345
Allgemeine Zeitung, Die 286
Amelia of Prussia 358
Amur, River 13, 249–53, 264, 364
Ancelot, J.-A. 66
Andreyev, A. N. 95, 352
Andreyevich, Ya.M. 219, 297, 300
Angara, River 219, 319
Anna Ivanovna, Empress 248
Anichkov Palace, The 35, 368
Annenkov, I.A. 240, 268, 276, 298
Annenkov, Ya.A. 73, 93
Annenkova, P.E. 251, 268, 293, 343,
  364, 366
'Apollon', ship 364
Arakcheyev, A.A. 6, 25, 110, 240,
  347, 362
Arbuzov, A.P. 59, 77, 191, 204, 218,
  247, 298, 349
Arbuzov, E.P. 218
Archangel 16, 42, 83, 312
Argun', River 231, 233, 264
Arkhipov, V.A. 346
Armenia 365
Arsen'yev, A.I. 284, 290

Arzamas, Society of 359
Atamanovka 252
Athenaeum, The 45
Augsburg Gazette, The 289
Austerlitz 355
d'Ayanger, le chevalier 144
Azadovsky, M.K. 343, 345, 363

Baikal, Lake 13, 107, 209, 213, 245,
  253, 284, 305, 308, 318–20
Bakunin, M. 75
Baltic, The 46, 356
Bancroft, H.H. 346
Bantysh-Kamensky, D.N. 237
Baranov, D.I. 161, 178, 181
Barguzina 257
Bartenev, P.I. 130
Baryatinsky, A.I., Prince 20, 113, 170,
  304, 354, 361, 364
Basargin, N.V. *passim;* esp. 128–31
Basargina, E.K. 128
Bashutsky, P.Ya. 85, 99, 133
Baten'kov, G.S. 14, 31, 35, 189, 196,
  266, 343
Batyushkov, K.N. 278
Bedryaga, courtesan 41
Belaya Tserkov' 2
Beleyev, D.N. 71
Belosel'skaya, Princess 183
Belyayev, A.P. 59, 168, 207, 277, 303,
  306, 342, 366
Belyayev, P.P. 59, 168, 207, 277, 303,
  306, 349, 358
Belyy Klyuch 68
Benkendorf, A.Kh. 16, 108, 141, 152, 155,
  157, 161, 166–67, 173–74, 178, 181,
  191, 271, 278, 358
Bentham, J. 356
Berdichev; *see also* Ukraine 114, 354
Beryosov 212
Beschasnov, V.A. 365
Besenkovichi 20, 345
Bestuzhev(-Marlinsky), A.A. 4, 11, 22,
  39, 59, 90, 139, 145, 179, 204, 219,
  273, 343, 350